W. E. B.
DU BOIS

Black Radical Democrat

TWAYNE'S TWENTIETH-CENTURY AMERICAN BIOGRAPHY SERIES

_____

John Milton Cooper, Jr., General Editor

W. E. B.
DU BOIS

Black Radical Democrat

Manning Marable

TWAYNE PUBLISHERS • BOSTON
A Division of G.K. Hall & Co.

Twayne's Twentieth-Century
American Biography Series No. 3

All photographs are from the archives of the University Library,
University of Massachusetts at Amherst

Designed by Marne B. Sultz
Produced by Elizabeth Todesco
Copyediting supervised by Lewis DeSimone
Typeset in 10/12 Century Oldstyle by Compset, Inc.

Printed on permanent/durable acid-free paper
and bound in the United States of America

Library of Congress Cataloging-in-Publication Data

Marable, Manning, 1950–
W. E. B. DuBois, Black Radical Democrat.

(Twayne's twentieth-century American biography
series ; no. 3)
Bibliography: p. 274
Includes index.
1. Du Bois, W. E. B. (William Edward Burghardt),
1868–1963.   2. Afro-Americans—Biography.   I. Title.
II. Series.
E185.97.D73M37   1986   303.4'84'0924   [B]   86-14881
ISBN 0-8057-7750-4
ISBN 0-8057-7771-7 (pbk.)

CONTENTS

FOREWORD

In 1969, the playwright Lorraine Hansberry's autobiography was posthumously published under the title *To Be Young, Gifted and Black*. That title highlighted one of the more poignant aspects of life for black Americans. What has become of the talent and work of gifted men and women who have been trapped by slavery and caste, deprived of freedom and opportunity, judged inferior from the start because of their color, and denied the worth of their achievements? What if a biologist, with abilities equal to a Thomas Henry Huxley, had been born the son of former slaves in the American South in the 1880s? The case is not hypothetical. Ernest Everett Just was such a biologist, and his career bore witness to the blighting impact of racism even in the "objective" world of science. Or what if a social observer and theorist, with the insights of an Alexis de Tocqueville, and the literary gifts of a Walt Whitman had been born in the American North three years after the end of the Civil War and lived almost a century? Again, the case is not conjectural. William Edward Burghardt Du Bois was such a social thinker and writer. His long life, as Manning Marable shows in this incisive biography, illustrates the trials and triumphs of a genius who was a black American.

W. E. B. Du Bois ranks, along with Frederick Douglass, Booker T. Washington, and Martin Luther King, Jr., as one of the four greatest black Americans in the nation's history. Like them, he was a leader of his people and a man who sought to share fully in their lot. Unlike them, however, with the possible exception of Douglass, Du Bois could easily have become an expatriate to Europe, where he would have enjoyed the honor and recognition to which his awesome intellectual gifts entitled him. A Ph.D. graduate of Harvard University and author of twenty-one books, Du Bois taught only in black colleges, never received an honorary degree from a major American university, and found his writings either patronized or ignored by whites. Although he was not sweet-tempered or acquiescent, Du Bois refused to allow racism to daunt him and turned his racial identity to advantage. This biography illuminates how, more than any other person, he uncovered and interpreted black Americans' African roots and theorized about their ties to the larger nonwhite world. Du Bois deserves the title of first and greatest Afro-American.

John Milton Cooper, Jr.

PREFACE

Few intellectuals have done more to shape the twentieth century than W. E. B. Du Bois. Only Frederick Douglass and Martin Luther King, Jr., equalled Du Bois's role in the social movement for civil rights in the United States. But in other respects, Du Bois's diverse activities over nearly a century left a larger legacy. Du Bois was the "father of Pan-Africanism" and a central theoretician of African independence; the major social scientist, educator, critic, and political journalist of black America for two generations; and an important figure in the international movements for peace and socialism.

This study is not designed as a comprehensive biography of Du Bois. It is an introduction that focuses on the main themes of Du Bois's social thought. Large omissions were inevitable, although recent studies have begun to address aspects of Du Bois's writings that are not discussed in detail in this book. I have also attempted to present Du Bois as much as possible in his own words, employing materials from his private correspondence, published and unpublished works.

PREFACE

The central thesis of this study advances a general revisionist interpretation of Du Bois's life and thought. Some historians and sociologists have emphasized the "paradoxical" behavior of Du Bois: that he was at various stages, a supporter of racial integration and voluntary racial segregation, an African nationalist, socialist, Communist, and pacifist. This "paradox" begins to unravel if one considers the central insight of Du Bois's close friend and colleague, Herbert Aptheker: "Du Bois was a Du Boisite. His political affiliations or affinities varied as times changes, as programs altered, and as he changed. . . . These were, however, political choices and not defining marks of his philosophical approaches. All his life Du Bois was a radical democrat."

There was a basic coherence and unity to Du Bois's entire public career. More than anything else, he remained a radical democrat. The bulk of his vast writings are a search to advance the democratic rights of peoples of African descent, of those in the nonwestern world, and by extension, of the world's working people. "Du Boisite" social theory embraced several other key elements. Du Bois was a cultural pluralist. He always opposed all forms of coercive discrimination and segregation based on race. But simultaneously, he was a leading proponent of black cultural pride and a founder of what today is termed *black studies*. Du Bois vigorously opposed any manifestation of human intolerance and social inequality—especially anti-Semitism and women's oppression. One critical component of Du Bois's thought frequently ignored was his profound sense of morality and his black prophetic Christianity. Du Bois was a harsh critic of orthodox Christianity, but any careful reading of his writings indicates a striking familiarity with the Bible. For Du Bois, politics were largely inseparable from moral imperatives. His opposition to racial inequality, European colonialism, and American capitalism was both moral and political. Even Du Bois's costly decision to defend the Communist party during the period of McCarthyism was both a political and a moral act. He would affirm his basic faith in democratic principles, even if his government would not.

From its inception, this book was the product of the collective insights from many colleagues and scholars. Since 1979, I have discussed the life and thought of Du Bois with Herbert Aptheker, whose special knowledge of the subject remains unsurpassed. Without his extensive research and the editing of Du Bois's published and unpublished works, this study would not have been possible. Among my former associates at Colgate University, Rhonda Levine and Arnold Sio reviewed the entire manuscript and provided helpful criticism. Gerald Horne, the National Director of the National Conference of Black Lawyers and noted Du Bois scholar, also gave critical encouragement and suggestions. Melanie Goldstein, Jennifer Braak, Mary

Smith, and Patricia Ryan were instrumental in preparing the manuscript. For her energetic and always timely efforts, my research assistant, Lisa Eiseman, was invaluable. I am particularly grateful to John Cooper, the editor of this series, for his careful reading of the final draft and for his support throughout this project.

However, my major debt is to my wife, Hazel Ann, who has a closer understanding of the central relationship between black faith and social transformation than I shall ever have. Through her life, her sacrifices, and her spirituality, I acquired fresh insight into a fundamental dimension of Du Bois's social thought. This short acknowledgment cannot fully express her vital contributions to this work.

1

A
GREAT
AMBITION

My boyhood seems, if my memory serves me rightly, to have been filled with incidents of surprisingly little importance. . . . In early youth a great bitterness entered my life and kindled a great ambition. I wanted to go to college because others did. I came and graduated and am now in search of a Ph.D. and bread. I believe, foolishly perhaps but sincerely, that I have something to say to the world.

> W. E. B. Du Bois,
> 3 October 1890

The greatest casualty of racism is democracy. Afro-Americans have understood this for many decades, and their leaders have attempted to redefine the American political system for the benefit of all citizens, regardless of race, gender, and social class. Most of the pivotal figures in the black experience who pursued the goal of multicultural democracy were charismatic leaders and orators—from Frederick Douglass and Sojourner Truth to Martin Luther King, Jr., and Fannie Lou Hamer. But the most complex social theoretician of this black tradition was William Edward Burghardt Du Bois. A social scientist who reluctantly entered politics, Du Bois was preoccupied with the relationship between race, class, and democracy throughout his long and productive life. He was an intellectual driven by his Calvinist upbringing and deep democratic ideals, who frequently opposed the dominant currents of his times. A cultural pluralist and Pan-Africanist who expressed "a New England conscience on a tropical heart," Du Bois embodied the tensions and paradoxes within America's cultural fabric.[1] His career was a long sojourn toward the aim of black cultural integrity, political emancipation, and democratic freedom for every sector of American society.

Du Bois was born "by a golden river and in the shadow of two great hills," in the village of Great Barrington, Massachusetts, on 23 February 1868.[2] His mother, Mary Burghardt Du Bois, was thirty-six years old, the youngest of at least ten children. The Burghardt extended family, located in the Berkshires for nearly 150 years, was responsible for young Du Bois's Negro identity. The family patriarch, Tom, had been born in West Africa and brought as a slave into the region by a Dutch family. During the American Revolution, Tom enlisted into the ranks of the Berkshire County regiments. One of his sons, Jack Burghardt, was a participant in Shays' rebellion. By the middle of the nineteenth century, the Burghardt clan was a well-established part of the community. Some family members worked as housemaids, waiters, and small farmers; one industrious cousin in nearby Lenox ran a laundry, and another owned the only barbershop in West Stockbridge. Mary's father, Othello, the owner of a modest farm on Egremont Plain near Great Barrington, was later described by his grandson as a "good-natured but not energetic" black man, "strong-voiced and redolent with tobacco." Othello's wife, Sally, was a "thin, tall, yellow and hawk-faced woman" with some Dutch and perhaps native American ancestry. Both tended to be overly protective toward their youngest child. Mary Burghardt had an affair with her first cousin, John Burghardt, that led to the birth of a son, Idelbert. The parents broke up the relationship, and Mary went to work in Great Barrington as a household domestic. The daughter had become a "silent, repressed woman" when Alfred Du Bois came to town early in 1867.[3]

The Du Bois heritage was traced to a physician and Bahamian plantation owner, James Du Bois. His eldest son by a black woman, Alexander, had been educated in a private school in Connecticut and lived for a time in Santo Domingo. Something of an entrepreneur, Alexander Du Bois eventually settled in New Haven, and managed a small grocery store while also working as a steward on a passenger boat serving New York City. A strict and domineering man—who eventually married four times—Alexander Du Bois refused to accept any form of racial discrimination. When black communicants at the Trinity Episcopal Church in New Haven were confronted with white hostility, Du Bois helped to create an all-black church, St. Luke's. His only son, Alfred, unfortunately shared many of his father's worst traits. Born in Haiti in 1825, Alfred was a romantic yet stubborn individualist, who constantly challenged parental authority. After a stint as a private in the Union army, he drifted into Great Barrington with little money, few skills, and no job. The Burghardts instantly disliked him, and questioned his itinerant background and lack of family ties. Without permission, Du Bois and Mary Burghardt were married, and the rebellious couple "carried on a more or less open feud" with the Burghardts until the birth of their son. About one year after Will's birth, Alfred Du Bois left town in search of permanent employment. Although he lived for a time only thirty-six miles from Great Barrington, he never returned to his wife and child.[4]

Mary Burghardt Du Bois and her infant son lived for several years on her parents' farm and later moved into a small house in town. Life was difficult, and frequently Mary suffered from severe depression. During Willie's childhood, Mary was partially paralyzed by a stroke that crippled her left leg and hand. Yet she still continued to work occasionally as a maid in the households of local white families. Despite the care and assistance by Mary's many sisters and brothers, she focused her hopes and aspirations on her young child. Perhaps, she may have thought, her son would have all the opportunities she had not found for herself. Despite her physical handicap and near penury, she wanted Willie to obtain a good education and to have a childhood without hunger and deprivation. With quiet determination, she consciously reinforced the boy's desire to excel.

In most respects, Mary Burghardt Du Bois's son had a pleasant childhood. He was enrolled in the local public school at the age of five or six and quickly became a favorite of his teachers. Will was obedient and highly motivated, and he soon advanced to upper grades. Usually he was several years younger than his classmates, and the boy soon sensed his intellectual superiority. "Art Benham could draw pictures" better, Du Bois reflected years later, but as a boy Will "could express meaning in words better than he. Mike Gibbons was a perfect marble player, but dumb in Latin." Will was not particularly good in football, and was one of the few children in town not permitted to ice-skate, since his "mother was afraid of the water." But he won praise as a fine singer and among his peers was usually the leader of intricate games, mountain climbing, and cave expeditions. Will had many friends, virtually all from middle-class, white households. George Beebe, a child of an affluent family, was one close companion, "because with all his clothes he was rather dumb in class and knew it, while I was bright and just this side of shabby, so that we balanced each other." Mary worked occasionally for the farm family of Will Beckwith, and the two boys frequently played together over weekends. Perhaps Will Du Bois's closest friend, Louis Russell, was the mentally retarded child of the mill owner. Most of the girls in Will's class made few impressions on him. His stern mother, and local opinion in general, frowned upon social affairs such as school dances, and juvenile dating was nonexistent. Even older boys did not escort girls to school or walk together on streets. Will had virtually no serious contacts with any females other than his mother. Friends commented about Will's close companionship with Mary, but he had no apologies. "This seemed quite normal to me; my mother was lame, why should I not guide her steps?" Du Bois later wrote, "And who knew better about my thoughts and ambitions?" After a day's household work at a white residence, Mary found

3

her son frequently waiting at the front door to assist her to their home. Mother and son, walking slowly together, were a familiar sight to town residents.[5]

As Will entered high school, he began to shoulder a greater share of the burden for maintaining their small family. He had learned from the Burghardts that no self-respecting individual could accept public charity, and he sought out odd jobs wherever work needed to be done. On Saturday mornings, he split wood and did chores for two elderly women. Every morning before walking to school he shoveled coal into the stove of the millinery shop. During afternoons he worked as a tea salesman for the A & P store, and in the summers he mowed lawns. Despite these tasks, Will continued to do well in his academic work, and he even found time to engage in other activities. He was briefly the coeditor of the high school newspaper, the *Howler.* With his mother, Will regularly attended services at the local Congregational church and participated in its social events. White teachers and neighbors provided important support for Will's future development. When Mary Du Bois lacked the funds to purchase her son's textbooks for Greek, Louis Russell's mother promptly paid for them. Johnny Morgan, a Welshman who ran the community bookstore, permitted Will to read his periodicals and books. Morgan secured for young Du Bois an appointment as Great Barrington correspondent to the *Springfield Republican,* and several of his articles and notes may have been published in 1884 and 1885. Frank Hosmer, the high school principal, also took charge of the young man's curriculum, recommending a college preparatory course including Latin, algebra, and geometry.

The stolid citizens of Great Barrington took pride in their local government, and here Du Bois received his first lessons in democracy. Every spring a town meeting was held to discuss expenditures for public education, street maintenance, and other issues of general concern. Will Du Bois began to attend these meetings by the age of thirteen, and took a distinct interest in the political process. Occasionally he became annoyed with the lengthy debates concerning the extravagance of high school appropriations, but gradually he came to conclude that the "essence of democracy" was in "listening to the other man's opinion and then voting your own, honestly and intelligently." Great Barrington had no "conscious socialist tendencies," but it owned its own water supply, which freely serviced all residences; the poor had little difficulty in obtaining private contributions, and health care was "mainly a matter of friendly charity among relatives and neighbors."[6] New England politics was cast largely in Calvinist terms, especially in small towns like Great Barrington. Few made any distinctions between the strict moral code that governed personal life and the duties and obligations of the political process. Perhaps here Du Bois began to draw the correlations between politics and ethics that would inform his entire career.

However, even as a high school pupil, Du Bois sensed the subtle distinctions of social class and political power that functioned within the village's democratic system. "Certain well-known and well-to-do citizens were always elected to office," Du Bois observed, "not the poorest or the Irish Catholics." Almost all citizens were Republicans, with the prominent exception of one local attorney: as a Democrat, he was suspected "of low origin and questionable designs." A small private school was maintained only for the children of prosperous families. Great Barrington's social outcasts were not blacks, but the Irish Catholics who dwelled in slums in the upper section of town near the woolen mills. Irish workers were casually made "the basis of jokes and ridicule in town." Young Irish women comprised almost all domestic workers, and their husbands and fathers were contemptuously described as "sloven," habitually drunken, unreliable laborers. Another oppressed group were women. None were permitted to vote, and with few exceptions, most working women were "housekeepers." Female students were not expected to engage in academic competition, and few in Du Bois's circle went beyond high school. At that time such gender and class categories remained vague to Du Bois, because he still subscribed to the hegemonic ideology of the town's middle class. He believed that "wealth was the result of work and saving and the rich rightly inherited the earth. The poor, on the whole, were themselves to be blamed."[7] Democracy was, in the context of Great Barrington, structured upon a hierarchical social order, and only those with talent, education, and property merited the right to voice opinions. As in Calvinist dogma, only the elect had the moral and intellectual capability to direct public discourse and policies.

As a child, Will Du Bois had little experience of racial discrimination, even though almost all his playmates were white. He recognized that the Burghardt clan was certainly less affluent than most of the town's established families and that they owned little property. But they were not as impoverished as the Irish working class. One of Du Bois's cousins married a young white woman, but the Burghardt family's major criticism was that her family history was unknown. There were about twenty-five Afro-American families who lived in Great Barrington out of a population of five thousand, and some were intermarried with whites. "The colored folk were not set aside in the sense that the Irish were, but were a part of the community of longstanding." Nevertheless, young Du Bois always sensed a degree of racial alienation and isolation. On one occasion, when students decided to exchange visiting cards, a white girl curtly rejected his gift. After other incidents, he became aware that his color permanently separated him from his friends. At first Du Bois reacted with a mood of "exaltation and high disdain. They were the losers who did not ardently court me, and not I, which seemed to be proven by the fact that I had no difficulty in outdoing them in nearly all competition, especially intellectual."[8] Adding to his isolation was the absence of his father and the depressed condition of his mother. As a Harvard graduate student, Du Bois later reflected that he could claim "no line of distinguished ancestors—indeed I have often been in a quandary as to how those revered ones spent their time." He had come to prefer friendships with men "who have no grandfathers. . . . In early youth a great bitterness entered my life and kindled a great ambition."[9] To discover himself, Will Du Bois gradually began to turn toward race.

A small number of Afro-Americans migrating from the South arrived in town and in the fall of 1884 established a small African Methodist Episcopal Zion Church. The Burghardts took no part in initiating this all-black congregation, but both Mary and Will Du Bois occasionally attended Sunday services and the ladies' monthly suppers. Will organized a literary and "social improvement" club, the "Sons of Freedom," which was dedicated to the "advancement of the colored race" in the town. The "Sons of Freedom" held debates, scheduled lectures, and studied the history of the United States. Somewhat earlier, Du Bois had been named local correspondent for the Afro-American weekly, the *Globe,* published in New York. *Globe* editor T. Thomas Fortune, then a leading black radical, wrote Du Bois "an encouraging letter," and the journalist's "fierce, brave voice" inspired him to provide some direction to the small black community of Great Barrington.[10] In the pages of the *Globe,* Du Bois criticized blacks for not participating in local town meetings, noting that "they do not take as much interest in politics as is necessary for the protection of their rights."[11] Like Fortune, who urged blacks to initiate political actions outside both major parties, Du Bois urged his elders to do the same. "Colored men of the town should prepare themselves" to contest for public office. We "hold the balance of power," Du Bois asserted. If Afro-Americans "will only act in concert, they may become a power not to be despised."[12] By the age of sixteen, Du Bois had reached an insight that would help to shape his political activities in future years: black Americans could not exercise their full democratic rights unless they organized themselves within a race-conscious bloc. In later decades, this observation would be expanded to include other sectors of society that experienced structural inequality. Democracy could not be colorblind in a racist society, nor could it extend full rights to workers or women when the state was dominated by a narrow elite. Group cooperation was essential to advance democratic reforms.

Du Bois's racial identity was reinforced during the summer of 1883, when he experienced his "greatest boyhood trip." The fourth wife of Alexander Du Bois invited her grandson to visit his paternal grandfather, then living in New Bedford, Massachusetts. Alfred Du Bois had died several years before, and Mary hoped that the Du Bois family might provide funds for her son's education. With some difficulty she raised the funds for the "great

6

excursion." When Will arrived at the train station, no one was there to welcome him. After a few frantic inquiries, the young man finally found the house. Alexander Du Bois proved to be rather intimidating at first. Still stern, "always he held his head high, took no insults, made few friends. He was not a 'Negro'; he was a man!"[13] Will was rather put off by his grandfather's ceremonious behavior and pretensions. But in a letter to his mother he confided, "I like him better than I thought I would. He says very little but speaks civily when I say anything to him."[14] More profound was Will's sojourn at a black festival on Narragansett Bay at Rocky Point, Rhode Island. Afro-Americans from three states gathered there annually for a picnic. Du Bois was deeply stirred by the event: "I viewed with astonishment ten thousand Negroes of every hue and bearing, saw in open-mouthed astonishment the whole gorgeous gamut of the American Negro world; the swaggering men, the beautiful girls, the laughter and gaiety, the unhampered self expression."[15] Reporting his travels in Fortune's newspaper, Du Bois was filled with black pride. But in keeping with his Calvinist upbringing, he duly noted areas in which Afro-Americans needed improvement. He had been "pleased to see the industry and wealth" of many blacks, but regretted the "absence of literary societies" in their communities.[16]

The next spring Du Bois graduated from high school with high honors and delivered his oration on the abolitionist, and later, socialist leader Wendell Phillips. Du Bois was the first black graduate in the school's history, and the entire black community was proud of him. Leaving school, he obtained employment as a timekeeper on a construction project. While saving his wages, he began to pore through college catalogues. Finally Harvard University was selected as Du Bois's first choice for a college education. But on 23 March 1885, Mary died suddenly, leaving Will's future plans in turmoil. His entire academic career might have ended there had it not been for the intervention of four white men: Frank Hosmer, Du Bois's former principal; the Reverend Evarts Scudder, pastor of the Congregational church; Edward Van Lennep, superintendent of the Congregational church's Sunday schools and principal of Great Barrington's private academy; and the Reverend C. C. Painter, a retired federal Indian agent and former pastor of several Congregational churches in Connecticut. As community leaders, they took a paternal interest in Will's plight, and without directly consulting the Burghardts they began to make certain decisions. The church in Great Barrington and Painter's churches agreed to donate one hundred dollars annually for Du Bois's college education. Dismissing Will's desires to attend Harvard, Painter insisted that the black youth's place was at Fisk University in Nashville, Tennessee. The Burghardts and other black citizens strongly disagreed with Painter's plan to send Du Bois to a predominantly black school in the South, but without funds of their own, they had little control over the situation. It seems likely that the town's liberal white elite believed that the proper training for Negroes was among their own people. But Du Bois, with a budding race consciousness and a desire to see the South, voiced no objections. He had once been moved to tears when a black quartet from Hampton Institute had visited the Congregational church. He recognized that he had the potential to become an effective leader for Afro-American people, and an experience in the South would prove invaluable. He could attend Harvard, after all, following his undergraduate studies at Fisk University. Leaving behind no debts, collecting his personal items and his grandfather's wrought iron tongs and shovel, Du Bois arrived in Nashville in the fall of 1885.

Fisk represented a new world of color to Du Bois. "I was thrilled to be for the first time among so many people of my own color. . . . Never before had I seen young men so self-assured and who gave themselves such airs, and colored men at that; and above all for the first time I saw beautiful girls."[17] But in early October typhoid fever struck Nashville, and Du Bois became "deathly sick." After weeks under intensive care, Du Bois "crept out, thin and pale" and quickly became "the school favorite." Another sort of crisis occurred when Du Bois learned that his male classmates had "loose sex morals," and not a few regularly drank alcohol. Years of sexual repression and Calvinist training instantly placed Du Bois at odds with other students. Long afterward Du Bois admitted frankly, "I actually did not know the physical difference between men and women. At first my fellows jeered in disbelief and then became sorry and made many offers to guide my abysmal ignorance. This built for me inexcusable and startling temptations."[18] Regarded as a "liar or freak" when he asserted his virginity, he sought familiar refuge in the arms of the church. Dutifully attending church services, revivals, and morning prayers at the beginning of each school day, Du Bois tried desperately to find inner tranquility. Writing to Reverent Scudder in February 1886, the young man observed that he had "united with the Church and hope that the prayers of my Sunday-School may help guide me in the path of Christian duty." Du Bois continued to correspond with members of the Great Barrington Sunday school class until at least 1892.[19] But in Nashville, he encountered opposition from "fundamentalist" quarters. One of Du Bois's classmates, "Pop" Miller, brought him before the congregation and accused him of "a particularly heinous form of sin," public "dancing." Du Bois protested in vain that he had "never attended public dance halls" and had only engaged in the "innocent pastime . . . at the homes of colored friends in the city." Fisk University professors supported Miller, warning the young sinner "that my dancing might well be quite innocent, but . . . my example might lead others astray." Du Bois deeply resented their intervention and much later concluded that his little tempest "led to my eventual refusal to join a religious organization." But for the moment, he still "never questioned [his] religious upbringing. Its theory had presented no particular difficulties: God ruled the world, Christ loved it, and men did right, or tried to; otherwise they were rightly punished."[20]

Problems also surfaced in the college. In the annual English examination, Du Bois placed second in the university. Despite his first year status, he was disappointed with his failure to claim the customary top prize. The daughter of a white German instructor had outranked him. "I could not quite forgive her as a girl and a white one at that." Moreover, Du Bois was upset that most of the school's black pupils were placed at an unfair disadvantage, since they had lacked "decent elementary school training in the colored public schools of the South."[21] Despite these minor setbacks, Du Bois soon established a solid reputation as a diligent student. His previous studies in Greek and Latin placed him in good stead with the well-respected professor of classics Adam Spence. Accepted into the sophomore class, Du Bois mastered the *Odyssey* and the *Iliad* in his first academic year. Other first-year studies included courses in French, botany, rhetoric, and calculus. Du Bois's major extracurricular activity was his involvement with the campus newspaper, the *Fisk Herald*. In November 1885, he was named editor of the "Exchanges" column. In 1886 he became the *Herald*'s literary editor and during his senior year was editor-in-chief. Under Spence's guidance, Du Bois became a member of the Mozart Society, a choral group that gave renditions of classical music. During his senior year, with the assistance of the *Herald*'s enterprising business manager, Tom Calloway, Du Bois solicited donations to finance the college's first gymnasium. Du Bois recognized that Fisk represented that tremendous yet unfulfilled potential of the entire black world that had been "held back by race prejudice and legal bonds, as well as by deep ignorance and dire poverty. . . . Into this world I leapt with enthusiasm. A new loyalty and allegiance replaced my Americanism: henceforward I was a Negro."[22]

Against the advice of his professors and some Fisk students, Du Bois ventured into the east Tennessee countryside to teach summer school in 1886 and 1887. The university campus, perched on a hill overlooking the city, provided no vantage point from which to study the actual problems of rural blacks. Du Bois obtained a minor position as an instructor at twenty eight dollars per month. Finally he encountered "the real seat of slavery. . . . I touched intimately the lives of the commonest of mankind—people who ranged from barefooted dwellers on dirt floors, with patched rags for clothes, to rough hard-working farmers, with plain, clean plenty."[23] His schoolhouse was nothing but a log hut with no door, "a massive rickety fireplace," and little furniture. "I was haunted by a New England vision of neat little desks and chairs, but alas the reality was rough plank benches without backs, and at times without legs," Du Bois noted. "They had the one virtue of making naps dangerous, possibly fatal, for the floor was not to be trusted."[24] Among his class of nearly thirty youths, many older than himself, was "a thin, homely girl of 20," Josie—later to be described as an unforgettable figure in *The Souls of Black Folk*.[25] The crucible of southern black life and labor was opened to Du Bois. Here he found warmth and unpretentious friendship he had not thought possible. Frequently after classes were finished he visited the families of his pupils: sitting on the porch eating fresh peaches with Josie and her talkative mother; visiting Doc Burke's farm, helping himself to fried chicken, wheat biscuits, string beans, and plump berries. Here he also discovered the mystery of sex, as Du Bois slept with an "unhappy wife who was my landlady." Time for these folk seemingly stood still. To be sure, life "was dull and humdrum," Du Bois wrote in his last *Autobiography*. "I have called my community a world, and so its isolation made it. There was among us but a half-awakened common consciousness, sprung from common joy and grief, at burial, birth or wedding; from a common hardship in poverty, poor land and low wages; and, above all, from the sight of the Veil that hung between us and Opportunity."[26]

But the essence of black life was to be found on Sunday mornings, as the dawn broke above the rural countryside. In the center of Alexandria, Tennessee's colored district were "the twin temples of the hamlet, the Methodist and Hard-Shell Baptist churches." In these unadorned wooden halls the black rural folk made "the weekly sacrifice with frenzied priest at the altar of the 'old-time religion'"; it was here that the families of his students sang in "soft melody and mighty cadences" the black spirituals of slavery. At first Du Bois was baffled by this experience. "We in Berkshire . . . were very quiet and subdued, and I know not what would have happened those clear Sabbath mornings had someone punctuated the sermon with a scream, or interrupted the long prayer with a loud Amen!" Such deep expressions of spirituality were utterly new to him. But in later years, Du Bois would document the black religious experience as comprising three essential elements—"the Preacher, the Music, and the Frenzy." The Afro-American minister was at once "a leader, a politician, an orator, a 'boss,' an intriguer, an idealist." The spirituals were simultaneously sorrowful and yet filled with hope, expressing "a faith in the ultimate justice of things." And the "frenzy," when the "Spirit of the Lord passed by, and, seizing the devotee, made him mad with supernatural joy," was at once an act of purgation of the believer's anxieties and fears created by racial oppression. It was a catharsis, the expression of transcendence, a cry of faith and hope, a physical and collective explosion that was essential for a people wedged in the vise of social frustration and material exploitation. The spirituality and sensuality, the shouting and swaying had awakened within Du Bois a commitment to black Christianity and had nearly shattered his former beliefs.[27]

When Du Bois returned to Fisk, he viewed orthodox religion somewhat differently. When assigned a text on Christian logic, it now "affronted my logic. It was to my mind, then and since, a cheap piece of special pleading." In 1888 university president Erastus Cravath secured a scholarship for Du Bois's postgraduate studies at Hartford Theological Seminary. But Du Bois rejected it, knowing that he "believed too little in Christian dogma to become a minister."[28] Du Bois's racial views also hardened into a general aversion of contact with southern whites. One small incident on a Nashville street was never forgotten. Du Bois accidentally bumped into a white woman and immediately offered his apologies. The woman became "furious" at Du Bois's polite gesture and cried: "How dare you speak to me, you impudent nigger!" Du Bois was deeply disturbed. "Was it because I showed no submissiveness? Did I fail to debase myself utterly and eat spiritual dirt?" Du Bois asked himself. Brooding over her visage of scorn and hatred, Du Bois decided that henceforth he would avoid "the necessity of showing them courtesy of any sort," beyond that demanded by his own strict "standards of decency." He followed statistics on southern lynchings; each racial atrocity "was a scar upon my soul." In an "Open Letter to the Southern People," which was unpublished, Du Bois criticized whites for their opposition to blacks' civil rights and educational opportunities. He believed that interracial cooperation was possible and that blacks should not be "foolish enough to demand social equality or amalgamation. . . . What we demand is to be recognized as men, and to be given those civil rights which pertain to our manhood."[29] To his fellow students, Du Bois projected a militant belief in black pride. "I am a Negro; and I glory in the name!" he declared in one public speech. "I am proud of the black blood that flows in my veins. From all the recollections dear to my boyhood have I come here, not to pose as a critic but to join hands with this, my people."[30]

Early in his senior year, Du Bois forwarded his application to the secretary of Harvard University. He observed that his ultimate goal was "a course of study for the degree of Ph.D. in Political Science after graduation." In support of Du Bois's application, letters of recommendation were submitted by Hosmer, Cravath, Spence, and several members of the Fisk faculty. Cravath affirmed that Du Bois possessed "an unusually quick, active mind" and had "maintained a high rank in all branches of study." Professor Frederick A. Chase of the physical sciences department sent a six-page letter, noting that the black youth gave "the impression of being conceited"; nevertheless, he believed with guidance Du Bois "would develop into an earnest and hard-working student."[31] On the strength of his record, Du Bois was admitted to Harvard College as a junior and was awarded a grant of $250 from the Price Greenleaf Fund. Graduating in June 1888, Du Bois delivered his commencement address on the subject "Bismarck," leader of German unification and proponent of the "blood and iron" political philosophy. Years later, Du Bois reflected that his selection of Bismarck "showed the abyss between my education and the truth in the world. Bismarck was my hero. He had made a nation out of a mass of bickering peoples." Du Bois may have perceived himself as a future black Bismarck, organizing Afro-Americans beneath the banner of inevitable progress. Fisk had emancipated his racial identity, but it had also reinforced elitist tendencies and an aversion to the struggles of workers. He knew little about economics, and his vague attitude toward trade unionism was "unfavorable." Despite his racial beliefs, Du Bois recalled himself as "blithely European and imperialist in outlook; democratic as democracy was conceived in America."[32] He had become something of a woman's rights advocate, even predicting in December 1887 that "the Age of Woman is surely dawning."[33] But his preoccupation was the clash between the races. In a *Fisk Herald* editorial of February 1888, Du Bois noted that he had dedicated himself "toward a life that shall be an honor to the Race."[34]

Upon graduation, Du Bois needed to raise additional funds for travel and living expenses at Harvard. Several Fisk students conceived a plan to generate money by forming a small glee club, for which Du Bois would serve as business manager. The group would work as waiters at a summer resort hotel at Lake Minnetonka, Minnesota, for several months, and in the last weeks of August schedule a set of performances in the Midwest. The proposal was at first repugnant to Du Bois, who had "instinctively hated such work" from his birth. His mother had been a "menial," and his paternal grandfather "had to fight hard to be a man and not a lackey." He did not wish to feel the "sting" of the "talons," hustling as a humble waiter. Yet he sadly agreed to the scheme and traveled to the hotel with "distinct forebodings." The experience was an ordeal that Du Bois would long recall. Waiters were poorly paid, confined to a filthy table in the kitchen quarters, and received "uneatable scraps." The guests were not "well-bred," smelled of liquor, and "spent a great deal of money. . . . Husbands arrived with other men's wives and gay women without husbands were in evidence." Waiters competed for gratuities by playing clowns before wealthy white patrons, "crouching, grinning, assuming a broad dialect." To eat, waiters stole portions of guests' meals and gave false orders to cooks. Du Bois was "too cowardly" to steal but "not coward enough to refuse what others stole." Du

Bois's hostility toward white bourgeois culture was certainly reinforced. He detested the "business men and their prostitutes" and tried to maintain his self respect:

> I did not mind the actual work or the kind of work, but was the dishonesty and deception, the flattery and cajolery, the unnatural assumption that worker and diner had no common humanity. . . . I stood staring and thinking, while the other boys hustled about. Then I noticed one fat hog, feeding at a heavily gilded trough, who could not find his waiter. He beckoned me. It was not his voice, for his mouth was too full. It was his way, his air, his assumption. Thus Caesar ordered his legionaires or Cleopatra her slaves. Dogs recognize the gesture. I did not. He may be beckoning yet for all I know, for something froze within me. I did not look his way again. Then and there I disowned menial service for me and my people. . . . When I finally walked out of that hotel and out of menial service forever, I felt as though, in a field of flowers, my nose had been held unpleasantly long to the worms and manure at their roots.[35]

When Du Bois began classes at Harvard, he had lost most of his illusions about the institution and the prospects for fraternal relations with white classmates. He had gone to Harvard "as a Negro, not simply by birth, but recognizing myself as a member of a segregated caste whose situation I accepted but was determined to work from within that caste to find my way out."[36] He selected a broad range of courses necessary for his projected role as an intellectual leader for his race. During his junior year, he scored A's in geology, qualitative analysis, and economics, but obtained a C in English composition. The next year he studied French and German philosophy with George Santayana and enrolled in William James's course on logic. In Albert Bushnell Hart's course, "Constitutional and Political History of the United States, 1783–1861," Du Bois received a rare A-plus.

Several Harvard professors had a lasting influence on Du Bois's thought. As Arnold Rampersad observed, Du Bois acquired from Hart an appreciation for scholarly documentation and rigorous research, as well as literary restraint. William James and Josiah Royce were just beginning to articulate their pragmatist philosophy, which would have an impact upon Du Bois's earliest writings in sociology. In his composition courses, Du Bois was tutored in the late Victorian style of Adams Sherman Hill that was "grounded squarely on the classical tradition of Aristotle's *Rhetoric* and Cicero's speeches," Rampersad noted. Hill's elegant syntax and reverence for Latin sharply affected Du Bois's prose style.[37] Du Bois developed a close personal relationship with James, who invited him into his home for dinners and receptions. He also joined the students' Philosophical Club. But he maintained a distinct distance from most students. Du Bois knew fewer than a dozen of the three hundred students in his graduating class. White students from the South avoided his company and sometimes refused to sit beside him in classes. There were inevitable racial insults and rejections. Despite a fine singing voice, his application to join the Harvard Glee Club was refused. At a reception, one white matron deliberately insisted that Du Bois had to be a waiter. Sensitive to any racial slur, he became "desperately afraid of intruding" into white student life. Several black undergraduates, notably William Monroe Trotter, had many white friends and experienced few difficulties engaging in social events. Not Du Bois. Retreating quietly from campus, he lived for a time in the second story flat of a home owned by a black woman. He sought little companionship with whites as a group and devoted himself largely to research and reflection.

But in the Boston black community, Du Bois did find support and comfort. He became a friend of Josephine St. Pierre Ruffin, a national leader of the black women's club movement and editor of the Boston *Courant,* a black weekly. A number of Du Bois's classroom theme papers were printed in the *Courant,* and he quickly became well known within the Negro community. He attended local black affairs and initiated cultural events. In 1891 Du Bois and other black students organized a rendition of Aristophanes' "Birds" in a black church. The play was somewhat amateurish and "not quite appreciated by the colored audience." In his personal life, Du Bois was attracted to Maud Cuney, the daughter of the Collector of Customs at Galveston, Texas. Cuney had "gold-bronze skin, brilliant eyes and coils of black hair" and was a bright and talented musical performer. When officials at the New England Conservatory of Music placed Cuney in a racially segregated section of their dormitory, Du Bois and other black students rallied in protest and overturned the decision. For a time Du Bois and Cuney were "deeply in love" and were engaged to be married. "I was encased in a completely colored world, self-sufficient and provincial, and ignoring just as far as possible the white world which conditioned it," Du Bois later commented. "This was self-protective coloration, with perhaps an inferiority complex, but with belief in the ability and future of Black folk."[38] Although Du Bois identified with Boston's blacks, he did not romanticize their political and social condition. Black churches were too reluctant to initiate community welfare projects; neighborhoods had too few libraries and reading circles. Du Bois believed that Afro-Americans had to hold themselves to higher criteria in cultural, social, and intellectual endeavors: "No Negro can afford to stoop to an Anglo-Saxon standard of morality."[39]

Academically, Du Bois continued to live up to the expectations of his former instructors. In October 1889 he was awarded a Matthews Scholarship; he competed for the Boylston prizes in oratory and placed second behind another black student Clement Morgan. At his undergraduate commencement on 25 June 1890, Du Bois was selected to give one of several brief orations. Rather boldly, he selected the topic "Jefferson Davis" for his speech. Du Bois attempted to give a fair critique of Davis as a "typical Teutonic Hero." Davis was a "naturally brave and generous man" who became "the peculiar champion of a people fighting to be free in order that another people should not be free." The entire logic of his career was "the advance of a part of the world at the expense of the whole; the overweening sense of the I, and the consequent forgetting of the Thou." The lecture's success brought Du Bois to national attention for the first time. The *Nation* commented that the "slender, intellectual-looking mulatto" had "handled his difficult and hazardous subject with absolute good taste, great moderation, and almost contemptuous fairness."[40] During his first two years of graduate level studies in 1890–92, Du Bois continued to make progress, earning five A's and five B's in his course work. Much of 1890–91 was devoted to library research on the topic of "the Suppression of the African Slave Trade." By mid-March 1891, he had collected materials on 146 "colonial laws suppressing . . . the traffic from 1638 to 1788," and about 100 similar acts introduced into Congress between 1789 and 1830. Professor Hart continued to provide direction and encouragement for Du Bois's historical research. In 1891 Du Bois delivered his first academic paper at the American Historical Association meeting, and he received his M.A. degree the same year.

Despite these successes, Du Bois maintained his distance from most whites. The "veil" of segregation and racism still set him apart from his colleagues. He was not permitted to join the Graduates Club, a social group, solely on racial grounds. He could win the H. B. Rogers Memorial Fellowship in Political Science in 1890–92 but still fail to obtain genuine social equality and respect from most white students with lesser abilities. Occasionally Du Bois expressed his bitterness in his papers. In an English composition class directed by Professor Barrett Wendell, Du Bois submitted a brutal essay entitled "The American Girl" that revealed both his disgust with white bourgeois culture and his progressive ideas on women's emancipation: "When I wish to meet the American Hog in its native simplicity; when I wish to realize the world-pervading presence of the Fool; when I wish to be reminded that whatever rights some have I have none. . . . I seek the company of the American girl." Du Bois may have been characterizing the girlfriends of white Harvard students: "her face . . . is apt to be more shrewd than intelligent, arrogant than dignified, silly than pleasant." White women of the upper classes stood in "horror of being 'mannish'" and were afraid to take "rational" steps to demand their rights. To "cure this eye-sore," Du Bois suggested that the woman must "emancipate herself from the rule of the Ribbon," obtain an education, and "lastly, go to work." Du Bois's instructor was nonplussed. "Such truculence as yours is thoroughly injudicious. Nothing could more certainly induce an average reader to disagree," Wendell warned.[41] Du Bois was scarcely less hostile toward orthodox white Christianity. In his private papers, he condemned the "high Episcopal Nicene creed" as a rationale for white supremacy. God may still have been real to blacks and possibly to Quakers, but most whites had long since buried any identification with Christian morality and ethics.

While at Fisk, Du Bois probably decided to spend one or more years abroad during his graduate school studies. His sharp sense of racial alienation and isolation probably reinforced this determination to leave the United States. Du Bois learned that the Slater Fund for the Education of Negroes, chaired by former President Rutherford B. Hayes, was willing to provide educational grants for advanced studies in Europe. On 4 November 1890, Du Bois wrote Hayes, noting that he had "no money or property" but had a desire "to pursue my work in the continental universities." In early 1891, Du Bois forwarded two more letters to Hayes. The former president responded casually in May 1891, informing Du Bois that the "plan had been given up." Frustrated and upset, Du Bois wrote an abrasive reply. "The outcome of the matter is as I expected it would be. . . . I am perfectly capable of fighting alone for an education if the trustees do not see fit to help me," he noted. "On the other hand the injury you have—unwittingly I trust—done the race I represent, and am not ashamed of, is almost irreparable." Already Du Bois identified his own fortunes with those of the entire black American people. "I find men willing to help me thro' cheap theological schools, I find men willing to help me use my hands before I have got my brains in working order, I have an abundance of good wishes on hand, but I never found a man willing to help me get a Harvard Ph.D."[42] It is surprising that Hayes did not discard the letter. Perhaps half ashamed, Hayes promised to bring the matter before the board of trustees in 1892. In April 1892, the Slater Fund notified Du Bois that it would award him the sum of seven hundred fifty dollars, one half of which had to be repaid with interest, and promised to consider renewing the grant for a second year. Du Bois celebrated by purchasing a shirt that cost "three dollars, which was about four times as much as I had ever paid for a shirt in my life."[43] The young scholar was bound for Europe and had to dress appropriately.

Du Bois "crossed the ocean in a trance," repeatedly questioning whether his dream was actually coming true. Arriving in Rotterdam on 1 August 1892 on a Dutch steamer, Du Bois had over two months for sightseeing before classes began at Friedrich Wilhelm University in Berlin. During his travels, he was befriended by a German family in Eisenach. Du Bois was astonished that he was perceived simply as another human being by the Germans. One young woman, Dora Marbach, was particularly attracted to Du Bois and escorted him to dances and outings. After several weeks, Dora and Will expressed their love for each other, and she wanted to get married "at once." But Du Bois knew that "this would be unfair to her and fatal for my work at home, where I had neither property nor social standing for this blue-eyed stranger. She could not quite understand." This brief but important love affair left its mark on Du Bois. The warm friendship eroded some of the mistrust that had dictated his cool behavior toward whites. Emerging from "the extremes of racial provincialism," Du Bois later observed, "I became more human; learned the place in life of 'Wine, Women, and Song' . . . and above all I began to understand the real meaning of scientific research . . . for the settlement of the Negro problem in America."[44] The color line need not be permanent, if human beings understood the reasons for hatred, poverty, and ignorance. Enrolling at the university in October, Du Bois again felt little or no color prejudice. He attended the operas and made friends within the student body. And he acquired new affectations: a beard and mustache, fashioned after that of Kaiser Wilhelm, a cane and gloves, and a habit of stylish dress that he never lost. Only after several months of student life did Du Bois recognize another sort of "veil" within German culture, the poison of anti-Semitism. Intrigued with this unforeseen aspect of intolerance, he concluded that German anti-Semitism had "much in common with our own race question."[45]

As at Harvard, Du Bois established fairly good relations with some of his professors. With Gustav Schmoller, he did research on the patterns of plantation economics and peonage in the U.S. South; he studied the structure of the Prussian state under Rudolph von Gneist; he heard a lecture by young sociologist Max Weber, and studied political economy with Adolph Wagner. Du Bois was offended when a "fire-eating" professor, Heinrich von Treitschke, thundered an attack against "mulattoes" as "inferior." Most of the professors, however, seemed to have little recognition of Du Bois's race. But Du Bois's real education took place outside the university. He attended local meetings of the German Social Democratic party, then the largest socialist party in the world. Only recently permitted to function legally, the Social Democrats had received 1.4 million votes, roughly 20 percent of the total, in the Reichstag elections of 1890. Berlin was a stronghold of socialist support, and Du Bois became vaguely sympathetic with the movement.[46] Du Bois's first opportunity to see other parts of Europe came in late 1893, during the Christmas holidays. Traveling with two students,, Du Bois visited Strassburg, Munich, Prague, Dresden, and other central European cities. Much of the time was spent at the major art galleries and cultural sites, but along the way they conversed and lived with dozens of "peasant folk," drinking and feasting, attending "social assemblies," and listening "to their gossip." With an English student, Du Bois journeyed to Italy to visit historical monuments and paintings. Trouble arose in Rome when Du Bois and his companion, "mistaken for Frenchmen," were stoned by angry Italian youth in the central city.

Traveling alone, Du Bois left Vienna to see a school friend in Crakow, and encountered other peoples whose oppressed political and social conditions bore a "far-off likeness" to those of Afro-Americans. In Budapest, he was surprised at the "hostility" between Hungarians and their Austrian rulers. The "poverty and despair" throughout Hungary was profound, and on more than one occasion he was "mistaken for a Jew." In one small Slovenian town, Du Bois related later, "the driver of a rickety cab whispered in my ear, *'Unter die Juden?'* . . . I stared and then said yes. I stayed in a little Jewish inn." Crossing into Poland on foot, he finally arrived in Crakow. Du Bois's Polish classmate, Stanislaus Ritter von Estreicher, had warned him of the "race antagonism" within Austrian-occupied Poland. But Du Bois was still saddened by what he observed. "Tyranny in school and work; insult in home and on the street," he later noted. Some Poles in the upper classes managed to escape "personal insult." But the masses of workers and peasants were trapped within a "degradation" that was "only too familiar."[47] Returning by way of Prague and Dresden, Du Bois may have begun to perceive the broader class dimensions of national oppression. Racism in the United States was only one virulent example of ethnic and national minority subordination.

Always conscious of his personal and intellectual obligations to the Afro-American community, Du Bois periodically communicated with friends and associates in the United States, sharing his observations about European culture and political life. Forwarding a lengthy letter to the *Fisk Herald* in May 1893, he urged Fisk students to study abroad. European intellectuals and culture would provide assistance and direction in "the rise of the Negro people."[48] Fortune published several of Du Bois's letters in his newspaper, the New York *Age,* that were not always well received. As one critic in the Cleveland *Gazette* noted, "Much of W. E. B. Du Bois's letters from Europe . . . make one very tired. 'I, I, I, I, Me, me, me, Black bread and butter', Scat!"[49] What Du Bois could not share with American readers was the impact of the European trip upon his personal life. There were petty temptations along the way, detours from the art galleries and lecture halls, that shaped his mind and mood. One minor peccadillo occurred on a French train, when Du Bois "played the pea in a shell game and lost two dollars." Chastened by his loss, he did not gamble again for forty years. Visiting Paris in the spring of 1894, Du Bois became "fascinated by the glory of French culture in painting, sculpture, architecture and historical monument." He "haunted" the Louvre and walked pleasantly along the Champs Elysées. But he also dared to visit a house of prostitution and after "a brief trial" left questioning his "sense of decency." Throughout his stay in Europe, Du Bois "went through a desperately recurring fight to keep the sex instinct in control." His longest relationship was with a young woman who worked in a Berlin shop. Although Du Bois never revealed her name in his writings, he "lived more or less regularly" with her for at least one year. The dilemma was identical to that in his earlier romance with Dora Marbach: he opposed the marriage because of the hardships a biracial couple would suffer within the United States. Perhaps a second factor was Du Bois's profound sense of guilt about premarital sex. Faced with the contradictions of "virginity and motherhood . . . prostitution and adultery," Du Bois "fought and feared amid what should have been a climax of true living."[50]

The clearest indication of how Du Bois viewed himself at this time occurred on his twenty-fifth birthday. Characteristically, he planned the event meticulously as a "Sacrifice to the Zeitgeist." It was, Du Bois wrote, "one of the happiest days of my happy life." Alone in his small flat, he sang "Jesus, Lover of My Soul" and "America"; he visited an art gallery and had coffee with "a pretty girl"; he dined on cocoa, oranges, and Greek wine. In his reflections that evening, Du Bois revealed his deepest ambitions and fears. He questioned an "egotism" that made him feel "royal and that beneath my sceptre a world of kings shall bow." Du Bois dedicated himself to the search for scientific "Truth," the "cold and indisputable" research that was necessary to advance the interests of all black people, "taking for granted that their best development means the best development of the world." Nothing would deter him from the challenge, and neither "Heaven nor Hell, God nor Devil shall turn me from my purpose till I die." His years of "apprenticeship" at Great Barrington, Harvard, and Berlin had prepared him for a life's work of scholarship and struggle that would embrace the color line across the globe. "These are my plans: to make a name in science, to make a name in literature and thus to raise my race. Or perhaps," Du Bois added, "to raise a visible empire in Africa thro' England, France or Germany . . . I will go unto the king—which is not according to the law and if I perish—I PERISH."[51] Du Bois's remarks reveal not simply a transcendent faith in his own abilities but an intimate connection between his fate and that of all Afro-Americans. His future task was to harness his skills and training to resolve the burden of race, and to instill in others the intellectual and moral capacity to devote their energies toward black advancement. Three weeks after his twenty-fifth birthday, in correspondence with the trustees of the Slater Fund, Du Bois explained that his ultimate goal was "to get a position in one of the Negro universities, and to seek to build up there a department of history and social science, with two objectives in view: (a) to study scientifically the Negro question past and present with a view to its best solution. (b) to collect capable young Negro students, and to see how far they are capable of furthering, by independent study and research, the best scientific work of the day."[52]

Despite the efforts of professors Wagner and Schmoller, Du Bois was unable to obtain a doctorate from the University of Berlin when the faculty refused to give him an oral examination. Technically Du Bois had attended classes for only three semesters, and a minimum of five semesters was mandatory for doctoral candidates. Du Bois was tempted to remain in Germany for another year, but the Slater Fund's director, President Daniel Coit Gilman of Johns Hopkins University, advised him to return to the United States. Du Bois's funding was not renewed, but the Slater trustees expressed "with great earnestness" the hope that the black scholar would ultimately "devote" his talents "to the good of the colored race."[53] After spending several months in France, nearly without funds, Du Bois booked passage in the steerage section of a ship out of Southampton in June 1894. The man who returned was quite different from the one who left two years before. Passionately a Negro, yet he now felt no need to have his racial identity reinforced by others. Five blacks were among the eight hundred passengers aboard the ship, but Du Bois did not seek their company or even speak to them. The whites on the vessel, mostly of "the lower classes," had no "trace of deception and desire to injure or envy others."[54] Europe had introduced him to social classes that expressed little or no racial prejudice. They had become for Du Bois "not white folks, but folks. The unity beneath all life clutched me." His education abroad did not reduce his opposition to racial segregation at home: he knew that ahead of him was "'nigger'-hating America." But Du Bois also understood that the fight against the color line could not be waged in isolation. "I felt myself standing, not against the world, but simply against American narrowness and color prejudice, with the greater, finer world at my back urging me on."[55] Du Bois's confidence in his intellectual equipment was rooted in a pragmatic faith in social science as a tool for social reform. Or, as he had observed in his diary several years before: "The Universe is Truth. The Best ought to be. On these postulates hang all the law and prophets."[56] Now with the awareness of larger cultural patterns beyond the United States, the young scholar felt prepared to initiate his life's work.

2

THE
IVORY TOWER
OF RACE

The Negro is a sort of seventh son, born with a veil, and gifted with second sight in this American world—a world which yields him no self-consciousness, but only lets him see himself through the revelation of the other world. . . . One ever feels his twoness—an American, a Negro; two souls, two thoughts, two unreconciled strivings; two warring ideals in one dark body, whose dogged strength alone keeps it from being torn asunder.

W. E. B. Du Bois,
"Strivings of the Negro People," 1897

Du Bois arrived in New York with exactly two dollars in his pocket, plus fare for a train ticket to Great Barrington. Throughout the months of July and August he penned letters to dozens of black colleges in search of employment. One distinct possibility was a small industrial school in the Alabama Black Belt, Tuskegee Institute. Tuskegee's principal, Booker T. Washington, had recently married a Fisk classmate of Du Bois's, Margaret Murray. In his correspondence to Washington, Du Bois mentioned this relationship, adding that "my specialty is history and social science but I can teach German, philosophy, natural science, classics, etc."[1] But there were few replies, all unfavorable. Finally in mid-August he received an offer to teach Greek and Latin at Wilberforce University, an African Methodist Episcopal church school in central Ohio. The position would pay eight hundred dollars annually. Du Bois immediately accepted, and began to prepare for his long train ride to the Midwest. Within one week, several additional offers arrived, including a telegram from Tuskegee Institute: "Can give mathematics here if terms suit. Will you accept."[2] Du Bois informed Washington that he was no longer available for the job. With great expectations, Du Bois arrived at the small train depot in Xenia, Ohio, in late August 1894.

From his first months on the campus, Du Bois presented problems for the administration. There was the matter of his appearance: his high silk hat, gloves and walking cane, and his dapper Vandyke beard. Du Bois was tactless and thoughtlessly blunt. He complained about the absence of books in the library and criticized the school's curriculum. When he attended a local religious gathering out of curiosity, Du Bois was asked by a student leader to "lead us in prayer." Astonished, Du Bois replied, "No, he won't." In his *Autobiography,* Du Bois noted this his curt remarks "nearly lost my new job. It took a great deal of explaining to the board of bishops why a professor of Wilberforce should not be able at all times and sundry to address God in extemporaneous prayer."[3] Du Bois's willingness to work proved to be his salvation. He agreed to teach courses in English and German, as well as in Latin and Greek. He urged the administration to permit him to give a course in sociology but failed to obtain permission. He also served as the university's official "Keeper of Marks" and even occasionally supervised disciplinary matters. Du Bois did not make friends easily, and the religious dogmatism of the institution prevented him from reaching out to many faculty members. During one week-long revival, Du Bois shut himself away in his room, fearing "mental imbecility" due to the "wild screams, cries, groans and shrieks" from the campus chapel.[4] But he made several acquaintances during these years that lasted for decades to come. A talented young poet from Dayton, Paul Laurence Dunbar, read poetry to Wilberforce students. Impressed with his work, Du Bois was "astonished to find that he was a Negro." West Point graduate Charles Young, who worked as the school's military instructor, became particularly close to Du Bois. They refused to take part in religious revival sessions, and both men "dreamed of a great future for this Negro school." Yet on balance, Du Bois was increasingly frustrated. "I found myself against a stone wall," he later admitted. "Nothing stirred before my impatient pounding!"[5] Wilberforce was frequently late in paying Du Bois's salary, and in June 1895 he notified the Slater Fund that he would be unable to repay his graduate school loan for the year.

Most of Du Bois's spare time was devoted to the revision of his doctoral dissertation. *The Suppression of the African Slave-Trade to the United States of America, 1638–1870* was accepted by Harvard, and Du Bois obtained his Ph.D. in 1895. In October 1896, the dissertation was published as the initial volume in the Harvard Historical Studies Series. The literary style and methodology of the monograph clearly indicate Du Bois's training by Hart and his graduate studies in Germany. Cool and precise, *Suppression* appeared to be a detached legalistic study. But, beneath the data was a sharp moral and ethical repudiation of chattel slavery. Du Bois began the book with a brief historical sketch of the slave trade, noting that "crucifixion, burning and starvation were legal modes of punishment" for rebellious blacks.[6] Du Bois then explained the differences in legal codes affecting the importation and supervision of slaves in the plantation colonies of the South, the middle colonies, and New England. The bulk of the text examined the political and legal dimensions of the growing attempt to abolish the slave trade. Du Bois illustrated that the Constitutional Convention of 1787 "had no desire really to enter upon a general slavery argument." The South still "apologized for slavery," and the East "could only tolerate it from afar," but "instead of calling the whole moral energy of the people into action, so as gradually to crush this portentous evil, the Federal Convention lulled the nation to sleep by a 'bargain,' and left to the vacillating and unripe judgement of the States one of the most threatening of the social and political ills." Du Bois briefly mentioned the impact of slave revolts and the actions of rebels such as Haitian leader Toussaint L'Ouverture upon the debate to abolish slavery. The book repeatedly condemned the moral and political hypocrisy of American democracy, its inability to check "this real, existent, growing evil," which paved "the highway that led straight to the Civil War."[7]

Du Bois's emphasis on moral factors in the evolution of slavery was largely in keeping with the state of American historiography of that period. Indeed, as the president of the University of Michigan observed to the president of Johns Hopkins University in 1885, "I should not want a man who would not make his historical judgements and interpretations from a Christian standpoint." The writing of history was directly related "to Ethics."[8] Although Du Bois had distanced himself from his Calvinist origins, the effects of his earlier ideological indoctrination were still apparent in *Suppression*. Consequently he minimized economic factors at the expense of moral issues. He recognized that "the primary excuse for the rise of the African slave-trade to America" was the decision of early colonists to regard "this land as existing chiefly for the benefit of Europe, and as designed to be exploited, as rapidly and ruthlessly as possible." But he emphasized the ethical dimensions of this social process of exploitation. Du Bois noted that the slavery regime had created a southern "oligarchy," but he did not fully explore social class divisions within the white population. His description of abolitionism was primarily that of "a rising moral crusade," rather than a political movement. *Suppression* essentially subordinated political and social class conflict to the ethical question elevated by slavery: "How far in a State can a recognized moral wrong safely be compromised?"[9] Most reviewers were impressed with the monograph. The Nation predicted that *Suppression* would "long remain the authoritative work on the subject." Another viewer disliked Du Bois's "moralistic attitude," yet admitted that the author had been "most industrious in gathering and arranging his material."[10]

While rewriting his manuscript for publication, Du Bois came under renewed pressure at Wilberforce. Several faculty members began to make veiled hints concerning Du Bois's status as an unmarried male. For Du Bois, any sexual encounter with a married woman was distinctly impossible. But he had already "carefully calculated" that he should marry before the age of thirty, and that his paltry salary was "sufficient for two—if paid." And there was one special woman whom Du Bois found attractive. Nina Gomer, a "slender, quiet, and dark-eyed girl," was an undergraduate student at the university. Nina's father was a black chef in Cedar Rapids, Iowa, and her late mother had been an immigrant from Alsace. By the spring of 1896, both were deeply in love, and they made secret plans to be married. Nina took a train to Iowa, while Du Bois petitioned the university's treasurer to provide his back wages. The treasurer dismissed Du Bois's pleas, explaining that he was preparing to leave for the A.M.E. church's "General Conference where he had more weighty matters to discuss than teachers' salaries." Outraged and "penniless," the young professor "waylaid him and firmly persuaded him that until my salary due was paid, he was unlikely to see General Conference." With funds in hand, Du Bois traveled to Cedar Rapids, was married, and returned to the college "with a very tired young bride." Many of the faculty were "critical" of Du Bois's abrupt behavior, but the students were "hilarious." The young couple settled in a small two-room apartment in the men's dormitory. Both were quite happy, despite the different expectations they held about married life. Nina's "life-long training as a virgin," Du Bois later noted, "made it almost impossible for her ever to regard sexual intercourse as not fundamentally indecent. It took careful restraint on my part not to make her unhappy. . . . This was no easy task for a normal and lusty young man."[11]

Du Bois had also alienated the administration by protesting the proposed appointment to the faculty of the son of Bishop Benjamin Arnett, who was the president of the university. Although this protest was successful, Du Bois understood that his "days at Wilberforce were numbered." He had published his first book but was "doing nothing directly in the social sciences and saw no immediate prospect. Then the door of opportunity opened."[12] In the spring of 1896, Du Bois received an offer from the University of Pennsylvania to conduct an extensive study on the "social condition of the Colored People of the Seventh Ward of Philadelphia." The project was initially suggested by Susan B. Wharton, a member of the Philadelphia Settlement's executive committee. Charles C. Harrison, the university provost, succinctly outlined the project: "We want to know precisely how this class of people live; what occupations they follow; from what occupations they are excluded; how many of their children go to school; and to ascertain every fact which will throw light on this social problem."[13] The salary was nine hundred dollars, but the appointment was only for one year. Du Bois promptly accepted, and by late July the Du Bois household had moved into Philadelphia's black ghetto, finding a one-room apartment above a cafeteria. Du Bois did not anticipate a warm welcome from the University of Pennsylvania's faculty, and he was not disappointed. Given the curious title of "assistant instructor," he received no office on the campus. His name was even omitted from the university catalogue, and he did "no instructing save once to pilot a pack of idiots through the Negro slums."[14]

From 1 August 1896 until the end of 1897, with the exception of two months in the summer of 1897, Du Bois worked on the project. A task that should have required the intensive labor of a team of scholars over a three-year period was completed by the young "assistant instructor." Du Bois studied published volumes on Philadelphia's historical and socioeconomic conditions and reviewed archival materials. He developed comprehensive questionnaires on family units, individuals, and domestic workers. He personally interviewed five thousand people. Du Bois "labored morning, noon, and night."[15] The compiled results were *The Philadelphia Negro,* the first sociological text on an Afro-American community published in the United States. Nearly a half century later, Swedish sociologist Gunnar Myrdal, author of *An American Dilemma,* described Du Bois's monograph as "a study of a Negro community . . . which best meets our requirements."[16]

The Philadelphia Negro shares some basic methodological and stylistic traits with *The Suppression of the African Slave Trade.* The rigorous research again reflected the influence of historian Albert Bushnell Hart and the standards of late nineteenth-century German scholarship. Exhaustive data was presented on the character and social institutions of the black community, including statistics on health, marital and family relations, crime, education, vocational status, and literacy. But quite deliberately, Du Bois began the book with a detailed historical analysis of Afro-American people in the city of Philadelphia. Sociology was more than a concrete assessment of present socioeconomic realities. As Du Bois explained in 1897, "one cannot study the Negro in freedom and come to general conclusions about his destiny without knowing his history in slavery."[17] The only worthwhile sociology was historical sociology, research that examined the constant evolution of social structure, cultural values, and economic life of people. Du Bois was especially convinced that careful sociological measurement, combined with a proper cultural and historical understanding of a social group, could lead to the construction of a social agenda for reform. As in *Suppression,* the monograph exhibits a strong moral or Calvinist undercurrent, which is manifested in blunt criticisms of the black community's social contraditions. Du Bois deplored the vice and "sexual looseness" that was "the prevailing sin of the mass of the Negro population." He criticized the black criminal element, noting with some dismay: "it is not well to clean a cesspool until one knows where the refuse can be disposed of without general harm." Black parents were censured for not reinforcing sufficiently the value of formal education, and the Negro church was charged with failing to combat social corruption and moral decay.

However, *The Philadelphia Negro* also represented a major shift in Du Bois's assessment of black American society. Within Philadelphia's forty thousand black Americans, a basic class stratification could be discerned, which revealed the systemic impact of racial discrimination and the lack of economic justice. For the black poor and jobless, the city was a "social environment of excuse, listless despair, careless indulgence and lack of inspiration to work." Thousands of black young adults, denied educational and vocational opportunity, had been unable to develop "fully the feeling of responsibility and personal worth." Du Bois observed that the ghetto functioned as a social entity for economic and social subordination: blacks were "a people receiving a little lower wages than usual for less desirable work, and compelled, in order to do that work, to live in a little less pleasant quarters than most people, and pay for them somewhat higher rents. . . . The Negro who ventures away from the mass of his people and their organized life, finds himself alone, shunned and taunted, stared at, and made uncomfortable." Du Bois's assessment of the Negro middle class was critical yet hopeful. The black "aristocracy" did not exhibit a clear race consciousness, a political and social commitment to uplift the masses of poor blacks. The Negro elite usually consumed more than it produced, and it had not begun to generate a program to accumulate capital and to initiate economic enterprises that could employ black workers. "The better classes of Negroes," Du Bois commented, "should recognize their duty toward the masses. They should not forget that the spirit of the twentieth century is to be the turning of the high toward the lowly, the bending of Humanity to all that is human; the recognition that in the slums of modern society lie the answers to most of our puzzling problems and life." Implicitly, Du Bois was expressing the kernel of his famous "Talented Tenth" thesis, developed several years later.

The major weakness of *The Philadelphia Negro* is the absence of a coherent political and economic strategy for black advancement. Once more, blacks are urged to engage in "work, continuous and intensive; work, although it be menial and poorly rewarded work." White paternalists interested in interracial problems were advised to "recognize the existence of the better class of Negroes" and to solicit "their active aid and co-operation."[18] Despite this flaw, Du Bois presented a powerful sociological and moral argument against institutional racism. By discouraging blacks from entering certain trades and labor unions, and by the perpetuation of housing segregation and political and social oppression, white society condemned all Negroes behind a wall of social injustice. Du Bois observed that his study "revealed the Negro group as a symptom, not a cause; as a striving, palpitating group and not an inert, sick body of crime; as a long historic development and not a transient occurrence." When the bulk of the research was finished, in the spring of 1897, Du Bois realized his future goals for his "life program. . . . I became painfully aware that merely being born in a group, does not necessarily make one possessed of complete knowledge concerning it. I had learned far more from the Philadelphia Negroes than I had taught them concerning the Negro Problem."[19]

Even before the publication of *The Philadelphia Negro* in 1899, Du Bois's scholarship had come to the attention of President Horace Bumstead of Atlanta University. The college had initiated several conferences on the social and health problems of urban blacks, that paralleled similar work on rural blacks that was being done at Hampton Institute in Virginia and at Tuskegee Institute. Du Bois's academic training and research interests made him the ideal candidate to direct the conferences. However, several trustees and prominent friends of Atlanta University expressed severe reservations. Some had heard that Du Bois was an "agnostic." When Du Bois was interviewed for the position, he was "reluctant to speak of his religion or to say what he would do at Atlanta," Bumstead later recalled. It was only "in spite of objections and misgivings" that Du Bois received the appointment as professor of history and economics in late 1897. Upon his arrival, Du Bois was predictably at odds with the university's religious orthodoxy. Bumstead graciously permitted Du Bois to use the Episcopal prayer book to select readings for formal gatherings, a text that was less rigidly evangelical than most. During the next thirteen years he and Nina lived on the cloistered college campus. "Here I found myself," Du Bois reflected. "I lost most of my mannerisms. I grew broadly human, made my closest and most holy friendships . . . [and] became widely acquainted with the real condition of my people." He had come to an "ivory tower of race" in order "to explain the difficulties of race and the ways in which these difficulties caused political and economic troubles."[20]

Du Bois's scholarly activities assumed three major forms. First, drawing upon his experiences in Philadelphia, he initiated a series of sociological studies of various Afro-American communities. Even before moving to Atlanta, Du Bois spent July and August 1897 in Farmville, Virginia, collecting data for a detailed assessment of black life and labor in that rural town. The study was commissioned by Carroll Davidson Wright, head of the U.S. Bureau of Labor, and was published in January 1898. As in *The Philadelphia*

Negro, Du Bois noted the existence of "the usual substratum of loafers and semicriminals who will not work." But the masses of black workers in Farmville suffered not from moral laxity but from "irregular employment. A really industrious man who desires work is apt to be thrown out of employment from one-third to one-half of the year by the shutting up of the tobacco factories, the brickyard, or the cannery." Du Bois distinguished several "differentiated social classes" in the town. The black upper class of "farmers, teachers, grocers, and artisans, who own their own homes," exhibited exemplary social behavior: "no drinking, no lewdness [and] no questionable conversation." A number of Negro families did exist "below the line of ordinary respectability, living in loose sexual relationship . . . and furnishing a half-dozen street walkers and numerous gamblers and rowdies." But the overall social trends in Farmville, as Du Bois depicted them, were positive: "The industrious and property accumulating class of the Negro citizens best represents, on the whole, the general tendencies of the group. . . . No black woman can to-day be concubine to a white man without losing all social position—a vast revolution in twenty years; no black girl of the town can have an illegitimate child without being shut off from the best class of people and looked askance by ordinary folks."[21]

During these years, Du Bois established the foundations for the field of black sociology. In May 1899, the Department of Labor published Du Bois's "Negro in the Black Belt," a brief survey based primarily on interviews with Atlanta University students.[22] More ambitious was "The Negro Landholder of Georgia," published in July 1901. One hundred thirty pages in length, the essay presented a historical and sociological analysis of the struggle of blacks to acquire land and property in the Deep South. The racial and political history of Georgia was outlined, with figures of the black population given by county since 1790. The economic status of blacks was discussed and determined in each Georgia county as of 1900.[23]

Du Bois's second area of research focused on the Atlanta University conferences. Without consulting his colleagues or Bumstead, Du Bois decided to alter the orientation of the annual conferences. The new aim would be to carry out "a plan of social study by means of recurring decennial inquiries into the same general set of human problems" that confronted black Americans.[24] Ambitiously, Du Bois proposed a program that would be carried out over a period of one hundred years. In May 1898, the conference theme was devoted to "efforts of American Negroes for their own social betterment." A series of formal papers was delivered, including presentations by the Reverend H. H. Proctor of Atlanta, Du Bois's former classmate at Fisk; Helen A. Cook, a leader of the Washington, D.C. "Women's League"; and Professor J. M. Colson of Virginia Normal Institute, who described black self-help efforts in Petersburg, Virginia. Du Bois collected information on social improvement activities from black college graduates, churches, benevolent societies, and businesses across the country.[25] This theme was repeated in a conference held in May 1909. "The Negro in Business" was the theme of the May 1899 conference. John Hope, a black educator who was soon to become Du Bois's closest friend, presented a lecture on "The Meaning of Business." During the year, Du Bois had sent inquiries to black entrepreneurs; the final publication listed tables on the "characteristics of the different Black businesses in major cities."[26]

Through these conferences, Du Bois established a national reputation as the leading social scientist on black America. In the preparation of the volume on *The College-Bred Negro*, the theme for the conference in May 1900, Du Bois identified and contacted twenty-six hundred Afro-American college graduates. Nearly half responded, supplying important biographical data.[27] The 1902 conference volume on the black artisan was the most detailed survey of the status of black labor written in the early twentieth century. Data obtained from detailed questionnaires sent to thirteen hundred black "skilled workers" was summarized. Information was forwarded from hundreds of labor union affiliates on their policies toward blacks; data on blacks' involvement in strikes was also reproduced. The major speaker at the 1902 conference, Booker T. Washington, observed that he had a "keen interest and appreciation" for Du Bois's research, and predicted that his efforts "will stand for years as a monument to his ability, wisdom and faithfulness."[28] Du Bois was never completely satisfied with the publications from these meetings. He had a small subsidy provided by the university to conduct his investigations and conferences, but the lack of an adequate staff and philanthropic support often compromised his work. Many of the volumes lack the comprehensive scope and intimate detail that characterized *The Philadelphia Negro* and even Du Bois's brief survey of Farmville, Virginia. But the lasting significance of the Atlanta University series must be understood within its historical context. Du Bois's sociological studies on Negro life stood virtually alone against a flood of nonscientific and virulently racist dogma—which included Charles Carroll's *'The Negro a Beast'; or 'In the Image of God'* (1900); Thomas Dixon's *Leopard's Spots* (1902); Robert W. Shufeldt's *The Negro, A Menace to American Civilization* (1907); and William Graham Sumner's *Folkways* (1907). The latter explained that racial "folkways" were "uniform, universal in the group, imperative, and invariable."[29] At a period when white social scientists and novelists denied the humanity of Afro-Americans, Du Bois established their sociological diversity and integrity. Despite criticisms from some white academics, the general reception to Atlanta University's "Annual Publications" was positive. The London *Spectator* commented in 1900 that Du Bois's studies were "being done with much intelligence, discrimination and assiduity." The New

York *Evening Post* noted in 1905, "the only scientific studies on the Negro question being made today are those carried on by Atlanta University."[30]

The third direction Du Bois's scholarly activity took was to overture white intellectuals and government agencies on behalf of the socioeconomic concerns of black Americans. Speaking before a conference of the American Academy of Political and Social Science in November 1897, Du Bois proposed a scientific, national study of the Afro-American condition. He urged the "endowment of a Negro college" that would be the focus of all "careful historical and statistical research" on Afro-Americans. Such an institute would work "in close connection and co-operation with Harvard, Columbia, Johns Hopkins, and University of Pennsylvania."[31] Testifying before the House of Representatives' Industrial Commission in February 1901, Du Bois discussed his research on blacks in rural Virginia and Georgia. He urged federal authorities to take direct measures to improve black educational systems in the South.[32] In Georgia, Du Bois joined with local leaders to stem the popular movement toward black disfranchisement and Jim Crow. When a bill was introduced in the state legislature in November 1899 that was designed to disfranchise blacks by literary tests and property restrictions, Du Bois wrote and published a "Memorial" defending blacks' democratic rights. It was signed by twenty-four black politicians, clergy, and educators, including John Hope. "No Nation or State can advance faster than its laboring classes," Du Bois insisted. "Whatever hinders, degrades or discourages the Negroes weakens and injures the State."[33]

These were productive yet difficult years for the Du Bois family. Racial segregation and white vigilante violence was becoming more widespread across the South. The Georgia legislature passed legislation segregating all public streetcars in 1891, and by 1900 most Southern states had similar codes. Between 1889 and 1899 the average number of lynchings was 187.5 per year. Atlanta and other southern cities began to pass laws requiring Jim Crow restrictions in public accommodations. Atlanta's public buildings soon had racially segregated elevators.[34] In 1905 the "Separate Park Law" was adopted by the Georgia legislature; it restricted blacks from public parks.[35] Du Bois and his wife tried to avoid contact with local whites whenever possible and essentially lived on the campus. In October 1897 Nina gave birth to a boy, who was proudly christened Burghardt Gomer. Nina especially loved the baby. "Her own life builded and moulded itself upon the child," Du Bois wrote in *The Souls of Black Folk*. "No hands but hers must touch and garnish those little limbs; no dress or frill must touch them that had not wearied her fingers; no voice but hers could coax him off to dreamland." At the age of eighteen months the infant died, a victim of the sewage pollution in the city's water system. "Blithe was the morning of his burial, with birth and song and sweet-smelling flowers." Du Bois recalled. "The busy city dinned about us; they did not say much, those pale-faced hurrying men and women. . . . They only glanced and said, 'Niggers!'" Du Bois was in agony: "I am no coward, to shrink before the rugged rush of the storm, nor even quail before the awful shadow of the Veil. But harken, O Death! Is not this life hard enough . . . is not all the world beyond these four little walls pitiless enough, but that thou must needs enter here,—thou, O Death?"[36] The child's death "tore our lives in two," Du Bois wrote. "I threw myself more completely into my work, while most reason for living left the soul of my wife. Another child, a girl, came later, but my wife never forgave God for the unhealable wound."[37]

Perhaps in his deep sorrow, Du Bois came to a new understanding of the meaning of black faith. In December 1900, he contributed a brief essay, "The Religion of the American Negro," to the Boston publication *New World*. "The Negro church antedates the Negro home," he noted, an historical fact that created "the expression of the inner ethical life of a people in a sense seldom true elsewhere." The church was a haven in a heartless world, as blacks searched for meaning in a segregated and politically oppressive society. "Conscious of his impotence, and pessimistic," the Negro "often becomes bitter and vindictive; and his religion, instead of a worship, is a complaint and a curse, a wail rather than a hope, a sneer rather than a faith." And at these moments, "one type of Negro stands almost ready to curse God and die." Yet he finds salvation within the veil and a spiritual deliverance from earthly suffering. Silently, as ever, broods "the deep religious feeling of the real Negro heart, the stirring, unguided might of powerful human souls who have lost the guiding star of the past and seek in the great night a new religious ideal. Some day the Awakening will come," Du Bois predicted, "when the pent-up vigor of ten million souls shall sweep irresistibly toward the Goal, out of the Valley of the Shadow of Death . . . [toward] Liberty, Justice, and Right."[38] As black theologian Cornel West observed, Du Bois embraced a version of prophetic black Christianity, which suggested that the spiritual "exceptionalism" of black people, a quality of pietism and innate endowment, permitted the race to transcend the death and destruction of the racist social order.[39] Du Bois remained throughout his life a harsh critic of Western Christianity, but he retained a deep spiritual identification with the radical, messianic tradition of black faith.

Du Bois's activities at Atlanta University were one dimension of a broader trend among the small black middle class toward professional organization and race-conscious development. Under the increasing pressure of racial segregation, black professionals began to create their own associations. Black newspaper editors were among the first, establishing the Colored Press Association in 1880. Black school teachers initiated a national association in 1889, and in 1894 the National Medical Association was formed by black physicians. Black middle-class women, led by Josephine St. Pierre Ruffin, sponsored the first National Conference of Colored Women in Boston in 1895. From this gathering came the National Federation of Afro-American Women, which elected Margaret Murray Washington its first president. The following year the National League of Colored Women was established in Washington, D.C., led by Mary Church Terrell. The National Bar Association was initiated by black lawyers in 1903, and the National Negro Bankers' Association was started in 1906. Most black professionals, like Du Bois, favored the expansion of civil rights and opposed most forms of racial segregation. But the conditions of the period made resolution of blacks' social and economic problems impossible without the existence of black-controlled institutions that functioned in the collective interests of Negroes. The rise of these race-conscious organizations reinforced an interest in Afro-American history and culture among the black middle class and intelligentsia. In the early 1880s, A.M.E. bishop Daniel A. Payne helped to initiate the Bethel Literary and Historical Association in Washington, D.C. Other northern blacks established similar local groups, such as the American Negro Historical Society of Philadelphia, and the Society for the Collection of Negro Folklore in Boston. These local forums stimulated a growing identification with Africa's cultural heritage, while providing an ideological justification for race-conscious, separatist organizations in American political and economic life.

Two black intellectuals who assumed critical roles influencing Afro-American thought at this period were Edward Wilmot Blyden and Alexander Crummell. Born in the Danish West Indies in 1832, Blyden migrated to Liberia at age eighteen. One of the earliest and most widely read Pan-Africanists of the nineteenth century, Blyden served as Liberian Secretary of State from 1864 to 1866, ambassador to Great Britain from 1877 to 1878, and was later president of Liberia College. Blyden promoted research in African history and culture and suggested that the basic distinctive characteristics of black people were their spirituality and rejection of materialism. Blyden gave lectures in the United States in 1880, 1882, 1889–90, and 1895, and was a contributor to the A.M.E. *Review*.

Crummell had been born of a free black family in New York City. As an Episcopal minister in the 1840s, he participated in the political conventions of black abolitionists in the North. After receiving his A.B. degree at Cambridge University in 1853, he moved to Liberia and remained in Africa for the next twenty years. In 1864, Blyden and Crummell had established the Atheneum Club of Monrovia, a debating and literary society for Liberian intellectuals. Returning to the United States in the 1870s, Crummell became the pastor of St. Luke's Episcopal Church in Washington, D.C., and several years later created the first organization of black Episcopal clergy. Crummell's ideology of racial solidarity and black pride had a profound impact upon younger Afro-American intellectuals of Du Bois's generation. In a collection of essays published in 1882, Crummell observed that the majority of white Americans had become "so poisoned and stimulated by the noxious influence of caste" that any social movement designed to destroy racism "in the present day" could not succeed. This did not mean that Afro-Americans had to accept racial injustices. "The special duty before us is to strive for footing and for superiority in this land, on the line of race, as a temporary but needed expedient, for the ultimate extinction of caste, and all race distinctions," Crummell advised. "For if *we* do not look after our own interests as a people, and strive for advantage, no other people will." Yet Crummell was not a racial separatist. He strongly opposed all forms of racial segregation, but as a realist, he understood that Afro-Americans required their own economic, educational, and cultural institutions. Like Blyden, he recognized the unique cultural heritage of African peoples; but along with this pride in his race, he advocated a conscious struggle for political rights. "What this race needs in this country is POWER . . . and that comes from character, and character is the product of religion, intelligence, virtue, family order, superiority, wealth, and the show of industrial forces. These are the forces which we do not possess."[40] To abolish the color line, in short, racial solidarity and the development of all-black economic and political institutions were required.

Du Bois had known of Crummell for many years. In 1847, Crummell had been the first rector of the Episcopal parish of St. Luke's in New Haven, where Du Bois's paternal grandfather had been senior warden. Du Bois first met Crummell at a Wilberforce commencement and cherished the occasion. "Tall, frail and black he stood, with simple dignity and an unmistakable air of good breeding," Du Bois reflected later. The young professor talked "eagerly" with this legendary figure of black history. "Instinctively I bowed before this man, as one bows before the prophets of the world." Crummell embodied the wisdom and integrity which Du Bois sought to give to his oppressed people. Crummell had "bent to all the gibes and prejudices, to all hatred and discrimination, with that rare courtesy which is the armor of pure souls. . . . He never faltered, he seldom complained; he simply worked, inspiring the young, rebuking the old, helping the weak, guiding the strong."[41] Du Bois wrote many tributes of his associates and colleagues in later years, but his essay on Crummell in *The Souls of Black Folk* is the

most lyrical and powerful. It is curious, therefore, that many researchers
of Du Bois have not examined the important relationship between Crummell's ideology and the emerging social thought of Du Bois. It is no exaggeration to suggest that Crummell became Du Bois's "spiritual father," the
personification of the young scholar's image of what all Afro-American intellectuals should be. Crummell represented the politics of pan-Negroism,
abolitionism, and ethical sacrifice. At a moment in his intellectual life when
Du Bois was attempting to define his own identity, Crummell provided many
critical insights.

Other young Afro-American intellectuals also deeply respected Crummell
and relied upon his advice. In 1894, two young college professors, Richard
R. Wright of Savannah and William H. Crogman of Atlanta's Clark University, contacted Crummell concerning their plans to initiate a national society
of black intellectuals. Crummell's response was thoughtful and comprehensive. He proposed the creation of an "African institute composed of say fifty
colored scholars, the best we have; devoted to literary, statistical, ethno-
graphical, folklore investigation, pertaining wholly and entirely to Africa and
to the world-wide Negro race." Two years later, Crummell presided over a
small group of black scholars in Washington, D.C. to form the structure of
the organization. At the suggestion of poet Paul Laurence Dunbar, the name
of the society became the 'American Negro Academy.' The original members selected for the academy included some of the most prominent intellectuals and educators in black America: Presbyterian minister Francis
James Grimké; newspaper publisher John Wesley Cromwell, a Howard University law graduate; Wilberforce University professors William S. Scarborough and Edward E. Clarke; Howard University sociologist Kelly Miller;
Tuskegee Institute principal Booker T. Washington; and Du Bois. [42]

On 5 March 1897, the American Negro Academy held its first formal
session in Washington, D.C. Crummell was the unanimous choice for the
presidency of the academy, but the seventy-eight-year-old scholar declined
the nomination due to his advanced age. Du Bois vigorously protested, noting that the academy's presidency should reflect a "reverence for age and
. . . the performance of past duties." [43] Supported by Grimké and other
members, Crummell reluctantly accepted the position. Du Bois was elected
first vice-president. Crummell's presentation, "Civilization, the Primal Need
of the Negro Race," was a restatement of many of the themes he had developed over previous decades. Black Americans had not begun to develop
their own cultural institutions: "we have no art; we have no science; we
have no philosophy; we have no scholarship." False prophets within the
black community proposed that "property is the source of power" and that
"official position" would lead to "the elevation of the race." The real task of
black scholars was "to transform and stimulate the souls of a race." The

members of the academy had to "bring forth, stimulate, and uplift all the latent genius, garnered up, in the by-places and sequestered corners of this neglected Race." But academic research, achievement in the humanities and social sciences, for its own sake, was not enough. For Crummell, black intellectuals had to become the vanguard in the struggle for political power and human equality: "In all the great revolutions . . . scholars have been conspicuous; in the re-construction of society, in formulating laws, in producing great emancipations, in the revival of letters, in the advancement of science, in the renaissance of art, in the destruction of gross superstitions and the restoration of true and enlightened religion."[44] Crummell's speech reiterated many of Du Bois's ideas expressed in *The Philadelphia Negro* and his sociological essays: the necessity for moral and cultural uplift, a rejection of crass materialism, and a firm belief in the exceptional role of the Negro intelligentsia in assisting the black masses.

That evening, Du Bois presented a paper, "The Conservation of Races," that not only helped to establish his position as the leading young black intellectual in America, but also determined much of his future cultural and social orientation. Du Bois asserted that each of the world's great racial groups had distinct cultural and "spiritual" characteristics. Some racial groups, such as Negroes, Orientals, and Slavs, had only begun to give "to civilization the full spiritual message which they are capable of giving." The challenge of any race's leading intellectuals in the realization of their "ideals" was to promote collective action among their own people. "For the development of Negro genius, of Negro literature and art, of Negro spirit, only Negroes bound and welded together, Negroes inspired by one vast ideal, can work out in its fullness the great message we have for humanity." Du Bois believed that Afro-Americans had "to take their just place in the van of Pan-Negroism." In order to do so, blacks had to reject the goal of racial "absorption" and assimilation into white American society. "If in America it is to be proven for the first time in the modern world that not only Negroes are capable of evolving individual men like Toussaint, the Savior, but are a nation stored with wonderful possibilities of culture, then their destiny is not a servile imitation of Anglo-Saxon culture, but a stalwart originality which shall unswervingly follow Negro ideals." The problem with this strategy, Du Bois readily admitted, was the ambiguity of the Negro's political and social status within American society. Black Americans had been confused historically about their own self-definition. Most had asked themselves: "What, after all, am I? Am I an American or am I a Negro? Can I be both? Or is it my duty to cease to be a Negro as soon as possible and be an American?" This issue was the central cultural contradiction dividing black Americans. And Du Bois offered his own resolution to "the riddle that puzzles so many of us":

> We are Americans, not only by birth and by citizenship, but by our
> political ideals, our language, our religion. Farther than that, our Amer-
> icanism does not go. At that point, we are Negroes, members of a vast
> historic race that from the very dawn of creation has slept, but half
> awakening in the dark forests of its African fatherland. We are the first
> fruits of this new nation, the harbinger of that black to-morrow which
> is yet destined to soften the whiteness of the Teutonic to-day. We are
> that people whose subtle sense of song has given America its only
> American music, its only American fairy tales, its only touch of pathos
> and humor amid its mad money-getting plutocracy. As such, it is our
> duty to conserve our physical powers, our intellectual endowments,
> our spiritual ideals; as a race we must strive by race organization, by
> race solidarity . . . to the realization of that broader humanity which
> freely recognizes differences in men, but sternly deprecates inequality
> in their opportunities of development.[45]

The American Negro Academy, combining its activities with black colleges, business associations, and newspapers, could promote a cultural and
spiritual renaissance in black America, and across the black world. Within
this massive effort to uplift the race, Du Bois added, certain political realities could not be ignored. Negros were "hard pressed in the economic world
by foreign immigrants and native prejudice, hated here, despised there and
pitied everywhere." Given the level of racism and political oppression inside
the United States, blacks could not "expect to have things done for them—
they MUST DO FOR THEMSELVES. . . . A little less complaint and whining,
and a little more dogged work and manly striving would do us more credit
and benefit than a thousand Force or Civil Rights bills." "The Conservation
of Races" lecture was not a plea for parochial racial chauvinism, but an appeal for the preservation of the Negro's cultural integrity and identity. Du
Bois's entire speech was rooted in the conception of race as an "ethical"
rather than biological category; each "race" possessed specific aesthetic and
moral gifts. Dialectically, as the Negro race came to full self-consciousness,
it would be able to partake in broader relationships with the other races that
comprised the human family. Du Bois's central thesis is that of cultural pluralism, not black nationalism, and its philosophical point of departure owes
as much to Josiah Royce and William James as to Crummell.[46]

A comparison between Crummell's and Du Bois's addresses provides interesting parallels and discontinuities. With Crummell, Du Bois believed
that the black intelligentsia was capable of the reconstruction of black civil
society. Both men spoke in idealistic, spiritual terms. Du Bois departed
from Crummell's ideology only in one major respect. The elder scholar did
not depreciate the long-term goal of the abolition of the "caste system" of
racial segregation. Du Bois, on the other hand, described the issues of seg-

regated schools, "wage-discrimination and lynch law" as "smaller questions" that were distinctly secondary to an examination of "the whole question of race in human philosophy." Du Bois supported the battle to win political reforms and greater "personal liberty" for blacks, but only as "the second great step toward a better adjustment" of race relations. He did not advocate "social equality" but favored "a social equilibrium," that would permit blacks and whites to "develop side by side in peace and mutual happiness."[47] Implicitly, Du Bois's position accepted the temporary existence of racial segregation. This does not mean that Du Bois denied the necessity for full democratic rights. But on balance, culture and ethics rather than politics dominated Du Bois's concerns. Du Bois was "conservative" in that he did not perceive the necessity to engage overtly in politics in order to fulfill his cultural and social program.

Du Bois's lecture received "prolonged applause" from academy members, but several participants in the audience voiced criticisms. R. R. Wright, William S. Scarborough, and several others did not believe that the American Negro could preserve a distinct racial identity, given the pressure to integrate within the larger society. The debate over Du Bois's remarks did not end within the academy. A number of newspapers, including the Lagos *Weekly Record* in West Africa, published reports on the academy's proceedings. The most bitter polemics came from Du Bois's former patron, T. Thomas Fortune. He opposed the society's emphasis on "Negro" identity and took issue with Du Bois's call for pan-Africanism. The development of a "Negro genius, of Negro literature and art" was not possible "in a country where Anglo-Saxon ideals . . . predominate." Crummell privately dismissed Fortune's attack as "contemptible."[48] The Lagos *Weekly Record* reprinted Du Bois's entire paper and Fortune's rejoinder, and in an editorial sided with Du Bois.

During the late spring of 1897, Du Bois restructured some of the major concepts in "The Conservation of Races" and drafted another short essay. Accepted for publication in the *Atlantic Monthly,* "Strivings of the Negro People" was the first article written by Du Bois to receive a national audience. This essay contains the central theme of Du Bois's intellectual life, the theory of double consciousness. The American Negro "is a sort of seventh son, born with a veil, and gifted with second sight in this American world—a world which yields him no self-consciousness, but only lets him see himself through the revelation of the other world." This "double consciousness" separated the Negro from all other Americans. "One ever feels his twoness,—an American, a Negro; two souls, two thoughts, two unreconciled strivings; two warring ideals in one dark body, whose dogged strength alone keeps it from being torn asunder." The entire history of the Negro in America was symbolized by this inner spiritual conflict, "this longing to attain self-conscious manhood, merge his double self into a better and truer self."

Du Bois found himself between two conflicting black political and cultural traditions. Black nationalists such as Martin Delany in the mid-nineteenth century, and Blyden during Du Bois's early professional years, had espoused racial solidarity, glorified Africa's cultural heritage, and rejected racial integration. Frederick Douglass, the central black leader of the abolitionist era, ultimately accepted the goal of racial assimilation into white society, but staunchly fought for blacks' full democratic rights. Du Bois, the cultural pluralist, proposed a third alternative. The Negro "does not wish to Africanize America, for America has too much to teach the world and Africa." He would not "bleach his Negro soul in a flood of white Americanism, for he believes—foolishly, perhaps, but fervently—that Negro blood has yet a message for the world. He simply wishes to make it possible for a man to be both a Negro and an American without being cursed and spit upon by his fellows, without losing the opportunity of development." The Afro-American might become a "co-worker in the kingdom of culture" and "escape both death and isolation," if he appreciated this "waste of double aims," which has "sent them often wooing false gods and invoking false means of salvation, and has even at times seemed destined to make them ashamed of themselves." Like "The Conservation of Races," the 1897 essay placed ethical and spiritual conflict above politics. Du Bois's concern about the need for the franchise and civil rights is secondary. "The power of the ballot we need in sheer self-defense, and as a guarantee of good faith," Du Bois suggested. "We may misuse it, but we can scarce do worse in this respect" than white Americans.[49]

Du Bois's growing affinity for "Pan-Negroism" and the cultural image of Africa was shared by many Afro-American intellectuals in the 1890s. A.M.E. Bishop Alexander Walters and Crummell participated in the Chicago Congress on Africa in August 1893. The week-long conference featured a presentation by A.M.E. Bishop Henry M. Turner, who urged Afro-Americans to emigrate to the continent. Another conference on African affairs was sponsored by the Stewart Missionary Foundation and held at Gammon Theological Seminary in Atlanta in December 1895. A.M.E. church leader T. McCants Stewart, a member of the Brooklyn Board of Education in 1891–95, lived in Liberia for two years. Although an opponent of mass colonization, the influential Democrat urged black entrepreneurs "to build up a new Christian Negro Nationality in the 'Fatherland'" through commercial ventures.[50] Du Bois's first Pan-Africanist proposal illustrates his political conservatism. In 1897, he drafted a lengthy memorandum to Paul Hagemans, the Consul General of Belgium to the United States, on the "question of the emigration of American Negroes to the Congo Free State." Du Bois ob-

served that the "general emigration of American Negroes to Africa is neither possible nor desirable." Nevertheless, the Afro-American was
inevitably part of the larger black world. The Negro recognized "that Africa
was in truth" his "fatherland," and that "as the advance guard of Pan-Negroism the future development of Africa will depend more or less on his efforts." The problem with previous colonization schemes lay in an absence
of intelligent planning, Du Bois believed. "There was no proper preparation,
no equipment of tools and capital, no proper idea of the country and climate—simply an indiscriminate invitation to the lazy, vicious, and ignorant
to go to a land of milk and honey." Du Bois proposed that the Belgian government work with the American Negro Academy, "an organization which
represents a better class of educated Negroes," to develop scientific literature on the Congo Free State. A second step would be the promotion of
"commercial intercourse" among the Congo, the West Indies, and black
America. Simultaneously a "small but steady stream of carefully selected
classes" of blacks could emigrate to the Congo.[51] Nothing came of Du Bois's
plans, but the draft reveals his considerable naiveté about the nature of
European colonialism.

Once more, Crummell played a decisive role in preparing Du Bois's future
as a leading Pan-Africanist. Touring England in the summer of 1897, Crummell met with Henry Sylvester Williams of Trinidad and T. J. Thompson of
Sierra Leone, two law students who had just formed an "African Association" in London. Upon his return, the academy passed a resolution of
congratulations to the African Association, and information about this organization was publicized in the black press. When Williams called an international Pan-African conference, to be held in London in July 1900, Du Bois
and several black American intellectuals were prepared to participate. Only
thirty-two delegates attended this meeting, radical representatives of the
black diaspora's radical petty bourgeoisie. From Liberia came F. R. S. Johnson, the country's former attorney general; from Ethiopia, Benito Sylvain,
assistant to Emperor Menelik II. Sylvain was selected vice-chairman of the
conference. The Afro-American delegation included Bishop Alexander Walters, Washington, D.C., educator Anna Cooper, Anna H. Jones of Missouri,
and Du Bois. After the presentation of papers, the conference formed a
permanent Pan-African association. The body's stated purposes included
the achievement of full "civil and political rights for Africans and their descendants throughout the world," and the fostering of black educational and
business enterprises.[52] The conference adopted a brief appeal drafted by Du
Bois that called upon Britain to grant "the rights of responsible government
to the black colonies of Africa and the West Indies." The statement deplored
the "dishonesty and unrighteous oppression toward the American Negro"
and demanded the "right of franchise, security of person and property." The

national integrity of "the free Negro States of Abyssinia, Liberia, Haiti, and the rest" should be respected by other states. Most significant were the initial words of the appeal, which became the most famous prediction Du Bois ever made: "the problem of the twentieth century is the problem of the colour line."[53]

Du Bois's activities in the American Negro Academy and the Pan-African Association were both aspects of his deepening identification with African culture and political nationalism. When Crummell died in September 1898, Du Bois was unanimously elected to replace him as the academy's president. For several years he continued to work actively with John W. Cromwell to coordinate the academy's business. In August 1900, Du Bois and another academy member, Thomas Junius Calloway, organized an American Negro exhibit at the Paris Exposition. At the London conference, Du Bois was selected to direct the branch of the Pan-African Association in the United States. But by late 1901 Du Bois's involvement in both organizations had declined considerably. Although the next Pan-African Association conference was scheduled to take place in the United States, the group had disintegrated by 1902. Du Bois's location in Atlanta and his extensive research and publication commitments made frequent trips to the academy's meetings in Washington, D.C., difficult. In December 1903, Archibald H. Grimké, a noted author and attorney, succeeded Du Bois as president. The academy continued to function until 1928, and it inspired the creation of other black academic formations. Historian Carter G. Woodson, elected to the academy in 1914, for example, later established the Association for the Study of Negro Life and History and initiated the *Journal of Negro History*. Du Bois's subsequent relations with the academy were usually cordial; in 1911 he wrote an essay, *The Social Evolution of the Black South*, edited by Cromwell as the academy's fourth contribution to its "American Negro Monographs" series. Du Bois's primary debt to the academy was the lasting influence of Crummell. Under his influence, Du Bois developed most of the major themes that informed his future scholarship.

Throughout Afro-American history, a succession of leaders have emerged who have symbolically represented entire generations and classes, especially during periods of intense social change. Historian Thomas Carlyle once characterized decisive historical figures as "beginners." Social theorist George Plekhanov concurred: "A great man is a beginner precisely because he sees further than others and desires things more strongly than others. . . . He points to the new social needs created by the preceding development of social relationships; he takes the initiative in satisfying these needs."[54] In black social history some leaders were prophetic, dynamic, and visionary: Frederick Douglass, Paul Robeson, Malcolm X, Martin Luther King, Jr. Others acquired public prominence and power by articulating widespread grievances, and by addressing short-term practical needs in a pragmatic manner. Du Bois was one of the former; he gradually assumed the mantle of the prophetic leader of black America—a role, however, with which he was never fully comfortable.

Booker T. Washington was an example of the second type of leader. Popular and powerful, he symbolized the strengths and critical weaknesses within the Afro-American community at the turn of the century. As historian Louis R. Harlan observed, Washington "was not an intellectual, but a man of action. Ideas he cared little for. Power was his game, and he used ideas simply as instruments to gain power."[55] What Washington lacked in vision, he compensated through hard work, determination, and ambition. His public acclaim came not from the espousal of original ideas, but from his uncanny ability to appeal simultaneously to blacks and affluent whites, and from his personal identification with the spirit of entrepreneurialism that dominated the culture of early twentieth-century America. To appreciate Du Bois's role in Afro-American history, it is necessary to review briefly Washington's rise to power.

Born a slave in 1856, Booker T. Washington was educated at Hampton Institute in Virginia. At the age of twenty-five he became the founder of Tuskegee Institute in the heart of Alabama's Black Belt. With few resources, Washington and his dedicated assistants—notably his second wife, Olivia Davidson Washington—established Tuskegee as a major center for technical and agricultural education. By 1901, the institute had 109 full-time faculty, 1,095 pupils, and owned property valued at nearly $330,000. Many of black America's leading researchers and scholars found employment at the institute: gifted agricultural chemist George Washington Carver; architect Robert R. Taylor; dramatist Charles Winter Wood; and Monroe N. Work, director of records and research and the editor of the *Negro Year Book*. During the 1880s and early 1890s, Washington became an effective orator, and he was able to secure limited philanthropic aid for his school. Washington was a cautious man, but by no means was he an "Uncle Tom." During the 1880s he had openly condemned racial segregation laws on public transportation, and as late as 1894, he encouraged blacks to boycott Jim Crowed streetcars.

Washington's sudden emergence as a major figure came in September 1895, when he delivered a short address at the Cotton States and International Exposition in Atlanta. Little in the speech, which Du Bois later termed the "Atlanta Compromise," represented a radical departure from what other moderate black educators and elected officials had already argued. He observed that one-third of the South's population was black, and that any "enterprise seeking the material, civil, or moral welfare" of the region could not disregard the Negro. Blacks should remain in the South—"Cast down your bucket where you are"—and participate in the capitalist economic development of that area. During the Reconstruction era, blacks had erred in their priorities. "Ignorant and inexperienced," blacks had tried to start "at the top instead of at the bottom"; a Congressional seat "was more sought than real estate or industrial skill." To the white South, Washington pledged the fidelity of his race, "the most patient, law-abiding, and unresentful people that the world has seen." And on the sensitive issue of racial integration and the protection of blacks' political rights, Washington made a dramatic concession: "In all things that are purely social we can be as separate as the fingers, yet one as the hand in all things essential to mutual progress. . . . The wisest among my race understand that the agitation of questions of social equality is the extremest folly."[56] Washington's "compromise" was this: blacks would disavow open agitation for desegregation and the political franchise; in return, they would be permitted to develop their own parallel economic, educational, and social institutions within the framework of expanding Southern capitalism. Obscured by accommodationist rhetoric, Washington's statement nevertheless accurately expressed the feelings of the nascent black entrepreneurial elite, many black landholders, and some educators.

White America responded to Washington's address with universal acclaim. President Grover Cleveland remarked that the speech was the foundation for "new hope" for black Americans. More accurate was the editorial of the Atlanta *Constitution:* "The speech stamps Booker T. Washington as a wise counselor and a safe leader." Black reactions were decidedly mixed. Fortune termed Washington black America's new "Douglass," the "best equipped of the lot of us to be the single figure ahead of the procession." But black editor W. Calvin Chase described the speech as "death to the Afro-American and elevating to the white people." A.M.E. Bishop Henry M. Turner believed that Tuskegee's principal "will have to live a long time to undo the harm he has done our race." The Atlanta *Advocate* condemned Washington's "sycophantic attitude," and a writer in the *Voice of Missions* characterized him as "an instrument in the hands of an organization seeking money gain."[57] By the late 1890s, Washington's leap into prominence had helped to create a powerful political organization, the "Tuskegee Machine." With the advice of his able secretary and counselor Emmett Jay Scott, Washington began to exercise tremendous authority. Through Washington's patronage, his black and white supporters were able to secure posts in the federal government. Washington's influence with white philanthropists largely determined which Negro colleges would receive funds. The Tuskegee Machine never acquiesced in the complete political disfranchisement of blacks, however, and behind the scenes Washington used his resources to fight for civil rights. In 1900 he requested funds from white philanthropists to lobby against racist election provisions in the Louisiana state constitution. He privately fought Alabama's disfranchisement laws in federal courts, and in 1903–04 personally spent "at least four thousand dollars in cash" to promote the legal struggle against Jim Crow.[58] Nevertheless, the general impression Washington projected to the white South was the Negro's subservience to Jim Crow, lynchings, and political terror. One of Washington's strongest critics in this regard was Alexander Crummell. The black scholar disliked Washington's emphasis on Afro-American industrial training at the expense of higher education. But more important, he viewed Washington's entire accommodationist political program as opportunistic, and believed that Tuskegee's principal was nothing but a "white man's nigger."[59]

Du Bois was at first sympathetic toward Washington. Less than one week after the Atlanta Compromise speech, Du Bois wrote Washington, "Let me heartily congratulate you upon your phenomenal success in Atlanta—it was a word fitly spoken."[60] Du Bois had noticed the criticisms of Washington published in the black press, and he promptly forwarded a letter to Fortune's *New York Age*. The proposed Atlanta Compromise, Du Bois thought, "might be the basis of a real settlement between whites and blacks in the South, if the South opened to the Negroes the doors of economic opportunity and the Negroes co-operated with the South in political sympathy."[61] In January 1896 Du Bois again inquired about a teaching position at Tuskegee Institute, before accepting the position at the University of Pennsylvania. At the 1899 conference of the Afro-American Council, the major civil rights organization prior to the creation of the Niagara Movement, a core of northern dissidents led by A.M.E. minister Reverdy C. Ransom, attacked Washington's philosophy. A majority of blacks at the meeting, including Du Bois, however, issued a strong "endorsement" for the "noble efforts" of Booker T. Washington."[62] At the 1899 Atlanta University conference, Du Bois had urged Afro-American entrepreneurs to create a series of "Negro Business Men's Leagues" and to foster a "Negro money for Negro merchants" strategy in their communities. Washington essentially took over Du Bois's idea—even obtaining mailing lists of black businessmen from him—and established the National Negro Business League in 1900, one of the strongest elements of the Tuskegee Machine.[63] In early 1900, the post of Superintendent of Negro Schools in Washington, D.C. became available, and Washington lobbied to secure the appointment for Du Bois. Although Du Bois did not seek the job, Washington informed him privately that he had "recommended" him "as strongly as I could."[64] In the summer of 1901, Washington invited Du

Bois to be his "house guest" at his West Virginia residence.[65] And in July 1902, Washington again personally praised Du Bois for his research "on the condition of the public schools in the South. . . . I know it is hard work," he wrote, but "constantly putting such facts before the public cannot but help our cause greatly in the long run."[66]

The compatibility between both men was not simply based on personal self-interest, but was rooted in the dominant ideology of the small Negro middle class of this historical period: racial self-sufficiency, education as a means of upward social mobility, black cultural pride, the support of "Pan-Negroism," and entrepreneurialism. Like Washington, Du Bois was a product of his age. In 1899, he was prepared to accept property and literacy qualifications on the Georgia franchise, in order to save voting rights for a minority of blacks. In his 1898 address before Fisk University graduates, Du Bois repeated the concepts of racial self-sufficiency popularized by Washington. "The German works for Germany, the Englishman serves England," Du Bois declared, "and it is the duty of the Negro to serve his blood and lineage, and so working, each for each, and all for each, we realize the goal of each for all."[67] Du Bois initially supported Washington, in part because many of his colleagues in the American Negro Academy and in the broader circles of the black intelligentsia were also inclined to favor most, if not all, of his programs. Cromwell vigorously supported Washington's Atlanta Compromise before a hostile audience at the Bethel Literary Association in 1895. Although at first critical of Washington, sociologist Kelly Miller was by 1899 largely in Tuskegee's camp. W. S. Scarborough told a 1900 conference at Hampton Institute that blacks should adopt Washington's "sound philosophy."[68]

Even on the vital issue of pan-Africanism, Washington's credentials were in order. In 1899, during a London visit, Washington had promoted the proposed Pan-African conference as a "most effective and far reaching event."[69] Henry Sylvester Williams corresponded with Washington in 1899 and 1900 and had asked him to distribute materials on the "proposed conference . . . as widely as is possible."[70] Washington established an economic partnership with a private German firm that held concessions in Germany's African colonies, and in January 1900, three Tuskegee graduates and one faculty member initiated an agricultural project in Togo. Tuskegee graduates were employed in the Sudan, Nigeria, and the Congo Free State. Inspired by Washington, Zulu minister John Langalibalele Dube spoke at Tuskegee's commencement in 1897 and four years later started the Zulu Christian Industrial School in Natal, South Africa.[71] The sage of "Pan-Negroism," Edward Wilmot Blyden, also endorsed Washington's leadership. After reading the 1895 Atlanta address, Blyden declared that Washington's "words" and "work will tend to free two races from prejudice and false views of life."[72]

Several factors eroded the temporary bonds between Du Bois and Washington. As historian Joel Williamson observed, one major reason was "the change in the interracial environment in which they labored. In effect, the white people with whom Washington had negotiated a modus vivendi in 1895 were, by 1900, rapidly losing control to people who had radically different ideas about the proper state of relations between the races."[73] Segregation codes had become more rigid; the number of lynchings had started to decline slightly, yet blacks' access to voting had all but disappeared. Washington's frequent criticisms of black higher education won few friends among the faculty at Atlanta University and Fisk University. The trend toward agricultural and industrial training jeopardized the continued existence of these institutions, as philanthropists shifted their funds to schools structured along the Hampton-Tuskegee model. Du Bois was also deeply worried about Washington's abuse of power. Through the National Negro Press Bureau in Washington, D.C., pro-Washington press releases were distributed across the nation. Most of the prominent black politicians in the Republican party, such as J. C. Napier of Nashville, and J. C. Daney, the federal recorder of deeds in 1901–10, were firm advocates of the Tuskegee philosophy. Critics of Washington sometimes lost their jobs or found the doors of white benefactors closed to them. As Du Bois noted, "Few political appointments of Negroes were made anywhere in the United States without his consent. Even the careers of rising young colored men were very often determined by his advice and certainly his opposition was fatal."[74]

Washington never succeeded in silencing his black opponents. In Chicago, the leading black "radical" was Ida B. Wells-Barnett, fiery journalist, feminist, and antilynching activist. Her husband, Ferdinand Barnett, used his newspaper, the *Conservator*, as a principal vehicle for attacks on Tuskegee. In Cleveland, the editor of the *Gazette*, H. C. Smith, was that city's major opponent of Washington's organization. The Reverend William J. White of Augusta, Georgia, a veteran of Reconstruction era politics and journalist, was a staunch critic of Washington. In Atlanta, one of the chief opponents of the Tuskegee Machine was John Hope, who was named president of Atlanta Baptist College in 1905. Hope consistently emphasized that Negro advancement depended upon higher education and that blacks' political demands must lead to full "social equality." The most bitter and controversial critics of the Tuskegee philosophy were William Monroe Trotter and George W. Forbes of Boston, the editors of the *Boston Guardian*. Trotter detested Washington, describing him as a "coward" and unprincipled "self-seeker."[75] Forbes declared that "it would be a blessing to the race if the Tuskegee school should burn down." In early 1903 one of Trotter's radical protégés, William H. Ferris, debated Washington supporters at a Washington, D.C. meeting of the Bethel Literary Society. The "Trotterites" established a militant organization, the Massachusetts Racial Protective Association, to mobilize black radicals across their state.[76] But taken collectively, the early opponents of Tuskegee were a small minority of the Negro middle class. All black leaders recognized Washington's influence, and few were prepared to risk their careers by challenging his views publicly. Moreover, none of Washington's critics had developed a comprehensive alternative to the Tuskegee philosophy, a critique that included educational, social, political, and economic strategies to promote blacks' vital interests. By 1903, the majority of black Americans seemed to speak with one voice—that of Booker T. Washington.

Du Bois was an unlikely candidate to lead the campaign against Tuskegee. A detached social scientist and humanist, Du Bois seemed fairly moderate by the radicals' standards. Ida B. Wells-Barnett had described Du Bois in 1900 as "the most scholarly and one of the most conservative members" of the Afro-American Council.[77] At the council's 1902 meeting in St. Paul, Washington's forces seized control of the organization, removing Wells-Barnett from her position as secretary. Fortune replaced Bishop Walters as council president. The Trotterites criticized Du Bois for his failure to assist the opposition. In the *Guardian* Trotter complained, "We might have expected Prof. Du Bois to have stood in the breach here, but like the others who are trying to get into the band wagon of the Tuskegeean, he is no longer to be relied upon."[78] But Du Bois was also experiencing a degree of "discomfort and resentment" caused by the Tuskegee Machine. While attending a conference at Hampton Institute, several prominent white supporters of Washington—Hampton principal Hollis Burke Frissell, Episcopal Bishop William McVickar, and *Atlantic Monthly* editor Walter Hines Page—proposed the establishment of a national black journal. Du Bois was enthusiastic about the prospect of editing the publication, and he outlined his "dreams and plans" in careful detail. But when Du Bois insisted on controlling all editorial policies, the project was promptly dropped. Du Bois sensed that Washington's allies wanted a publication "dominated by and subservient to the Tuskegee philosophy."[79]

Du Bois began to hint at his reservations concerning the Tuskegee philosophy in his published writings. When Du Bois reviewed Washington's autobiography, *Up From Slavery*, for *Dial* magazine in July 1901, he was mildly critical of Washington's educational and economic outlook.[80] "Hopeful Signs for the Negro," published in October 1902, was an explicit rejection of accommodationist politics. Du Bois insisted that the Negro would never "abate one jot" from his "determination to attain in this land perfect equality before the law."[81] Perhaps sensing Du Bois's drift toward Trotter's radicalism, Washington recognized his error in failing to hire Du Bois in previous years. Tuskegee now made several lucrative offers to the black scholar. In late 1902, William Henry Baldwin, Tuskegee Institute's most influential trustee, invited Du Bois to attend a New York conference "regarding the condition of the Colored people" in that city. Du Bois prepared specific proposals for a social study along the lines of his Philadelphia project. This meeting marked the beginning of a process that led to the establishment of the National Urban League in 1911.[82] Baldwin's primary object, however, was the recruitment of Du Bois. Transporting Du Bois to his Long Island estate, Baldwin and his wife "insisted" that his place "was at Tuskegee." It was also clear that Du Bois could name his own salary. This session led to two interviews with Washington. Tuskegee's principal "was not an easy person to know," Du Bois wrote later. "He never expressed himself frankly or clearly until he knew exactly to whom he was talking and just what their wishes and desires were. . . . On the other hand, I was quick, fast-speaking and voluble."[83] Du Bois eventually agreed to lecture at Tuskegee Institute during its summer session in 1903. He also accepted Washington's invitation to participate in a private conference with a carefully selected group of black leaders. "All shades of opinion," according to Washington, should be represented at the meeting. The "main object" would be "to agree upon certain fundamental principles and to see in what way we understand or misunderstand each other and correct mistakes as far as possible."[84]

A small Chicago publishing house, A. C. McClurg, had contacted Du Bois concerning the possible publication of a collection of essays. Du Bois drew together his "fugitive pieces" from the *Atlantic Monthly,* the *New World,* and other publications. He also included a chapter, "Of Mr. Booker T. Washington and Others," that provided a "frank evaluation" of the Tuskegee philosophy. Published in April 1903, *The Souls of Black Folk: Essays and Sketches* has since become a classic in the English language. Its grace and power are still overwhelming. The book soon sparked a national controversy among black intellectuals. In early May, Wells-Barnett and her husband defended the book's thesis in a literary debate that included Monroe Work, Negro club leader Fannie Barrier Williams, and her husband S. Laing Williams, a leader of Tuskegee's forces in Chicago. Three weeks later, Wells-Barnett wrote Du Bois, "We are still reading your book with the same delighted appreciation."[85] As the book reached an international audience, others came to similar conclusions. From the Gold Coast, West African author and nationalist Casely Hayford congratulated Du Bois after having "the pleasure of reading your great book *The Souls of Black Folk.*"[86]

The collection of fourteen essays represents the three major areas of Du Bois's research up to 1903—political history, sociology, and cultural criticism. The title and composition of the book are of extreme importance. As Rampersad comments, "The 'souls' of the title is a play on words, referring to the 'twoness' of the black American." In the use of the term "folk," Du emphasis on the preservation of democratic rights for Afro-Americans implied the necessity to develop a political reform movement against Jim Crow.[89]

Du Bois's criticisms of Washington were far more effective than Trotter's, precisely because of his profound respect for the Tuskegee principal. Indeed, until the end of his life, Du Bois comprehended fully the "circumstances of the South" that dictated Washington's moderation, and he genuinely valued his "achievements."[90] The author of the "Atlanta Compromise" was "certainly the most distinguished Southerner since Jefferson Davis, and the one with the largest personal following," Du Bois commented. "One hesitates, therefore, to criticize a life which, beginning with so little, has done so much." Du Bois then skillfully attacked the major contradictions of the Tuskegee philosophy. Washington had learned "the speech and thought of triumphant commercialism," and his program was "a gospel of Work and Money to such an extent" that it nearly obscured "the higher aims of life." His call for industrial training jeopardized black higher education. In politics, Washington represented "the old attitude of adjustment and submission" that permitted the erosion of blacks' civil rights. His rise to national power had led to "the hushing of the criticism of honest opponents." In brief, the Tuskegee approach to race relations had "tended to shift the burden of the Negro problem to the Negro's shoulders," while whites "stand aside as critical and rather pessimistic spectators." Du Bois called upon blacks to perform "a duty stern and delicate . . . to oppose a part of the work of their greatest leader. So far as Mr. Washington preaches Thrift, Patience, and Industrial Training for the masses, we must hold up his hands and strive with him, rejoicing in his honors. . . . But so far as Mr. Washington apologizes for injustice, North or South, does not rightly value the privilege and duty of voting, belittles the emasculating effects of caste distinctions . . . we must unceasingly and firmly oppose them."[91] Du Bois's objections to Washington were simultaneously ethical and political—a moral rejection of Tuskegee's narrow "Mammonism" and a political affirmation for the Douglass tradition of democratic protest.

James Weldon Johnson noted that *The Souls of Black Folk* had "a greater effect upon and within the black race in America than any other single book published in this country since *Uncle Tom's Cabin.*"[92] Washington was stunned, but his agents promptly went to work to discredit Du Bois. The *Outlook* declared that Du Bois was "half ashamed of being a Negro." The *Colored American* characterized Du Bois's perspectives on Washington as "petty annoyances," and urged President Bumstead to curb "the outgivings and ill-advised criticisms of the learned Doctor who is now in his employ."[93] Du Bois was still permitted to work at Tuskegee Institute during the summer of 1903, but a final break was yet to come. He was still trying "to occupy middle ground" by appeasing "the *Guardian* on one hand and the Hampton-Tuskegee idea on the other."[94]

On the night of 30 July 1903, Washington spoke before an audience of two thousand in Boston. A group of radicals led by Trotter disrupted the meeting, and the police were called. Four people were arrested, and Trotter spent one month in jail, the maximum sentence. Du Bois had no prior knowledge of Trotter's plans, and when the "Boston Riot" took place he was not in the city. But Du Bois stayed at the Trotter home as a guest that August and expressed his opposition to Trotter's jail term. Washington consequently believed that Du Bois was behind the "conspiracy to riot." In October 1903, Washington wrote to Robert C. Ogden, an owner of Wanamaker's department store in Philadelphia and a major financial supporter of black education. "I have evidence which is indisputable showing that Dr. Du Bois is very largely behind the mean and underhanded attacks that have been made upon me," Washington stated. Ogden wrote to Bumstead and demanded an explanation.[95] George Foster Peabody, another millionaire and member of the Tuskegee Board of Trustees, also pressured Atlanta University. In December, Du Bois answered Peabody's charges, explaining that he had "steadfastly condemned" Trotter's actions in the Boston Riot. However, he also admired the black radical and agreed "with him in his main contentions."[96] Washington had no "evidence" against Du Bois. But he succeeded in alerting northern philanthropists to avoid making donations to Atlanta University. Du Bois had to be punished.

The Boston Riot of 1903 represented a turning point in Afro-American political history. Many black intellectuals, such as Kelly Miller, continued to express the position that the "conservatives" and "radicals" disagreed over tactics but were fundamentally similar on most issues. Du Bois's friend H. H. Proctor continued to work with Washington on local political affairs. But for Du Bois, the differences with Washington had become questions of principle. He retained faint hope that compromise with Tuskegee would be possible. He had no political machine or organization to combat Washington. But Du Bois began to look to the educated Negro elite, his "Talented Tenth," as a constituency to assert his political and cultural ideals. Only the segregated Negro colleges, not Tuskegee and Hampton, had the ability to produce such an elite. Indeed, "to attempt to establish any sort of a system of common and industrial school training, without *first* (and I say *first* advisedly) without *first* providing for the higher training of the very best teachers, is simply throwing your money away to the winds," Du Bois argued in 1903. Black America would only be "saved by its exceptional men," those who possessed "intelligence, broad sympathy, knowledge of the world that was and is, and of the relation of men to it." The Talented Tenth must "guide the Mass away from the contamination and death of the Worst, in their own

Bois "was making a strong claim for the recognition" of the "dignity and separate identity" of Afro-Americans. Taken together, the text blends the main themes that comprised Du Bois's emerging social theory: "double consciousness"; the beauty and originality of Negroes' "sorrow songs" and black religion; the unique spirituality of the Negro people; the necessity to develop black educational institutions; the general division of the modern world along the "color line." As in Du Bois's first books, *The Souls of Black Folk* retains a profoundly ethical and religious character. There was a frequent use of Biblical language, evident in Du Bois's description of the Georgia Black Belt as "the Egypt of the Confederacy," or in his use of the phrase "house of bondage." Throughout the book, Rampersad observes, "a patriarchal tone is encouraged by Du Bois's frequent borrowing from the King James Bible.[87] Like a prophet from the Old Testament, Du Bois expressed fears for the salvation of his people. In an age of expanding capitalism across the South, the false god of "Mammonism" was threatening to destroy the higher platonic ideals of "Truth, Beauty, and Goodness." Du Bois affirmed his support for economic development—"work and wealth are the mighty levers to lift this old new land"—but warned that the black world might "suddenly sink to a question of cash and a lust for gold." More than wealth, the South required "knowledge and culture. . . . The function of the university is not simply to teach bread-winning . . . it is, above all, to be the organ of that fine adjustment between real life and the growing knowledge of life, an adjustment which forms the secret of civilization."[88]

Two important features of *The Souls of Black Folk* were the metaphorical use of the "veil" as a description of institutional racism, and the greater emphasis placed by Du Bois on democratic political engagement to preserve blacks' rights. The "veil" reappeared in several passages: for example, as the "Veil that hung between us and Opportunity" in Du Bois's description of his east Tennessee teaching experiences. The veil of racial segregation made blacks virtually invisible to white America, and it inhibited Negro Americans from acquiring a unified perspective on their own conditions. This insight became a major theme of twentieth-century Afro-American literature. But the main theoretical transition in Du Bois's thinking involved politics. Writing with greater passion, he made subtle yet important changes in his "Strivings of the Negro People," republished as chapter one, "Of Our Spiritual Strivings." The Negro's belief that he "has a message for the world" is no longer described as being "perhaps foolish"; the goal of becoming "both a Negro and an American" requires that "the doors of Opportunity" should no longer be "closed roughly in his face." Du Bois added several brief passages denouncing racial disfranchisement and the "atmosphere of contempt and hate" across the nation. The "power of the ballot" was now defined as a means to "save us from a second slavery." Du Bois's greater ton wrote Du Bois, "otherwise the conference will be a failure from the beginning."[1] Du Bois recognized that most of the twenty-five or so delegates would be pro-Washington, and he urged Archibald Grimké and other allies to come prepared. "Bring every speech or letter or record of Washington men you can lay hands on so he can face his record in print," Du Bois advised. "The main issue of this meeting is *Washington,* refuse to be sidetracked."[2] Washington obviously anticipated such petty maneuvers and was far better organized. He consulted with President Theodore Roosevelt and several white philanthropists, including Baldwin and Andrew Carnegie. Trotter was excluded from the guest list—although when he learned of the location of the meeting, he attempted to enter Carnegie Hall but was barred. Pliable Kelly Miller served as secretary, and over Du Bois's objections, Fortune was in attendance, as was Emmett Scott. Du Bois's chief supporter at the conference was Massachusetts leader Clement G. Morgan.

Given Washington's orchestration, the Tuskegee faction was able to deflect most of Du Bois's criticisms. Du Bois emphasized that his objections to Washington did not extend to industrial education, but only on "his attacks upon higher training and upon his general attitude of belittling the race and not putting enough stress upon voting."[3] After the initial exchanges, the group appointed three members—Washington-supporter H. M. Browne, Washington, and Du Bois—to act as an executive committee that in turn would select a "Committee of Twelve." This body would function as a secretariat for national Negro action. Despite this decision, which may have helped to bridge some distance between radicals and the Tuskegee Machine, Washington nearly destroyed Du Bois's hopes by ushering several powerful white allies into the meeting. Du Bois recognized most of these individuals: Lyman Abbott, editor of the *Outlook,* Andrew Carnegie, Robert Ogden, George Foster Peabody, William Baldwin, and the pro-Tuskegee editor of the *Nation,* Oswald Garrison Villard, grandson of the abolitionist William Lloyd Garrison. One or more of these men had been coached by Washington, and all vigorously reminded their captive audience of their firm support for the Tuskegee philosophy. "Their words were lyric, almost fulsome in praise of Mr. Washington," Du Bois recalled in his *Autobiography.* "Even if all they said had been true, it was a wrong note to strike in a conference of conciliation."[4]

For the next three months, Du Bois attempted to work with the Committee of Twelve, trying to suppress his doubts. In February 1904, Du Bois drafted a bold, democratic model for creating a national formation. A "Committee of Safety" consisting of twelve leaders would meet every third month. A national "General Committee" would come together annually, and the socioeconomic and political decisions made by both organs would be carried out by "Committees of Correspondence" in every Negro community.[5] Washington and Browne vetoed this plan. At the executive committee's secret session in New York in March, all of Washington's initiatives were approved by a margin of two to one. For the Committee of Twelve, only Du Bois, Charles E. Bentley of Chicago and Archibald Grimké were selected to represent the radicals. It finally became clear to Du Bois that Washington was simply using the new organization to control his critics. During Du Bois's lecture tour in early 1904, he carefully refrained from personal attacks on Washington. But in his essays, he condemned the policy of accommodation. In "The Parting of the Ways," published in April, he warned that Afro-Americans should "refuse to kiss the hands that smite us." In language similar in style to Frederick Douglass, Du Bois stated, "The way for Black men today to make these rights the heritage of their children is to struggle for them unceasingly, and if they fail, die trying."[6] In one national magazine, *Collier's,* he called for a militant fight to achieve racial justice.[7] When the first official meeting of the Committee of Twelve was held in July, Du Bois did not attend. Du Bois submitted his resignation, as did Grimké. But the latter soon reversed himself and rejoined the organization. The Committee of Twelve continued to exist, financed by an annual subsidy of twenty-seven hundred dollars from Carnegie. Beyond publishing several pamphlets and engaging in limited suffrage issues, it did little to advance the cause of civil rights during the next ten years. The committee was just one small cog in the Tuskegee Machine.

Hostilities between Washington and Du Bois became more serious in early 1905. In a brief essay for an Atlanta publication, the *Voice of the Negro,* Du Bois charged that several black newspapers had obtained "hush money" totaling three thousand dollars during the previous year. All these publications "in five leading cities" were being dominated by Washington for political purposes.[8] The Tuskegee Machine used these undocumented charges to smear Du Bois. Fortune's *New York Age* termed Du Bois the "Professor of hysterics." To his white supporters, Washington innocently declared that he had never purchased "a dollar's worth" of any black newspaper and ridiculed Du Bois's assertion that Emmett Scott served as his "press agent."[9] Villard was amazed by Du Bois's "charge without having proofs" and demanded that Du Bois provide him with the evidence. With materials supplied by Trotter and others, Du Bois pieced together his case. Villard read through the information and admitted that Scott had been "extremely injudicious." Nevertheless, Du Bois had "failed to substantiate" the balance of his charges. For Villard, such matters were minor compared to the great contribution Washington played within society. "I do not think that there are any essential differences between your positions," Villard observed. "I do believe that for the masses of the negro race industrialization is the all-important question of the hour." Du Bois replied that any basis for cooperation with Washington had disintegrated. He still believed "that by means of downright bribery and intimidation" Washington was "influencing men to do his will . . . that he was seeking not the welfare of the Negro race but personal power."[10]

Du Bois actually underestimated Washington's manipulation of the national black press. After running Du Bois's original charges, the *Voice of the Negro* promptly lost one of its advertising accounts from a black businessman; Scott had persuaded him to withdraw his patronage. In Boston, the Tuskegee Machine largely financed two newspapers, the *Colored Citizen* and later the *Alexander's Magazine,* to push Trotter's *Guardian* out of business. In Washington, D.C., Washington provided funds to E. E. Cooper, editor of the *Colored American,* until it folded in early 1905. Soon afterward, Tuskegee Machine lieutenant Melvin J. Chisum began to court W. Calvin Chase, the militant editor of the Washington *Bee.* Chisum obtained a job on the *Bee*'s staff, and gradually convinced his employer to switch sides. Chisum informed Washington privately that Chase was "at heart a vile, malicious, jealous-heartless 'cuss'" but that he would work well for him. Washington began to funnel money to Chase, and in mid-1906 the *Bee* repudiated its previous positions by backing Tuskegee.[11] In Chicago, Washington provided funding for the *Leader,* and in 1906–07 attempted to buy up stock in the radical publication, the *Conservator.* Tuskegee's strategy backfired in Atlanta, however, when Washington helped to establish the *Voice of the Negro* in January 1904. Scott was placed on the editorial staff, and Professor J. W. E. Bowen of Gammon Theological Seminary, an old ally, became editor. Unfortunately for Washington, young radical journalist J. Max Barber was hired, and he soon moved the publication to the left with his sharp editorials.

The controversy over the Afro-American press pushed Du Bois and other radicals toward the establishment of their own organization. In June 1905, Du Bois secretly circulated a call "for organized determination and aggressive action on the part of men who believe in Negro freedom and growth." A conference would be held to organize those Negro leaders who opposed "present methods of strangling honest criticism." Fifty-nine Afro-Americans signed the statement, and in early July twenty-nine black men from fourteen states caucused at a hotel in Fort Erie, Ontario. They decided to create a militant civil rights formation to be called the Niagara Movement. Its stated objectives included: "freedom of speech and criticism"; "manhood suffrage"; "the abolition of all caste distinctions based simply on race or color"; "the recognition of the principle of human brotherhood as a practical present creed."[12] Du Bois was elected general secretary of the organization, and in January 1906, the Niagara Movement was incorporated in Washington, D.C. Booker T. Washington did what he could to disrupt the conference. After discovering the meeting's proposed location, he sent two agents to the Buffalo area. One lieutenant, attorney Clifford Plummer, was able to get the Associated Press bureau in Buffalo to halt its coverage. After the Niagara Movement's statements were circulated, Scott ordered Richard W. Thompson's National Negro Press Bureau to suppress any information about the group. But as the radicals grew in number, Tuskegee's counterstrategy shifted. Scott informed his agents to begin "to hammer" against the Niagara Movement.[13] Tactically, Tuskegee tried to project itself as the innocent victim. "The movement exists for the sole purpose of opposing Mr. Washington and the work he is trying to do," explained Scott to one college president. Privately, Washington fumed to Scott that Du Bois and the Niagara members were "scoundrels."[14]

By mid-1906, about one hundred seventy men had joined the Niagara Movement. Without exception, they were part of Du Bois's Talented Tenth, but they represented several ideological tendencies. Some had been quite close to Washington in previous years. Minnesota attorney Frederick L. McGhee had been Washington's supporter on the Afro-American Council's legislative committee; Episcopalian minister George F. Bragg of Baltimore had cooperated with the Tuskegee faction in opposing racial discrimination laws. Some were identified politically as Trotterites, such as the Reverend Byron Gunner of Newport and the Reverend J. Milton Waldron, founder of the Afro-American Industrial Insurance Society. Others were personal friends of Du Bois, like John Hope and Clement Morgan of Massachusetts. Many of these men were intellectuals: Lafayette Hershaw and J. R. L. Diggs would later join the American Negro Academy; Waldron had been trained at Newton Theological Seminary; the Reverend Reverdy C. Ransom was a product of Wilberforce; Morgan had been educated at Harvard. But some high school graduates in the Niagara Movement were far more radical than their college-trained colleagues. The best representative of this group was Cleveland editor H. C. Smith, who had served three terms in the Ohio House of Representatives and had authored the state's 1894 civil rights act. A number of these men were sympathetic to socialism, especially Ransom, Waldron, and J. Max Barber. Such leaders also tended to influence Du Bois toward the left; as Du Bois explained in his correspondence in November 1904, he would "scarcely describe" himself as a socialist, but he possessed "many socialistic beliefs."[15] Over all, the Niagara Movement was the most progressive faction of the Negro middle class, the group most willing to jeopardize its material and political security in the effort to achieve democratic rights for the Afro-American people.

The Niagarites held their second conference at Harper's Ferry, West Virginia, in August 1906. Throughout the year members were engaged in numerous reform activities. In Chicago, branch members protested the opening of a racist play, "The Clansman," and were instrumental in placing a black leader on the New Chicago Charter Committee. The Massachusetts branch had defeated local legislation that would have created racially segregated railroad cars. In Georgia, Du Bois and other Niagarites took part in the state's Equal Rights Convention, held in Macon in February, 1906. In the convention's manifesto, Du Bois spoke boldly for the principle of racial equality: "Disfranchisement and oppression will not . . . settle the race problem. We do not desire association with any one who does not wish our company, but we do expect in a Christian, civilized land, to live under a system of law and order, to be secure in life, limb and property . . . yet we are the victims of the most unreasoning sort of caste legislation."[16] The official documents issued by the Niagara conventions expressed the same beliefs. "We will not be satisfied to take one jot or tittle less than our full manhood rights," stated the Niagara Address of 1906. "We claim for ourselves every single right that belongs to a freeborn American, political, civil, and social; and until we get these rights we will never cease to protest and assail the ears of America."[17]

Du Bois understood that any successful challenge against the Tuskegee Machine required the creation of a national publication. He discussed the matter with Edward L. Simons, an Atlanta University graduate with considerable skill as a printer. In March 1904, the two men paid sixteen hundred dollars for a small printing shop in Memphis. During the first eight months of operation, the firm recorded over thirteen hundred dollars in gross receipts. Optimistic about their entrepreneurial chances, they secured a five-year lease on their building and tried to gain white philanthropic support for a national journal. Despite their inability to obtain adequate capital, Du Bois thought their publication would succeed. In December 1905, the first issue of the *Moon: Illustrated Weekly* appeared with Du Bois as editor, and Harry H. Pace as managing editor. Problems surfaced almost immediately. Du Bois's teaching commitments in Atlanta reduced his ability to provide editorial direction for the journal. The *Moon*'s content was designed to appeal to the liberal wing of the Talented Tenth, but its circulation was probably below five hundred. Few black middle-class intellectuals were prepared to back the magazine, and by July 1906, the enterprise was halted. Several months later, Du Bois was ready to try again, this time in partnership with Niagarites F. H. M. Murray and Lafayette Hershaw. The first issue of the *Horizon*, printed in Washington, D.C., appeared in January 1907.

The Tuskegee Machine initiated several complex tactics to crush and confuse its opponents. It had already taken steps to recruit leading radicals. For example, in the late 1890s, Massachusetts attorney William H. Lewis, a Harvard Law School graduate, was a stern critic of Washington's accommodationism. At that time Du Bois was so concerned about Lewis's hostility towards Tuskegee that he personally introduced him to Washington. When

President Roosevelt decided to name Lewis as Boston's assistant district attorney, Washington gave Lewis the false impression that he had arranged the appointment. Thereafter, Lewis became a strong advocate for Tuskegee. Washington was successful in obtaining a federal appointment for Robert Terrell, a Washington D.C. high school principal and husband of civil rights activist Mary Church Terrell. Becoming the district's first black judge in 1901, the liberal educator was forced to comply with most of Tuskegee's wishes. Washington also cultivated individuals who would later become leaders of the desegregation movement. A prime example was the early career of artist/writer James Weldon Johnson. In Johnson's December 1905 correspondence with Du Bois, he mentioned the possibility of organizing a group of black artists "in connection with the Niagara Movement." He even requested a photograph of Du Bois.[18] All along, however, he was Washington's man. Through the Tuskegee Machine, he obtained posts as United States Consul to Venezuela and Nicaragua. In a March 1907 letter to Washington, Johnson termed the Tuskegee's black critics "the enemy."[19]

A more aggressive method was the removal of enemies from their jobs. When Judson W. Lyons, register of the U.S. Treasury, voiced modest support for Trotter, Washington decided to obtain his dismissal. In 1905, Scott authored an anonymous press release that claimed that Lyons's office was used by Niagara Movement member Lafayette Hershaw for partisan politics. The charges were picked up by the press, and Roosevelt sacked Lyons. Two years later, Tuskegee Machine boss Charles W. Anderson met with President Roosevelt in an effort to secure the dismissal of Hershaw and F. H. M. Murray from their federal jobs. Du Bois came under special scrutiny. Washington's aides secretly checked Atlanta's tax records to learn "whether or not Dr. D. is actually a registered voter."[20] When the superintendent of the District of Columbia schools offered Du Bois the post of assistant superintendent in 1906, the Tuskegee Machine was mobilized. One local black leader "took the matter straight to President Theodore Roosevelt and emphasized the 'danger' of my appointment," Du Bois later noted. "The offer was never actually withdrawn, but it was not pressed, and I finally realized that it probably would not have gone through even if I had indicated my acceptance."[21] The position eventually went to Tuskegee advocate Roscoe Conkling Bruce. Even within his own ranks, Washington cautiously looked for signs of insubordination. One Tuskegee Institute instructor expressed misgivings about Washington's authoritarian behavior to his pastor in Boston. Washington's aides managed to steal these personal letters, and the teacher in question was promptly humiliated for actions which "were disloyal to the Institution."[22] Mary Church Terrell's militant speeches for civil rights also caused constant grief. One of Tuskegee's lieutenants, R. W. Tyler, warned that "some one ought to muzzle Mary Church

Terrell." Tyler attempted to do so in the *New York Age,* arguing that the race needed "less agitators and more constructors."[23]

A principled political movement seldom defeats an opponent who employs unscrupulous means. Before Melvin Chisum was placed at the Washington *Bee,* he had been assigned to spy on Trotter. Two months after the Boston Riot, Chisum was present at two secret strategy meetings in Trotter's home. In 1905–06 Chisum was a member of the Brooklyn branch of the Niagarites, and he continued to give Washington valuable information. Chisum's longtime friend, Emmett Scott, explained to Washington, "I do not think Chisum is a very brainy man, but I do know he is resourceful." After Washington's death, Chisum continued his career as a spy for the Pullman Company in its campaign to destroy the Brotherhood of Sleeping Car Porters.[24] Another Tuskegee Machine "mole" was Richard T. Greener, a Harvard graduate and a former United States consul in Bombay and Vladivostok. Before the Harper's Ferry meeting, Washington explained to Greener, "I have done all I could to work in harmony with Du Bois, but he has permitted Trotter and others to fool him into the idea that he was some sort of a leader." Greener was asked to "spare no pains" to acquire "inside" information on the Niagara Movement.[25] In need of a new appointment, Greener probably agreed to Washington's demands. Greener gave a speech at the Harper's Ferry meeting, and several weeks later he arrived on Tuskegee's campus. Washington's many efforts to suppress free speech and civil rights reveal his determination to play an aggressive role as "collaborator" with white corporations, the state, and segregationists in controlling the status of the Negro. As sociologist Oliver C. Cox suggested, "the term 'Uncle Tom' does not seem to describe the role of the leadership of Washington. The 'Uncle Tom' is a passive figure; he is so thoroughly inured to his condition of subordination that he has become tame and obsequious." Washington, by contrast, projected himself as a mass leader, but his effective power was obtained from white elites. Washington was "an intercessor between his group and the dominant class," Cox noted. He was "given wide publicity as a phenomenal leader" precisely because "he demanded less for the Negro people than that which the ruling class had already conceded."[26]

Washington cannot be held responsible for the racial violence that swept across the South during his public prominence, but his accommodationist rhetoric did nothing to check the regional trend toward vigilantism. In September 1906, Atlanta's newspapers ran a series of articles that presented in lurid detail imaginary Negro male attacks against white women. The play "The Clansman" had been performed in the city, and one paper urged racists to revive the then-defunct Ku Klux Klan organization locally. On 22 September the pogrom began. A black shoeshine boy, chosen arbitrarily, was dragged into a downtown street by several whites and literally beaten to

death. Afro-Americans who worked in downtown areas were most vulnerable. Black laborers were thrown through windows; Negro barbers waiting
on white customers were pulled from their chairs and assaulted; whites
destroyed Negro-owned restaurants and shops. The police frequently
joined the rioters. In one instance, they entered the home of a black man
who had been wounded during the previous night. "He was in bed; they
opened his shirt, placed their revolvers at his breast, and in cold blood shot
him through the body several times in the presence of his relatives." The
mob made no distinction between black "radicals" or "conservatives." J. W.
E. Bowen, Washington's most loyal supporter in Atlanta, was "beaten over
the head by one of the police with his rifle-butt."[27] Ten Afro-Americans and
two whites were killed; another sixty blacks and ten whites were wounded,
and hundreds received minor injuries. Booker T. Washington's response
was typical. He arrived in the city after the hostilities had stopped. Appealing for law and order, he wrote that "one is just as safe in Atlanta at present
as in New York." To the battered Bowen he explained, "I believe good in
the end will result from the present trials through which, we as a race, are
passing."[28] Within two months, Washington had secured the presidency of
Gammon Theological Seminary for his trusted friend.

Du Bois's response was different. Working on a sociological project in
Alabama's Black Belt, Du Bois immediately boarded a train for Atlanta after
learning about the pogrom. Worried about family and friends, he quickly
penned a poem, "A Litany at Atlanta." The lyrical lines capture his thoughts
of the moment: "Bewildered we are and passioned-tossed, made with the
madness of a mobbed and mocked and murdered people. . . . / Keep not
Thou silent, O God! / Sit no longer blind, Lord God, deaf to our prayer and
dumb to our dumb suffering. Surely Thou, too, art not white, O Lord, a
pale, bloodless, heartless thing!"[29] Du Bois rushed to his home, and found
Nina and their six-year-old daughter Yolande secure. Du Bois hated violence
and could not conceive of himself "killing a human being." But he purchased
a "Winchester double-barreled shotgun and two dozen rounds of shells filled
with buckshot." He waited for the white vigilantes on his front porch. "If a
white mob had stepped on the campus where I lived," Du Bois wrote later,
"I would without hesitation have sprayed their guts over the grass. They
did not come."[30]

Scott had learned that Du Bois was in Alabama when the riot erupted,
and in October 1906 he wrote an anonymous editorial that claimed that
Washington had fearlessly entered Atlanta. Du Bois, by contrast, had shown
his cowardice by hiding safely in Alabama. The *New York Age* and other
Negro papers under Washington's control ran the story. Du Bois's account
of the pogrom appeared in *World Today*, and he charged that police brutality,
political corruption, and racial prejudice were the causes of the violence. He

also applauded those blacks who had armed themselves to protect their communities.[31] The battle between the radicals and the Tuskegee Machine continued.

Du Bois's entry into politics was not entirely to his "liking." "My career as a scientist," he observed ruefully, was being "swallowed up in my role as a master of propaganda."[32] With considerable difficulty, he attempted to maintain his social science research projects. The Atlanta University conferences were continued as in previous years. In May 1905, the conference was on the topic "Methods and Results of Ten Years' Study on the American Negro." The participants included Hershaw, Professor Walter F. Willcox of Cornell University, and Mary White Ovington, a young socialist and social worker.[33] In 1904–05 Ovington held a fellowship through New York's Greenwich House to research the socioeconomic conditions of Afro-Americans in that city. Du Bois provided extensive advice to her, and soon a warm personal and political relationship developed. At the 1906 conference on the "Health and Physique of the Negro-American," Du Bois brought together some of the leading scholars in the field. R. R. Wright, Jr., an A.M.E. minister who had published articles on blacks in the American Southwest, prepared a paper on Negro mortality rates in urban areas. Monroe N. Work contributed research to the final conference document, and Professor Franz Boas of Columbia University presented a brief paper.[34] The Carnegie Institution financed the 1907 studies on "Economic Co-Operation Among Negro Americans." The conference document was the most detailed economic sketch of black America yet produced. Du Bois obtained data on hundreds of Negro-owned banks, fraternal societies, consumer and producer cooperatives, and religious and educational institutions. The major attempt of the volume was to illustrate collective activity within the private sector and to suggest methods for stimulating "the group economy" of black Americans. Segregation had forced Afro-Americans to develop their own structures of "religious ministration, medical care, legal advice, and education of children," Du Bois noted. The possibility for using internal economic organization to help destroy institutional racism was a theme Du Bois returned to during the Great Depression.[35]

Although the conference volumes were a major contribution to American sociology, Du Bois perceived that relatively few people beyond some liberal academicians appreciated his work. Partially to generate attention for fundraising purposes, Du Bois began to write short essays describing Atlanta University's research activities. For the *Annals of the American Academy of*

Political and Social Science, he submitted an article outlining the "Laboratory in Sociology" at Atlanta University. He explained the serious limitations of his studies: "Although our researches have cost less than $500 a year, yet we find it difficult and sometimes impossible to raise that meager sum. We lack proper appliances for statistical work and proper clerical aid." But the challenge of a black university was to conduct "a systematic and thoroughgoing study" of the Negro "problems as would gradually raise many of the questions above the realm of opinion and guess into that of scientific knowledge." Du Bois was discouraged that the studies had "not received as much criticism as they deserved," but overall took pride that they had "undoubtedly exerted a wholesome influence" and a "healthy self-criticism based on accurate knowledge."[36] A similar essay, entitled "The Atlanta University Conferences," was printed in the New York-based magazine *Charities* in May 1903.[37] In 1905 Du Bois contributed a lengthy article on Atlanta University to an edited volume on black education, which was printed by the American Unitarian Association. The tone of this later essay is much more political. Writing for a white audience, Du Bois reminded his readers: "Most men in this world are colored. A faith in humanity . . . must, if honest, be primarily a belief in colored men." Atlanta University was a major "bulwark against the assaults of all forces within and without the race, which consciously or unconsciously work to narrow the opportunities and to curb the righteous ambitions of black men." The college had been a "social settlement" where blacks had been "brought into contact with the standards of modern culture in school and home and campus." Du Bois stated the case for black higher education in stark terms: "Force and fear and representation have hitherto marked our attitude toward darker races. Shall this continue or be replaced by freedom and friendship and open opportunity?"[38]

Du Bois's public opposition to Booker T. Washington was a central factor in the growing financial difficulties of both the research conferences and Atlanta University. As early as January 1904, an editor of *Collier's* magazine commented to Du Bois: "If I am not mistaken, your views and those of my friend, Mr. Washington, are diametrically opposed, or at least in that you feel that his program in all particulars is not in harmony with the modern spirit."[39] Washington encouraged the misperception that Du Bois and Atlanta University were hostile toward industrial education—a myth that still persists nearly ninety years later. In the wake of the Boston Riot, Robert C. Ogden complained to philanthropist George Foster Peabody that Du Bois was not "intellectually honest. . . . Too many of our colored friends are bumptious for much of which we may thank Bumstead."[40] Money from northern friends gradually began to diminish. In March 1904 Du Bois issued an urgent appeal for support in the *Voice of the Negro.* "If Negroes were lost in Africa, money would be available," he observed, "but $500 a year is hard to raise for Atlanta."[41] By 1905 Du Bois speculated that the Atlanta University conferences would soon have to become biennial events. As Du Bois completed final details for his 1908 conference on the black family, Atlanta University's new president, E. T. Ware, informed him that the conference series was to be halted indefinitely. Continued funding from the John F. Slater Fund was obtained, and the May 1909 conference on black social welfare programs was held as scheduled. "Young President Ware had received almost categorical promise that under certain circumstances increased contributions from the General Education Board and other sources might be expected, which would make the University secure," Du Bois wrote. It was apparent that Du Bois was one of the "circumstances," and only his removal or dismissal would be sufficient. He became "acutely conscious of the difficulty which my attitudes and beliefs were making for Atlanta University."[42]

If Du Bois's research received few plaudits from white American intellectuals and philanthropists, his growing reputation abroad was another matter. European sociologists were well aware of Du Bois's sociological studies. When Max Weber came to the United States in 1904, he met with Du Bois. In a March 1905 letter, Weber emphasized, "Your splendid work 'The Souls of Black Folk' *ought to be translated in German.*"[43] Weber edited a journal, *Archiv für Sozialwissenschaft und Sozialpolitik,* and requested a contribution from Du Bois. Du Bois's essay "The Negro Question in the United States" was published in Weber's journal in 1906. In November 1906, Du Bois's article, "L'Ouvrier nègre en Amérique," appeared in the Brussels academic journal *Revue Économique Intérnationale.* For a New Zealand publication, Du Bois presented an essay on racism and the political conditions of Negro Americans. Five years later, the *Sociological Review* of Manchester printed Du Bois's "Economics of Negro Emancipation in the United States." The article was perhaps the most radical statement Du Bois had yet presented to an academic audience. In it he maintained the struggle for black freedom required economic strategies, chiefly the unity of the working class across racial lines. The oppression of the Negro was part of an international economic dynamic that had reduced "human labor to the lowest depth in order to derive the greatest personal profit."[44]

Despite his controversial political affinities, Du Bois continued to write popular essays for the white public on race relations. To the *Nation,* he forwarded a detailed note on the decline of "Negro illiteracy."[45] In October 1906, *Collier's* magazine published Du Bois's "The Color Line Belts the World," which connected the oppression of Afro-Americans with the plight of other peoples of color under European colonialism. The logic behind this short essay was evident in Du Bois's famous "color line" statement of 1900, but here it is made more cogently as a political argument against imperialism.[46] For the *American Journal of Sociology* Du Bois wrote "Race Friction Between Black and White," as a critique of a paper by Alfred Holt Stone, a Mississippi cotton planter and an "expert" on Negro "problems." Du Bois criticized white academic institutions for failure to support any "serious study of the race problem." He predicted that "race segregation in the future" would be impossible "primarily because these races are needed more and more in the world's economy. . . . What we ought to do in America is seek to bind the races together rather than to accentuate differences."[47]

In August 1910, Du Bois's witty and important article on "The Souls of White Folk" appeared in the magazine *Independent*. "High in the tower" where Du Bois sat, he was most perplexed by those "souls . . . that have become painfully conscious of their whiteness." Du Bois makes the historical observation that constantly escaped his contemporaries: "The discovery of personal whiteness among the world's people is a very modern thing—a ninteenth-and twentieth-century matter, indeed. The ancient world would have laughed at such a distinction. The Middle Ages regarded it with mild curiosity." Racism had produced the powerful social equation within white minds: "I am white and you are black. . . . I am white and you are nothing." Despite the inherent absurdity of the situation, the racist's "descent to Hell is easy." In the effort to justify white supremacy, American science "has repeatedly suppressed evidence, misquoted authority, distorted fact and deliberately lied. It is wonderful that in the very lines of social study, where America should shine, it has done nothing."[48]

Although the bulk of Du Bois's writings between 1903 and 1910 were in the field of sociology, he also produced many works of political and social history. In the *Voice of the Negro,* he wrote a four-part series on the history of slavery, spanning from its African and Mediterranean roots through black American "serfdom."[49] In a book review essay for *Dial* magazine in 1906, he again focused on "slavery and its aftermath."[50] Du Bois's struggles against white racism and Washington's machine revived an academic interest in the abolitionist movement and in the black Reconstruction period after the Civil War. In the *Independent,* Du Bois submitted a short statement on "Garrison and the Negro," which largely criticized the contemporary shortcomings of white liberals.[51] Niagarite J. R. L. Diggs, the president of Virginia Theological Seminary, urged Du Bois to "take the lead" in writing an accurate historical description of Reconstruction. "The series of works by southern writers present our white brothers' side of the question," Diggs wrote, "but I do not find the proper credit given our people for what good they really did in those days."[52] Five months after Diggs's correspondence, Du Bois presented a paper, "Reconstruction and Its Benefits," at the American Historical Association's annual meeting. The thesis of Du Bois's paper was radically at odds with the dominant school of Reconstruction historiography. Du Bois noted the achievements of the Reconstruction state governments, which included the construction of the South's first public school systems, democratic political rights for all citizens, and social welfare legislation. Undoubtedly with some irony, Du Bois concluded that black suffrage had established the basis for "practically the whole new growth of the South" since the war. Black participation in southern governments had benefited the entire population of the region.[53] The white historical profession totally ignored this paper for over three decades—although by the 1950s Du Bois's interpretation became the consensus view of scholars. His failure to dislodge the racism of his professional colleagues did not, in itself, distress him too much. What did bother Du Bois was the *American Historical Review*'s stern refusal to permit him "to capitalize the word Negro" in his published paper.[54]

Du Bois's major work of this period was also in the field of history—a biography of abolitionist John Brown. Both the origins of the book and its public reception are of interest. Originally Du Bois had been asked by Ellis Paxon Oberholtzer, the editor of a biographical series for George W. Jacobs and Company, to write a biography of Frederick Douglass. In November 1903, Du Bois agreed to write the book. Two months later, Oberholtzer informed Du Bois that Booker T. Washington had also expressed interest in the same topic. Despite Du Bois's "superior historical training," Oberholtzer wrote, "I regret to tell you that I must give it to him."[55] Du Bois then proposed to write a biography of Nat Turner, which Oberholtzer rejected. Finally, at Oberholtzer's suggestion, Du Bois agreed to select John Brown. He began to write the biography of the white abolitionist in 1905, but it was not until 1909 that *John Brown* was published.

In some respects, *John Brown* was similar to the *Suppression of the African Slave-Trade*. Both books are studies in the ethical and moral aspects of American society during the period of slavery; both maintain Hart's standards for rigorous documentation. One critical difference in *John Brown* was the absence of much original research. Du Bois relied on several secondary sources, including an 1885 study by F. B. Sanborn and the 1894 work, *John Brown and His Men*, by R. J. Hinton, to present a fresh interpretation of the white abolitionist. Du Bois's interest in Brown stemmed from historical and contemporary factors. Like Du Bois, Brown viewed himself as an exceptional man who possessed a moral and political vision of a just, democratic society. Brown had been trained in Puritanism, "the last white flower of the Lutheran revolt," and was familiar with "the cruel grandeur of the Old Testament." He shared Du Bois's hatred of mammonism and conceived of business as a "philanthropy." Most of all, Brown came to hate slavery as a moral abomination and political crime against the black masses. Brown saw himself as an "instrument in the hands of Providence," a messenger sent to strike down the institution of black inequality. For Du Bois, Brown represented the capacity of white progressives to transcend the racist culture and to place their lives in the movement for biracial democracy. In *John Brown,* Du Bois explains the activities and views of the black abolitionists—Douglass, Harriet Tubman, Martin Delany, Henry Highland Garnet, and others—whom he viewed as the forerunners of the Niagara Movement. That Brown was unable to spark a general slave uprising at Harper's Ferry was interpreted not as a failure but as a "blow" for democracy and a higher good. "That John Brown was legally a lawbreaker and a murderer all men knew," Du Bois commented. But Brown's "lawlessness was in obedience to the highest call of self-sacrifice for the welfare of his fellow men." Brown believed "that all men are created free and equal, and that the cost of liberty is less than the price of repression." Du Bois's argument here, that temporal laws were subordinate to a transcendent moral law, was the foundation for the politics of Mohandas Gandhi and Martin Luther King, Jr. Du Bois still deplored violent social change, observing that "revolution is not a test of capacity; it is always a loss and a lowering of ideals." But Brown's death and legacy indicated that "the price of repressing the world's darker races is shown in a moral retrogression and an economic waste unparalleled since the age of the African slave-trade."[56]

John Brown would always remain Du Bois's favorite of his works. Its weakness as a conventional history was transcended by its powerful political interpretation, and even more, by its literary artistry. But written during the high tide of Jim Crow, many white reviewers had little difficulty in ignoring the book. Fewer than seven hundred copies of *John Brown* were sold from 1909 to 1916. Part of the reason for the biography's poor reception may be attributed to Oswald Garrison Villard. For several years, Villard had been at work on a biography of Brown, and Du Bois's latest work received a harshly negative review in the *Nation.* Du Bois wrote a lengthy rebuttal and requested that it be printed in the journal. The *Nation* not only refused to publish Du Bois's statement, but Villard replied arrogantly: "The appearance of your book, so far from injuring the chances of my own . . . improves them, and would have improved them still more if it had reached the standard we have a right to expect from you."[57]

Du Bois had begun to reject the sterility of detached social science and sought new avenues to express his ideas. "The Negro is primarily an artist," Du Bois observed in 1913. "The only race which has held at bay the life-destroying forces of the tropics has gained therefrom in some slight compensation a sense of beauty, particularly for sound and color, which characterizes the race."[58] In 1903 he compiled and published a *Bibliography of Negro Folk Songs.*[59] Between 1904 and 1906 he wrote most of the first draft of a novel, *The Quest of the Silver Fleece,* which was not completed until 1911. Although the basic story consists of a romance between two characters—Blessed Alwyn, an ambitious yet naive black man, and Zora, the daughter of a conjure woman—*The Quest of the Silver Fleece* was an attempt to present the South's racial and economic conflicts to a popular audience. In some ways the novel parallels the works of Frank Norris and Upton Sinclair. Zora and Blessed are caught in the destructive social forces that were then transforming the South: conservative northern philanthropy, which was aligned with the South's ruling class; the rise of racist lynch mobs; the corrupt maneuvers of politicians, both black and white. As Arlene A. Elder illustrated, the novel's central motif is the link between the "swamp" and the "cotton fields." The swamp, which provides a home to Zora's mother, Elspeth, symbolizes human decay, the lowering of ideals and cultural backwardness. Here Zora is raped by a racist plantation owner. "Cotton" represents the road forward for blacks, the means to acquire property and an education, the "silver fleece" for a rising people. The struggle for self sufficiency is not simply economic but moral. A secondary but important feature of the novel is Du Bois's development of strong female characters, particularly Sarah Smith, a hardworking white New England school teacher in the black community, and Zora, who mobilizes the masses of illiterate rural blacks against their white landlords. Du Bois later described his first novel as "an economic study of some merit," but like *John Brown,* it illustrated the political achievement of individuals who dedicated themselves to a moral struggle.[60]

Du Bois's most lasting contributions to Negro literature before 1910 were his "Credo" and the poem "The Song of the Smoke." "Credo" was a prose poem of barely five hundred words that was first published in *Independent* magazine in October 1904. In it Du Bois outlines the central principles that motivate his political and cultural work: "I believe in God, who made of one blood all nations that on earth do dwell. . . . Especially do I believe in the Negro Race: in the beauty of its genius, the sweetness of its soul, and its strength in that meekness which shall yet inherit this turbulent earth." The "Credo" embodies Du Bois's hopes—a world without war, the "training of Children," the achievement of political liberty "for all men: the space to stretch their arms and their souls, the right to breathe and the right to vote."[61] The statement captured the deep cultural and political yearnings of black people, and within several years it became widely known. The prose poem was memorized by many black children; it was frequently framed and prominently placed in Negro homes.

"The Song of the Smoke" was published in the second issue of the *Horizon* in February 1907. The poem was a reminder of the cultural distance between Du Bois and some of the Niagarites. Many early proponents of desegregation equated their struggle for equal rights with cultural assimilation. In that limited sense, Du Bois was never an integrationist. As an advocate for pan-Africanism and black identity—which ultimately gave birth to *Négritude* as a literary movement—Du Bois made no distinction between art and political engagement. A movement to abolish racism required a positive cultural consciousness among the oppressed. For its time, the poem was both shocking and inspirational: "I am the smoke king, I am black. I am darkening with song, I am hearkening to wrong; I will be black as blackness can, The blacker the mantle the mightier the man."[62] Gradually, the social scientist was becoming both poet and man of action.

The Niagara Movement never acquired a large constituency among black Americans. The *Horizon* consistently lost money and attracted few advertisers. Eighteen months after the magazine started, Du Bois appealed for donations: "As a straight out, independent, business proposition a national Negro magazine will not pay yet. . . . Yet we need a journal, not as a matter of business, but as a matter of spiritual life and death."[63] The Niagarites challenged racist legislation in the courts with limited success. But members were frequently behind in their dues, and the organization had raised less than thirteen hundred dollars in its first two years. Tensions soon surfaced among the leaders. At the August 1907 conference in Boston, Trotter quarreled sharply with Du Bois and Clement Morgan. In November 1907, Trotter demanded Morgan's removal as Massachusetts branch leader. The Niagara Movement executive committee supported Trotter, but Du Bois threatened to resign his post as general secretary if Morgan were deposed. Trotter complained to one associate that Du Bois's followers were "self-seekers" to be avoided.[64] During 1908 many of the branches ceased to hold regular meetings. Some members began to work primarily in other local organizations or independently.

Du Bois's inexperience as a political leader was an obvious factor in the organization's decline. "I was no natural leader of men," Du Bois wrote later. "I could not slap people on the back and make friends of strangers. I could not easily break down an inherited reserve; or at all times curb a biting, critical tongue."[65] Trotterite William H. Ferris effectively compared Du Bois with Booker T. Washington: "Du Bois is gifted with a more powerful intellect than Washington, is a more uncompromising idealist, and is a more brilliant writer. . . . But Washington is a more magnetic speaker and more astute politician, a greater humorist, and less of an aristocrat." Du Bois's strength was his singular power as an intellectual in a "struggle for the supremacy of rival theories." But unlike Washington, he "had no aspiration of becoming a race leader."[66] Du Bois was now the second most prominent black leader in the country. "Du Bois Clubs" were started by students at the University of Pennsylvania and by Afro-American women in Baltimore. One student society at Cornell University purchased "a large order" of *The Souls of Black Folk*, using the text as a means "toward broadening the racial spirit" at the institution.[67] Trotter and some other radicals may have had misgivings about their elevation of this scholar who seemed so aloof and formal. They had helped to create his political prestige; had they made a mistake?

In 1908, Trotter, J. Milton Waldron, the Reverend Alexander Walters, and other radicals formed the National Negro American Political League, which campaigned against the Republican party presidential candidate William Howard Taft. Washington's Tuskegee Machine backed Taft; and after some hesitation, Du Bois advised blacks to support Democratic candidate William Jennings Bryan. "An avowed enemy," Du Bois reasoned, was "better" than a "false friend."[68] Following the 1908 election, Walters and Trotter renamed their new formation the National Independent Political League. Although Du Bois was sympathetic to this display of political independence among black voters, such activism did little to build the Niagara Movement. Other organizations had begun to take the lead on civil rights issues. The major reform group was the Constitution League, founded in 1903 by a white liberal Republican, John E. Milholland. Like Villard and other liberals, Milholland had long supported Tuskegee Institute. He had donated funds to help black tenant farmers near the school; in 1904 the Constitution League cooperated with Washington on legislative issues. The relationship between Washington and Milholland soured in 1906, when the Constitution League actively criticized the Roosevelt administration's mass dishonorable discharges of black troops after the Brownsville, Texas, riot. In retaliation, Washington informed Roosevelt's postmaster general "that it was Milholland, who derived most of his income from selling pneumatic tube equipment to the post office department," who was largely "responsible for stirring up the Brownsville agitation."[69] Even before the Atlanta and Brownsville riots, many Niagarites had worked with the interracial Constitution League. In March 1907, the Niagara Movement created a formal committee to cooperate with the League. By mid-1907, Du Bois had become a league director. The national movement against racism was gaining strength, but the Niagara Movement's organizational identity was weakening steadily.

Many observers thought throughout its short existence that the Niagara Movement should be merged with other groups. One curious proposal was advanced by the Washington *Bee*—the union of the Niagara Movement with the National Negro Business League. Some called for a merger between the Afro-American Council and the Niagarites. In late 1905, Du Bois indicated that he was distinctly "not enthusiastic" about any merger negotiations. But in September 1906, Hershaw was sent to an Afro-American Council meeting as the Niagara Movement's representative.[70] And by June 1908, recognizing his organization's severe limitations and internal divisions, Du Bois made the most ambitious proposal for black unity. In the *Horizon*, he advocated a union of the American Negro Academy, the Afro-American Council, the National Negro American Political League, and the Niagara Movement. "Each of the four organizations once had its raison d'etre," Du Bois noted, but all these groups "want the same things." As a measure of good faith, he pledged to refuse all official positions in this "united organization."[71] Technically, what Du Bois sought was a united front of radical-to-moderate Negroes that could pool financial resources and personnel in the struggle for racial equality. Had the proposal been accepted by all parties, Washington would have had little room for maneuver. But strategies of this type seldom work when one formation's leader has a broad, national identity. Archibald Grimké promptly opposed the proposal, arguing that the academy should remain politically neutral. Obviously Trotter would have been skeptical, since he had already developed a political vehicle of his own.

The Tuskegee Machine sensed the Niagara Movement's deterioration and moved rapidly to push it into extinction. Black newspapers took turns ridiculing Du Bois. The *New York Age* termed the Niagarites an "aggregation of soreheads." The Indianapolis *Freeman* described the Niagara Movement's 1907 "Address to the World" as a "final shriek of despair." Washington secured the cooperation of white newspapers to delete any information on the movement's 1908 conference in Oberlin, Ohio. He even asked the *Age* to print "an obituary which he prepared" on the organization.[72] The machine continued to harass its critics in other ways. When Kelly Miller tried to obtain a faculty position at Howard University for Du Bois in 1909, Washington used his influence as a Howard trustee to block the appointment.[73] Some Niagara Movement members were particularly vulnerable. After the Atlanta riot, J. Max Barber moved to Chicago and in February 1908 became editor of the *Conservator*. Washington knew that Barber was "to the point of nearly starving" when he was hired. But through the paper's largest stockholder, a member of the National Negro Business League, Washington obtained his removal. Barber soon fled to Philadelphia and acquired a teaching position at an industrial school. When Washington learned about it, he wrote to the school describing Barber as a misfit. Barber would teach "colored people to hate white people," Washington warned. The Negro was "about as unfitted for such work . . . as any man that I can think of."[74] Barber finally entered dental school and after several years started his private practice: at least Washington could not control his patients. This episode indicates the great lengths Washington sometimes took to destroy his black opponents, personally and professionally.

The struggle took its measure of Du Bois. Frequently Nina took their daughter Yolande away from the South, and the extended separations were painful to Du Bois. Nina often attended Niagara conferences and political meetings with her husband, and softly offered her advice on different matters. But life under Jim Crow conditions was difficult, and her health had begun to decline. Du Bois's friends experienced similar personal and economic hardships. David Wallace, a member of the Niagara Movement's Chicago branch, obtained a job in Chattanooga. Forwarding a letter of resignation to Du Bois in 1908, Wallace explained: "There are many who dare not, for good reasons, speak or contribute openly . . . to a cause which lies close to really all Negroes' and many white men's hearts. . . . You shall have a secret comrade in me. My private prayers shall go up for you who dare, and when opportunity affords I shall be a secret subscriber to our common cause."[75] Fear dictated the actions of many who had been influenced by Du Bois's writings. Ministers were concerned about losing their churches; teachers feared being dismissed from their schools. Even John Hope, who was now president of Atlanta Baptist College, was plagued with doubts. For his powerful stance against racial injustice, philanthropic aid to his institution was halted. With the critical assistance of Hampton Institute educator Robert Russa Moton, Washington's friend and later successor as principal at Tuskegee, Hope acquired ten thousand dollars from Carnegie for his college. Some radicals claimed that Hope had betrayed their cause. But Hope knew that only to Du Bois did he owe any explanation: "Why Du Bois? Because I have followed him; believed in him; tried even, where he was not understood, to interpret him and show that he is right; because I have been loyal to him . . . and because, in spite of appearances, I am just as truly as ever a disciple of the teachings of Du Bois regarding Negro freedom." Du Bois understood, and his friendship with Hope was not easily shaken. "Of course I am sorry to see you or anyone in Washington's net," he replied. "One thing alone you must not, however, forget: Washington stands for Negro submission and slavery."[76]

It was perhaps inevitable that some formal merger would be proposed between the white and Afro-American radicals. The catalyst for this was an assault on blacks in Springfield, Illinois. A white socialist, William English Walling, described the pogrom in a September 1908 essay, and challenged white liberals to build a new social movement: "Either the spirit of the abolitionists, of Lincoln and of Lovejoy, must be revived and we must come to treat the Negro on a plane of absolute political or social equality or Vardaman and Tillman will soon have transferred the Race War to the North."

Mary White Ovington took the initiative. Contacting Walling and Dr. Henry Moskowitz, the three progressives decided to organize a conference for May 1909, to "discuss the Negro's status in the United States." Villard was brought into the discussions, and he volunteered to write a conference "call" statement. Fortunately, Villard had experienced some political disagreements with Washington, and he was prepared to agree that the moment had arrived for a "radical political movement" against racial inequality. Most of the leading whites who endorsed the "call" or who would participate in the conference were socialists or liberal reformers: pioneer social workers Jane Addams and Florence Kelley; writer William Dean Howells; educator John Dewey; historian John Spencer Bassett; and Milholland. According to Ovington, many whites involved had little real understanding of "the Negro problem" and tended to view blacks as objects of "pity."[77] Although Villard invited Washington's "sympathetic interest and help," the Tuskegee Machine had little difficulty in recognizing a potential threat. The new group, called the "National Negro Committee," might become another Niagara Movement. Carnegie and other white philanthropists were informed to boycott the committee's initial conference, scheduled on 31 May–1 June 1909, in New York.[78]

Black delegates at the conference were motivated by other considerations. There was ample reason to distrust Villard and the more moderate white participants. Du Bois's presentation to the conference was a masterful critique of the contradictions of Washington's philosophy. As in his *Souls of Black Folk* essay, he did not resort to Trotter's caustic rhetoric. The basic argument was that democratic political rights and economic opportunity were directly related; the absence of the Negro franchise condemned blacks to a subordinate economic status. Most of the whites who had adopted Washington's version of the Niagara-Tuskegee debate were visibly moved, including Villard. Compared to Trotter, who was "behaving very badly," Villard noted privately, Du Bois came off rather well. "All through our committee sessions, Du Bois was most useful; his attitude and bearing were faultless and his spirit of the best. I was more impressed with him than ever before."[79] During the selection of the group's steering committee and the adoption of resolutions, conflicts erupted between black and white participants. On one occasion, a black woman "leapt to her feet and cried in passionate, almost tearful earnestness. . . . 'They are betraying us again— these white friends of ours,'" Du Bois wrote in *Survey* magazine.[80] Trotter and Waldron were especially discouraged by the results of the meeting. Negroes with marginal ties to Washington, such as Mary Church Terrell, were named to the steering committee, and a few black radicals had been omitted. Washington was also disgruntled, although well informed about the dynamics of the conference. His lieutenants had already tried to "discredit" the meeting with local reporters.[81] But both Washington and Du Bois may have sensed a new turning point in their protracted political confrontation. The "net result" of the conference, Du Bois perceived, "was the vision of future co-operation, not simply, as in the past, between giver and beggar . . . but a new alliance between social workers and reformers in touch, on one hand, with scientific philanthropy, and on the other hand, with the great struggling mass of laborers of all kinds, whose condition and needs know no color line."[82]

Within less than a year, a consensus was reached within the steering committee to launch a permanent organization—the National Association for the Advancement of Colored People (NAACP). All of the national officers elected at the May 1910 conference were white, except Du Bois. Liberal reformer Moorfield Storey was elected national president; Walling, chair of the executive committee; Milholland was named national treasurer; and Villard was disbursing treasurer. Although there was no formal merger between the NAACP and the Niagara Movement, most of the Niagarites joined the interracial formation from the beginning. Trotter's participation was tenuous. Several NAACP leaders, especially Villard and Storey, were too compromising toward Washington. It was also evident that Du Bois and his close supporters from the Niagara Movement would become the dominant black constituency within the organization. The Tuskegee Machine, conversely, now recognized the potential danger of a powerful rival machine. Washington privately believed that his former white allies had been "deceived" by the radicals, and that the NAACP's 1910 resolutions were "nonsense."[83] He resorted to his usual tactics. He ordered the *New York Age* to "burn Walling up in an editorial." The *Age* complied with this broadside: "We hope that no colored man or woman will in the future disgrace our race by inviting Mr. Walling in their home or ask him to speak at any public meeting." Machine lieutenants were ordered to criticize blacks who were joining the NAACP or creating local branches; at least one spy was sent to take notes at the 1910 conference. Although Washington no longer trusted Mary Church Terrell, on at least one occasion she divulged confidential information about dissention inside the NAACP's national leadership to him. He was pleased that Terrell and Du Bois "have absolutely nothing to do with each other," and he hoped to find other ways to divide the organization.[84]

Du Bois was unwilling to sever his ties with the academy and to plunge into a full-time career of political propaganda. Even after accepting the position as NAACP Director of Publicity and Research, he continued to coedit volumes from the Atlanta University conferences with sociology professor Augustus G. Dill until 1913. "At last, forbear and waver as I would, I faced the great Decision," Du Bois wrote in *Darkwater*. "My life's last and greatest door stood ajar."[85] There were no guarantees. The NAACP could disappear in the coming months, leaving Du Bois without the means to support his family. It says much about this man that he chose to express his inner thoughts in 1909–10 in a series of prayers, delivered to students at Atlanta University. Most of the prayers were drafted in pencil, and nearly all were inspired by a Biblical passage. The prayers were political and spiritual, in the great prophetic tradition of the black church: "Let the Christ spirit be born anew in this our home and in this land of ours. Out of the depths of selfishness and languor and envy, let spring the spirit of humility and poverty, of gentleness and sacrifice—the eternal dawn of Peace, good-will toward men." The human condition need not be bound to the materialism and avarice of society. Through social reform and sacrifice, the Lord's voice could be manifested within the temporal world: "Give us grace, O God, to dare to do the deed which we well know cries to be done. Let us not hesitate because of ease, or the words of men's mouths, or our own lives. Mighty causes are calling us—the freeing of women, the training of children, the putting down of hate and murder and poverty." At the conclusion of this prayer, Du Bois repeated the final sentence of his 1893 autobiographical statement: "Mercifully grant us, O God, the spirit of Esther, that we say: I will go unto the King and if I perish, I perish—Amen."[86] The final door had been opened, and Du Bois was now prepared to enter a new arena.

4

THE *CRISIS*
AND THE NAACP:
SOCIAL REFORM IN
THE PROGRESSIVE ERA

The policy of the *Crisis* will be simple and well defined. It will, first and foremost, be a newspaper: it will record important happenings and movements in the world which bear on the great problem of interracial relations, and especially those which affect the Negro American. . . . Its editorial page will stand for the rights of men, irrespective of color or race, for the highest ideals of American democracy, and for reasonable but earnest and persistent attempt to gain these rights and realize these ideals.

W. E. B. Du Bois,
November 1910

Du Bois arrived in New York City on 1 August 1910, and immediately went to work for the NAACP. No one was precisely clear what Du Bois's responsibilities were or what he should do. Villard greeted him laconically: "I don't know who is going to pay your salary; I have no money." Frances Blascoer, the Association's first secretary, was a liberal white woman who seemed to Du Bois to be "alarmed about her own job and suspicious of my designs." Since the last issue of the *Horizon,* published in February 1910, Du Bois had already made plans to initiate a new journal for the NAACP. But even on this issue, many friends expressed their doubts. "If you have not decided upon a periodical, for heaven's sake don't," pleaded Albert E. Pillsbury, then Massachusetts attorney general. "They are as numerous as flies."[1] As at Atlanta University, Du Bois followed his own mind and began to write material for the first issue. Mary Dunlop Maclean, a journalist at the *New York Times,* organized the "makeup" of the periodical; Walling suggested "the

Crisis" for the title. The sixteen-page magazine was ready for publication by November 1910. Without consulting his colleagues, Du Bois ordered one thousand copies of the first issue, "in a fit of wild adventure."[2] The *Crisis* bore a great resemblance to the *Horizon* and advocated the same militant political perspective. Du Bois's initial editorial established its future direction: "The object of this publication is to set forth those facts and arguments which show the danger of race prejudice, particularly as manifested toward colored people. It takes its name from the fact that the editors believe that this is a critical time in the history of the advancement of men."[3]

The central political theme of Du Bois's editorials in the *Crisis* from 1910 to 1934 was the relationship between racism and American democracy. Racial inequality was not the product of "inborn antipathy" between whites and blacks, but a function of "social and economic caste."[4] The struggle for "social equality" was absolutely essential to erode the walls of racial segregation and to expand the political and economic opportunities of black Americans. Implicitly, the Tuskegee philosophy reinforced Negro "subordination" and gave racists the prerogative to eliminate democratic rights for all oppressed people. "The nemesis of every forward movement in the United States is the Negro question," Du Bois argued in October 1911.[5] A major aspect of Du Bois's critique of American democracy was a repetitious condemnation of the South. Du Bois repeatedly attacked the white primary laws that blocked Negro participation in the selection of Democratic party candidates. He criticized the convict leasing system and viewed the South's refusal to admit its existence as "a deliberate attempt to deceive the public."[6] Du Bois took special pleasure in assailing southern values. One particularly effective polemic appeared in the *Crisis* in November 1913: "A 'Southerner,' it seems, must be a man who has assimilated no new ideas as to democracy and social classes since 1863 . . . he hates Niggers; he pursues them vindictively; he chases a drop of Negro blood like a sleuth. He makes it his chief business in life to hound, oppress and insult black folk, and to tell them personally as often as he can how utterly he despises them—except their women, privately. These he likes."[7] On other occasions, Du Bois interpreted the South's absence of democratic institutions as a failure of culture. "Is the South a land of barbarism leavened with culture, or a land of culture leavened with barbarism?" Du Bois asked in March 1917. "What sort of a culture is it that cannot control itself in the most fundamental of human relations, that is given over to mobs, reactionary legislation and cruel practices?"[8] Not surprisingly, the distribution of the *Crisis* in the South was difficult and often dangerous work. Southern racist politicians knew about the "radical" periodical, and several years later the Bureau of Investigation monitored the *Crisis*.[9]

The pursuit of biracial democracy required allies. Du Bois was discouraged by the racist behavior of many white workers, but he recognized other potential friends in the struggle against inequality. In the *Horizon,* Du Bois had frequently noted works on Jewish people, and in the *Crisis,* he outlined more specifically the necessity for a black-Jewish alliance. Repeatedly Du Bois denounced anti-Semitism, and praised Jewish Americans as a "tremendous force for good and for uplift . . . in this country."[10] However, Afro-Americans had the immediate task of initiating strategies that preserved their rights. In September 1911, Du Bois shocked white liberal supporters by urging blacks to arm themselves when subjected to racist attacks. "We have crawled and pleaded for justice and we have been cheerfully spat upon and murdered and burned. If we are to die," Du Bois declared, "in God's name let us perish like men and not like bales of hay."[11] Racial self-defense also included the development of all-black economic and social organizations. Integrationists—and later, some of Du Bois's biographers—charged Du Bois with inconsistency; how could a movement for racial equality tolerate any form of segregation, voluntary or otherwise? As a cultural pluralist, Du Bois made the critical distinction between racial "subordination," or the Jim Crow system, and voluntary, planned development along all-black lines. In "The Strength of Segregation," published in December 1913, Du Bois urged blacks to weld themselves "together like one great fist for their own ends, with secret understanding, with pitiless efficiency and with resources for defense which will make their freedom incapable of attack from without." The abolition of lynching, political disfranchisement, and Jim Crow required a race-conscious policy that would generate "one great unity" among blacks in the struggle for democracy. "What can America do against a mass of people who move through their world but are not of it and stand as one unshaken group in their battle? Nothing."[12]

From the beginning, the *Crisis* represented a type of militant Negro journalism that was distinct. Written primarily for the Talented Tenth, it also spoke to a broad spectrum of Americans, from rural southern blacks to white northern liberals. Its commentaries covered all aspects of the Afro-American community—churches, businesses, schools, health care, political and civil associations, literature, and music. The *Crisis* was bold and uncompromising. As Irene Diggs noted, "Du Bois analyzed, interpreted, denounced, condemned what he believed was wrong whether perpetrated by president, royalty, or commoner."[13] At first, some of Du Bois's closest associates believed that eventually the *Crisis* would fail. In late 1910, for example, Du Bois wrote to the American Negro Academy twice, requesting its attention to the *Crisis* "as an advertising medium." The academy's executive committee discussed the matter and refused, noting privately that an advertisement for its occasional papers in the *Crisis* "was not a good business proposition."[14] But the periodical was successful. In February 1911, four thousand copies of the fourth issue were printed. The circulation of the *Crisis* reached fifteen thousand by July 1911, and thirty-five thousand by November 1915. Largely through Du Bois's voice, the NAACP experienced unexpected growth. In 1912 it had ten branches; four years later it had sixty-seven, including six branches in the South, and a total of nine thousand members.

Villard, Storey, and other moderate NAACP leaders stressed to Du Bois that the *Crisis* should not become an anti-Tuskegee periodical. With occasional polemical exceptions, Du Bois usually tried to abide by this understanding. Washington, however, was not so generous. He worried about the journal's circulation and urged his aides to promote the *New York Age* as an alternative, national publication. Increasingly insecure, he resorted to tactics that could be described as unscrupulous. He explained to author Ray Stannard Baker that the NAACP's whites had fooled some Negroes into believing that civil rights would be gained "by merely making demands, passing resolutions and cursing somebody." In March 1911, he described the NAACP's function as solely for "tearing down our work wherever possible . . . none of our friends should give it comfort." His relations with the NAACP's white leaders degenerated. Milholland described Washington's book *The Man Farthest Down* as a set of "platitudinous, narcotic deliverances"; Washington replied bitterly that Milholland had never raised money for Tuskegee Institute. Washington also continued to slander Du Bois and Ovington. In a January 1911 letter to Fortune, Washington returned to Scott's old untruths concerning Du Bois's behavior in the 1906 Atlanta riot: "Du Bois did run away from Atlanta. All the time that the riot was going on, Du Bois was hiding." Fortune promptly published a fresh series of essays slurring his former protégé. Washington gloated, "When we get done with Dr. Du Bois, I am sure that he will have some trouble in handing over leadership of the race to white men." When Ovington planned several large banquets in 1908 and 1911, which were designed to promote interracial harmony, Washington employed the services of New York lieutenant Charles W. Anderson to humiliate her. Anderson obtained the cooperation of New York reporters to smear these events. One paper later attacked the "banquet for mixed marriage"; another edition described "white women . . . fashionably attired in low-cut gowns" who "leaned over the tables to chat confidentially with negro men of the true African type." Although these sensationalist reports generated racist and obscene mail to Ovington, she never learned the real originator of the attacks.[15]

Washington's major mistake in his efforts to destroy the NAACP was his failure to distinguish the political moderates like Villard from the radical democrats, led by Du Bois. Even as late as 1914, when Villard compared Washington to "Nero, fiddling while Rome burns," he still described himself as "a loyal supporter of Tuskegee."[16] The Villard-Du Bois relationship parallels that of Villard's grandfather, William Lloyd Garrison, with Frederick Douglass. When Douglass broke with Garrison's narrow political orbit and established his newspaper the *North Star,* Garrison denounced him as "destitute of every principle of honor, ungrateful to the last degree and malevolent in spirit."[17] Villard lacked Garrison's radical ideology; his father, Henry Villard, had been the first president of General Electric and owner of the *New York Evening Post,* which the son inherited in 1897. Villard's wife, a Georgian, would not tolerate blacks or Jews in their home. Consequently, even before Villard became chairman of the NAACP's executive board, his relationship with Du Bois was, at best, tenuous. Although he had a public commitment to black equality, Villard tended to treat blacks in a paternalistic manner. Instinctively, he distrusted Du Bois's militancy, and he sought to curb the radical currents inside the NAACP. Association secretary May Childs Nerney, a white librarian hired in June 1912, shared Villard's racial attitudes to a great extent. Both were troubled by Du Bois's dual role as a member of the board of directors and employee of the Association. The *Crisis* had quickly become Du Bois's autonomous instrument, and they wanted the board to assert its full authority over the Negro editor.

In a March 1913 board meeting, Villard ordered Du Bois to print "a list of Negro crimes" beside the "monthly record of lynchings" in the *Crisis.* Du Bois refused and engaged Villard in a heated argument. Villard had little experience in receiving negative responses from Negroes, and curtly informed the board that "further cooperation" with Du Bois "in the work of the association" was impossible. Du Bois stood firm. "I count myself not as your subordinate but as a fellow officer," Du Bois wrote Villard. "Any suggestions made to me by you will always receive careful attention, but I decline to receive orders from anyone but the board." Du Bois noted that Villard had "no right to imply" that his "independence of action is a breach of discipline."[18] Disagreements continued to fester. When Du Bois recruited Atlanta University professor Augustus G. Dill as the *Crisis* business manager in September 1913, Dill soon quarreled with Villard. Dill refused to apologize, and Du Bois was somehow credited with the dispute. In late 1913, Du Bois prepared an essay for *Survey* magazine, "Black Man's Program for 1914." The article included the assertion that a black man should be able "to marry any sane grown person who wants to marry him." *Survey* tentatively accepted the essay but then checked with Villard and Nerney. One or both perceived that the controversial statement "would be regarded as the semi-official utterance of the Association" regarding racial intermarriage. *Survey* returned Du Bois's article, and Nerney was asked to submit an essay in its place.[19] Du Bois concluded that his article was "refused" because of its radical political content and published the piece in the February 1914 issue of the *Crisis*.[20] Nerney and Villard consequently accused Du Bois of "doubledealing." Du Bois attacked both for having "discredited me behind my back and without my knowledge."[21]

Villard resigned as NAACP board chairman in January 1914, and Joel E. Spingarn replaced him. Villard still retained his membership on the board, however, and in April 1914 proposed that Du Bois's authority be sharply curtailed. Du Bois appealed to Ovington for her support: "The Association has come to the parting of the ways. . . . I should regard the adoption of the proposed provision a vote of lack of confidence and I should immediately resign my position. Meanwhile, while the matter is under discussion I shall oppose the adoption of the measure before the board, before the membership and before the colored people." Du Bois addressed two related concerns. He insisted that his differences with Villard were, to an extent, political. The NAACP could "stand on its original radical platform" under Du Bois, or "go that way of conservative compromise." The second and more important issue, Ovington was informed, was racism. Villard was "not democratic," Du Bois observed. "He is used to advising colored men and giving them orders and he simply cannot bring himself to work with one as an equal." If the NAACP "is unable to treat its black officials with the same lease of power as white, can we fight a successful battle against race prejudice in the world?"[22] The proposal to limit Du Bois's influence failed, but tensions became worse. Joel Spingarn suggested that Du Bois preferred to have his "own way rather than accept another way, even when no sacrifice of principle is involved." The editor confused "obstinancy for strength of character." People "yield to you," Spingarn wrote in October 1914, "for the reason that parents yield to spoilt children in company, for fear of creating a scene: they were less willing than you to wreck our cause before the colored world."[23]

Some historians have attributed much of the Association's early turmoil to Du Bois's "stubbornness," "arrogance," and even "Negro racism."[24] Few of his colleagues would have disagreed that Du Bois was an extremely difficult man to have as a close associate. He remained a highly sensitive intellectual with a fine antenna for any racial slight, real or imaginary. But Du Bois was not blind. As he explained to Spingarn, Nerney "accepts your judgment without question" but feels "quite at liberty to oppose [me]" "because none of my type ever spoke to her or her friends with authority."[25] Most white liberals in the NAACP, with the prominent exception of Ovington, made no genuine effort to question their racial chauvinism. The decision of Du Bois to appeal his case to the NAACP's members and the black community generally was not an exaggerated or elitist response. His willingness to jeopardize the existence of the young organization was based on his higher commitment to oppose any manifestations of racial prejudice and undemocratic procedures. Du Bois was so perturbed by the conduct of the white liberals that he considered starting a "secret organization," perhaps staffed entirely by Afro-Americans, that would work in concert with the white-dominated NAACP.[26] In January 1916, the executive board voted to grant Du Bois control over the *Crisis* editorials. Villard, Nerney, and Spingarn insisted that Du Bois should be nothing but "a paid employee, subject to the disciplining of the Chairman"; however, a majority of the board members sided with Du Bois. Nerney promptly resigned; Spingarn and Villard also submitted their resignations from the board but soon withdrew them.[27] Nevertheless, the basic issue of Du Bois's accountability went unresolved. Du Bois was still convinced that the *Crisis* should be an organ of "personal opinion" that stood in "general agreement" with the Association.[28] So long as the *Crisis* was self-supporting financially, the matter was not pressing.

Booker T. Washington's power was still formidable, but two events initiated his decline as black America's dominant figure. On the night of 19 March 1911 in New York City, Washington was the victim of a racist attack by a white man, Henry A. Ulrich. Claiming that Washington had insulted his "wife" and had attempted to burglarize his apartment, Ulrich beat the college principal with a heavy walking cane. Although Ulrich was charged with felonious assault, he was later acquitted in court. After this humiliation, Washington was informed that he would be barred from the Hotel Manhattan as a future guest. The *Atlanta Constitution* criticized Washington's questionable behavior, and one Tuskegee Institute trustee who doubted the principal's "evasive" answers was replaced on the school's board. Black conservatives and radicals alike expressed sympathy for Washington. The NAACP passed a modest resolution of "our profound regret at the recent assault." For a few weeks even Trotter expressed support for his archenemy. Washington's influence inside the federal government also diminished after the election of Democratic president Woodrow Wilson in 1912. Almost all the Tuskegee Machine's lieutenants were dismissed, and Washington had few direct contacts with Wilson. Segregation laws across the South continued to be tightened, despite Washington's extensive but covert efforts to combat Jim Crow. Between 1909 and 1915, an average of seventy Negroes were lynched each year across the South. Gradually, Washington found it necessary to move closer to the NAACP's platform in speeches and writings. In his last article, published posthumously in December 1915, Washington issued his strongest public attack on racial inequality. "If the Negro is segregated," Washington noted, the Negro sewage systems, streets, and lights "will be inferior," and that "section of the city will not be kept in order." Jim Crow residential codes would one day be declared illegal, he predicted. Blacks and whites could only develop on the basis of social justice: "in the gain or loss of one race, all the rest have equal claim." Overworked, Washington suffered a "nervous breakdown" in early November 1915. On the morning of 13 November, he died in Tuskegee.[29]

Du Bois's obituary in the *Crisis* was a generally fair assessment of Washington's career: "He was the greatest Negro leader since Frederick Douglass. . . . Of the good that he accomplished there can be no doubt: he directed the attention of the Negro race in America to the pressing necessity of economic development; he emphasized technical education and he did much to pave the way for [interracial] understanding. . . . On the other hand, in stern justice, we must lay on the soul of this man, a heavy responsibility for the consummation of Negro disfranchisement, the decline of the Negro college and public school and the firmer establishment of color caste."[30] With Washington's death, members of both the radical and conservative factions of Negro opinion moved toward reconciliation. The Tuskegee Institute board of trustees was expected to select Emmett Scott or institute treasurer Warren Logan as Washington's successor. Instead, the principal's position was given to Robert R. Moton, the commandant of the Hampton Institute cadet corps. Moton lacked Scott's Machiavellian political instincts and had no burning ambitions as a national leader. And throughout the Washington-Du Bois debate, he had maintained civil relations with the radicals. Moton had once acted as a salesman for the American Negro Academy occasional papers; in 1909–11 he had tried to get Washington to accept the legitimacy of the NAACP's policy positions. In an "Open Letter" to Moton, Du Bois noted that Tuskegee's new principal "substantially" supported the NAACP program.[31] Du Bois had proposed John Hope as the Association's new secretary, but he declined the post. Spingarn then suggested the leading intellectual within the Tuskegee Machine ranks, James Weldon Johnson. Ovington expressed doubts about Johnson's "hopelessly reactionary" posture on "labor and other problems," but Du Bois supported the move.[32] Johnson was appointed by the board in 1917, and with the brief exception of John R. Shillady's tenure in 1918–20, served as NAACP secretary until January 1931.

The most important event to promote black rapproachment was the Amenia Conference of 24–26 August 1916, hosted by Spingarn. Unlike Washington's abortive 1904 conference, Amenia brought together all the major exponents of black middle-class political thought—from radicals Trotter and Hope to conservatives Fred R. Moore and Emmett Scott. Nearly sixty leaders attended, and at first "there was just a little sense of stiffness and care in conversation when people met who for ten years had been saying hard things about each other," Du Bois wrote later. "None of us held uncompromising and unchangeable views. It was after all a matter of emphasis. We all believed in thrift, we all wanted the Negro to vote, we all wanted the laws enforced." In these intimate surroundings, a general consensus was obtained. The Amenia Conference resolutions endorsed both industrial education and higher education for Afro-Americans; they recognized the "peculiar difficulties" that confronted leaders like Moton and Scott in the Deep South. However, the conference explicitly affirmed what Washington had been so reluctant to state publicly: "The Negro, in common with all other races, cannot achieve its highest development without complete political freedom." The Amenia Conference did not heal all old wounds; Scott continued to heap abuse on Du Bois's theories, and the *Crisis* editor still peppered Hampton and Tuskegee too often. Nevertheless, Amenia "not only marked the end of the old things and the old thoughts and the old ways of attacking the race problem, but in addition to this it was the beginning of the new things."[33] Within a decade, nearly all Washington's former supporters had accepted most of the NAACP's views, and the Du Bois-Washington controversy receded into history. As Du Bois observed in 1923: "There is no reason for retaining much of Mr. Washington's philosophy except as an interesting historical fact. No Negro dreams to-day that he can protect himself in industry and business without a vote and without a fighting aggressive organization."[34]

Radicalism is always a relative term: to become a proponent of racial equality and political rights for Negroes before World War I was to be identified as extremely radical by most white Americans. But the NAACP and the *Crisis* were only one democratic current among many movements of social unrest, which included woman suffragists, trade unionists, anarchists, socialists, advocates of birth control, pacifists, and radical intellectuals. The heart of this political and cultural ferment was Greenwich Village in New York City. Between 1911 and 1917, the village was filled with avant-garde and countercultural institutions—new schools, art galleries, free love colonies, clusters of militant socialists, new radical journals. One central gathering point was 23 Fifth Avenue, the celebrated salon of Mabel Dodge, "a pioneer in the cult of the orgasm."[35] Dodge was not involved in the NAACP but was an important patron and advisor to white liberals and radicals who related both to the early desegregation movement and to other social protest currents. Most of the major American radical intellectuals and activists of the period gave talks in her home: birth control advocate Margaret Sanger, writer Carl Van Vechten, anarchist Emma Goldman, feminist Charlotte Perkins Gilman, radical labor leader "Big Bill" Haywood. Two young intellectuals in Dodge's coterie, Walter Lippmann and William English Walling, were associates of Du Bois. Along with socialist editor Max Eastman, these young rebels—called by their contemporaries the "New Intellectuals"— shared many of Du Bois's beliefs and ideals.[36]

Walling's involvement in the NAACP was secondary to his role as a "pragmatic" theoretician of the American Socialist party. With Dodge's financial support, Walling established the *New Review,* a popular socialist journal, in January 1913. Lippmann was, like Du Bois, a Harvard graduate and student of William James. Lippmann had worked as an aide for a socialist mayor and before the age of thirty was editor of the *New Republic.* Both editors and other intellectuals in the "Lyrical Left" were deeply influenced by James and, to some extent, the pragmatic philosophy of John Dewey. They viewed politics as a holistic endeavor that included new creative forms of poetry, art, economic organization, and racial justice. Du Bois had come to many of the views of the New Intellectuals, and he welcomed the advent of the Lyrical Left. He contributed three essays to the *New Review* in 1913–14 and joined Ovington on the journal's editorial board. Du Bois took an early interest in the *New Republic* and persuaded Lippmann to alter the magazine's policy to capitalize the word "Negro." Lippmann expressed awareness of Du Bois's activities in Pan-Africanism, and in 1920 the black editor contributed an essay to the *New Republic.*[37] Du Bois was also connected directly or peripherally with other reformists. When the Christian-pacifist Fellowship of Reconciliation was initiated in 1915, many NAACP members, including Villard and Jane Addams, became leading supporters. On at least one occasion, Du Bois participated in a fellowship demonstration as a major speaker.[38] Even on the controversial issue of birth control, Du Bois was an outspoken advocate. In a statement to an international birth control conference, Du Bois declared: "Next to the abolition of war in modern civilization comes the regulation of birth by reason and common sense instead of by chance and ignorance." In the *Crisis* Du Bois condemned the political persecution of Margaret Sanger, and later he contributed an article to the *Birth Control Review.*[39]

Du Bois's response to these social protest movements was shaped by his double consciousness theory. As an American radical, he frequently gave political support to trade unionist, suffragist, and progressive causes. He sought to advance theoretical concepts on the meaning of each movement to the reconstruction of American democracy. But as a Negro, Du Bois was always aware of the veil of color that inhibited many white radicals from pursuing creative reform strategies challenging racial inequality. He believed that the central contradiction in democratic society was the burden of racism, and that if left unchallenged, racial prejudice would compromise the goals of social reformers.

This duality is apparent in Du Bois's analysis of women's oppression. Like Douglass, Du Bois was probably the most advanced male leader of his era on the question of gender inequality. In the *Voice of the Negro,* he had called for full "equality" for all women in the political system.[40] As editor of the *Crisis,* he promptly threw his energies behind the woman suffrage movement. The September 1912 issue of the *Crisis* was devoted to women's voting rights, and Du Bois's editorial explained the reasons that black men should join the struggle: "First, it is a great human question. . . . Whatever concerns half mankind concerns us. Secondly, any agitation, discussion or opening of the problem of voting must inevitably be a discussion of the right of black folk to vote in America and Africa. . . . Finally, votes for women means votes for black women."[41] In the April 1913 essay "Hail Columbia!" Du Bois penned a witty condemnation of "Anglo-Saxon manhood" and the suppression of the suffragists.[42] Theoretically, Du Bois emphasized the direct links between Afro-American and women's liberation: "Every argument for Negro suffrage is an argument for woman's suffrage; every argument for woman's suffrage is an argument for Negro suffrage; both are great movements in democracy."[43] After the *Crisis* ran a second issue devoted to woman suffrage in August 1915, Kelly Miller submitted a critical rejoinder. Miller argued that suffrage was not "a natural right"; that "woman's sphere of activity falls mainly within while man's field of action lies largely without the domestic circle"; and that little "common ground" existed between "Negro suffrage and woman suffrage." Du Bois described Miller's thesis as "ancient" and insisted that "difference, either physical or spiritual, does not argue weakness or inferiority." The struggle for complete democracy required the emancipation of all women and black people.[44]

Though Du Bois's support for woman suffrage was consistent, he was troubled by racism within the white women's movement. Since the late 1890s, many white women leaders such as Carrie Chapman Catt, president of the National American Woman Suffrage Association, had argued that democratic rights had been granted to "the negro . . . with possibly ill advised haste. . . . Perilous conditions" in society were the result of introducing "into the body politic vast numbers of irresponsible citizens." Mississippi suffragist leader Belle Kearney was even more explicit and advocated women's enfranchisement as a guarantee for "immediate and durable white supremacy."[45] Two prominent NAACP supporters, socialist attorney Florence Kelley and Jane Addams, served as vice-presidents of the National American Woman Suffrage Association. But Du Bois believed that the organization's frequent compromise on racial issues had to be openly confronted. In an important October 1911 editorial, "Forward Backward," he criticized the "war cry" of "Votes for White Women Only." Racism was the "nemesis of every forward movement in the United States," and the white middle-class women's failure to address the question undermined their cause.[46] Du Bois returned to this issue in "Votes for Women," published in the *Crisis* in November 1917. Du Bois was "particularly bitter at the attitude of many white women" who assumed that the "height" of the black male's ambition "is to marry them." He predicted that "the women's vote, particularly in the South, will be cast almost unanimously, at first, for every reactionary Negro-hating piece of legislation." Despite this, Du Bois believed that the long-term interests of blacks favored the abolition of gender restrictions on the franchise. "As an intelligent, self-supporting human being," Du Bois wrote, "a woman had just as good a right to a voice in her own government as has any man."[47]

Du Bois took special care to address the double oppression of Afro-American women and to challenge the gender chauvinism of black males. And like many members of the Lyrical Left, his political device was often prose and poetry. In his 1911 parable "The Woman" and in "The Black Mother," he honored the beauty and power of black womanhood.[48] "The Burden of Black Women," published in the November 1914 issue of the *Crisis,* combined Du Bois's abiding love for black women with his deep hatred of racism and war: "Dark daughter of the lotus leaves that watch the Southern Sea! Wan spirit of a prisoned soul a-panting to be free! The muttered music of thy streams, the whisper of the deep, have kissed each other in God's name and kissed a world to sleep."[49] In the *Crisis* "Men of the Month" column, Du Bois frequently publicized the activities of talented black women artists and civic leaders—educators Bessie B. Bruington, Dora J. Holmes, Coralie F. Cook, Hallie Quinn Brown, and Fanny Jackson Coppin; pianist Hazel Harrison; Negro women's clubleader Josephine Silone-Yates; and sculptor Mary Howard Jackson.[50] Du Bois's most significant essay on the subject was "The Damnation of Women," published in *Darkwater.* Du Bois emphasizes the central role of women in the development of African and black American culture. His chief indictment against American racism is the systemic degradation of black women: "I shall forgive the white South much in its final judgement day: I shall forgive its slavery, for slavery is a world-old habit; I shall forgive its fighting for a well-lost cause . . . but one thing I shall never forgive, neither in this world nor the world to come: its wanton and continued and persistent insulting of the black womanhood which it sought and seeks to prostitute to its lust."[51]

The labor movement presented different problems to Du Bois and many black radicals. After 1900, organized labor had largely accommodated itself to Jim Crow. The leader of the American Federation of Labor (AFL), Samuel Gompers, vowed in 1881 never to "exclude any workingman who believes in and belongs to organized labor." But by 1900, Gompers refused to denounce black disfranchisement and lynchings on the grounds that labor could not interfere in the South's "internal affairs." The labor movement became in many states a proletarian drive for white supremacy. The AFL admitted unions that had antiblack exclusion clauses in their constitutions. By 1912, many unions—the Iron, Steel and Tin Workers, the Glass Workers, the Potters, the Printers, the Lithographers, the Pressmen, and the Printers— were either lily white or had only a handful of black members. Even in the more progressive unions, conditions for blacks were grim. Black membership in the United Mine Workers stood above twenty thousand in 1900 but fell to between four thousand and nine thousand ten years later. The socialist founder of the American Railway Union, Eugene V. Debs, refused to speak before segregated audiences. But his union, by a narrow margin, voted to ban black membership. The only egalitarian exception in the house of labor was the radical Industrial Workers of the World (IWW) founded in 1905 by Debs, Bill Haywood, and socialist theoretician Daniel De Leon. The IWW denounced Jim Crow laws and lynching, and upheld the common unity of the entire working class. Thousands of black laborers joined the IWW, which maintained no racially segregated locals. Ovington was perhaps the strongest defender of the IWW among the NAACP's white leaders. In 1913, she proclaimed that the NAACP and the IWW were the only "two organizations in this country that have shown they do care about full rights for the Negro."[52]

Du Bois's Atlanta University research on black labor problems had convinced him that class oppression was a vital element in the general exploitation of black people. "It is only a question of time," Du Bois observed in 1907, "when white working men and black working men will see their common cause against the aggressions of exploiting capitalists." Southern white workers may be "befuddled by prejudice," but the "economic strength of the Negro" required black-white unity inside the labor movement.[53] Du Bois viewed the struggle of working people as critical to the development of a more democratic society, but felt that the tendency toward racism among white labor leaders had to be denounced. In the *Crisis,* Du Bois criticized Gompers's hostility to black workers. In a July 1912 article "Organized Labor," he stated that the *Crisis* "believes in organized labor. . . . All American labor to-day, white, black and yellow, benefits from this great movement." However, the *Crisis* also deplored the "deliberate exclusion from decent-paying jobs" of black laborers, and the policy of whites who "beat or starve the Negro out of his job if you can by keeping him out of the union."[54] Du Bois urged black workers to initiate their own independent unions whenever possible. In 1914, he proposed that Afro-American porters organize themselves on Pullman railroad cars. A decade later, Du Bois became a strong supporter of A. Philip Randolph's Brotherhood of Sleeping Car Porters, the first successful Afro-American union.[55] Du Bois also thought highly of the IWW, applauding it as "one of the social and political movements in modern times that draws no color line."[56] However, it is doubtful that he would have supported the IWW's refusal to participate in electoral politics.

Du Bois's involvement in radical politics directly coincided with the growth of the Socialist party. The Socialists' national membership soared from about 10,000 in 1902 to 118,000 in 1912. Several hundred socialists were elected to city councils and as mayors, and at one point over three hundred socialist magazines and newspapers were regularly published. During these years the Socialist party was a collection of radically diverse tendencies. The Socialists' charismatic national leader, Debs, seldom tried to direct the party's policies. The socialist intellectual who presents the closest parallels to Du Bois's political development was Daniel De Leon. Like Du Bois, De Leon had admired Bismarck as a youth, studied in Europe, and was a professor of political science for a time. Both men had supported the Democratic party at one point, and had a deep interest in the "single tax" theories of middle-class radical Henry George.[57] During the pre–World War I years, De Leon advanced a theory of social change that bears a rough resemblance to Du Bois's Talented Tenth thesis. De Leon insisted that only a dedicated core of workers, steeled in socialist theory, could lead a mass movement to eradicate capitalism: "In all revolutionary movements, as in the storming of fortresses, the thing depends upon the head of the column— upon that minority that is so intense in its convictions, so soundly based in its principles, so determined in its actions, that it carries the masses with it, storms the breastworks and captures the fort."[58] Given De Leon's position as Americas's most radical socialist intellectual, cofounder of the IWW, and perpetual Socialist candidate for various state offices in New York, it would have been extremely unlikely that Du Bois had not encountered some of his work. What separated the two social theorists in part was their perspective on racism. De Leon attacked Gompers not on the grounds of racial bigotry but because of his "bourgeois" values and political reformism. He supported equal rights for women and blacks but considered issues of gender and racial oppression secondary to the class struggle. De Leon believed that Jim Crow and disfranchisement were not "aimed at the Negro ostensibly as a Negro" but were part of the economic dynamic designed to make "him a wage slave."[59] Like Debs, De Leon was unable or unwilling to accept the particularity of black oppression.

Many radical blacks had joined the Socialists' ranks before Du Bois. Black nationalist minister James Theodore Holly had advocated the use of "biblical socialism" to attack the moral and economic problems of American capitalism in 1892.[60] Almost a decade before joining the Niagara Movement, the Reverend Reverdy C. Ransom urged blacks to join the class struggle. "That the Negro will enthusiastically espouse the cause of socialism we cannot doubt," Ransom wrote in 1896. "When he comes to realize that socialism offers him freedom of opportunity to cooperate with all men upon terms of equality in every avenue of life, he will not be slow to accept his social emancipation."[61] The leading black Socialist in the United States immediately after 1900 was the Reverend George Washington Woodbey. Several weeks after *The Souls of Black Folk* was published, Woodbey gave a far more radical critique of the Tuskegee philosophy, denouncing Washington as "a good servant of capitalism."[62] Despite Woodbey's prominence, Afro-Americans were largely ignored inside the party. The right wing of the Socialist party, led by Victor Berger, was as racist as Gompers. As Berger informed the party's members in 1902: "There can be no doubt that the negroes and mulattoes constitute a lower race—that the Caucasians and indeed even the Mongolians have the start on them in civilization by many thousand years."[63] The Socialists did little to combat white supremacy within their own party, and with the exception of radicals like Walling, were not particularly interested in civil rights issues.

Du Bois's introduction to Marxism and socialism was extremely fragmentary. At Harvard, Marx's work was briefly discussed, "but only incidentally and as one whose doubtful theories had long since been refuted," Du Bois wrote later. "Socialism as dream of philanthropy or as will-o-wisp of hotheads was dismissed as unimportant." At Berlin, "Karl Marx was mentioned, only to point out how thoroughly his theses had been disproven; of his theory itself almost nothing was said."[64] Only at Atlanta University did Du Bois begin to acquaint himself with writings by socialists and radical liberals. He was soon familiar with the works of Jack London, John Spargo, and Henry George—but he did not study Marx's *Capital* or the writings of Friedrich Engels. He obtained copies of a Chicago socialist publication, *Tomorrow,* which he considered "rather unconventional."[65] In the second issue of the *Horizon,* in February 1907, Du Bois stated that he considered himself a "Socialist-of-the-Path." Du Bois had certain misgivings about the Socialist party, but still believed that "the socialist trend" represented the "one great hope of the Negro American."[66] As the Socialist party acquired a mass following, Du Bois monitored its progress as an ally to the democratic struggles of blacks. In February 1908, Du Bois advised readers of the *Horizon* that "the only party today which treats Negroes as men, North and South, are the Socialists."[67] After he moved to New York City, Du Bois became a reader of the New York *Call,* established in 1908. Du Bois praised the social democratic publication in the *Crisis,* noting its staunch opposition to racism.

Most of the white socialists in the NAACP were positioned ideologically between Debs and De Leon on the left and Berger's conservative tendency. They were either nominal members of the party—such as Jane Addams and

Florence Kelley—or they belonged to the Greenwich Village Lyrical Left, which had repudiated the basic elements of classical Marxism. NAACP leader Charles Edward Russell, for example, had joined the Socialist party only in 1908. But four years later, some conservatives selected Russell as their candidate to block the party's 1912 presidential nomination from Debs. Du Bois's January 1911 speech before one thousand New York Socialists was fully covered in the *Call;* but in early 1916, when Debs submitted an article to the periodical, the editor refused to publish it because of its radical content.[68] Thus when Du Bois became a member of the Socialist party in 1911, this decision did not mark any significant turn to radicalism. He did not join the tendency of Debs and Haywood. His entry was conditioned by his previous NAACP association with Walling, Ovington, and Russell, and by his overriding commitment to racial and economic justice. Socialism was integrated into his larger struggle against racial inequality. As Du Bois explained in December 1911, the Socialists were "the only party which openly recognizes Negro manhood. . . . Is it not time for black voters to carefully consider the claims of this party?"[69]

Du Bois's commitment to the Socialist party lasted only one year. He was fully aware that some of his comrades "openly excluded Negroes and Asiatics" from their definition of socialism.[70] Du Bois urged the party to attack racism inside its ranks and to make genuine efforts to recruit Afro-Americans as candidates for elective office. Du Bois's early departure from the party was caused by his support for Woodrow Wilson in the 1912 presidential election. Villard, Trotter, and J. Milton Waldron favored Wilson, and Du Bois was persuaded to support the Democratic candidate. Du Bois did so with grave reservations: he had attacked Wilson two years before for failing to admit Negro students during his tenure as Princeton University president. Du Bois drafted a statement committing the candidate to blacks civil and political rights, but Wilson refused to sign it. Nevertheless, Du Bois endorsed Wilson in the August 1912 issue of the *Crisis,* but added that Debs was the only candidate "by word and deed" who stood "squarely on a platform of human rights regardless of race or class." Wilson, however, was the lesser evil who could actually be elected, and Debs had no chance.[71] Many Socialists criticized Du Bois's endorsement of Wilson, and in November 1912 he left the party.[72] Only later did Du Bois recognize his mistake, when Wilson sanctioned racial segregation throughout the federal government. In early 1915, Du Bois condemned Wilson as a racist, "one of the most grievous disappointments that a disappointed people must bear."[73]

Du Bois may have resigned from the Socialist party, but he remained a Socialist. Less than two months after the 1912 election, he was contributing essays to Walling's *New Review.* In late 1917, he contributed an article on the responsibility of Socialists to oppose racism in the magazine *Intercolle-*

giate Socialist.[74] He followed the rise of the British Labour Party and met some of its leaders. When Du Bois decided to send his daughter Yolande to a liberal private school in England, he contacted Labour party leader Ramsay MacDonald. Britain's future prime minister provided a personal letter of reference, and Yolande was admitted in 1914.[75] When Socialist Upton Sinclair was preparing an anthology of social protest literature and music, he contacted "Comrade Du Bois" for help; his fellow Socialist provided the words to several Negro slave songs.[76] Lyrical Left concepts of political art also influenced Du Bois. Socialists staged plays and pageants to dramatize the class struggle. The most famous was the Patterson Strike Pageant of June 1913, held in Madison Square Garden. Thousands of IWW workers and Greenwich Village artists participated in the event, which culminated in the singing of "The International."[77] Du Bois wrote a similar pageant based on the spiritual and social struggles of black people, "The Star of Ethiopia," in 1911. First performed before an audience of fourteen thousand in New York in 1913, it was repeated in Washington, D.C. in late 1915, and in Philadelphia the next year. "The Star of Ethiopia" was also performed in the Hollywood Bowl in Los Angeles in 1925.[78]

As an artist and black Christian, radical democrat, and cultural pluralist, Du Bois viewed socialism as a humanistic enterprise. It proposed a radical reconstruction of world society on the basis of "a high, ethical ideal." The movement drew its energy from the collective contributions of all cultures and ethnic groups, in the struggle to uproot elitism. Du Bois was still unclear how this mass movement would relate to the special concerns of Negro Americans, and was disappointed when white Socialists retreated from racial egalitarianism. Yet his vision of the future was by this time based in part on socialist principles. As Du Bois noted in *Darkwater:* "All humanity must share in the future industrial democracy of the world. . . . Present Big Business—that Science of Human Wants—must be perfected by eliminating the price paid for waste, which is Interest, and for Chance, which is Profit, and making all income a personal wage for service rendered by the recipient."[79]

Despite Du Bois's intense involvement in domestic civil rights activities, he had never relinquished his interest in Pan-Africanism. In early 1902, Du Bois briefly served as secretary to an abortive project, the African Development Company, that proposed to raise fifty thousand dollars "to acquire land in East Central Africa to be used for the cultivation of coffee and other products; to establish and maintain the means for transport by land, river, lakes, and ocean; to establish and maintain trading stations, and to develop the natural resources of the lands acquired."[80] Although the company was never incorporated, Du Bois's continuing concern about African affairs was expressed in his political work and writings. At the 1906 Niagara Movement conference, a permanent standing committee on Pan-Africanism was initiated. The *Horizon* seldom failed to carry at least one note on African issues on its pages. The projects of the Aborigines Protection Society were discussed in the June 1907 issue; three journal articles on Africa were mentioned in the November 1907 issue; and the writings of Pan-Africanists Edward Blyden and Casely Hayford were discussed in July 1908.[81] The *Crisis* continued this pattern: the January 1912 issue included a note on Edward Blyden, the "leading representative of his race in West Africa"; the 1913 issues had several brief essays on Liberia and Afro-American involvement in that country; and in February 1914 the periodical presented a commentary on the death of Abyssinian emperor Menelik II.[82] Much of Du Bois's writing on Africa, especially his prose, foreshadowed the romanticism of the *Négritude* poets Léopold Sédar Senghor and David Diop. Their image of Africa was both mystical and mighty; it was a place where "the empire of the Songhay rivaled the empires of the world," a continent of dark humanity whose "pyramids and temples dotted the land and dared the heavens. . . . The thought of [its] souls and cities was the beginning of the world."[83] Africa was both the origin and the future of human progress, and Du Bois often identified the continent with the black woman's spiritual image: "The father and his worship is Asia; Europe is the precocious, self-centered, forward-striving child; but the land of the mother is and was Africa."[84]

Du Bois's scholarly activity also focused increasingly on Africa. In 1909, he projected the development of an "Encyclopedia Africana covering the chief points in the history and condition of the Negro race," and he asked Blyden to serve on the editorial board. Although nothing came of the project at the time, Du Bois revived the plan a quarter century later.[85] Du Bois's participation in the Universal Races Congress, a conference held in London in July 1911, reinforced his belief that Africa and the nonwhite world would soon assert their power within an international context.[86]

Several years later Du Bois wrote a brief and pioneering work on the role of African people in world history, *The Negro*. Published in 1915, it is perhaps Du Bois's most underrated major work. Its theoretical departure was Pan-Africanist: no study of African history and culture could ignore both the impact of the transatlantic slave trade, and the extensive links between the continent and the peoples of African descent in the Caribbean and the Americas. Within this general framework, Du Bois sketched twelve brief chapters, eight of which focused on Africa, and the remainder on slavery and the black experience in the New World. A major task for Du Bois was to reestablish the cultural and political heritage of African people. Quoting Blyden and other scholars, he noted the black African identity of classical Egyptian culture and the role of Negro Muslims in the establishment of North African and Iberian societies. In West African history, Du Bois outlined the development of the savannah kingdoms of Ghana, Mali, Songhay, and the Hausa states. In these and other societies, African people illustrated complex cultural institutions, agricultural and technical abilities, and elaborate political systems. "Perhaps no race has shown in its earlier development a more magnificent art impulse than the Negro," Du Bois noted. The "Negro genius" in music, sculpture, ironwork, and other forms of creativity is explained in careful detail. Du Bois was also one of the first American scholars to advance the argument that slavery did not destroy all aspects of traditional African culture. The Afro-American church, in particular, was a "surviving social institution of the African fatherland."[87] This insight was expanded more fully three decades later in Melville Herskovitz's *Myth of the Negro Past.*

The Negro also reflected Du Bois's growing application of socialist insights to the black experience. On the issue of the slave trade, for example, Du Bois transcended the essentially moralistic argument employed in his doctoral dissertation. The abolition of slavery, Du Bois argued, took place largely for nonhumanitarian reasons. Furthermore, racism itself was a direct social consequence of enslavement and the material exploitation of nonwhite people. For Du Bois, "On Negro slavery in America was based, not simply the abortive cotton Kingdom, but the foundations of that modern imperialism which is based on the despising of backward men." Consequently, there was a systemic relationship between European colonialism in Africa and the West Indies, the Jim Crow system of political and social exploitation in the United States, and the economic oppression of white workers under American and European capitalism. Du Bois concluded *The Negro* with a political prophesy that went well beyond his 1900 "color line" statement: "The Pan-African movement when it comes will not . . . be merely a narrow racial propaganda. Already the more far-seeing Negroes sense the coming unities: a unity of the working classes everywhere, a unity of the colored races, a new unity of men. . . . As long as black laborers are slaves, white laborers cannot be free." As historian Rayford W. Logan observed, *The Negro* "popularized the history of the African kingdoms."[88] But its final chapters also established a tradition of black socialist historiography that would be enriched in subsequent decades by other Pan-Africanist scholars such as C. L. R. James and Walter Rodney.

The image of Africa was also central to Du Bois's response to World War I. His initial reaction to the conflict was a cry of anguish, informed by his deep commitment to pacifism. "The cause of preparation for war is the hatred and despising of men, your and my brothers," Du Bois observed.

"War is raped mothers and bleeding fathers . . . death, hate, hunger, and pain!"[89] Within two months after the hostilities began, he advanced the radical thesis that "the present war in Europe is one of the great disasters due to race and color prejudice and it but foreshadows greater disasters in the future." The "theory of the inferiority of the darker peoples" and the colonial competition for Africa had created the sources for European confrontation and war. Du Bois expressed some sympathy for the Allies over imperial Germany but held no illusions about the nature of the conflict. "Belgium has been as pitiless and grasping as Germany and in strict justice deserves every pang she is suffering after her unspeakable atrocities in the Congo. . . . The triumph of the allies would at least leave the plight of the colored races no worse than now."[90]

This argument was developed more fully in one of Du Bois's seminal essays, "The African Roots of the War," published in May 1915. Du Bois declared that whites of all classes benefited materially from the exploitation of Africa and the nonwhite world. "The white workingman," mobilized in the West, had demanded "to share the spoils of exploiting 'chinks and niggers.'" To ensure "industrial peace," capitalists looked to the world periphery to accumulate greater profits. Racism was an essential ideological tool to divide workers and to maintain the domination of capital. "All over the world there leaps to articulate speech and ready action that singular assumption that if white men do not throttle colored men, then China, India, and Africa will do to Europe what Europe has done and seeks to do to them," Du Bois noted. Thus the world war was "the result of jealousies engendered by the recent rise of armed national associations of labor and capital, whose aim is the exploitation of the wealth of the world."[91] Although the essay was basically an idealist interpretation, it marks Du Bois's first tentative step toward Marxism-Leninism. Without Du Bois's knowledge, V. I. Lenin was making similar observations. In 1916, Lenin noted that there was an "inseverable bond" between colonial exploitation in Africa and Asia, "between imperialism and the trusts, and, therefore between imperialism and the foundations of capitalism."[92]

Another "Leninist" insight developed independently by Du Bois was the belief that the war should be used by colonized peoples as the means to assert their national liberation. Du Bois expressed solidarity with the Irish Republican uprising in 1916 against the British and urged black Americans to imitate the "foolishness" displayed by the rebels. The case of Ireland illustrated that "no human group has ever achieved freedom without being compelled to murder thousands of members of other groups who were determined that they should be slaves."[93] In January 1917, Du Bois predicted that Poland would gain self-determination as a result of the war and declared that "another suppressed race will have a chance for self-development after a high noon of despair."[94] As the war progressed, Du Bois perceived that people of color might also acquire substantial political power with the defeat of one or more European states. In several articles, he suggested that an independent state in central Africa should be established after the conflict, consisting of the German colonies, the Belgian Congo, and possibly territories from French Equatorial Africa, Uganda, and the Portuguese colonies. "Out of this war," Du Bois wrote, "will rise, soon or late, an independent China, a self-governing India, and Egypt with representative institutions, an Africa for the Africans, and not merely for business exploitation."[95]

The American Socialist party's reaction to the war had a direct impact upon Du Bois and progressive elements in the NAACP. The party's 1915 convention passed an antiwar amendment by a vote of 11,000 to 780: "Any member of the Socialist Party, elected to an office, who shall in any way vote to appropriate moneys for military or naval purposes, or war, shall be expelled from the Party." In April 1917, following President Wilson's request for a declaration of war before Congress, the Socialists held an emergency convention in St. Louis. Again by an overwhelming majority, the party's leaders denounced the war "by our government as a crime against the people of the United States and against the nations of the world." The party's actions served to increase its membership by over twelve thousand within months, and many antiwar Socialists were elected to municipal offices in the 1917 elections. The only significant segment of the Socialist party that favored American involvement was the left intelligensia. William English Walling, Upton Sinclair, and John Spargo, the most talented socialist writers in the country, defected to support the war. Liberals like John Dewey, Joel Spingarn, and moderate Socialist Walter Lippmann also endorsed America's entry. Spingarn even joined the army as a major, and served in the intelligence division in Washington. The decision of liberal and socialist intellectuals to back the Wilson administration caused tremendous bitterness. Charles Edward Russell, who had recently run a strong race for mayor of New York on the Socialist ticket, not only resigned from the party but publicly urged that all antiwar Socialists "be driven out of the country." J. G. Phelps Stokes, a wealthy Socialist and former supporter of Booker T. Washington, stated that his old comrades should be "shot at once without an hour's delay." Under the June 1917 Espionage Act, Congress targeted the Socialist party and other radicals. IWW leaders were lynched, tarred and feathered, and jailed; many socialist newspapers ceased publication, and most of the party's leaders, including Debs, were eventually imprisoned. In some instances "patriotic socialists" actively participated in government suppression of the left. The assault against the American Socialist party in

1917–19 permanently crippled the organization and effectively reduced social democracy to a marginal political status through the remainder of the twentieth century.[96]

The social patriotism of Walling, Russell, and Sinclair influenced Du Bois's shifting attitudes about World War I. These left intellectuals were Du Bois's closest friends within the socialist movement, and he valued their judgment. Du Bois was still troubled by the Wilson administration's racist policies concerning the training and deployment of Negro troops, and he complained to Secretary of War Newton D. Baker that the government must "settle" as much of the "Negro problem" as it "interferes with winning the war."[97] He was outraged by the racist pogrom in East St. Louis and the lynching of thirteen Negro soldiers following racial unrest in Houston during 1917. But the vast majority of NAACP members and leadership still supported the war mobilization. The NAACP endorsed the creation of a segregated camp for the training of black officers and campaigned for decent conditions for all black draftees. Spingarn actively lobbied for Du Bois's appointment as a captain in the War Department, and Du Bois responded that he "would accept" such a position, so long as he could "retain general oversight of the *Crisis* magazine." The NAACP board of directors had difficulty with Du Bois's demand to continue editing the *Crisis* but recognized that he "must accept" the captaincy in the war effort. Although the offer was later withdrawn in 1918, Du Bois was by then caught up in the frenzy of mass patriotism. Spingarn "wanted me and my people not merely as a matter of policy, but in recognition of a fact, to join wholeheartedly in the war," Du Bois wrote in *Dusk of Dawn*. "It was due to his advice and influence that I became during the World War nearer to feeling myself a real and full American than ever before or since." Although he was still, "in principle, opposed to war," Du Bois was convinced that America's involvement would become a "fight for democracy including colored folk and not merely for war investments." He also believed that any "passive resistance" by the NAACP against the war "would have fallen flat and perhaps slaughtered the American Negro body and soul."[98]

In July 1918, Du Bois wrote a controversial *Crisis* editorial, "Close Ranks," that urged Afro-Americans to rally behind their country. In a sentence that he later deeply regretted, Du Bois declared: "Let us, while this war lasts, forget our special grievances and close our ranks shoulder to shoulder with our own white fellow citizens and the allied nations that are fighting for democracy."[99] Many Niagara Movement veterans could hardly believe Du Bois had written these words. Byron Gunner, then president of Trotter's National Equal Rights League, wrote Du Bois that he was "unable to conceive that said advice comes from you. It seems to me that the impossible has happened and I'm amazed beyond expression." Gunner insisted that the war was "the most opportune time for us to push and keep our 'special grievances' to the fore."[100] Other NAACP members in local branches debated Du Bois's editorial, and many criticized their leader's new accommodationism. Du Bois promptly attempted to clarify his position in the August 1918 issue of the *Crisis*. "This is our country: We have worked for it, we have suffered for it, we have fought for it," Du Bois argued. Since the nation was in the war, "then this is our war." The United States was not perfect, "but it has not sinned as Germany has sinned. Its continued existence and development is the hope of mankind and of black mankind, and not its menace." Negroes must not "bargain with our loyalty" or gain profit "with our country's blood." The sacrifices of black soldiers, Du Bois hoped, would "show the world again what the loyalty and bravery of black men means."[101] Du Bois's 1917–18 strategy was based upon two assumptions: that loyal participation by American Negroes in the conflict would lead to expanded democratic rights and a lessening of social injustices and lynchings in the postwar era, and that the war would promote the independence of the former German African colonies. Both assumptions proved tragically incorrect.

Du Bois turned fifty years old during World War I, and in some respects had reached a position of national influence he would never again attain. By 1919, the NAACP claimed 300 branches and 88,448 members; significantly, 155 of these branches, totaling 42,588 members, were in the South. Many of these new members had been supporters of Washington but had come to recognize the political preeminence of the NAACP and to accept Du Bois as their national spokesperson. In early 1917, the circulation of the *Crisis* exceeded 41,000, and before the end of the war the magazine's monthly sales reached 70,000. Du Bois had long been a familiar figure among the Negro 'Talented Tenth,' but after the death of Washington he was becoming more widely known among the black working class and rural poor. One indication of his popularity was a letter Du Bois received in August 1917, from the Garrett Distributing Company of Kentucky, which sold cigars: "Kindly permit us to use your name as one of our private brands of cigars, also your photograph on our box labels and cigar bands." With good humor, Du Bois replied that he had "no objection" to the use of his name "on one of your brands of cigars providing the cigar is not too bad."[102] More serious was the response of his colleagues when Du Bois experienced two serious operations in late 1916 and early 1917, in which he lost one of his kidneys. Spingarn was severely shaken: "I walked out of the hospital, thinking of all it would mean for 12 million people if this champion of theirs were not permitted to live. Others would take up the gage where he threw it down; others might wield brilliant pens; others would speak with something of his quiet eloquence. But never again could these millions find another leader exactly like him."[103] Even white America recognized Du Bois's leadership.

His occasional essays frequently appeared in the major academic journals, including the *American Journal of Sociology* and the *American Political Science Review;* he was quoted in the *New York Times,* the *Christian Science Monitor,* and the *Congressional Record.* The *New York Sun* described Du Bois in 1919 as the "leading factor in the race question."[104]

During the war Du Bois completed the bulk of his autobiographical *Darkwater,* finishing the last pages on his fiftieth birthday. To celebrate the occasion, his friends held a festive dinner in his honor. Albert Bushnell Hart offered warm praise for his former student, congratulating Du Bois as "always among the ablest and keenest of our teacher-scholars."[105] Du Bois perceived the occasion as a time "to take stock of myself and ask what I really was as a person." To many white associates, he still seemed "the isolated outsider," aloof and always "arrogant." Outside of the *Crisis* office, he maintained little contact with whites. "We belonged to no social clubs, and did not visit the same people or even stand at the same liquor bars," Du Bois later explained. "Naturally we could not share stories of sex. . . . I was fighting against my own degradation. I wanted to meet my fellows as an equal; they offered or seemed to offer only a status of inferiority and submission."[106] But black colleagues often viewed Du Bois in a similar light. James Weldon Johnson noted that the *Crisis* editor could be "the most jovial and fun-loving of men." But to many outsiders, Du Bois assumed a formal behavior that was "cold," "stiff," and "supercilious."[107] Even Du Bois's closest disciples did not accurately comprehend his complex social outlook, a synthesis of radical democracy, cultural pluralism, pan-Africanism, and socialism. He was a leader who sometimes chafed under his role as a political messiah, a poet who had been drafted into a social movement with which he was often at odds. Du Bois could not be the charismatic leader or the mesmerizing orator of the Douglass tradition. During the chaotic years that followed the armistice, his contradictions became glaringly apparent to a younger generation of black militants.

5

PAN-AFRICANISM, SOCIALISM, AND GARVEYISM

In his fifty-five years Du Bois personally has made a success of nothing. In all his journalistic, personal and other business efforts he has failed, and were it not for [his white associates], Du Bois, no doubt, would be eating his pork chops from the counter of the cheapest restaurant in Harlem like many other Negro graduates of Harvard and Fisk.

Marcus Garvey,
1923

[Du Bois is] a political opportunist . . . a good transition from Booker T. Washington's compromise methods to the era of the new Negro.

A. Philip Randolph and
Chandler Owen, 1919

Black agents of international capitalism like Du Bois . . . are all offering their services to their imperialist masters. . . . Du Bois, the ideological leader of the middle-class Negro Intellectuals, is trying to take away the lead from the revolutionary movement by playing with 'left phrases.' . . . What stupidity! What demagogy!

George Padmore,
1931

With the end of the war, Du Bois believed that an unprecedented opportunity existed to advance two of his principal goals, Pan-Africanism and socialism. The connections between these two themes had been made by other Negro intellectuals some years before. In 1908, Blyden had projected an independent African economic system in which "all work for each, and each works for all."[1] Early in 1919, Du Bois announced his aims in the *Crisis*. He planned to attend the Paris Peace Conference as a representative of the NAACP, to advance the agenda "of the colored peoples of the United States and of the world." He would also attempt to organize a Pan-African Congress bringing together representatives of black people across the world.[2] The NAACP officially endorsed Du Bois's plan for the establishment of political, economic, and educational reforms in Africa. Writing to President Wilson in late November 1918, Du Bois requested American government support for the Pan-African Congress. Wilson's secretary, Joseph P. Tumulty, replied curtly that the material would be "brought to the President's attention" but that a meeting between Du Bois and Wilson would "not be possible."[3] Securing passage abroad was a major problem; however, Du Bois learned that Wilson was sending Moton to France on the press boat *Orizaba*. "His duty was to speak to the returning Negro soldiers, pacify them and forestall any attempt at agitation or open expression of resentment on their return to the United States." As Du Bois noted later, "Under those circumstances my request also to go could hardly be denied."[4]

Even before his arrival in Paris in mid-December 1918, Du Bois wrote several statements explaining his purposes to both black and white Americans. He stated that his proposal for a Pan-African Congress was not a call for racial separatism. African emigration for the masses of American blacks was "absurd." However, Du Bois emphasized, "the African movement means to us what the Zionist movement must mean to the Jews, the centralization of race effort and the recognition of a racial fount."[5] Visiting members of the peace congress, Du Bois lobbied for his ambitious program without success. Colonel Edward M. House, Wilson's chief aide, listened patiently to Du Bois but promised nothing. Leaving nothing to chance, on 1 January 1919, Major F. P. Schoonmaker of the U.S. Army's Ninety-second Division ordered his intelligence officers to monitor "all of [Du Bois's] moves and actions while at station of any unit."[6] Secretly watched by his own government, Du Bois spent four unfruitful weeks in and around Paris, frustrated by his inability to obtain even French permission to schedule his Pan-Africanist meeting. The *Chicago Tribune* correspondent, observing Du Bois's plight, cabled home: "[Du Bois's] memorandum to President Wilson . . . is quite Utopian, and has less than a Chinaman's chance of getting anywhere in the Peace Conference, but it is nevertheless interesting. As self-determination is one of the words to conjure with Paris nowadays, the Negro leaders are seeking to have it applied, if possible, in a measure to their race in Africa."[7]

As Du Bois later recalled, "My plan to have Africa in some way voice its complaints to the world [was] . . . without political backing and indeed without widespread backing of any kind. Had it not been for one circumstance, it would have utterly failed; and that circumstance was that Black Africa had the right to send from Senegal a member to the French Parliament."[8] This deputy, Blaise Diagne, was "the most influential colonial politician in France at the time," according to Pan-Africanist leader George Padmore, and "a close friend" of French premier Georges Clemenceau.[9] Diagne had been born in Goree, Senegal, in 1872. Despite his origins in poverty, he had risen to acquire a position as a French colonial customs officer. In 1914, over the strenuous opposition of both the colored *métis* and local white entrepreneurs, the black man won election to the French Chamber of Deputies. Despite his radical rhetoric, as West Indian scholar C. L. R. James observed, Diagne was always "a Frenchman before being a Pan-African, and insisted upon praising French colonial rule, while attacking the other European powers' operations in Africa."[10] When the French faced "military disaster" in early 1917, Clemenceau named Diagne Commissaire-Général for French West Africa, and he was charged "with the responsibility of recruiting African troops for the Western front to help stem the German offensive." Within twelve months, under Diagne's direction, 680,000 soldiers and 238,000 laborers from French West Africa were in France.[11] Clemenceau was "overjoyed" and offered Diagne the French Legion of Honor. Diagne modestly declined, pleading that "he had only done his duty and that was reward enough." Many African militants, suffering under the domination of French imperialism, denounced Diagne as "a traitor for having brought the Africans to fight for France" and termed him "a tool of the rich white colonial interests."[12]

Nevertheless, when Du Bois approached Diagne for help in scheduling the Pan-Africanist session, he reluctantly agreed. Clemenceau could easily ignore the unknown Afro-American petitioner; but when Diagne personally requested the Pan-African Congress, the French prime minister replied, "Don't advertise it, but go ahead."[13] Arrangements were made to reserve suites at the Grant Hotel in Paris. Madame Calman-Levy, the widow of an influential French publisher, "became enthusiastic over the idea of [Du Bois's] congress and brought together in her salon groups of interested persons" from the French and Belgian governments.[14] Frantically, American officials objected to the Pan-African Congress; one state department official told the press that "no such conference would be held" and that, should it occur, "no passports would be issued for American delegates desiring to attend the meeting."[15]

Despite American opposition, fifty-seven delegates from fifteen countries met on 19 February 1919 for the Pan-African Congress. Among them were twenty-one West Indians, sixteen representatives from the United States, and twelve delegates from nine African states, including the Belgian Congo, Ethiopia, Liberia, and Egypt. Several European nations sent representatives, including M. Van Overgergh, a member of the Belgian peace delegation, and Freire d'Andrade, Portugal's former minister of foreign affairs. The potential connections between Pan-Africanism and social democracy were reinforced by the attendance of William English Walling and Charles Edward Russell. The three-day conference obtained considerable press coverage. According to the *New York Evening Globe,* the congress was "the first assembly of its kind in history, and has for its object the drafting of an appeal to the Peace Conference to give the Negro race of Africa a chance to develop unhindered by other races."[16] But from the outset, Diagne, who was selected president of the congress, and Du Bois, chosen as secretary, were in disagreement. Diagne had no reservations criticizing British colonial policies, but he carefully sought to protect French political and territorial interests. The chairman of the French Foreign Affairs Committee even lectured the delegation on his nation's "policy of equality and liberty for all men regardless of race."[17]

Du Bois drafted the principal report of the congress, which requested that the European and American powers turn over the former German colonies of Kamerun, Tanganyika, and Southwest Africa (Namibia) to an "international organization." The Allies were asked to "establish a code of law for the international protection of the natives of Africa, similar to the proposed international code of labor." Nowhere in the congress's demands were Europeans asked to grant Africans the immediate right to complete self-determination. Rather the congress, speaking for "the Negroes of the world," resolved that "hereafter the natives of Africa and the peoples of African descent" should be "governed" according to more humane and democratic rules. Land and other natural resources "should be held in trust for the natives" while they acquired the means to "effective ownership of as much land as they can profitably develop." Capital should be "regulated as to prevent the exploitation of the natives and the exhaustion of the natural wealth of the country." All forms of "slavery and corporal punishment" must be abolished, the resolutions urged. The "right" of every black "child to learn to read and write his own language" and access to "higher technical and cultural training" must be guaranteed. In terms of political rights, all Africans should "participate in the government as fast as their development permits." Educated blacks must be given the "higher offices of State," culminating in a future where "Africa [would be] ruled by consent of the Africans."[18] At best, the resolutions had only a minor impact upon the deliberations of the Paris Peace Conference. Despite the relative moderation of these demands, noted Kwame Nkrumah, for European leaders "the very idea of Pan-Africanism was so strange that it seemed unreal and yet at the same time perhaps potentially dangerous."[19]

Du Bois returned to the United States with the expectation of writing a definitive history of the "Black Man in the Great War" and published a lengthy excerpt from the projected manuscript in the June 1919 issue of the *Crisis*.[20] He also published a series of military directives and other documents that illustrated a deliberate policy of racism in the American army's treatment of black soldiers in Europe. Reversing his policy of moderation during the previous year, Du Bois urged black Americans to militant action: "We return from the slavery of the uniform which the world's madness demanded us to don to the freedom of civil garb. . . . We sing: This country of ours, despite all its better souls have done and dreamed, is yet a shameful land. . . . *We return. We return from fighting. We return fighting.* Make way for Democracy! We saved it in France, and by the Great Jehovah, we will save it in the United States of America, or know the reason why."[21] Racial conditions became dramatically worse, culminating in the "Red Summer" of 1919. Fourteen blacks were burned in public, over sixty were lynched, and more than two dozen major race riots erupted in the last eight months of that year. In September, Du Bois advocated that blacks defend themselves against racist violence—"when the armed lynchers gather, we too must gather armed."[22] Du Bois's activities in the Pan-Africanist movement and his militant rhetoric favoring black armed self-defense brought the *Crisis* under intense government surveillance. The postal service temporarily blocked distribution of the *Crisis*. Several southern Congressmen openly demanded the prosecution of Du Bois under the espionage act. South Carolina's James F. Byrnes attacked Du Bois in Congress for appealing to "the prejudice and the passions of the negro, which can have no other result than to incite him to deeds of violence."[23] Du Bois retorted that Byrnes was in Congress illegally, since blacks in South Carolina were denied the franchise. The "dark majority of mankind," Du Bois declared, would not always be "ruled by the white minority."[24]

The democratic struggles of blacks in the United States, Du Bois understood, made a strong pan-Africanist movement even more essential. "The one new Idea of the World War—the idea which may well stand in future years as the one thing that made the slaughter worthwhile . . . is the vision of great dreamers that *only those who work shall vote and rule*," Du Bois wrote in September 1919.[25] Any democratic advance for people of color or oppressed nations throughout the world would have a positive impact upon the condition of Negro Americans. Throughout 1920 and early 1921 Du Bois made preparations for a second Pan-African Congress. He still hoped to gain the approval, or at least the neutrality, of the U.S. government for the movement. In his June 1921 correspondence to Secretary of State Charles

Evans Hughes, Du Bois provided documents from the 1919 congress and emphasized that the conference "contemplates neither force nor revolution in its program. We have had the cordial cooperation of the French, Belgian and Portuguese governments and we hope to get the attention and sympathy of all colonial powers."[26]

One hundred and thirteen delegates attended the 1921 congress, which held sessions in London, Brussels, and Paris on 28 August–6 September 1921. Seven delegates came from the Caribbean, thirty five from the United States, forty one from Africa, and the remainder from Europe. About one thousand guests and observers also participated. The second congress attracted a number of black leaders who were as influential in their respective nations as Du Bois had become in the United States. A brief list of the more prominent participants included: Dantes Bellegarde, noted historian and Haitian ambassador to France and the League of Nations; José de Magalhaes of Sao Thomé, member of the Portuguese parliament and leader of Liga Africana, an early African nationalist organization; John Langalibalele Dube, former president of the South African National Congress; and T. A. Marryshow, founder of the independence movement in Grenada and editor of the *West Indian* newspaper. Accompanying Du Bois from the United States were two of his young protégés, Jessie Redmond Fauset and Walter White. Fauset had become the *Crisis* literary editor in late 1919 and later became a major figure in the Harlem Renaissance literary movement of the 1920s; White had been a leader of the Association's Atlanta branch and in 1918 became its assistant secretary. The London session, held at Central Hall, Westminster, on 28–29 August, reflected Du Bois's increasing radicalism. France was criticized for "compelling black men without a voice in their own government to fight in France," and Belgium was condemned for its crimes in the Congo. The congress urged the adoption of one of two alternatives by the great powers: "either the complete assimilation of Africa with two or three of the great world states, with political, civil and social power and privileges absolutely equal for its black and white citizens, or the rise of a great black African State founded in Peace and Goodwill, based on popular education, natural art and industry and freedom of trade; autonomous and sovereign in its internal policy."[27]

Diagne desperately attempted to check the radicalism of the congress. In the Brussels sessions, Diagne refused to grant the validity of the London resolutions, and substituted what Du Bois termed "an innocuous statement concerning [the] goodwill" of both French and Belgian colonialists.[28] Had Du Bois pressed the issue, the pan-Africanist movement could have splintered, although he controlled a firm majority of the delegates. The final sessions in the Palais Mondial in Paris upheld a revised draft of the London documents. Following the meeting, a small delegation of participants led by Bellegarde traveled to the League of Nations in Geneva and presented the congress's "Manifesto." The League's Mandates Commission studied the congress's proposals and soon published them with favorable commentary: "Consciously or subconsciously there is in the world today a widespread and growing feeling that it is permissible to treat civilized men as uncivilized if they are colored and more especially of Negro descent. . . . [We] urge that the League of Nations take a firm stand on the absolute equality of races and that it . . . form an International Institute for the study of the Negro problem, and for the evolution and protection of the Negro race."[29]

The second Pan-African Congress's success in attracting a level of international support also generated, for the first time, extensive criticism in European newspapers. British Africanist Sir Harry Johnston chided the pan-Africanist intellectuals, noting smugly that American "colored people . . . know so *little about real* Africa." The British humor magazine *Punch* parodied the "Pan-African Manifesto."[30] More seriously, the *Neptune,* a major Brussels newspaper, leveled the accusation that the Pan-Africanist Congress was "an agency of Moscow and the cause of native unrest in the Congo." It asserted that the congress leaders had "received remuneration" from the Bolsheviks, and predicted darkly that Pan-Africanist propaganda would "some day [cause] grave difficulties in the Negro village of Kinshasa."[31] The *Manchester Dispatch* expressed the fears of many European colonialists: "the time may come when we shall have to submit ourselves to the tender mercies of our dusky conquerors." But even most racists recognized the grace and power of the writings by the *Crisis* editor. The Belgian journal *Echo de la Bourse* admitted that one must "bow to [Du Bois's] brilliant intellect and his devotion to the black race."[32] Du Bois was satisfied with the progress of the congress, and saw the movement's advance in terms of both color and class. The Congress's proposal to the League of Nations' International Bureau of Labor to establish a special section "to deal with the conditions and needs of native Negro labor especially in Africa" would assist the interests of all workers. "The labor problems of the world cannot be understood or properly settled," Du Bois argued, "so long as colored and especially Negro labor is enslaved and neglected, and that first step toward the world emancipation of labor would be through investigation of native labor."[33]

The 1921 Pan-African Congress was in many respects the high point of the movement in the 1920s. An international secretariat established in Paris to facilitate correspondence soon closed due to the absence of funds. Diagne postponed the scheduled 1923 Congress until "finally without proper notice or preparation" the sessions were held in London and Lisbon.[34] British author H. G. Wells and socialist Harold Laski attended the London sessions, held on 7–8 November 1923. Labour Party leader Ramsey MacDonald was unable to attend but expressed his support for the movement in a personal letter to Du Bois.[35] The London session called for "home rule and responsible government" for the "civilised British subjects in West Africa and in the West Indies" and demanded the initiation of educational, social, and economic reforms in all colonies.[36] The Lisbon sessions were perhaps more productive, with delegates from eleven nations in attendance. Two former colonial administrators of Portugal "promised to use their influence in getting their Government to abolish conscript labour and other much overdue reforms in the African colonies." In their manifesto, the delegates repeated their demands of two years before, concluding, "In fine, we ask in all the world, that black folk be treated as men. We can see no other road to peace and progress."[37] Nkrumah would later observe that the 1923 congress "lacked funds and membership was limited. The delegates were idealists rather than men of action. However, a certain amount of publicity was achieved, and Africans and men of African descent for the first time gained valuable experience in working together."[38] Du Bois openly admitted in the *Crisis* that the third congress had nearly failed for lack of financial resources. But he was convinced that blacks had to keep the "idea alive. . . . Someday when unity and cooperation come, the importance of these early steps will be recognized."[39]

Du Bois's political and spiritual identification with pan-Africanism was reinforced in 1923–24, when he was appointed by President Calvin Coolidge as "minister plenipotentiary" and official representative to the inauguration of President Charles King of Liberia. Ironically, the appointment was secured by former Tuskegee Machine leader William H. Lewis, who still exercised political authority in the Republican party. Even Du Bois's old nemesis Emmett Scott, voiced no objections when consulted on the matter.[40] Du Bois's tour along the coast of West Africa included five countries. In every port, he employed his experiences as a sociologist to analyze the social and economic structures of African societies. In the marketplace of St. Louis, Senegal, Du Bois was fascinated by the mixture of Islamic, traditional African, and French cultures. But as he examined Senegalese society more closely, he found the existence of class exploitation without color "caste lines." The mulatto and black elites of Senegal "were also exploiters," Du Bois noted: "They had the psychology of the exploiters. They looked upon the mass of people as means of wealth. The mass therefore had no leadership." The major black leader of Senegal, Diagne, was merely "a Frenchman who is accidentally black." In Sierra Leone, Du Bois was confronted with a system of rigid white supremacy. "Everything that America has done crudely and shamelessly to suppress the Negro," Du Bois observed, "England in Sierra Leone has done legally and suavely so that the Negroes themselves sometimes doubt the evidence of their own senses: segregation, disfranchisement, trial without jury, over-taxation, 'Jim Crow' cars, neglect of education, economic serfdom."[41] Du Bois urged President King of Liberia to solicit the "aid of American Negro capital and of colored technical experts to help Liberians in the development of agriculture, industry and commerce." Du Bois did not fully comprehend the oppressive existence of a colored elite in Liberia, but he emphasized that the country should develop strategies to avoid being "at the mercy" of European and American nations.[42] The African journey clarified to Du Bois the relationship between black exploitation throughout the world and working people's movements: "The chief hope lies in the gradual but inevitable spread of the knowledge that the denial of democracy in Asia and Africa hinders its complete realization in Europe. It is this that makes the Color Problem and the Labor Problem to so great an extent two sides of the same human tangle. How far does white labor see this? Not far, as yet."[43]

Du Bois's effort to popularize pan-Africanism with black America's "Talented Tenth" were extensive but not particularly successful. The *Crisis* continued to publish reports on every sector of the African diaspora. In February 1924, the magazine documented the struggle against British colonial rule in East Africa, warning that the system "will cause endless bloodshed and misery before it falls."[44] The *Crisis* noted the existence of labor unrest in South Africa and condemned the British government for its policies of "starving miners" and "child-slavery."[45] In "Italy and Abyssinia," published in June 1926, Du Bois predicted that fascist Italy was preparing to invade that African state. Mussolini's agenda for Africa was a "high-handed program of theft, lying and slavery."[46] The *Crisis* constantly defended Haiti's right to self-determination and praised West Indian social protest movements against colonialism. However, most of the NAACP leaders expressed scant interest in pan-African affairs, and the association's executive board viewed Du Bois's continuing concern for Africa and the Caribbean as irrelevant to the immediate conditions of Negro Americans. Du Bois also observed that some black board members "had inherited the fierce repugnance toward anything African." These Negroes "felt themselves Americans, not Africans. They resented and feared any coupling with Africa."[47] But Du Bois's theory of double consciousness dictated a strong affinity for the cultural and political links with African people. As Du Bois wrote in 1926: "Africa appears as the Father of mankind. . . . The sense of beauty is the last and best gift of Africa to the world and the true essence of the Black man's soul."[48] Through the ideals of Pan-Africanism, black Americans could rediscover and reaffirm themselves.

Du Bois was an advocate of radical democratic movements throughout the world, and he frequently compared the status of black Americans with other oppressed peoples. As early as 1907, in the *Horizon,* Du Bois noted the work of I. M. Rubinow on the high mortality rates of poor people in Russia.[49] In a prayer before Atlanta University students in 1909 or 1910, Du Bois emphasized that "our brothers" in Russia and other nations were also struggling "for better government and freer institutions."[50] In October 1916, Du Bois compared the similarities between Jewish migration from Russian persecution and the flight of Afro-Americans from the South.[51] Du Bois detested the Tsarist government and believed that Russia's political overtures to nonwhite nations were guided by "ulterior motives."[52] But Du Bois was not prepared for the February 1917 revolution in Russia. The Tsar's armies were allied with the West against Germany, and Du Bois may have feared Russia's withdrawal from the war. In March 1917, the *Crisis* expressed uncertainty about the revolution, which "makes us wonder whether the German menace is to be followed by a Russian menace or not."[53] The triumph of the Bolshevik Revolution eight months later was warmly praised by American Socialists who had opposed U.S. involvement in World War I—Debs, Haywood, journalist John Reed, and others. But Du Bois reserved full judgment of the revolutionary left and particularly the Communist government of V. I. Lenin.

Du Bois's primary attraction to all socialist movements was their appeals to universal "brotherhood" beyond the veil of color. "Perhaps the finest contribution of current Socialism to the world is neither its light nor its dogma," he commented in *Darkwater,* "but the idea back of its one mighty word— Comrade!"[54] Yet Du Bois was bothered by the inconsistencies between socialist theory and practice. He continued to criticize the American Socialist party's "unfortunate" refusal to support antiracist agitation.[55] But the Communist model of social change was unacceptable to Du Bois for several reasons. Armed revolution might be appropriate in Africa and Asia, Du Bois noted in June 1919, but "War, Force, Revolution are impossible, unthinkable" for the United States.[56] Socialism had to be "evolutionary," Du Bois insisted: "I do decidedly think that many proposals made by Socialists and Communists and even by the present rulers of Russia would improve the world if they could be adopted; but I do not believe that such adoption can successfully come through war or force or murder, and I do not believe that the sudden attempt to impose a new industrial system and new ideas of industrial life can be successful without the long training of human beings."[57] As the international socialist movement divided between the Communists and Social Democrats, Du Bois expressed support for the moderates. In

December 1920, he congratulated the British Labour Party and Italy's "right wing Socialists" for providing a "real path, leaving on the one side intransigent communism and on the other, organized and reactionary theft."[58] A peaceful transition to socialism in America could be gained through the development of economic cooperatives. The *Crisis* asserted repeatedly that "consumers' co-operation" and other collective economic endeavors were absolutely essential for Negro advancement.[59]

Du Bois's version of pragmatic, Fabian socialism and his advocacy of the war in 1917–18 placed him firmly to the right of many younger black radicals. The two leading critics of Du Bois on the left were the editors of the *Messenger,* A. Philip Randolph and Chandler Owen. Both black socialists were southerners and born in 1889. In 1916 they had formed the Independent Political Council in Harlem, which was designed to propagate socialism among Negroes and to support black candidates in electoral politics. Both men were arrested in September 1918 for the *Messenger*'s antiwar and radical statements. The *Messenger* initially attacked the *Crisis* editor in a January 1918 editorial. Du Bois condemned lynching, Owen noted, "but he has seldom, if ever, shown a grasp of its true causes and the probable remedy." Du Bois's hostility toward labor unions was described as "a gospel of hate . . . in criminal ignorance of the trend of the modern working world." Randolph and Owen intensely condemned Du Bois's leadership after his 1918 "Close Ranks" editorial. In 1919, the *Messenger* declared that Du Bois was a craven "misleader" who lacked "intelligence and courage." Du Bois "is conservative, reactionary on economic and political questions, and compromising in the face of cheap honors and extended epaulets." The NAACP leader's failure to extend uncritical solidarity to the Russian revolution was also taken as evidence of its "reactionary" politics. In December 1919, the *Messenger* openly gave thanks for the Soviet revolution, calling it "the greatest achievement of the twentieth century." Du Bois and the NAACP represented "the Old Crowd Negro," clients of the capitalist system. The *Messenger* placed itself in the vanguard of the "New Negro" movement, which "has become popular with the masses in every nook and corner of the world."[60] Throughout Harlem, Randolph and Owen became widely known as "Lenin and Trotsky," the most radical blacks in the city. Although their streetcorner speeches and militant publications attracted only small numbers of black workers, they were successful in projecting the concept of a "New Negro" who was to the left of the moderate NAACP. As The *Messenger* declared in 1918, Du Bois was simply a transitional figure "from Booker Washington's compromise methods to the era of the new Negro."[61]

Du Bois was by then accustomed to acrimonious attacks from the black press, and had little desire to debate Randolph and Owen. In December 1919, the *Crisis* criticized the government's harassment and suppression of the *Messenger* and defended the right of these "radicals" to a free press.[62] Du Bois subsequently made several attempts to explain his critical position on revolutionary socialism. In August 1921, Du Bois observed that the NAACP did "not believe in revolution. We expect revolutionary changes in many parts of this life and this world, but we expect these changes to come mainly through reason, human sympathy, and the education of children, and not by murder." The theory of "class struggle" did not apply to black America, because "the colored group is not yet divided into capitalists and laborers. Our professional classes are sons and daughters of porters, washerwomen, and laborers."[63] In October 1921, Du Bois went further to criticize revolutionary Marxism. "The workers of the world are, through no fault of their own, ignorant, inexperienced men," he argued. "It is not for a moment to be assumed that movements into which they are drawn or which they themselves initiate are necessarily the best for them." Du Bois insisted that all white workers benefited materially from imperialism and that "they are consciously submitting themselves to the leadership" of the capitalists.[64] The *Messenger* described Du Bois's thesis as "sheer cheap demagogy," "tawdry scholarship," and "fragmentary thinking." Once more, the "superficial sociologist" had presented an "effete and forceless argument."[65]

Randolph ran as the Socialist party's candidate for New York state comptroller in 1920 and received over two hundred thousand votes. In the same year Owen ran unsuccessfully for New York state assemblyman. But between 1921 and 1923, both activists reevaluated their radical political ideas. Owen became embittered by the racism in the Socialist party and in 1923 withdrew from radical politics. Under Randolph, the *Messenger* began to reflect a more moderate political tone. In 1923, Randolph unsuccessfully tried to initiate the United Negro Trades, which was designed to bring black workers into labor unions. Two years later, Randolph became general organizer of the Brotherhood of Sleeping Car Porters, and the *Messenger* became the union's publication. Although Randolph had long since disavowed his earlier support for Bolshevism, many black newspapers attacked him as a "Communist." The St. Louis *Argus* charged that Randolph was manipulating the porters "only to raise money" for the Soviet Union. The nation's major black newspaper, the *Chicago Defender*, condemned the brotherhood as a subversive organization. Other than the *Pittsburgh Courier*, the major black publication that consistently defended Randolph and the fledgling black union was the *Crisis*.[66] Du Bois wrote a series of editorials praising Randolph and criticizing the activities of federal authorities and the Pullman Company in their attempts to suppress the brotherhood.[67] The episode with Randolph reveals one of Du Bois's most attractive qualities as a political leader—his capacity to overcome personal disagreements to work for the greater interests of black people. As Du Bois reflected in his *Autobiography:*

"I tried to give the other fellow his due even when I disliked him personally and disagreed with him logically. It became to me a point of honor never to refuse appreciation to one who had earned it, no matter who he was."[68]

There were other black radicals who presented challenges to Du Bois and the NAACP. One of the earliest proponents of "revolutionary black nationalism" was Hubert Henry Harrison. Born in the Virgin Islands in 1883, Harrison had joined the Socialist party by 1910 and worked briefly with the IWW. Leaving the party in 1914 because of its failure to combat racism, he formed his own organization, the "Harlem People's Forum." Harrison's militant newspaper, the *Voice,* advocated a doctrine of "Race First," and assumed the primacy of racism over social class struggles. Randolph and Owen learned much of their early rhetoric and tactics from Harrison. A consistent critic of the NAACP, Harrison attacked the Association as a "capitalist" organization that did not reflect black workers' interests.[69] More influential was another West Indian radical, Cyril V. Briggs. Born in 1887, Briggs migrated to the United States in 1905. After working for Harlem's *Amsterdam News,* Briggs and other black militants established the *Crusader* newspaper in 1918. The following year Briggs initiated the African Blood Brotherhood (ABB), a secret, revolutionary society that adhered to an ideology of Pan-Africanism and radical socialism. Between 1921–23 the ABB had approximately seven thousand members throughout the Caribbean and the United States. Like Randolph and Harrison, Briggs condemned Du Bois and the NAACP as "Old Negroes" whose "abject crawling and pleading have availed the Cause nothing.." Some leaders of the ABB joined the Workers party, forerunner of the Communist party, as early as 1922. During these years members of the ABB included poet Claude McKay, radical journalist W. A. Domingo, and Richard B. Moore, a leading black Communist during the Great Depression. In 1925, Briggs became national secretary of a black workers' formation, the American Negro Labor Congress, and in 1929 he was elected to the American Communist party's central executive committee.[70]

Du Bois's relations with black Communists were strained from the beginning. In July 1921, McKay challenged Du Bois on several grounds. The NAACP "cannot function as a revolutionary working-class organization," he maintained, and although its aim was "noble," it could not lead a social revolution for all oppressed peoples. Black Americans suffered not just from color prejudice, McKay wrote, "in reality the Negro is discriminated against because he is of the lowest type of worker." Du Bois's response began with his reservations about the Russian revolution. "Russia is incredibly vast," Du Bois noted, and although much positive activity had occurred under communism, there were "other things which frighten us." He praised the Communist International's racial egalitarianism but questioned whether Negroes should "assume on the part of unlettered and suppressed masses of white workers, a clearness of thought, a sense of human brotherhood, that is sadly lacking in the most educated classes." Du Bois informed McKay that he was "not prepared to dogmatize with Marx or Lenin" and that it was "foolish . . . to join a revolution which we do not at present understand."[71] Throughout the 1920s, Du Bois's general attitude toward American communism did not change significantly. In 1926, he declared that Negro support for communism would be curtailed if racial prejudice were abolished.[72] Five years later Du Bois severely criticized the tactics of American Communists in the *Crisis:* "American Negroes do not propose to be the shock troops of the Communist Revolution, driven out in front to death, cruelty and humiliation in order to win victories for white workers. They are picking no chestnuts from the fire, neither for capital nor white labor. Negroes know perfectly well that whenever they try to lead revolution in America, the nation will unite as one fist to crush them and them alone."[73] Black Marxists occasionally responded to Du Bois in similar fashion. One of the most prominent black Communists of the period was a young Trinidadian, Malcolm Nurse. Acquiring the political nom de guerre "George Padmore," he attacked Du Bois in the Communist publication *Negro Worker:* "Du Bois, the ideological leader of the middle-class Negro Intellectuals, is trying to take away the lead of the revolutionary movement by playing with 'left phrases.' . . . What demagogy! This only shows the utter bankruptcy of the men at the head of the NAACP. They have no program to lead the masses out of their misery."[74]

The socialist organization that came closest to Du Bois's political expectations was the British Labour party. He applauded its moderately reformists program several times in the *Crisis.* When the MacDonald government fell in 1932, Du Bois described the event as a "failure for liberal, peaceful reform throughout the world."[75] But in one respect, Du Bois's understanding of socialism did change—his view of the Soviet Union became increasingly positive. In June 1922, Du Bois noted that the Soviets were excellent negotiators in international politics, adding that they "may be dreamers, but they are not fools."[76] Du Bois received an informative letter from a black American student visiting the USSR in 1924; he explained that "under the Soviet System there are no race problems."[77] By 1925 Du Bois had decided to visit the Soviet Union at the first opportunity. His writings expressed the strong hope that the Soviet experiment would succeed. "Russia has been seeking a *rapprochement* with colored labor," he observed. "She is making her peace with China and Japan. Her leaders have come in close touch with the leaders of India."[78] In the December 1925 issue of the *Crisis,* Du Bois insisted: "We should stand before the astounding effort of

Soviet Russia to reorganize the industrial world with open minds and listening ears."[79]

"In Black American history there are two personal feuds which stand out beyond all others," observed Theodore Vincent, "W. E. B. Du Bois vs. Booker T. Washington and W. E. B. Du Bois vs. Marcus Garvey."[80] Many historians have commented extensively upon Du Bois's famous conflict with Garvey, the most dynamic black nationalist of the twentieth century and have perpetuated the view that Du Bois was Garvey's "arch-enemy" and "fiercest" critic.[81] Actually, Du Bois's public criticisms of Garvey's Universal Negro Improvement Association (UNIA) were fairly balanced and restrained, at least until September 1922. Garvey's "fiercest" critics tended to be former members of the UNIA, or his political associates: W. A. Domingo, the first editor of the UNIA newspaper, the *Negro World*, later condemned Garvey's procedures as "medieval, obscure and dishonest"; and A. Philip Randolph, who actively collaborated with Garvey from 1916 to 1919, soon termed the black nationalist an "unquestioned fool and ignoramus." A majority of the Afro-American intelligentsia, radicals and moderates alike, also opposed Garveyism. Kelly Miller described Garvey as a "crass pragmatist" possessed by a "frenzied fanaticism"; young radical sociologist E. Franklin Frazier compared the UNIA to the Ku Klux Klan; and Cyril Briggs called Garvey a "Judas Iscariot" who was "the Moses that was to have been" in 1921.[82] It is important to consider three factors in any analysis of the Garvey-Du Bois controversy: the ideological relationship between Garvey and Booker T. Washington; the similarities and differences between Garvey's pan-Africanism and Du Bois's movement; and Garvey's "retreat from radicalism" after mid-1921, which coincided with the rapid expansion of the Ku Klux Klan across the United States.[83]

Born in Jamaica in 1887, Garvey first worked as a printer and journalist in the Caribbean, Central America, and England. In 1914, he established the UNIA and African Communities League in Jamaica as a black nationalist, self-help organization. Garvey read extensively but seems to have been most influenced by the writings of Blyden and Booker T. Washington. In November 1915, the UNIA held a memorial service in the Tuskegeean's honor. Garvey spoke more than one hour praising him as "the greatest hero sprung from the stock of scattered Ethiopia." Du Bois first met Garvey in April 1915 during a visit to Jamaica. In a public address, Du Bois implied that Jamaica had "settled the race question" and that the island's fundamental difficulties were economic rather than racial. To Garvey, Du Bois's statements were an admission of "the utter insignificance of the black man." Garvey wrote to Moton in February 1916, observing that the "one true friend" of the Negro was "the white man" and that any solution to the problem of racism must be based "on the platform of Dr. Booker T. Washington."[84] When Garvey arrived in New York in late March 1916, his original intention was to raise funds for an industrial farm and trade school in Jamaica, modeled after the Tuskegee Institute. Visiting the NAACP office, he was shocked to discover a number of white employees. But a distinct rupture between Garvey and Du Bois did not occur. In April 1916, Garvey invited Du Bois to chair his first public lecture in New York, and the *Crisis* announced Garvey's fundraising efforts in its May 1916 issue.

The upheaval of World War I and the Red Summer of 1919 catapulted Garvey into international prominence. Garvey was a gifted orator, and to many poor and working class Afro-Americans, the UNIA represented a militant alternative to the NAACP. Garvey's charismatic appeals to black nationalism, Pan-Africanism, and racial pride attracted thousands of followers. Within several brief years, the UNIA initiated the Black Star steamship line, the Universal African Legion, and the *Negro World* newspaper. The popularity of "Garveyism" spread at a phenomenal rate. At its peak, the UNIA had fifty two branches in Cuba, over thirty in Trinidad and Tobago, eleven in Jamaica, six in the Dominican Republic, forty six in Panama, and four in British Honduras. Garveyites established branches throughout Africa but were particularly successful in South Africa, South West Africa (Namibia), and Nigeria. Garvey's greatest successes occurred in North America, which had more than seven hundred official UNIA branches by the early 1920s. The organization claimed thirty five thousand dues-paying members in New York City alone. Garvey's charisma and talent for building a mass movement was not the sole factor in the rapid rise of the UNIA. As E. Franklin Frazier astutely observed in 1926, the NAACP, "which has fought uncompromisingly for equality for the Negro, has never secured, except locally and occasionally, the support of the masses. It has lacked the dramatic element." Garvey's genius was the ability to make "the Negro an important person in his immediate environment."[85] Garvey's achievement was in many respects unequaled in modern black history, but like most mass leaders, he possessed certain limitations. Richard B. Moore comments that Garvey's "egocentric and aggressive personality could brook no other leaders and intellectual figures standing beside himself nor tolerate anything short of total dominance." Garvey frequently tended to "underestimate, and often disregard, the primary opposition" of white "racists to all significant endeavors to improve the condition of people of African descent."[86] Moreover, Garvey largely perceived American race relations through the context of his formative Jamaican experiences. Sociologist Charles S. Johnson suggested in 1923 that Garvey "hated intensely things white and more intensely things near white."[87]

Garvey's hostility to Du Bois surfaced openly at the end of World War I. Speaking before the Baltimore UNIA branch on 18 December 1918, Garvey declared erroneously that Du Bois and Moton were sent jointly "to France to prevent Negroes from getting the fruits of their sacrifices on the battle-fields. . . . Negroes should enjoy [democracy]," Garvey stated, but whites had "sent for men like Du Bois and Moton to prevent us from getting it."[88] The UNIA appointed three black activists to attend the peace conference: A. Philip Randolph, Ida B. Wells-Barnett, and a nineteen-year-old Haitian, Eliezer Cadet. Only Cadet was able to secure a passport, but he arrived in Paris on 1 March 1919, several days after the Pan-African Congress had ended. Cadet's failure to attract the attention of the French press and authorities was falsely attributed to Du Bois's efforts. At a mass meeting of three thousand UNIA supporters held in New York on 25 March, Garvey, Randolph, Owen, and *Negro World* editor W. A. Domingo jointly denounced Du Bois as a "reactionary under [the] pay of white men." Garvey announced that Du Bois had placed "obstacles in the way of the elected representative efficiently discharging his already difficult duties on behalf of the Negro race." Owen asserted that only "good niggers" like Du Bois had been permitted to go to Paris. And the *Negro World* continued the attack on Du Bois, describing him as an agent of "the capitalist class" who had attacked the UNIA aims "in the French papers."[89]

Du Bois was perplexed by Garvey and the UNIA and for several years made no public comments about the organization. The mass movement seemed to combine many paradoxical currents—black nationalism, pan-Africanism, socialism, and Booker T. Washington's self-help ideas. The UNIA had attracted the interest of several American Negro Academy members, notably William H. Ferris, who edited the *Negro World* for a time, and John E. Bruce, who wrote a regular column for the paper and was knighted "Duke of Uganda" by Garvey in 1921. Former Niagara Movement member J. R. L. Diggs became the UNIA chaplain general in 1922; but the Tuskegee Machine's major journalist, T. Thomas Fortune, was an early defender of Garvey and edited the *Negro World* from 1923 until his death in 1928. Garvey's devotion to Booker T. Washington was well known, but the movement won the support of many New Negro radicals: Hubert H. Harrison was associate editor of the *Negro World* in 1920–21, and Claude McKay also wrote for the publication.[90] Du Bois attended the UNIA's August 1920 convention, which attracted twenty five thousand people. When Garvey learned about Du Bois's presence at an earlier session, he informed his audience: "We believe Negroes are big, not by the size of their pocketbook, not by the alien company they keep but by their being for their race. You cannot advocate 'close ranks' today and talk 'dark water' tomorrow; you must be a hundred percent Negro." Garvey considered Du Bois an "ante-bellum Negro" who had "obligated himself to the white folks, and is in no sense or way free to break with them now."[91]

By mid-1920, Du Bois reached several negative conclusions about Garveyism. He solicited information from T. K. Gibson, a Columbus, Ohio, black businessman, on the UNIA's activities in the state. He began to investigate the Black Star Line's financial records. Du Bois expected to uncover "that Garvey is financially more or less a fraud."[92] He was also worried that Garvey's black nationalist version of Pan-Africanism would undermine his own more elitist movement. Even as the 1919 Pan-African Congress met in Paris, the *Negro World* was banned by the acting governor in British Honduras and by the Trinidadian governor "on grounds that it [was] seditious." In May 1919, the British Guianan government seized and destroyed the *Negro World;* on 6 August 1919, the acting governor of Jamaica ordered postal agents to seize copies of the newspaper; and on 19 August, "legislation to ban the *Negro World* in the Windward Islands [was] advocated by the governor, G. B. Haddon-Smith."[93] Du Bois concluded that Garveyism was closely aligned with the Communists, whom he then distrusted. In an unpublished interview in August 1920, Du Bois described Garvey as a "demagogue" and termed his supporters "the lowest type of Negroes. . . . They are allied with the Bolsheviks and the Sinn Feiners in their world revolution." Du Bois was still unwilling to "raise a hand to stop" the UNIA, but he thought that the "movement will collapse in a short time."[94]

The *Crisis* commented on the Garvey movement only twice before December 1920: it defended the *Negro World* against federal government repression and presented a general overview of West Indian political activism in the United States, noting that the "cry 'Africa for the Africans' strikes with a startling surprise upon America's darker millions."[95] Du Bois's two-part essay on Garveyism was generally a balanced, and even favorable critique of "one of the most interesting spiritual movements of the modern Negro world." Du Bois commented that Garvey possessed "very serious defects of temperament and training: he is dictatorial, domineering, inordinately vain and very suspicious." The UNIA's business ventures, especially the Black Star Line, were beset with financial problems. However, Du Bois also emphasized that Garvey was also "an extraordinary leader of men. Thousands of people believe in him." The charges that the black nationalist was dishonest or that "he was consciously diverting money to his own uses" were groundless. Garvey's basic economic strategy was "perfectly feasible," Du Bois declared. "What he is trying to say and do is this: American Negroes can, by accumulating and ministering their own capital, organize industry, join the black centers of the south Atlantic by commercial enterprise and in this way ultimately redeem Africa as a fit and free home for black men. This is true."[96] Garvey characterized Du Bois's article as "75 percent criticism and 25 percent appreciation." Throughout his academic career, Du Bois "could rarely get close to the heart of colored people." He was "the idol of the drawing room aristocrats," Garvey noted, "while the UNIA appeals to the self reliant yeomanry."[97] Du Bois did not debate Garvey, but attempted to distinguish his pan-Africanist activities from those of the UNIA. In Du Bois's correspondence with Secretary of State Hughes, for example, he observed that the Pan-African Congress "has nothing to do with the so called Garvey movement."[98] But when Du Bois traveled to Europe in 1921 for the second congress, he discovered that "news of [Garvey's] astonishing plans reached Europe and the various colonial offices, even before my much more modest proposals. Often the Pan-African Congress was confounded with the Garvey movement with consequent suspicion and attack."[99]

Historian Robert A. Hill has recently illustrated that Garvey entered "a new political phase" after July 1921. During the period 1918–21, Garvey was profoundly sympathetic with the international left and with mass workers' movements against capital. In 1919, Garvey urged black supporters "to have a white man lynched for every Negro who was lynched"; in 1920, he claimed that the color red in the UNIA flag "showed their sympathy with the 'Reds' of the world, and the Green their sympathy for the Irish in their fight for freedom." But in early 1921, federal authorities directed by J. Edgar Hoover were able to block Garvey's return to the United States for five months, after the black nationalist's trip to the Caribbean. Upon his return, noted Hill, "Garvey abandoned his earlier espousal of resistance" and initiated a "dogma of racial purity," which became the UNIA central theme. At the UNIA's August 1921 convention, Garvey denounced the NAACP's commitment to "social equality" in language strikingly similar to Booker T. Washington's Atlanta Compromise: "We sincerely feel that the white race like the Black and Yellow Races should maintain the purity of self. . . . [The Negro] therefore denounces any attempt on the part of dissatisfied individuals who by accident are members of the said Negro Race, in their attempts to foster a campaign of miscegenation to the destruction of the Race's purity."[100] Some black leftists had already left the UNIA or had ceased to work with Garvey. In 1921 many progressive UNIA leaders joined Briggs's ABB, including UNIA secretary general James D. Brooks, UNIA commissioner to Liberia Cyril Crichlow, and UNIA chaplain general George A. McGuire. Former NAACP member James W. H. Eason, elected "Leader of American Negroes" by the UNIA in 1920, also broke with Garvey. In 1921, Randolph expressed his "disillusionment" with the "magic romanticism of color" projected by Garvey.[101] Briggs later explained the UNIA retreat from militancy in these terms: "The movement began as a radical petty bourgeois national movement, reflecting to a great extent in its early stages the militancy of the toiling masses. . . . From the very beginning there were two sides inherent to the movement: a democratic side and a reactionary side."[102]

In the United States, Garveyism coincided with the rebirth and rapid expansion of the Ku Klux Klan as a mass reactionary movement. In early 1920, the Klan had under two thousand members nationally. In less than six years, the "Invisible Empire" enrolled over two million white Americans on a program of white supremacy, anti-Semitism, and anti-Catholicism. About two-thirds of all Klan members were outside the South: total KKK membership reached fifty thousand in Chicago, thirty five thousand in Philadelphia, sixteen thousand in New York City, and thirty eight thousand in Indianapolis.[103] As the Klan's political and vigilante terror increased, Garvey's attitude toward the white supremacists became more conciliatory. He made political overtures to Klan leaders in 1922, which were later followed by alliances with Earnest S. Cox, leader of the White America Society, and John Powell of the Anglo-Saxon Clubs of America. Garvey soon declared that the Ku Klux Klan and other racist societies were "better friends of the race" than the NAACP, because of their "honesty of purpose towards the Negro."[104]

Du Bois first underestimated the strength of the Klan, writing in November 1921 that the racist organization's "power is ended." But he quickly recognized the fascist and antidemocratic potential of the KKK and wrote a series of articles calling for the Klan's destruction.[105] More than anything else, Garvey's flirtation with groups that committed murder and political violence against blacks, Jews, and other minorities motivated Du Bois to censure the UNIA. Unfortunately, Du Bois also committed Garvey's rhetorical errors by resorting to personal attacks. In his February 1923 essay "Back to Africa," Du Bois characterized Garvey as "a little, fat Black man, ugly, but with intelligent eyes and big head." The UNIA's "African program was made impossible" by Garvey's "pigheadedness. . . . [He was] a liar and blatant fool." His "unholy alliance" with the "notorious Ku Klux Klan" was a product of Garvey's hopes that the racists would "finance the Black Star Line."[106] Garvey retorted that Du Bois hated "the black blood in his veins. . . . That is why he likes to dance with white people, and dine with them, and sometimes sleep with them." Du Bois was a "lazy dependent mulatto" whose education "fits him for no better service than being a lackey for good white people."[107] Du Bois received death threats from Garveyites and letters that he termed "of such unbelievable filth that they were absolutely unprintable." Upon his return from Africa in early 1924 he "learned with disgust" that his friends were so "stirred by Garvey's threats" that they secured police protection for him "on the dock."[108]

118

The polemics between Du Bois and Garvey during 1923–24 overshadowed the UNIA leader's constant debates with all others. In a classic June 1924 editorial in the *Messenger,* Randolph described the feud as the "Heavyweight Championship Bout for Afro-American-West Indian Belt, Between Battling Du Bois and Kid Garvey."[109] But this obscures the fact that Du Bois took no leading role in the anti-Garvey movement. Randolph, Owen, and Domingo organized the "Garvey Must Go" campaign in Harlem; Briggs coordinated anti-UNIA street rallies as early as 1921; and Garvey's major critic in the black press was not the *Crisis* but Robert Abbott's influential *Chicago Defender.* Former Garvey supporters William Pickens and James Eason mobilized dissidents against the movement's founder, and Eason was assassinated by loyal Garveyites in January 1923. The UNIA's demise was due, in part, to internal financial mismanagement and to the relentless efforts of the federal government to destroy the organization. In January 1922, Garvey and several Black Star Line officials were arrested on mail fraud charges. The following year Garvey was convicted, and the Black Star Line went bankrupt. After an unsuccessful appeal, Garvey was sent to federal prison in Atlanta in 1925. Pardoned by President Coolidge, Garvey was deported to Jamaica in November 1927. Du Bois did not mince words in urging Garvey's removal from public life: "Marcus Garvey is, without doubt, the most dangerous enemy of the Negro race in America and in the world. He is either a lunatic or a traitor. . . . this open ally of the Ku Klux Klan should be locked up or sent home."[110]

Du Bois attributed the decline of his Pan-African Congress movement to "the unfortunate words and career of Marcus Garvey," who had "dampened" Afro-American interest in African affairs.[111] His plans for a fourth congress in 1925, scheduled for the Caribbean, failed to materialize. Addie W. Hunton, an NAACP field organizer and black women's club leader, worked with Du Bois to coordinate the fourth congress, held in New York City in August 1927. The sessions attracted five thousand people, more than the number of participants at all previous congresses combined. There were 208 paid delegates from 22 states and the District of Columbia. Representatives from India, Egypt, Liberia, Nigeria, the Gold Coast, and China were also present. The congress ratified a series of resolutions, including demands for black political rights and "the development of Africa for the Africans and not merely for the profit of Europeans." The Soviet Union was also supported "for its liberal attitude toward the colored races."[112] The fifth congress, scheduled in Tunisia in 1929, was blocked by the French government. Du Bois recognized that "the importance of these [Pan-African] meetings is not yet realized by educated and thinking Negroes" in the United States. "Nevertheless, the idea back of the Pan-African Congress is sound, and in less than a hundred years, it is going to be recognized."[113] Within several years, Du Bois's attitude toward Garveyism also became more generous. In February 1928, following Garvey's release from prison, the *Crisis* stated: "We have today no enmity against Marcus Garvey. He has a great and worthy dream. . . . We will be the first to applaud any success that he may have."[114] In 1944 Du Bois corresponded with Garvey's widow, Amy Jacques-Garvey, to coordinate the fifth Pan-African Congress, held after World War II.[115]

Many historians have interpreted the Du Bois-Garvey conflict as the product of these leaders' different social class and educational backgrounds—the "introspective scholar" versus the "self educated mass leader."[116] There is an element of truth here but far more important was the social composition of their respective Pan-African movements, and Garvey's unmistakable retreat from radicalism after 1921. Du Bois's Pan-African Congresses were an international "version" of the Niagara Movement—small, reform-minded black elites who sought to extend the principles of democracy and self-determination to colonial Africa and the Caribbean. Garvey's Pan-Africanism was an ideological extension of his black nationalism; during its early stages, it expressed an anticapitalist and anticolonialist politics and literally mobilized several million blacks in Africa, the Caribbean, and the United States. Du Bois's Pan-Africanism was based on cultural pluralism, a fervent belief in democratic ideals and socialism, and opposition to all forms of colonial rule. Nevertheless, as George Padmore later commented, Du Bois and Garvey were "the two outstanding Negro leaders in the Western Hemisphere" during the 1920s. Both provided essential contributions to the emergence of national democratic movements in the Caribbean and Africa after 1945.[117]

Mary Burghardt Du Bois
with her small son, William
Edward Burghardt Du
Bois, circa 1869–70.

Graduation speakers at Harvard University's
commencement, 1890. Du Bois is seated at far right.

Fisk University's graduating class, 1888. Du Bois is seated on the left.

Du Bois, Nina Gomer Du Bois (Du Bois's first wife), and their son
Burghardt. Photograph was probably taken in Atlanta, Georgia, in 1897,
only months before the child's death.

Atlanta University's faculty and administrative staff, 1906. Du Bois is at the
right in the upper row; Nina Du Bois is located in the center in the fourth
row; and Yolande Du Bois is seated in the front row.

Participants at the Niagara Movement's third national conference, held in Boston in 1907.

Key leaders of the Niagara Movement. With Du Bois are, left to right, F. H. M. Murray, L. M. Hershaw, and William Monroe Trotter. Photograph was taken in 1906 or 1907.

Portrait of Du Bois taken
in 1907; Du Bois was
thirty-nine years old.

NAACP protest march against lynching, held in New York City, 1917. Du
Bois is in the upper right, walking with a cane.

Du Bois and Paul Robeson, taken about 1949.

Du Bois portrait photographed by Carl Van Vechten, about 1940.

Shirley Graham Du Bois, photographed by Carl Van Vechten.

Du Bois and Mao Tse-tung in China, April 1959.

Du Bois's marriage to Shirley Graham, 27 February 1951.

President Kwame Nkrumah congratulates Du Bois on his
ninety-fifth birthday, 23 February 1963, in Accra, Ghana.

Portrait of Du Bois, 1950s.

6

THE
NEW
NEGRO

It must be remembered that in the last quarter of a century, the advance of the colored people has been mainly in the lines where they themselves working by and for themselves, have accomplished the greatest advance. . . . It is the class-conscious workingmen uniting together who will eventually emancipate labor throughout the world. It is the race-conscious Black [man] cooperating together in his own institutions and movements who will eventually emancipate the colored race.

W. E. B. Du Bois,
1934

Like cancer, segregation grows and must be, in my opinion, resisted wherever it shows its head.

Walter White,
1934

From its origins, the NAACP became the moral and political conscience of the nation on the issue of institutional racism. Much of the Association's reformist strategy rested on legal challenges to Jim Crow. As early as 1911, attorney Arthur Spingarn successfully led several cases against the use of violence by the New York City Police Department in the black community. In 1917, Association president Moorfield Storey came before the Supreme Court to argue against the residential segregation law in Louisville, and the Court ruled unanimously for the NAACP. In the 1920s, the Association led the unsuccessful campaign to secure congressional approval for the Dyer Anti-Lynching Bill. Perhaps more important, the NAACP provided political support and direction to hundreds of black communities, in their respective local struggles against segregation and disfranchisement. Despite criticisms from Randolph, the ABB, and the Garveyites, the leaders of the Association frequently risked their lives in the movement for social justice. NAACP member Martha Gruening was sent to East St. Louis to investigate the racist pogrom of 1917; Walter White traveled at risk throughout the South, and by 1921 he had investigated thirty six separate lynchings. In 1919, Association secretary John R. Shillady was viciously assaulted in Texas. Local NAACP organizers frequently experienced similar attacks. In 1920, one judge in Mississippi jailed a black minister who had sold copies of the *Crisis*. Southern racists condemned the Association as subversive, and often singled out Du Bois for special criticism. The governor of Mississippi challenged the black editor to come to his state, vowing to make Du Bois an "example . . . that would be a lasting benefit to the colored people of the South."[1] In 1923, a Dallas newspaper ran a front-page editorial against Du Bois, declaring that "the arrogant ebony-head, thick-lipped, kinky-haired Negro 'educator' must be put in his place and made to stay there."[2]

The national image of the NAACP and the writings of Du Bois were frequently merged in the public mind, a political reality that often created tensions inside the Association. One major difficulty was the common perception that Du Bois hated all whites. Even at the height of Garveyism, some contemporaries viewed Du Bois as a more hostile critic of white society than Garvey. In August 1920, for example, Randolph and Owen observed that the NAACP was "known as the 'Anti-White' organization"; and Frederick R. Moore, editor of the *New York Age,* termed the *Crisis* "the most anti-White Negro paper in the country."[3] As Du Bois remarked to one friend in 1927: "whites have borne the brunt of my attacks for thirty years. . . . They believe that I hate white folks. Even my nearest white friends shrink from me."[4] White leaders fretted over the *Crisis*'s fiery editorials but were unable to control Du Bois. A second problem developed in the early 1920s, when the *Crisis*'s circulation began to decline. The magazines's subscribers fell by one-third during the immediate postwar years, and in 1930 the *Crisis* sold fewer than thirty thousand copies. The magazine began to run in the red by several thousand dollars annually. Du Bois's colleagues sometimes blamed the decline of the publication on their editor's inflammatory style. But, in retrospect, as Theodore G. Vincent observed, the *Crisis* became a victim of its earlier successes. When the Association was established, the national circulation of all black newspapers was roughly three hundred thousand to five hundred thousand and most of these publications were hardly sympathetic to radicalism. Black journalism in the

1920s, however, reflected the political direction and style of the *Crisis*, and in some cases, went further to the left than the NAACP. The *Messenger*, at its peak, regularly sold fifty thousand copies; the *Crusader*, edited by Briggs, obtained thirty seven thousand readers; and the National Urban League's *Opportunity* edited by sociologist Charles S. Johnson, reached almost fifty thousand. Nationally, black publications had a combined circulation of 1.6 million in the late 1920s.[5]

Du Bois was frequently away from the *Crisis* office, and Association leaders increasingly urged him to "settle down to fewer lines of effort." For Du Bois, this was "impossible." "I was nervous and restless; in addition to all my activities, I ranged the country from North to South and from the Atlantic to the Pacific in series of lectures, conferences, and expositions," Du Bois noted in *Dusk of Dawn*. "I had to be part of the revolution through which the world was going and to feel in my soul the scars of its battle."[6] Du Bois's legendary sensitivity concerning matters of political and social decorum continued to exasperate friends. In April 1924, he informed Association secretary James Weldon Johnson that he would not attend the NAACP's annual conference. "In the last two or three years I seemed to sense on the part of you, Miss Ovington and Mr. White a feeling that I was not needed longer in this capacity and that my gradual elimination as a speaker on the platform of the NAACP was desirable," he wrote. In the previous year, NAACP officials had failed to consult him about the Association convention in Kansas City, and he had suggested to them that his "presence was not necessary." When he was taken off the 1923 program, Du Bois explained, "I was, I confess, surprised and hurt, but I took my medicine as a gentleman should. . . . If my services were unnecessary at Kansas City, no amount of argument can make me believe they are indispensable at Philadelphia." Johnson's reply was judicious. He informed Du Bois that no Association official had ever attempted to block his participation in the conferences. Johnson was "surprised and hurt" at Du Bois's implication that he had "conspired against" the editor. "I do not believe the services of any single individual are now indispensable to the NAACP," he added. Arthur Spingarn and other directors finally persuaded Du Bois to appear at the Philadelphia convention of the Association. But this petty dispute was not forgotten by either Du Bois or NAACP officials.[7]

Du Bois viewed himself as a "main factor in revolutionizing the attitude of the American Negro toward caste. My stinging hammer blows made Negroes aware of themselves, confident of their possibilities and determined in self-determination."[8] But Du Bois was more than simply a civil rights proponent. The *Crisis* was a forum of democratic opinion, and its editor consciously attempted to discuss problems of social inequality, poverty, and political rights that transcended the color line. He continued to campaign for women's rights throughout the 1920s and 1930s—and, indeed, until the end of his life. He hailed the ratification of the woman suffrage amendment in 1920, observing that "a civilization that required nineteen centuries to recognize the Rights of Women can confidently be expected some day to abolish the Color Line." Du Bois believed that black women would exercise the franchise more responsibly than black males. "They may beat and bribe our men," he noted, "but the political hope of the Negro rests on its intelligent and incorruptible womanhood." As in previous years, he criticized white women's organizations for their accommodation to racism. In February 1921, he denounced the racial insults directed at black women who took part in the International Council of Women. Du Bois recognized that the achievement of suffrage was only a partial step toward the eradication of women's inequality. He was particularly outraged by the chauvinism of male politicians. "Every statesman who yells about Children, Church and Kitchen," Du Bois commented in 1934, "ought to be made to bear twins, to listen to as many sermons as we have, and to wash dishes and diapers for at least ten years."[9]

Du Bois despised every form of social intolerance as a threat to democracy. The *Crisis*'s August 1922 editorial noted the growth of anti-Semitism across the country and criticized Yale, Harvard, and Columbia Universities for their discriminatory policies against Jews. Du Bois observed with alarm the initiation of anti-Semitic movements in postwar Europe. In Romania, the *Crisis* noted in September 1927, "Jew-baiting and stealing land from Russia are popular industries." The *Crisis* condemned anti-Semitic laws and pogroms in Poland and Hungary but expressed its greatest fears about the rise of National Socialism in Germany. "One has only to think of a hundred names like Mendelssohn, Heine, and Einstein, to remember but partially what the Jew has done for German civilization," Du Bois wrote in May 1933. All prejudice was to Du Bois "an ugly, dirty thing. It feeds on envy and hate."[10]

Du Bois continued to embarrass his Association colleagues by his private and public jeremiads against white Christianity. In his correspondence with the Reverend Samuel H. Bishop, general agent of the American Church Institute for Negroes, he criticized the Episcopal church for its "hypocrisy." Despite his nominal membership, "I have no particular affection for the Church," Du Bois informed Bishop. "I think its record on the Negro problem has been shameful. . . . So far as the Negro problem is concerned the southern branch of the Church is a moral dead weight and the northern branch of the Church never has had the moral courage to stand against it." The Episcopalian leadership was woefully "behind other churches in recognizing human manhood and Christian equality."[11] Such bluntness became common in the pages of the *Crisis*. In August 1920, he heartily congratulated the Methodist Episcopal Church for elevating two black men, Robert E. Jones and Matthew W. Clair, to the posts of bishop after "a fight of 25 years. . . . There are still white Christians in Zion," he added. But when the same northern Methodists attempted to merge with the southern Methodists, breaking off relations with the African Methodist Episcopal Church, the *Crisis* editor was filled with scorn. Unity between white Methodists was taking place at the sacrifice of racial equality, he declared. Sarcastically, he inquired if northern white Methodists still had "the present address of Jesus of Nazareth?"[12]

Du Bois's disputes with the Catholic church symbolized his strained relations with other denominations. In 1924 the Knights of Columbus published his book *The Gift of Black Folk*; Du Bois praised "Catholic priests and sisters teaching the colored South . . . for their unselfish work"; he "admired much" of the church's "mighty history." But in his private correspondence, Du Bois also charged that "the Catholic Church in America stands for color separation and discrimination to a degree equalled by no other church in America, and that is saying a very great deal." In hundreds of years, it had "ordained less than a half dozen black Catholic priests either because they have sent us poor teachers or because they think Negroes have neither brains nor morals." Catholic parochial schools rarely accepted black applicants, and "the Catholic University in Washington invites them elsewhere." In short, the "'nigger' haters" clothed in their episcopal robes "were promoting racism every degree as vicious" as "the Ku Klux Klan." The Catholic and Protestant churches failed generally on the race issue, Du Bois observed in the *Crisis,* because they had forgotten the living meaning of the teachings of "Jesus, the Jew." The ordeal of Christ who perished for all humanity was obscured by the coarse blinders of race hatred.[13]

Du Bois advocated what would later be termed "liberation theology," a prophetic faith that embraced the poor and the oppressed. The *Crisis* repeatedly declared that any acceptance of racial bigotry and labor exploitation was an abrogation of the teachings of the Son of God. "The church of John Pierpont Morgan [is] not the church of Jesus Christ," Du Bois wrote. For the special Christmas issue of the *Crisis* in December 1925, Du Bois imagined Jesus returning to earth and being immediately disillusioned with the gross spectacle of wealth and public avarice that was held in his name. Defiantly he spoke from the heights of the Woolworth Building in Manhattan to condemn the modern mob—"and the people were dumbfounded."[14] In one *Darkwater* essay, Jesus returned to earth in Waco, Texas, and taught white racists to "love" oppressed blacks. When an escaped black convict was unjustly burned alive, a voice came to him "out of the winds of the night, saying: 'This day thou shalt be with me in Paradise!' " During the Great Depression, Du Bois suggested that Christmas should be abolished, since "Jesus Christ is not usually invited to his birthday celebration." The living legacy of Christ could be realized only in a rededication to his historic example as a spiritual rebel against the established dogma and prejudice of the social order. Black and white opponents of South African racism, he believed, were truly "Christians" in the revolutionary tradition of Christ himself. Jesus was undoubtedly "the greatest of religious rebels," Du Bois affirmed in 1928.[16]

Perhaps the most frequent target of the *Crisis* was racism in organized labor. Consistently, Du Bois argued that the "masters of industry" benefited directly from the racial "hatreds" of working people. Afro-American laborers should enter unions wherever possible, the *Crisis* observed in May 1924. "Union labor has given the modern workman, white and black, whatever he has of decent wages and hours and conditions of work." If black and white workers ever achieved solidarity, Du Bois noted in August 1929, "the Solid South will crumble."[17] The inability of the AFL to transcend its policies of racial discrimination outraged Du Bois. "I am among the few colored men who have tried conscientiously to bring about understanding and co-operation between American Negroes and the Labor Unions," he wrote in March 1918. "I have sought to look upon the Sons of Freedom as simply a part of the great mass of the earth's Disinherited. . . . I carry on the title page, for instance, of this magazine the Union label, and yet as I know . . . the International Typographical Union systematically and deliberately excludes every Negro that it dares from membership."[18] By the time of the depression, Du Bois's patience had worn thin. A socialist printer complained to Du Bois when the union label was removed from the *Crisis*. Du Bois replied that he had "entirely lost faith in the American Federation of Labor and its attitude toward Negroes. . . . Until the trade-union movement stands heartily and unequivocally at the side of the Negro workers, I am through with it." In December 1933, the *Crisis* termed the AFL "a most sinister power. . . . Some time there is coming a great wave of demand from the mass of exploited laborers for an organization which represents their injuries and their wishes. And that new organization is going to sweep the AFL off the face of the earth."[19]

Du Bois's lifelong pattern of political independence continued through the 1920s and early 1930s. "The first and fundamental and inescapable problem of American democracy is Justice to the American Negro," Du Bois declared in March 1921. It was obvious to him that neither major party truly desired black freedom. "May God put us down as asses," the *Crisis* noted in May 1922, "if ever again we are found putting our trust in either the Republican or the Democratic Parties." In 1924, Du Bois decided to support the independent Progressive presidential candidate, Robert M. La Follette. Several years later, he joined the League for Independent Political Action, a liberal effort to develop a permanent third party. "Without the corrective of the Third Party," he commented in 1930, "party government degenerates into plutocracy."[20] Nevertheless, Du Bois doubted whether independent electoral movements could overturn the two-party system. At best, voting for third-party candidates was a showing of "moral" protest. Consequently, Du Bois's voting behavior frequently confused and confounded his critics. For example, in August 1928, the *Crisis* urged black voters to support Socialist party candidate Norman Thomas in the presidential elections. But less than six months later, Du Bois endorsed black Republican machine politician Oscar De Priest of Chicago for Congress. Du Bois lamented De Priest's "sorry" public record but insisted that "the only way in which the Negro can secure representation in local, state and national government, is by co-operating with a corrupt political machine." Racism "keeps white people from voting for Negroes or for their interests," he observed, and made it "impossible for Negroes to vote on the merits of the great problems confronting us."[21] Perhaps Du Bois's closest friend in electoral politics during the 1920s was attorney Ferdinand Q. Morton, the black leader of the Democratic party's Tammany Machine in New York City. Through Morton's offices, Du Bois lobbied against racism and anti-Semitism in the city government.[22] Du Bois deliberately advanced the interests of blacks and other oppressed people over the tradition of party loyalties; he was an important factor in moving many Afro-American voters away from the Republican party. As black educator Horace Mann Bond commented in 1925: "Not as an active leader, but as a consistent agitator for political activity of the bloc character, there can be no doubt but that [Du Bois's] views have profoundly influenced the course of events."[23]

Even when Du Bois left his office at the *Crisis,* he was actively involved in local community affairs. In 1922–23 he served on the "Fair-Play League" committee, which investigated the treatment of black prisoners in New York City police stations. In April 1923, Du Bois complained directly to the city police commissioner about the lack of police protection in Harlem.[24] At home, he continued to be a supportive and faithful husband and father. In his *Autobiography,* Du Bois observed that his marriage to Nina "was not an absolutely ideal union, but it was happier than most, so far as I could perceive." He tried to minimize the burdens of housework for his wife by regularly preparing his own breakfast. "I always leave a bathroom cleaner than when I enter," he noted: "I was not neglectful of my family; I furnished a good home. I educated the child and planned vacations and recreation. But my main work was out in the world and not at home." Du Bois cherished his daughter Yolande and frequently wrote to her during periods of absence. When Yolande married poet Countee Cullen in 1928, Du Bois wrote a beautiful essay, which illustrated his deep emotional attachment to her, in the

Crisis. Du Bois's extensive political responsibilities seldom came before the needs of his family.[25]

If a person "is over sixty years of age," Du Bois commented ruefully in *Dusk of Dawn,* "prevalent public opinion" dictates that he should have "had the grace to die." If not, "he ought . . . at least be willing to stop acting and thinking. I did not agree with that."[26] Du Bois turned sixty in 1928. Most of the leaders of the national black community during the 1890s were already dead, and others would be gone within another decade. Many of Du Bois's friends from Atlanta University, the Niagara Movement, and the Association died in these years: Colonel Charles Young (1922), John E. Milholland (1925), George W. Forbes (1927), Moorfield Storey (1929), Clement Morgan (1929), Ida B. Wells-Barnett (1931), Hugh H. Proctor (1933), and John Hope (1936). The American Negro Academy's last meeting was held in December 1928, as the number of founding members diminished. John E. Bruce died in 1925, followed by John W. Cromwell (1927), Francis Grimké (1927), Archibald Grimké (1930), and Kelly Miller (1939). Many early Pan-Africanists and African nationalists were also gone: Henry Sylvester Williams (1911), Edward Wilmot Blyden (1912), Casely Hayford (1930), and Blaise Diagne (1934). Trotter's death in 1934, possibly by suicide, was most painful for Du Bois. Although Trotter had renounced all association with the NAACP twenty years before, his former friend was "not an organization man," Du Bois noted in the *Crisis.* But Trotter had an "intense hatred" for racism, and no single publication "ever quite equalled" the *Boston Guardian.*[27]

Du Bois had been the most prominent intellectual of his generation. For young black scholars born after the Atlanta Compromise, however, Du Bois was literally an institution. Du Bois enjoyed the role of brahmin and was never reluctant to offer words of praise or advice to promising artists, social scientists, and political activists. In March 1918, he was one of the first critics to bring to national attention a talented "baritone soloist," a nineteen-year-old Rutgers University undergraduate named Paul Robeson.[28] Du Bois's correspondence was filled with early letters from black young adults who would later leave their mark on Afro-American society. In 1925, twenty-nine-year-old James W. Ford—soon to become a leading black Communist and vice-presidential candidate of the party—contacted Du Bois. Economist Abram L. Harris, at age twenty six, asked for Du Bois's opinion concerning his plans for black educational reform. A twenty-three-year-old college student at the University of California, Ralph J. Bunche, inquired if

Du Bois could help him to come "in closer contact with the leaders of our Race, so that I may better learn their methods." Mississippi-born Richmond Barthé, at the age of twenty seven, asked Du Bois for assistance in obtaining a Guggenheim fellowship "to continue my studies abroad." Although unsuccessful in his first attempt, Barthé subsequently won both the Rosenwald and Guggenheim fellowships and became one of the nation's great sculptors. St. Clair Drake, later an important social anthropologist, first wrote Du Bois at the age of nineteen, when he was attending the Hampton Institute. Robert C. Weaver, who in 1965 would become the first Afro-American cabinet member, consulted Du Bois during his doctoral studies at Harvard in 1931. For these and many others, Du Bois had become what Crummell, Blyden, and Douglass had been for their generation. As African historian William Leo Hansberry wrote Du Bois in 1933: "I consider myself a kind of spiritual son of yours, for it was your book *The Negro,* more than anything else, which was largely responsible for my determination to 'carry on' along my present lines of endeavor. I hope eventual accomplishments will prove me worthy of the self-appointed adoption."[29]

But black intellectuals who were between ten to twenty years younger than Du Bois often tended to view the black editor and scholar with less reverence than those whose careers had barely begun. William H. Ferris, who was only five years younger than Du Bois, anticipated the New Negro generation's criticisms of the NAACP leader. In his 1920 review of *Darkwater,* Ferris suggested that Du Bois may be "too aristocratic and hypercritical, too touchy and too sensitive, too dainty and fastidious, too high and holy to lead the masses of his race." Du Bois had committed "fatal blunders when he attempted to referee the work and worth of other coloured men," in an attempt "to determine 'who was who' in the Negro race."[30] Three dominant figures among the Afro-American intelligentsia between the world wars generally shared Ferris's views: Carter G. Woodson, editor of the *Journal of Negro History* and founder of the Association for the Study of Negro Life and History; Howard University philosophy professor Alain Locke, guiding critic of the Harlem Renaissance; and Charles S. Johnson, editor of *Opportunity* magazine and later founder of the Fisk University Race Relations Institute.

Du Bois's difficulties with these black scholars were both personal and theoretical. In 1925, Du Bois nominated Woodson for the NAACP Spingarn Medal, an annual award given for black achievement. In his letter to John Hope, Du Bois argued that Woodson had accomplished "the most striking piece of scientific work for the Negro race in the last ten years of any man that I know of." He admired Woodson's "integrity" and "his absolute independence of thought and action." But Du Bois added, "Woodson is not a popular man. He is, to put it mildly, cantankerous." In 1919, Du Bois had approached Woodson to serve as coauthor of his proposed volume on blacks during the war. Woodson tentatively agreed but soon retracted his commitment. In the *Crisis* and in his private correspondence, Du Bois unwisely wrote that Woodson "was afraid that he might be called upon to do most of the work and get the smaller part of the credit."[31] Du Bois's mildly negative critique of Woodson's 1922 book on the black church probably alienated the black historian again, and their relations were hardly fraternal thereafter. Woodson was never sympathetic to radicalism, and Du Bois's identification with socialism was also a factor in their mutual tensions. As Woodson commented in 1933, "To say that the Negro cannot develop sufficiently in the business world to measure arms with present-day capitalists is to deny actual facts, refute history, and discredit the Negro as a capable competitor in the economic battle of life." He dismissed "the so-called radical Negroes who have read and misunderstood Karl Marx."[32] Du Bois continued to value Woodson's important contributions to Afro-American historiography. However, the *Journal of Negro History* did not publish an article written by Du Bois until 1964, fourteen years after Woodson's death.[33]

Born in 1886, Locke graduated from Harvard College in 1907 and later studied at Oxford University and the University of Berlin. Locke collaborated with Du Bois in writing a brief essay on "The Younger Literary Movement," which appeared in the February 1924 issue of the *Crisis*. When Locke was briefly dismissed from Howard University in 1927, Du Bois rallied to his defense, observing that "Locke is by long odds the best trained man among the younger American Negroes." But candidly, Du Bois added, Locke was "not a particularly close friend." Du Bois strongly disagreed with Locke's view that "Beauty rather than Propaganda should be the object of Negro literature and art. . . . If Mr. Locke's thesis is insisted upon too much it is going to turn the Negro renaissance into decadence."[34] Charles S. Johnson had been the student of Robert Park at the University of Chicago and had acquired fairly conservative political and social views while working with the Urban League. The *Crisis*'s first review of Johnson's work was somewhat negative: Du Bois described Johnson's *Ebony and Topaz* as "a sort of big scrap book." Both men believed that Du Bois's stewardship over Afro-American intellectuals was no longer necessary or productive. "Old traditions are being shaken and rooted up by the percussion of new ideas," Johnson wrote in 1925. "Less is heard of the two historic 'schools of thought' clashing ceaselessly and loud over the question of industrial and higher education for the Negro." Locke agreed that a "metamorphosis" had taken place, and a "new spirit" was dawning for the Negro. The old debates and slogans were now passé. Perhaps thinking of Du Bois, Locke noted: "The Negro too, for his part, has idols of the tribe to smash."[35]

The greatest intellectual achievements of Afro-Americans in these years were in the arts. In poetry, the twenties saw the emergence of Claude McKay, Countee Cullen, and Langston Hughes; in the novel, Jessie Fauset, Rudolph Fisher, and Jean Toomer. The market for black artists' works was severely limited; Toomer's magnificent novel *Cane,* published in early 1923, sold only five hundred copies in its first year. The *Crisis* and *Opportunity* were the primary vehicles for artistic expression to reach mass audiences. But Du Bois also attempted to provide a cultural philosophy for the New Negro in literature. This proved difficult, because Du Bois's standards on art shifted with the development of the new literary movement. In June 1921, the *Crisis* observed that too many black Americans "want everything that is said about us to tell of the best and highest and noblest in us. We insist that our Art and Propaganda be one. This is wrong and in the end it is harmful." Du Bois encouraged black writers to "face the Truth of Art. We have criminals and prostitutes, ignorant and debased elements, just as all folk have. . . . The black Shakespeare must portray his black Iagos as well as his white Othellos." He returned to the central theme of the "Conservation of Races"—the Negro had a unique spiritual message for the world. "The great mission of the Negro to America," Du Bois wrote in November 1922, "is the development of Art and the appreciation of Beauty." Artists must ground their works in the cultural diversity of the black experience, "our love of life, the wild and beautiful desire of our women and men for each other."[36]

Du Bois also expressed an active interest in Afro-American music and theatre. As early as 1912, the *Crisis* noted with approval the development of "Ragtime" and congratulated popular black composer J. Rosamond Johnson for his contributions to "a new and distinct school of Negro music." In 1925 Du Bois praised the work of William Christopher Handy, the "father of the blues." He also drew to public attention the musical "labors" of John Wesley Work and Alice Work at Fisk University, in "resurrecting" the classic "Negro spiritual." Du Bois's July 1923 essay "Can the Negro Serve the Drama?" emphasized the need for black actors and playwrights to mine the "rich field" of their "own terrible history of experience. The somber pen of some black Ibsen, the religious fervor of some Negro Tolstoy, or the light sarcasm of a black Moliere have here a marvelous chance to develop." In 1925, Du Bois participated in the establishment of Harlem's Krigwa Players, a black theatrical company that performed for several years.[37]

As the Harlem Renaissance developed, however, Du Bois became uneasy with its political orientation. In late 1925, Du Bois again argued, "the art instinct is naturally and primarily individualistic. It is the cry of some caged soul yearning for expression and this individual impulse is, of course, back of Negro art." Du Bois criticized black audiences that wanted "no art that is not propaganda," but he expected the Negro artist to comprehend the oppressed social conditions of Afro-American people. However, at the June 1926 national conference of the NAACP, Du Bois delivered a blistering salvo against the aesthetic positions of Locke and some of the New Negro artists. "Do we want simply to be Americans?" Du Bois asked his audience. "We who are dark can see America in a way that white Americans cannot. . . . Thus, are we satisfied with its present goals and ideals?" Whites' approval for the writings of Cullen, Hughes, and other Renaissance artists indicated to some white critics that "there is no real color line." But to Du Bois, such "recognition" was rendered "because they think it is going to stop agitation of the Negro question. . . . And many colored people are all too eager to follow this advice; especially those who are weary of the eternal struggle along the color line, who are afraid to fight, and to whom the money of philanthropists and the alluring publicity are subtle and deadly bribes." The "apostle of Beauty" must also be bound to the "apostle of Truth and Right," if the goals of black liberation were to be served. "Thus all Art is propaganda and ever must be, despite the wailing of the purists," Du Bois declared. "I do not care a damn for any art that is not used for propaganda."[38]

Du Bois had declared moral war on any literature that degraded Afro-American culture and society. His June 1927 review of Julia Peterkin's novel *Black April* was fierce. People "who enjoy diving in the mud" would favor Peterkin's book, Du Bois declared. *Black April* was "a veritable cesspool of incest, adultery, fighting and poverty." Du Bois criticized H. L. Mencken's critique of Negro artists in October 1927: "White Americans are willing to read about Negroes, but they prefer to read about Negroes who are fools, clowns, prostitutes, or at any rate, in despair and contemplating suicide." But Du Bois's most vigorous statements were reserved for black writers. With the publication of McKay's *Home to Harlem* in 1928, Du Bois remarked that McKay had catered to the "prurient demand on the part of white folk for a portrayal in Negroes of that utter licentiousness which conventional civilization holds white folk back from enjoying." *Home to Harlem* "nauseates me," Du Bois wrote, "and after the dirtier parts of its filth, I felt distinctly like taking a bath. . . . As a picture of Harlem life or of Negro life anywhere, it is, of course, nonsense." McKay was furious, and promptly wrote Du Bois: "Nowhere in your writings do you reveal any comprehension of esthetics and therefore you are not competent nor qualified to pass judgement upon any work of art. . . . You mistake the art of life for nonsense and try to pass off propaganda as life in art!"[39]

The *Home to Harlem* controversy provided one of the few instances where Garvey and Du Bois found complete agreement. McKay's novel "is a damnable libel against the Negro," the black nationalist declared. "The time has come for us to boycott such Negro authors whom we may fairly designate as 'literary prostitutes.'" Predictably, Locke defended McKay, terming the book notable "for descriptive art and its reflection of the vital rhythms of Negro life. . . . *Home to Harlem* will stand as a challenging answer to the still too prevalent idea that the Negro can only be creatively spontaneous in music and poetry."[40] By the early 1930s, Du Bois had become fairly pessimistic about much Harlem Renaissance work. "Why was it that the Renaissance of literature which began among Negroes ten years ago has never taken real and lasting root?" Du Bois asked in 1933. "It was because it was a transplanted and exotic thing. It was a literature written for the benefit of white people and at the behest of white readers, and starting out primarily from the white point of view. It never had a real Negro constituency and it did not grow out the of the inmost heart and frank experience of Negros."[41]

Du Bois's major contribution to the Harlem Renaissance was his second novel, *Dark Princess,* published in 1928. The book can only be understood in its immediate historical context—written after Du Bois's polemics with the UNIA's version of black nationalism and Pan-Africanism and during his literary debates with Locke and younger black artists. Although the novel is a love story between a black American, Matthew Towns, and an Indian princess, Kautilya, the central theme is politics. The plot is based on an ambitious attempt by people of color throughout the world to conspire against white colonialism and imperialism. Three of the novel's more interesting characters are Perigua, a West Indian nationalist and "demagogue" designed roughly on Marcus Garvey; Sara Andrews, Towns's first wife, who represented the cold, unscrupulous elements within the Negro upper middle class; and Kautilya, who dedicated herself to the struggles of trade unionists and the nonwhite proletariat. The romance promoted a unity between moral and political transformation and a common effort between Asia, Africa, and black America to achieve spiritual unity. Renaissance critics were sharply divided over *Dark Princess.* Some viewed the novel as a melodramatic, spiritual fantasy, with a heavy dose of social realism. Others, like *Messenger* critic George S. Schuyler, termed it "a masterful piece of work" and a great "portrayal of the soul of our people."[42]

Du Bois was not content to focus solely on literary matters. With equal vigor, he attempted to influence Afro-American education—and again, his philosophy of cultural pluralism caused considerable debate within the Negro middle class. On the one hand, Du Bois firmly opposed the principle of racial segregation in schools. "The theory of the public school is that it should be the foundation of the democracy of the land," the *Crisis* stated in August 1921. "To separate children usually means their virtual separation through life. This means misunderstanding, friction; group, class, and racial hatred." When John Hopkins University initiated an extension course open solely to whites, Du Bois declared this "a tremendous surrender to provincialism and race discrimination."[43] But Du Bois also believed that wherever all-black educational institutions existed, they should be improved to provide quality instruction to black youth.

Speaking before an audience of three thousand in Philadelphia in 1923, Du Bois supported the existence of all-black Cheyney State Normal School. Ignorance was worse than Jim Crow, Du Bois declared, and blacks had to improve black institutions while struggling to achieve desegregation at white colleges. Many blacks charged Du Bois with inconsistency. Du Bois described the incident in *Dusk of Dawn:* "'It will be a Negro college!' shouted the audience, as though such a thing had never been heard of. 'It will be Segregation,' said a woman, who had given much of her life to furthering the fight for Negro equality. I can see her now, brown, tense, bitter, as she lashed me with the accusation of advocating the very segregation that I had been fighting." Du Bois was seen as retreating to the policies of Booker T. Washington. A group of black Baptist ministers contacted Du Bois, questioning whether he was "for Jim Crow schools or against them." Du Bois carefully outlined his position in his reply. "I believe that a 'Jim Crow' school system is the greatest possible menace to democracy and the greatest single hindrance to our advance in the United States. At the same time," Du Bois added, many all-black schools "are doing excellent work. . . . I believe in these schools in the sense that without them we could not have gotten our present education." Du Bois consistently maintained this perspective for the next four decades. In his July 1935 essay "Does the Negro Need Separate Schools?" Du Bois again urged Afro-Americans to achieve academic excellence within separate institutions, while supporting the long-term effort to abolish racism.[44]

Du Bois's defense of black colleges was always conditional: such institutions had to promote a liberal arts curriculum, acquainting students with Negro history, the humanities, and natural sciences. In 1908, Du Bois challenged Fisk University president James G. Merrill for introducing a modest vocational program including animal husbandry, farming, and mechanical arts at the college. "All this seemed to many of the alumni and to me as a Surrender and a Lie," Du Bois later reflected, "the surrender of college training to the current industrial fad, without the honest effort and equipment which this entailed." Du Bois and other Fisk alumni forced Merrill into retirement, and the college's "Department of Applied Sciences" was dropped in 1909. Du Bois continued to criticize the Hampton-Tuskegee model of industrial education. To Harvard professor Paul H. Hanus, Du Bois complained that his "chief difficulty with Hampton is that its ideals are low." Hampton's administrators "propose to develop the Negro race as a caste of efficient workers, [and] do not expect them to be co-workers in a modern cultured state." When Hampton Institute students initiated a strike against their administrators in October 1927, Du Bois aggressively supported the black youth. "There has always been at Hampton a degree of race discrimination and of repression that has been hateful and exasperating," the *Crisis* commented. "It has long been endured, just as beggars often endure the insult of impudent almsgiving. The time for an end to that endurance is surely at hand, unless we Negroes are willing to bring up our children in the same attitude of subserviency and uncomplaining submission to caste, which our fathers inherited from slavery."[45]

It was this deep concern for black higher education that engaged Du Bois in one of the most bitter educational confrontations of the 1920s. Yolande had been enrolled at Fisk in 1920, and she voiced no complaints about the college. But during a visit to the campus, a young undergraduate leader, George Streator, gave Du Bois "astonishing" details about the state of the institution. President Fayette McKenzie had surrendered "to Southern sentiment," Du Bois discovered, and "the student discipline at Fisk had retrograded so as to resemble in some aspects a reform school." Du Bois decided to speak at Fisk graduation exercises in 1924, "determined to do an unpleasant duty and do it thoroughly." In Fisk's chapel, Du Bois delivered a fiery address, "Diuturni Silenti," that denounced the McKenzie administration as undemocratic and accommodationist towards the white South. "In Fisk today," he declared, "discipline is choking freedom; threats are replacing inspiration, iron-clad rules, suspicion, tale bearing are almost universal." Du Bois was particularly outraged by McKenzie's acceptance of Jim Crow. The president had taken young black women from the school's glee club to perform "in a basement to Southern white men, while these men smoked and laughed and talked. If Erastus Cravath, the first president of this institution, knew that a thing like that had happened at Fisk University, he would, if it were any way possible, rise from the grave and protest against this disgrace and sacrilege." Any concession to the Hampton-Tuskegee "bargain" of second-class training had to be eliminated. "If any such bargain as I have outlined has been consciously or unconsciously, openly or secretly entered into by Fisk University," Du Bois thundered, "I would rather see every stone of its buildings leveled and every bit of its activity stopped before the Negro race consents."[46]

The conflict erupted immediately after Du Bois finished his speech and lasted one full year. Fisk students in the chapel "danced and celebrated in exuberant glee." Members of the board of trustees and alumni sympathetic to McKenzie charged that Du Bois "had done a cruel and unnecessary thing." The *Crisis* editor organized Fisk alumni in New York City and printed copies of a student publication banned by McKenzie. The following year Streator and several other student leaders were jailed when they mobilized a campus strike against the administration. Du Bois came to their defense in the *Crisis:* "Shall we surrender all control over the education of our children to those who despise Negroes and seek to hold them down by caste, or shall we drive this man and his methods from Fisk and from the colored educational field? . . . Men and women of Black America: *Let no decent Negro send his child to Fisk until Fayette McKenzie goes.*" Fisk alumni and other Negro educators rallied behind Du Bois and the student rebels. The trustees capitulated, and McKenzie was replaced by a liberal Quaker educator, Thomas E. Jones. Streater later was hired by Du Bois on the *Crisis* staff as business manager.[47]

Du Bois sensed that the Negro middle class did not fully appreciate the inherent duality of their culture and failed to comprehend the central role of education in giving young Afro-Americans a positive identity. *The Gift of Black Folk* provided a succinct survey of Afro-American contributions to American society. Particularly insightful was one chapter, "The Freedom of Womanhood," that outlined the special oppression of black women. In 1930, Du Bois wrote two brief pamphlets on African history and geography that offered roughly the same information as that given in *The Negro*. He hoped that black teachers would use these and other materials to instill a greater appreciation for the Negro's heritage. The clearest expression of this intention was Du Bois's lecture "The Field and Function of the Negro College," delivered at Fisk University in 1933. A black university must be centered on the particular economic, social, and political problems that confront Afro-Americans, Du Bois explained: "Starting with present conditions and using the facts and the knowledge of the present situation of American Negroes, the Negro university expands toward the possession and the conquest of all knowledge. It seeks from a beginning of the history of the Negro in America and in Africa to interpret all history; from a beginning of social development among Negro slaves and freedmen in America and Negro tribes and kingdoms in Africa, to interpret and understand the social development of all mankind in all ages."[48] There was no contradiction, for Du Bois, between black cultural pride and the campaign for desegregation—nor between the advocacy of Pan-Africanism and the pursuit of biracial democracy within higher education. Negroes would ultimately become full partners within American society through the destruction of Jim Crow—but not at the expense of sacrificing their heritage and special spiritual gifts.

Three factors explain Du Bois's resignation from the NAACP in 1934: his growing respect for Marxism and the Soviet Union; the impact of the depression on Black America, and especially upon the NAACP; and the emergence of Walter White as the Association's secretary in 1931. Du Bois spent six weeks in the Soviet Union in 1926 and was visibly impressed. He had never witnessed "such public interest in social matters on the part of men, women and children." There were the inevitable social problems that plagued any nation after revolution and civil war. "The people were poor and ill-clothed; food was scarce, and long lines stood hours to get their share," Du Bois observed. But the Soviet Union appeared to be making substantial progress. In the *Crisis,* Du Bois dismissed the claim that the Bolsheviks had a "dictatorship." All forms of government, Du Bois believed, were dictatorships of some form or another. "The real Russian question is: Can you make the worker and not the millionaire the center of modern power and culture? If you can, the Russian Revolution will sweep the world." From 1927 until 1934, the *Crisis* published a number of favorable comments about the Soviet government. In January and May 1928, Du Bois noted with approval the Soviet Union's support for world disarmament; in February 1929, he congratulated Russia's "ten years of reform"; in August 1929, the *Crisis* commented that "the collapse of Russia has been indefinitely postponed"; and in June 1930, Du Bois asked, "Why is it that May 1st is a day when all the world except Russia gets scared to death, mobilizes the police and keeps its soldiers ready in barracks?"[49]

Crisis subscribers noticed Du Bois's increasing radicalism, and some expressed disapproval. One white reader complained in November 1927, "It is deplorable that so excellent a magazine as the *Crisis* should have at its head a man who sneers at all forms of government—save the Soviet government of Russia." But Du Bois began to make a serious study of Marx's writings and moved further left. In May 1933, he observed that Marx was "a colossal genius of infinite sacrifice and monumental industry, and with a mind of extraordinary logical keenness and grasp." Marxism had a direct bearing on the liberation of Afro-Americans. Du Bois noted that "the shrill cry" of American Communists was not "listened to," but he believed that some form of "modified" Marxian philosophy did have relevance to the United States. "In the hearts of black laborers," Du Bois wrote, " . . . lie those ideals of democracy in politics and industry which may in time make the workers of the world effective dictators of civilization." In the summer of 1933, he taught a course, "Karl Marx and the Negro," at Atlanta University.[50]

Many white and black social democrats had been favorable to the Soviet Union in 1917–20. Randolph is only one example; Charles Edward Russell authored *Unchained Russia* in 1918, and Lincoln Steffens, returning from the young Soviet Union, announced, "I have been over into the future, and it works." But by the late 1920s, much of the Lyrical Left close to Du Bois had departed from radicalism. In 1929, for example, the *Crisis* published a harsh attack on Moulders Union leader John P. Frey's claim that Negroes experienced no greater discrimination from labor than other ethnic groups. Du Bois wrote that Frey's "whole thesis is untrue and unfair. The record of the American Federation of Labor toward the Negro is indefensible." Walling tried to mediate the dispute, and counseled Du Bois and Walter White to halt their criticisms of Frey and other union leaders. But privately in a letter to Frey, Walling condemned his black associates as "nasty reds. Labor's attitude on the color question is 100 percent o.k. and it has nothing to be ashamed of." Du Bois became more critical of the American Socialist party's failure to address racism and of its moderate views on class conflict. Speaking before a socialist educational forum in New York in February 1929, Du Bois charged that white social democrats "attribute" the lack of black support of their party "to the stupidity and backwardness of an undeveloped people who are not acquainted with the modern labor movement. . . . If American socialism cannot stand for the American Negro, the American Negro will not stand for American socialism." Four years later the *Crisis* editor observed that a young Socialist organization had "not only repudiated Socialism" but had changed "the name of their magazine 'Revolt.' Why not call it 'The Kiss'?"[51]

The impact of the Great Depression was devastating upon black America. As Langston Hughes commented, "The depression brought everybody down a peg or two. And the Negro had but few pegs to fall."[52] In early 1931, one out of seven black male workers in the North was jobless, and those fortunate enough to find work usually experienced sharp reductions in wages. In some sectors of the economy, especially manufacturing, black unemployment exceeded fifty percent. Many businesses dismissed black workers and hired whites in their place. And as the depression deepened, by early 1933, about half of the entire black labor force was unemployed, compared to one quarter of all white workers. The effect of the economic crisis on the *Crisis* and the NAACP was severe. The magazine was already losing money in the late 1920s, and in 1929 and 1930 the NAACP gave the *Crisis* almost five thousand dollars to continue publication. Soon Du Bois was placed on the NAACP payroll, and the Crisis Publication Company was created to protect the Association legally from the magazine's debts. The NAACP's board attempted to cut costs, and the *Crisis* began to be viewed as a liability rather than an asset. Ovington explained the new situation to Du Bois in December 1930. "Your personal liberty in handling the magazine" had created "many a bout" in the past, she noted, "and generally you won. But when you won the *Crisis* was more important than the Association. In the early days the magazine amounted to more than the organization." Ovington predicted that "the *Crisis* would either disappear or become distinctly an NAACP organ, and that means it must be under the secretary." Du Bois appreciated Ovington's concern but could not accept the conditions that she saw ahead. "I would not be at all interested in the work which you outline," Du Bois replied. "Either the *Crisis* is necessary to the work of the NAACP or it is not. . . . If it is necessary, then I have earned the right to conduct it under just and reasonable control."[53]

Du Bois's concerns increased when Walter White replaced Johnson as the Association's secretary in 1931. White was, in many ways, the most representative figure of the Talented Tenth. Born in 1893, White had graduated from Atlanta University in 1916 and became active in organizing the NAACP in Georgia. Because of his extremely fair complexion, White was able to conduct investigations of racial atrocities across the South. A talented writer, he established a reputation as a fine social critic during the Harlem Renaissance. Politically, White was a liberal reformer who opposed both racial segregation and radical Marxism. Although he had accompanied Du Bois to the 1921 Pan-African Congress, he did not share the elder man's enthusiasm for the movement. Culturally, White was closer to Alain Locke than to Du Bois in their debate over literary criticism; and on the issue of black education, White saw little redeeming value in separate schools of any kind, under any circumstances.[54] Du Bois commented on his *Autobiography:* "White could be one of the most charming of men. He was small in stature, appealing in approach, with a ready smile and a sense of humor. Also he was an indefatigable worker, who never seemed to tire." But like Charles S. Johnson, Locke, McKay, and many New Negro leaders of their generation, White believed that Du Bois was not in harmony with contemporary issues and trends. His polemics against black college administrators and renaissance authors seemed unnecessary, and even counterproductive. More important, Du Bois's support for the Soviet Union and espousal of Marx's writings was, in White's judgement, dangerous to the progress of the NAACP. Du Bois viewed their differences as both personal and political: "[White was] one of the most selfish men I ever knew. . . . He seemed really to believe that his personal interests and the interests of his race and organization were identical."[55]

Du Bois's weakness as a political tactician was never more apparent than in 1930–34. Du Bois urged the NAACP to develop a meaningful economic program to assist Afro-Americans during the depression. In May 1930, the *Crisis* repeated that the "first job" of the Association was "to fight color discrimination," but it also stated that "our fight for *economic equality*" must include economic cooperatives "and socialization of wealth." Du Bois believed that governmental and private agencies should be pressured to respond to the economic crisis. "The United States government ought to make appropriations for relief," he wrote in 1931. "There ought to be a national dole distributed without reference to the color line, and wherever there are considerable numbers of Negroes they ought to be represented on the Executive Boards of the distributing agency." While Du Bois was largely preoccupied with developing strategies to combat black unemployment, White quietly consolidated his position in the Association. In 1931, Du Bois tried unsuccessfully to persuade NAACP board members to permit the general membership to exercise greater power in the selection of future members. When this proposal died, Du Bois spoke directly to his constituents. The Association had to devise "a positive program rather than mere negative attempt to avoid segregation and discrimination," the *Crisis* reported in July 1932. "The interests of the masses are the interests of this Association, and the masses have got to voice themselves through it." Du Bois called for a general reformation of the organization and a decentralization of power from its executive body.[56]

However, Joel Spingarn, who then served as NAACP president, had become convinced that Du Bois "was turning radical." As Du Bois related in *Dusk of Dawn*, Spingarn used "his power and influence in order to curb my acts and forestall any change of program of the Association on my part." White secured the appointment of members on the board's nominating committee "who unfortunately were either absolutely reactionary in their social and economic outlook or basically ignorant." White also placed a young journalist, Roy Wilkins, as head of the Crisis Publishing Company. In effect, by late 1933, Du Bois lacked any institutional leverage to replace White, or to push the Association toward a more progressive agenda. Abram L. Harris, then a professor at Howard University, warned Du Bois in January 1934: "You can't rely upon the James Weldon Johnsons and the Walter Whites for any new program, for they represent just those values that I think stand in the way of thinking on the present relation of the Negro to world forces. . . . Now if this thing leads into a fight that brings into existence a new movement, there is no one to lead it but yourself. Should this come to pass I feel that you are going to [have] a much harder fight on your hands than you did against Booker T. Washington."[57]

White's opportunity to remove Du Bois from the Association came in January 1934, when the *Crisis* printed the essay "Segregation." Du Bois attempted to distinguish institutional racism, or "racial discrimination," from the existence of separate racial institutions. "It must be remembered that in the last quarter of a century, the advance of the colored people has been mainly in the lines where they themselves, working by and for themselves have accomplished the greatest advance." Du Bois argued that blacks should use "voluntary segregation" to establish black economic cooperatives and other enterprises to address black poverty and to save black schools. Black Americans "must stop being stampeded by the word segregation."

White's rejoinder appeared in the March 1934 issue of the magazine. He claimed that Du Bois's editorial had been used "by certain government officials at Washington to hold up admission to Negroes to one of the government-financed relief projects." The NAACP had always "resolutely fought" any form of racial segregation. "To accept the status of separateness," White declared, " . . . means inferior accommodations and a distinctly inferior position in the national and communal life, [and] means spiritual atrophy for the group segregated." Du Bois's replies, printed in the March and April issues, were sharply worded. "Let the NAACP and every upstanding Negro pound at the closed gates of opportunity and denounce caste and segregation," Du Bois explained; "but let us not punish our own children under the curious impression that we are punishing our white oppressors. . . . Let us not sit down and do nothing for self-defense and self-organization just because we are too stupid or too distrustful of ourselves to take vigorous and decisive action." And in a devastating comment, Du Bois reminded his readers that White was personally unaffected by Jim Crow: "in the first place, Walter White is white. He has more white companions and friends than colored."[58]

Du Bois won this skirmish, but he lost the battle. White's assertion that racial integration was crucial for obtaining government-sponsored projects was false. Equally untrue was the implication that the Association had always opposed racial separation—its endorsement of a Jim Crow officers' school during World War I was but one contrary example. Nothing in Du Bois's arguments represented a fundamental break with his cultural pluralist orientation. However, the general perception of the Du Bois-White debate was that the *Crisis* editor had become a later-day proponent of the Tuskegee philosophy of racial segregation. Du Bois was "slipping" as a leader, noted the Philadelphia *Tribune*. "The Editor of an official organ must agree with the policies of his organization. . . . Because of his former efforts in a glorious cause he should be permitted to resign." The *Chicago Defender* declared that the "Race Champion" had decided to "travel the path of least resistance." George Schuyler, then a columnist for the *Pittsburgh Courier*, condemned Du Bois's personal comments against White, declaring that the black editor had fought "like a punch drunk pugilist despairing of victory." Du Bois attempted to answer his critics and repeated his belief that "segregation was evil, and should be systematically fought." But Jim Crow would exist for decades to come, and black Americans must "make the best of their life" by collective and cooperative organization. The Association's board ended the debate in May 1934, by voting essentially to censure Du Bois: "The *Crisis* is the organ of the Association and no salaried officer of the Association shall criticize the policy, work, or officers of the Association in the pages of the *Crisis*." Du Bois promptly submitted his resignation, reminding the board sharply, "The *Crisis* never was and never was intended to be an organ of the Association in the sense of simply reflecting its official opinion."[59]

Du Bois sadly departed, knowing that the organization was "in a time of crisis and change, without a program, without effective organization, without executive officers who have either the ability or disposition to guide the (NAACP) in the right direction." Why did Du Bois refuse to initiate a democratic campaign against the Association's leadership? First, Du Bois had never been a "mass leader." In a humorous but prophetic *Crisis* essay published in 1929, Du Bois complained that he had extreme difficulty remembering "the names which are most illogically and inconsequently attached to human beings." This problem plagued Du Bois throughout his life. Colleagues at Atlanta University agreed that Du Bois "very seldom thought in terms of individuals" and tended to forget the names of students and former associates. Second, Du Bois did not believe that a mass black movement to the left of the NAACP could be successful. In August 1934, attorney Harrison S. Jackson contacted Du Bois concerning the creation of a National Negro Congress that would "promulgate racial solidarity and strength along our political, social, religious and economic lines." Du Bois's shortsighted response was, "I do not think that the time has yet come when such a movement is practical or advisable." However, Randolph recognized the opportunity to build a "united front of all Negro organizations." With the support of black Communist leader James W. Ford, New Negro intellectuals Alain Locke and Langston Hughes, and representatives from black workers' organizations, Randolph forged a militant formation in 1935–36. At the initial National Negro Congress convention in February 1936, in Chicago, delegates from nearly 600 organizations representing 1.2 million members established a political force that, unlike the NAACP, was based on the black working class.[60]

Another factor that limited Du Bois's maneuvers against the NAACP leadership was his isolation from the organized left. In the spring of 1931, nine young black men were falsely convicted of raping two white women in Scottsboro, Alabama. The NAACP was heavily involved in the legal defense of the "Scottsboro boys" and attacked Communist agitation around the case. "The ultimate object of the Communists," Du Bois insisted in September 1931, "was naturally not merely nor chiefly to save the boys accused at Scottsboro; it was to make this case a center of agitation to expose the helpless condition of Negroes, and to prove that anything less than the radical Communist program could not emancipate them." Periodically throughout the depression Du Bois criticized the American Communist party's tactics. In 1936, Du Bois was widely quoted—out of context—as claiming "the tactics of the Communist party in America in the past had 'given me a pain in the neck.'" But in August 1937, he argued in the *Pittsburgh Courier* against the Communist party's position on economic cooperatives. And in *Dusk of Dawn*, Du Bois explained his position in the 1930s as standing "between paths diverging to extreme communism and violence on the one hand, and extreme reaction toward plutocracy on the other." He believed that Communists ignored the intense racism of the white proletariat. "American Negroes were asked to accept a complete dogma without question or alteration," Du Bois wrote. "It was first of all emphasized that all racial thought and racial segregation must go and that Negroes must put themselves blindly under the dictatorship of the Communist Party." Given Du Bois's distance from the Marxist left, he still believed that the Negro middle class possessed the inherent capacity to pursue a socialist economic program for the black majority. "The charge of the Communists that the present set-up of Negro America is that of the petit-bourgeois minority dominating a helpless black proletariat, and surrendering to white profiteers is simply a fantastic falsehood," Du Bois stated in 1931. "The attempt to dominate Negro Americans by purely capitalistic ideas died with Booker T. Washington."[61]

At the invitation of Hope, Du Bois returned to Georgia and became chairman of the Department of Sociology at Atlanta University. Leaving the *Crisis* "was like giving up a child," Du Bois observed. Yet even the Association board recognized what Du Bois's twenty-four years of service had meant to the black freedom movement. Accepting his letter of resignation, the board commented: "He created, what never existed before, a Negro intelligentsia, and many who have never read a word of his writings are his spiritual disciples and descendants. Without him the Association could never have been what it was and is. . . . We shall be the poorer for his loss, in intellectual stimulus, and in the searching analysis of the vital problems of the American Negro; no one in the Association can fill his place with the same intellectual grasp."[62]

7

THE GREAT DEPRESSION AND WORLD WAR

This the American black man knows: his fight here is a fight to the finish. Either he dies or wins. If he wins it will be by no subterfuge or evasion of amalgamation. He will enter modern civilization here in America as a black man on terms of perfect and unlimited equality with any white man, or he will enter not at all. Either extermination root and branch, or absolute equality. There can be no compromise. This is the last great battle of the West.

W. E. B. Du Bois,
Black Reconstruction in America, 1935

With the clear "understanding" with President John Hope that his appointment to Atlanta University was "for life" or during his "ability to work," Du Bois returned to the South in 1934. Many of Du Bois's friends viewed his new position as being tantamount to retirement. "Having been in the thick of controversy and the fighting out of race issues for the last thirty years, you deserve an opportunity for rest and repose which you should embrace," suggested George W. Crawford, a former Niagarite and NAACP leader.[1] Du Bois had other ideas. He became a vigorous teacher, assigning one paper per week to his graduate students. Students later described him as a hard "task master." Although students were awed by his reputation and were reluctant at first to approach him, Du Bois became known as a "charming" and "thoughtful" instructor and colleague.[2] The bulk of Du Bois's activities during his second period at Atlanta University, from 1934 to 1944, involved a tremendous number of research projects, academic publications, public lectures, and popular essays for the Negro press. Du Bois's unfinished projects or unpublished works during these years, from "The Negro and Social

Reconstruction" to a book-length manuscript "The Sorcery of Color," were substantial.[3] The works he published during this period—including *Black Reconstruction in America, Black Folk Then And Now, Dusk of Dawn, Color and Democracy: Colonies and Peace,* the initiation of the journal *Phylon,* and more than 350 newspaper articles—would comprise the life's work of many scholars. During this decade, and especially in the war years, Du Bois clarified his concepts of democracy, socialism, and the nexus between peace and decolonialism. The political direction he assumed in the last twenty years of his public life was cast at this time.

Although Du Bois had written previously on the Reconstruction era, he did not give "continuous and concentrated time" to the new manuscript until 1930. In 1931 he received a grant from the Rosenwald Fund to work on the text, and in 1933 the Carnegie Corporation donated one thousand dollars to the research project. Du Bois revised the massive manuscript several times and at one point deleted 250 pages from the book. Publisher Alfred Harcourt was so "distressed" with Du Bois's extensive changes in the book's page proofs that *Black Reconstruction* nearly went unpublished. Du Bois forwarded a check for $250 to cover some of the additional corrections and explained to Harcourt that his "method of writing is a method of 'afterthoughts' . . . This is the crowning of my creative process."[4] The delays and extensive revisions were worthwhile. Du Bois's *Black Reconstruction* was more than a social history of the black experience: it was a great work of literature. Sterling Brown, author of *Southern Road* (1932) and then a young literature professor at Howard University, reviewed the book's galleys in 1934. Brown commented favorably: *"Black Reconstruction* is a first rate piece of work that has for a long time needed doing. . . . [It] belongs with the best historical interpretations I have read. I think it belongs with the best of your writings."[5]

Like the *Suppression of the African Slave-Trade* and *John Brown, Black Reconstruction* assumed a moral and political critique of the historical limitations of American democracy. "The true significance of slavery in the United States to the whole social development of America lay in the ultimate relationship of slaves to democracy," Du Bois observed. "What were to be the limits of democratic control in the United States? If all labor, black as well as white, became free—were given schools and the right to vote— what control could or should be set to the power and action of these laborers?" Du Bois argued that the North "went to war without the slightest idea of freeing the slaves." But the black Southern "proletariat" forced the question of general emancipation by covert and overt activities against the planter oligarchy. The slaves essentially staged a "general strike" against the master class, and hundreds of thousands of blacks joined the war effort against the South. After the conflict, black leaders created the institutions of effective democracy for both races across the region. The franchise was extended to poor white males and black freedmen. Public school systems were established, which in turn led to the creation of Negro colleges and industrial institutes. In great detail, Du Bois described the political and social experiences of the Reconstruction period in every southern state. He emphasized the educational and political backgrounds of black leaders and effectively refuted the charge that Reconstruction governments were plagued by corruption and graft.

The influence of Marx is apparent in *Black Reconstruction,* but the book cannot accurately be described as a Marxist analysis in the strictest sense. As Herbert Aptheker commented, the study "tends to ignore the former nonslaveholding whites who were landed—i.e., the yeomanry . . . and is weak, too, insofar as it accepts the concept of a monolithic white South from the pre–Civil War period to Reconstruction." Another theoretical difficulty involves Du Bois's repeated use of "caste," a static social category, in his definition of institutional racism, which is dynamic and dialectically related to the means of production of a given social formation. Conversely, *Black Reconstruction* broke new ground in many areas. It examined the distinct social history and class interests of poor whites after 1865 and illustrated the crucial role of racism in protecting the prerogatives of capital. Du Bois noted the importance of social class divisions inside the black community. Many black leaders "were petty bourgeois, seeking to climb into wealth. . . . In the minds of very few of them was there any clear and distinct plan for the development of a laboring class into a position of power and mastery over the modern industrial state." Du Bois observed that the real failure of Reconstruction was "the revolutionary suppression not only of Negro suffrage but of the economic development of Negro and white labor." Only in the 1880s did "white labor in the South [begin] to realize that they had lost a great opportunity, that when they united to disfranchise the black laborer they had cut the voting power of the laboring class in two." Finally, *Black Reconstruction* included a brief but devastating critique of the racism in American historiography: "The whole history of Reconstruction has with few exceptions been written by passionate believers in the inferiority of the Negro. The whole body of facts concerning what the Negro actually said and did . . . is masked in such a cloud of charges, exaggeration and biased testimony, that most students . . . simply [repeat] all the current legends of black buffoons in legislature, golden spittoons for fieldhands, bribery and extravagance on an unheard-of scale, and the collapse of civilization until an outraged nation rose in wrath and ended the ridiculous travesty."[6]

The initial public response to *Black Reconstruction* was quite positive. The book received favorable reviews in the *New York Times, New York Herald-Tribune,* the *Literary Digest* and other publications. Even Du Bois's critics were enthusiastic. Walter White forwarded a copy of the book to Eleanor Roosevelt, explaining to Du Bois that he "wanted her to get this more accurate picture of the Reconstruction period so that she would understand more clearly the southern scene as it is today." Charles S. Johnson termed the book "a brilliant brief" against "a vast conspiracy of silence." And Emmett J. Scott contacted Du Bois, declaring that "the colored peoples of the world owe you a sincere debt of gratitude for your monumental work." Within several months, however, a negative reaction against *Black Reconstruction* had begun. Historian Avery O. Craven incorrectly charged that Du Bois's work failed to employ primary source materials. Du Bois had written a distorted and bitter text, using "abolition propaganda and the biased statements of partisan politicians." The *American Historical Review* did not even review *Black Reconstruction*. During its first full year after publication, the book sold only 376 copies.[7]

Directly related to *Black Reconstruction* were a series of articles written by Du Bois in 1935–37 on the relationship between racism and democracy in the context of the Great Depression. Perhaps the most controversial was "A Negro Nation Within the Nation," published in June 1935. "The colored people of America are coming to face the fact quite calmly that most white Americans do not like them, and are planning neither for their survival, nor for their definite future if it involves free, self-assertive modern manhood," Du Bois declared. Afro-Americans had no choice except to develop their own program for economic development along collective lines. "With the use of their political power, their power as consumers . . . Negroes can develop in the United States an economic nation within a nation, able to work through inner cooperation, to found its own institutions, to educate its genius, and at the same time, without mob violence or extremes of race hatred." Du Bois insisted that such "segregation" did not mean the abandonment of the goal of full equality or the possibility of a future alliance of working people that transcended racial boundaries. Speaking before the National Baptist Convention in September 1935, Du Bois observed that Communist and Socialist concepts were of value in addressing blacks' economic problems. "But we cannot stop here, for the difficulty with us, even more than with the mass of the whites, is that our labor classes have neither the education, the technique, or the experience" to lead a program of radical economic reform. Du Bois insisted: "therefore, we must seek to raise a Talented Tenth among us who would become the intelligent leaders and directors of our masses. We must guard against the difficulty that such a Talented Tenth may easily think of itself as the object of its own efforts, and think of the masses of Negroes as existing for the aggrandizement of the few. . . . The [elite] must look upon themselves as the servants to do the work for the great mass of the uneducated and inexperienced."[8]

Although many of his contemporaries viewed Du Bois's call for "group segregation" and cooperative economics a departure from his previous policies, it was largely a restatement of many long-held views. He firmly believed that the Negro middle class could lead black workers to a moderate socialist program. In a series of articles in the *Pittsburgh Courier,* Du Bois explained that the entire working class could "make one assault upon poverty and race hate." But to begin this process, black Americans had to build their own separate organizations along cooperative lines. The black working class, left alone, could not advance itself; a "saving nucleus of a conscious dictatorship of intelligence" was necessary. Blacks must "try in every legal way" to achieve desegregation but not at the expense of their cultural and historical identity.[9] Du Bois's position was a synthesis of cultural pluralism and cooperative economics, balanced by a more radical perspective on the tasks of the Talented Tenth. To many younger black activists and intellectuals, notably Ralph Bunche, E. Franklin Frazier, and George Streator, Du Bois's arguments seemed contradictory and self-defeating. "There is no such thing as a separate consumers' economy," Streator informed Du Bois in April 1935. "You count on the Negro middle class to usher in this cooperation. What you need to do, Dr. Du Bois, is to cease dulling your vision to the fact that the Negro middle class is after all, a lousy minority bourgeoisie of which your late associates at the NAACP should have given you ample proof." Du Bois replied that this strategy was simply "to get Negroes thinking from the consumers' point of view, which is the only way to gauge their real power." Du Bois believed that the rise of black cooperativism would ultimately establish a unity between workers of both races. Streator was unconvinced: "You are in the same camp with McDonald, [Norman] Thomas . . . and the Mensheviki of Kerensky's brief regime. You want security, prestige, and the good life, and socialism without a sacrifice. And you are easily fooled by flatterers."[10]

The manuscript that best expressed Du Bois's political perspective during the depression was "The Negro and Social Reconstruction." Alain Locke was in charge of a textbook series on the Afro-American experience, which was funded by the Carnegie Corporation. In March 1935, Locke requested a contribution from Du Bois, and within two months the initial draft was completed. The thirty-thousand-word essay was a radical reinterpretation of black social history from the nineteenth century through the 1930s. It described Booker T. Washington in unflattering terms—"an opportunist, slow but keen-witted, with high ideals"—but also explained Tuskegee's role in cooperating with capitalist interests. "He hated caste and lawlessness and wanted the best for his people," Du Bois observed, "but he believed implicitly in his economic program and made the fatal mistake of trying to forestall criticism from Negroes and to disparage, if not to oppose Negro colleges." Du Bois illustrated the strategic weaknesses of a black capitalist strategy that had "no chance" for success in the future. "The old idea of accumulating small capital by thrift and going into business is largely unreal today." Black Americans had to initiate a transitional strategy toward socialism that made political sense within the system of Jim Crow. Toward this end, Du Bois again advocated the development of cooperatives. He carefully insisted that group segregation was a tactical maneuver: "if we move back to increased segregation it is for the sake of added strength to abolish race discrimination; if we move back to racial pride and loyalty, it is that eventually we may move forward to a great ideal of humanity and a patriotism that spans the world." Du Bois argued that the New Deal program of Franklin Roosevelt could not be depended upon to advance the material interests of workers and blacks, despite many meaningful reforms. And he issued a stern word of warning to the Talented Tenth: "if the leading Negro classes cannot assume and bear the uplift of their own proletariat, they are doomed for time and eternity."[11]

Locke reviewed the manuscript in early June 1935, judging it "interesting and adequate." But Du Bois heard nothing about the publication for several months. In February 1936, Du Bois wrote Locke, "What on earth has become of our booklets?" Du Bois finally received an honorarium for the manuscript, but Locke requested extensive revisions. He also suggested the deletion of Du Bois's "Basic American Negro Creed," a summary statement that was later published in *Dusk of Dawn,* on the "grounds" that it was "direct propaganda." Du Bois's final draft, submitted in May 1936, was deemed generally acceptable by Locke. However, Locke waited until Du Bois was out of the country in later 1936 before sending to Atlanta University a final letter of rejection. Although "The Negro and Social Reconstruction" is a landmark of black radical social theory, it was not published until 1985.[12]

Another major research project that occupied much of Du Bois's time and energy was the *Encyclopedia of the Negro.* With the initial support of the Phelps-Stokes Fund, a tentative organization for the *Encyclopedia* had developed by 1934. Du Bois was the principal figure in the project, but other scholars who served on the early board of directors included Monroe N. Work, James Weldon Johnson, Charles H. Wesley, Alain Locke, and Arthur A. Schomburg. Du Bois approached Edwin R. Embree, director of the Rosenwald Fund, to provide support for the *Encyclopedia.* "In this time of crisis and inquiry to postpone such an undertaking for half a generation or more, would be not only unwise but calamitous," Du Bois insisted. The case of "the Negro problem" required an "authoritative collection of the opinion and historical judgements" of leading scholars. Embree admitted that Du Bois had stated the case "clearly and persuasively" but refused to recommend any appropriation to the project. Du Bois contacted George Foster Peabody, Roscoe Pound, the dean of the Harvard Law School, and a number of philanthropic and academic leaders for financial assistance and support, but received few substantial commitments. Du Bois and his close friend, sociology professor Ira De A. Reid of Atlanta University, tried to obtain funding from the Federal Writers' Project, but had no success. By May 1937, Du Bois had completed a manuscript of 125 pages that listed potential topics for the *Encyclopedia of the Negro*. He was still optimistic about the project. In his correspondence with Anson Phelps Stokes, Du Bois projected a four-volume encyclopedia comprising "2,800 pages and 2,240,000 words."[13]

Du Bois perceived the *Encyclopedia of the Negro* as both a work of scholarship and a statement against racism. "An editorial board under my leadership would, of course, make certain assumptions concerning Negroes" that many "still regard as unproven," Du Bois noted in the late 1930s. "These assumptions would revolve around the belief that black folk are human beings, with reactions essentially the same as those of other human beings." Curiously, some Afro-Americans doubted the wisdom of the project. E. Franklin Frazier criticized Du Bois's prospectus in November 1936. The list of tentative contributors seemed to include too many "so-called 'big Negroes'" and "interracial 'politicians,'" Frazier noted. "The present syllabus should be discarded and a group of competent scholars should be called together to plan the general organization of the *Encyclopedia*." More hostile was the opinion of Carter G. Woodson. In January 1932, Du Bois requested Woodson's participation in the project. Woodson curtly replied that his Association for the Study of Negro Life and History also planned to "bring out its Encyclopedia Africana by the end of 1933. We welcome competition, because it is the spice of life." Woodson never completed his encyclopedia project. However, in May 1936, he wrote a strident attack on Du Bois's efforts in the Baltimore *Afro-American*. Du Bois explained to Professor Robert Park that Woodson was "angry," because he mistakenly believed that his idea for the encyclopedia has been usurped. "I conceived the idea in 1908," Du Bois recalled, but "my project never went far enough to give me any claim to exclusive occupation of the field." After repeated delays, an extensive bibliography was completed for the *Encyclopedia* in late 1942 and published by the Phelps-Stokes Fund in March 1945. No substantial funding ever became available, and the project became dormant until late 1956, when it was revived at the suggestion of Charles H. Wesley.[14]

More successful was the initiation of *Phylon*, a social science journal. In 1935 Du Bois approached President Hope with the concept of publishing a quarterly containing "valuable literary and scientific articles of permanent value." Hope died in February 1936, "without coming to any conclusion concerning this quarterly." Hope's successor as Atlanta University president, Rufus E. Clement, was never enthusiastic about the project. In May 1937, Du Bois and several young colleagues, including Rayford Logan and Ira De A. Reid, met with Charles S. Johnson at Fisk to plan the quarterly journal with joint control between their respective universities. Tentatively titled *Race and Culture*, the journal was to receive one thousand dollars annually from Fisk and Atlanta Universities, and it would solicit outside funding. Johnson later had second thoughts about the quarterly, and Fisk withdrew from the project. A proposal to the General Education fund in 1939 was also unsuccessful. Nevertheless, the first *Phylon* issue appeared in early 1940, with Du Bois as editor-in-chief. In his initial editorial, Du Bois observed that the quarterly would "proceed from the point of view and the experience of the black folk where we live and work, to the wider world." The Carnegie Corporation donated one thousand dollars to the "First Phylon Institute," a conference on race relations held in April 1941 at Atlanta University. During Du Bois's editorship in 1940–44, *Phylon* was established as a leading black social science publication, ranking with Woodson's *Journal of Negro History* and the *Journal of Negro Education*. [15]

Du Bois continued to play an active role shaping the direction of black education in the 1930s and early 1940s. In January 1935, Du Bois was consulted on the selection of the assistant to the superintendent for Negro pupils in the Los Angeles public school system; in April 1937 he spoke before the House Committee on Education in Washington, D.C., as a critic of Jim Crow schools in Georgia; and in September 1941, he reviewed materials on "Negro achievements" designed for the elementary school curriculum in Chicago. [16] Du Bois thought of "education" in the broadest possible social context. In black newspapers, he urged the development of a "Negro Book-of-the Year Club" and the widest distribution of the latest works by Negro intellectuals. Under Reid's direction, Du Bois participated in a "People's College" at Atlanta University that offered evening classes to Afro-American workers at a fee of only ten cents. In 1938, Du Bois served as a consultant for the Columbia Broadcasting System's "Americans All—Immigrants All" radio series. Several years later, he even made tentative plans to reestablish the defunct American Negro Academy. [17]

But it was in the field of black higher education that Du Bois exercised the greatest influence. At the fiftieth anniversary of Du Bois's graduation from Fisk University, he presented a commencement address, "The Revelation of Saint Orgne the Damned." "Orgne" was an anagram for "Negro." Du Bois urged students to reject the materialism of the dominant capitalist society, and he reaffirmed his support for "self-segregation" and "group culture." But significantly, he emphasized that Afro-American Negroes had to "examine anew the basic thesis of democracy":

> Democracy does not really mean to say that all men are equal; but it does assert that every individual who is a part of the state must have his experience and his necessities regarded by that state if the state survive. . . . Democracy then forms not merely a reservoir of complaint but of ability, hidden otherwise in poverty and ignorance. It is the astonishing result of an age of enlightenment, when the ruling classes of the world are the children of peasants, slaves and guttersnipes, that

151

> the still dominant thought is that education and ability are not today
> matters of chance, but mainly of individual desert and effort. . . . De-
> mocracy does not and cannot mean freedom. On the contrary it means
> coercion. It means submission of the individual will to the general will
> and it is justified in this compulsion only if the will is general and not
> the will of specific privilege.[18]

Du Bois continued to correlate the issues of black education and democratic social transformation in subsequent essays and lectures. In his 1939
article "The Position of the Negro and the American Social Order" Du Bois
urged blacks to denounce capitalist values and to develop strategies to
achieve fundamental socioeconomic change. At Lincoln University in January 1941, Du Bois denounced segregated colleges as "unfortunate," "idiot-
ic," and a political consequence of those upper classes that dominated black
life and labor. But he reminded his audience: "You have an extraordinary
opportunity . . . for planning and carrying out through methods by which,
without hatred, agitation, or upheaval, you can show how a minority can not
simply repeat the accomplishments of a majority, but can show the majority
the way of life." In November 1941, Du Bois proposed to the presidents of
seventeen black colleges a comprehensive program to study "the social and
economic conditions" of Negro working people. With modest support from
the Carnegie Corporation, Du Bois projected an ambitious series of conferences across the South "aimed toward the economic guidance of the Negro." Despite the lack of support from President Clement, a conference of
"Negro Land Grant Colleges" was held at Atlanta University in April 1943.[19]

Du Bois's major manuscripts of the late 1930s were the unpublished "Sorcery of Color," *Black Folk Then and Now: An Essay in the History and
Sociology of the Negro Race,* printed in 1939, and his autobiographical *Dusk
of Dawn,* which appeared in 1940. Although *Black Folk Then And Now* was
a survey of African and Afro-American history similar to *The Negro,* it reflected a distinctly Marxian perspective. Du Bois informed his old friend
Charles Edward Russell that the manuscript contained "enough of Marx
lugged in to make some of my friends unhappy." Nine chapters were devoted to Africa's ancient history and culture, the transatlantic slave trade,
and the rise of the abolitionist movement. But much of the book included a
critique of black American working people's struggles for democratic rights,
quality education, and land tenure. *Black Folk Then And Now* went much
further than *The Negro* in placing the movements for black equality within a
social context of struggles between the world's proletariat and the capitalist
class.

Dusk of Dawn was noteworthy in several respects. Although Du Bois
advocated the tactic of the Negro "segregated economy," he stressed that
the hegemony of the bourgeoisie was "breaking down." "We have lived to

see the collapse of capitalism," Du Bois observed. Negroes could not "follow the class structure of America. . . . We cannot permit ourselves simply to be the victims of exploitation and social exclusion." He criticized his earlier concept of the Talented Tenth as a "panacea" that had been made irrelevant by "the whole economic trend of the world." Du Bois expressed the hope that the Negro middle class could still assume a critical role in radical social change, but he also made stern criticisms of its ambiguous historical relationship with black workers and the poor: "The upper class Negro has almost never been nationalistic. He has never planned or thought of a Negro state or a Negro church or a Negro school. This solution has always been a thought up-surging from the mass, because of pressure which they could not withstand and which compelled a racial institution or chaos."[20]

The productivity of Du Bois during his years at Atlanta was quite remarkable. But equally impressive were his extensive informal contacts with scholars, labor leaders, workers, and teachers. When Gunnar Myrdal began preparations for his massive study *An American Dilemma,* Du Bois reviewed his basic memorandum for the project and delivered several constructive criticisms. Twenty-five-year-old John Hope Franklin, then a history instructor at St. Augustine's College in North Carolina, requested assistance from Du Bois in the preparation of an academic paper in 1940. Black social scientist Wilson Record, at age twenty-four, received help from Du Bois in developing a "bibliography on minority group strategies." Du Bois took a special interest in the early artistic career of Shirley Graham, whose father had been a strong supporter of Du Bois. In 1934, Du Bois assisted Graham during the writing of her master's thesis on "The Survivals of Africanism in Modern Music." Throughout the 1930s and 1940s they continued to correspond, and a warm friendship developed between them. With the passage of time, many of Du Bois's former critics came to appreciate his work. A. Philip Randolph, who had become the most prominent leader of the civil rights movement, informed Du Bois in 1935 that black Pullman workers were grateful for his continued support. And with the 1939 publication of E. Franklin Frazier's classic *Negro Family in the United States,* the black sociologist wrote Du Bois: "In this book I have noted your pioneer contribution to the study of the Negro family. . . . We are building upon a tradition inaugurated by you."[21]

One of the major reasons Du Bois regretted leaving the *Crisis* was his inability to reach large numbers of black Americans. In December 1935, *Pitts-*

burgh Courier publisher Robert L. Vann asked Du Bois to contribute a regular column for his newspaper. Du Bois quickly consented, and in early February 1936 his weekly series "A Forum of Fact and Opinion" began. The column ran for two years in the *Pittsburgh Courier,* and from October 1939 through October 1944, Du Bois's "As the Crow Flies" weekly series appeared in Harlem's *Amsterdam News.* The non-*Crisis* journalistic writings of Du Bois have received, to date, little analysis. But through these popular essays, Du Bois spoke to several million Afro-Americans over a period of eight years. They illustrate better than any other single source the evolution of Du Bois's political thought during the depression and World War II.

Du Bois's attitude toward Roosevelt and the New Deal, for example, changed markedly during these years. The first mention of Roosevelt in the *Crisis* came in October 1920. Du Bois pointedly criticized the New York Democrat as "impudent" and a "lackey" of the Wilson administration. Eleven years later, the *Crisis* editor predicted that Roosevelt "is about to buy the Democratic nomination." Throughout 1932 and 1933, Du Bois made critical comments about Roosevelt. "Mr. Roosevelt's record on the Negro problem is clear," stated the *Crisis* in August 1932. "He hasn't any."[22] Du Bois still believed that neither major party had any solutions to the crisis of the economy and racism. In March 1936, Du Bois's column in the *Pittsburgh Courier* charged that the New Deal had done "nothing for the tenant-farmer and sharecropper." However, in September 1936, Du Bois sharply criticized the Republican presidential candidate Alfred Landon. The following year Du Bois endorsed Roosevelt's unsuccessful "court-packing plan" to reduce the influence of conservatives on the Supreme Court. In 1940, Du Bois openly urged Afro-Americans to support Roosevelt's program. The New Deal had begun to address the problem of poverty, Du Bois insisted in the *Amsterdam News,* while the Republicans had not. By 1944, Du Bois's support for Roosevelt was enthusiastic but not completely uncritical. Roosevelt had pursued the goal of socialism "in such vast undertakings as the TVA; in providing jobs for the unemployed during the depression, and seeking to aid works of art and literature," Du Bois argued. "President Roosevelt has openly championed the cause and rights of union labor and fought race discrimination in employment. . . . If Roosevelt is defeated it will be because of his championship of organized labor and the Negro."[23]

The modification in Du Bois's assessment of the New Deal coincided with his seven-month global journey in June-December 1936, funded largely by the Oberlaender Trust. Technically, the Oberlaender proposal called for Du Bois to study German and Austrian school systems and their relation to industrial development. But Du Bois also used the opportunity to travel around the globe "during this most critical time perhaps in the world's history." Much of Du Bois's time was spent in Nazi Germany. He was in the country during the frightening spectacle of the 1936 Olympic games. Du Bois viewed Hitler as the latest "crude but logical exponent of white world race philosophy [that] since the Conference of Berlin in 1884" had culminated in the partition of Africa. He detested the regime's vulgarly racist and anti-Semitic philosophy, which he described as surpassing "in vindictive cruelty and public insult anything I have ever seen; and I have seen much." In his 19 December 1936 column in the *Pittsburgh Courier,* Du Bois declared, "There has been no tragedy in modern times equal in its awful effects to the fight on the Jew in Germany. It is an attack on civilization, comparable only to such horrors as the Spanish Inquisition and the African slave trade." Du Bois understood that fascism rested upon systematic terror, but like many social democrats, he had difficulty relating the Nazi regime with the dominant interest of monopoly capital. Because Du Bois tended to define socialism largely as state ownership of production, he was not clearly able to discern the broad prerogatives of industrialists and finance capitalists who supported the Nazi state. He also drew the highly debatable conclusion that the majority of Germans supported "Adolph Hitler today."[24]

Du Bois's travels through the Soviet Union provided a welcome change from fascist Germany. He was astonished by the economic and social development of the socialist state since his last visit a decade before. The nation seemed "sure of itself," he wrote later. "In Moscow the streets were widening and the city had crossed the river. . . . The folk were better dressed and food was much more plentiful. There were no unemployed, and all the children were in school; factories, shops and libraries had multiplied." In the *Pittsburgh Courier,* Du Bois wrote: "Russia says that the bread for the million masses is more important than diamond rings for the hundreds. . . . The only hope of human unity today lies in the common cause, the common interests of the working classes, in Europe, Africa and Asia."[25] The one significant event that concerned Du Bois after his stay in the Soviet Union was the initiation of Stalin's public trials against opponents of the state. In 1926, Du Bois had become familiar with Karl Radek, who was then provost of Sun Yat-sen University in Moscow. In September 1936, Radek's regular articles disappeared from the Soviet newspapers, and on 7 October 1936, *Pravda* announced his pending trial on grounds of treason. Radek was convicted on 30 January 1937 and died probably in 1939. Du Bois had little sympathy for the exiled Soviet leader Leon Trotsky; as early as March 1929 he had observed critically, "nothing in modern history is so touching as the sudden interest of the *New York Times* in Leon Trotsky." But Radek's removal was something different. In February 1940, Du Bois wrote, "I love the victim Radek more than the tyrant Stalin." But despite these political problems, the Soviets moved forward toward "their magnificent goal. . . . I still believe in Russia."[26]

China and Japan presented striking contrasts when Du Bois visited these nations in 1936. Du Bois had been quite critical of the regime of Chiang Kai-Shek since 1928, primarily because of Chiang's anti-Marxist policies. "It would have been magnificent providence of God if Russia and China could have made common ground for the emancipation of the working classes of the world," Du Bois commented in September 1937. But Chiang was dominated by Western interests that in turn perpetuated the exploitation of the Chinese people. Du Bois was struck by the "helpless, undefended welter of misery and toil" among the Chinese masses. The brutal imposition of European political controls in Shanghai reminded him of the racial inequality of Mississippi.[27] Du Bois had been an admirer of the Japanese for many years, and he tended to interpret the imperialist state's political actions in the best possible light. In 1922, Du Bois had hoped that Japan and China would create an "unbroken front to the aggressions of the whites"; in 1927 he criticized Japanese aggression in China but asserted that Japan might soon express solidarity "with the colored race"; and in 1932, he attacked Western governments for forcing Japan "to choose between militarism or suicide." In his newspaper column, Du Bois explained in 1936 that "Japanese imperialism" could foster "economic reform" in China. Surveying Japanese domination in Manchuria, Du Bois was at first convinced that their dictatorship was a distinct mode of "colonialism" without racial prejudice. The Japanese press widely commented on Du Bois's 1936 visit to the country, and the black scholar was popularly received. Du Bois was deeply grateful for the generous hospitality of the Japanese people. He remained critical of Japan's capitalist model of development but was impressed by the nation's social and material accomplishments. Du Bois's ideas on education and democracy continued to influence some liberal Japanese scholars, especially after World War II.[28]

Du Bois's experiences abroad had a profound impact upon his understanding of international politics. First, he was thoroughly convinced that the United States should not become involved in the next world war, which seemed inevitable. "[I am] bitterly opposed to [the] present effort of American and English capital to drive this nation into war," Du Bois observed in October 1937. "Such miserable war would be based on color prejudice." He viewed British colonialism in India and Africa as only slightly less odious than the Nazi regime. With the outbreak of war in 1939, he urged the continued agitation of Indian nationalists against British rule. He depicted Japanese imperialism in benign terms, almost to the point of apologetics. By 1939, it was "rumored" in Congress that Du Bois was "receiving funds for Japanese propaganda work." Du Bois responded to the rumors: "It is not that I sympathize with China less but that I hate white European and American propaganda, theft and insult more. I believe in Asia for the Asiatics and despite the hell of war and the fascism of capital, I see Japan the best agent for this end." In February 1941, Du Bois explained his antiwar views in greater detail to Andrew J. Allison, the alumni secretary of Fisk University. He was pleased that Fisk had not yet "yielded to War hysteria. . . . I utterly refuse to believe that there is any excuse for the United States entering the present war." Du Bois believed that American hostility to Japan was caused by "race prejudice" and declared that the "British Empire has caused more human misery than Hitler will cause if he lives a hundred years." In the *Amsterdam News,* Du Bois succinctly noted in May 1941: "If Hitler wins, down with the blacks! If the democracies win, the blacks are already down." It must be emphasized that Du Bois's antiwar sentiments were shared by millions of Americans. In 1940, the Congress of Industrial Organizations (CIO) adopted a resolution opposing "any foreign entanglements." Between late 1939 and mid-1941, the American Communist party vigorously denounced this "Second Imperialist War." Many black Americans agreed with journalist George S. Schuyler: "our war is not against Hitler in Europe, but against the Hitlers in America."[29]

Du Bois's attitude toward the Communist party in the United States was also substantially revised. Before his second visit to the Soviet Union, Du Bois remained an acerbic critic of American Marxist-Leninists. Du Bois's April 1935 correspondence with Streator makes this clear: "I do not believe in the verbal inspiration of the Marxism scriptures. . . . I am, therefore, absolutely and bitterly opposed to the American brand of communism which simply aims to stir up trouble and to make Negroes shock troops in a fight whose triumph may easily involve the utter annihilation of the American Negro. I, therefore, attack and shall continue to attack American communism in its present form, while at the same time, I regard Russia as the most promising modern country." In the late 1930s, he continued to criticize Communists for their agitation around the Scottsboro case and generally sided with Randolph in his political disagreements with Marxists inside the National Negro Congress. But Du Bois also recognized the important contributions of Communists in building the labor movement and in defending the interests of the unemployed and the poor. In a November 1938 letter to a young Communist worker, Du Bois noted, "I am not a communist but I appreciate what the communists are trying to do and endeavor always . . . to give a fair and balanced judgment concerning them." In March 1940, Du Bois backed the analysis of Earl Browder, general secretary of the Communist party, in his description of Western governments as "sham democracies." Later that year, Du Bois publicly opposed the American government's prosecution of Browder as a violation of free speech.[30]

The Communist party's view of Du Bois also changed sharply between 1935–45 for several reasons. In the early 1930s, black Communists had little to do with the NAACP. But with the emergence of Nazism, the international Communist movement revised its theses toward liberal democracies and non-Marxist political organizations like the NAACP. The Communist International, led by Georgi Dimitroff, developed the thesis of a "popular front" against fascism, consisting of Marxists, liberals, and other democratic forces. Consequently, American Marxist-Leninists approached the NAACP much more favorably after 1935. As veteran black Communist Hosea Hudson relates: "We members of the Party at every meeting, nearabouts, we'd hammer and hammer on our people, especially Negroes, to become members of the NAACP as a mass organization. Before, we just knew it was there, but we didn't go, that was the better class of folks was in the NAACP."[31] Marxists' criticisms of Du Bois's political positions still continued. In 1938, black Communists Cyril V. Briggs and Harry Haywood authored the pamphlet *Is Japan the Champion of the Colored Races?* But some of Du Bois's sharpest critics left the Communist movement during the 1930s. George Padmore was expelled in 1934 and subsequently initiated the International African Service Bureau in London, with the assistance of African nationalist Jomo Kenyatta and Trinidadian Trotskyist C. L. R. James. Briggs, Richard B. Moore, and other former ABB members were expelled from the American Communist party in 1939, on the grounds of their "Negro nationalist way of thinking."[32]

A rough convergence of opinion between Du Bois and the Communist party developed after 1938. Du Bois defended the August 1939 Molotov-Ribbentrop pact between the Soviets and Nazi Germany, seeing it as a result of British and French inaction against European fascism. Soviet neutrality, Du Bois observed, provided "the best promise" for the "future industrial democracy" throughout the world. When Nazi Germany invaded the Soviet Union in June 1941, Du Bois radically changed his thoughts about the conflict. "The war between Russia and Germany reorientates all our thinking," Du Bois wrote in the *Amsterdam News* on 26 July 1941. German aggression was ultimately aimed against communism. "The hopes of the modern world rest on the survival of the new conception of politics and industry which Russia represents." After the bombing of Pearl Harbor and America's entry into the war, Du Bois argued that Afro-Americans had to support the struggle. The world war could be waged to expand democratic rights for oppressed nations and peoples—and if so, "my gun is on my shoulder," Du Bois declared in May 1942. Du Bois valued the progressive political work of black Communists Benjamin Davis Jr. and Doxey Wilkerson, among many others. Du Bois retained some reservations about the Party's policies and tactics, and in 1944, he reflected: "I did not believe that the

Communism of the Russians was the program for America; least of all for a minority group like the Negroes; I saw that the program of the American Communist party was suicidal." In January 1945, a journalist for the Communist publication *Daily Worker* published a critical essay on Du Bois's views on colonialism. Ironically, the *Daily Worker* attacked Du Bois for expressing ultraleftist and sectarian positions. Black Communist leader James W. Ford promptly wrote Du Bois: "I want you to know that I disagree entirely with the manner and content of the criticism expressed in the *Daily Worker* article."[33]

The Second World War was as crucial as the period 1897–1904 in restructuring Du Bois's ideas on the pursuit of democracy for people of color. "The democracy which the white world seeks to defend does not exist," Du Bois wrote in 1940. "It has been splendidly conceived and discussed, but not realized." The destruction of fascism could bring about a new definition of democracy across the world, Du Bois thought. For this process to occur, democracy had to be distinguished from the political economy of capitalism. In 1943, Du Bois suggested the establishment of new democratic institutions within the United States, based on popular participation and open discussion, as an alternative to the segregationist-controlled Congress. Real democracy was more than universal suffrage and the abolition of Jim Crow laws. It also demanded state planning of production, the end of unemployment and poverty, and the abolition of women's inequality, anti-Semitism, and racist violence. More clearly than ever before, Du Bois recognized that the long-term goals of the civil rights movement should not be blacks' integration within the existing system but the transformation of the United States for the benefit of all Americans. In an unpublished essay drafted in May 1942, Du Bois observed: "Democracy is not, as so many of us are prone to think, simply the right of electing our rulers. It is not simply, as others think, the right of working people to have a choice in the conduct of industry. It is much more than this; it is a vaster and more inclusive ideal; it is the right to accumulate and use a great reservoir of human thought and experience, out of which a people may choose . . . the wisest and best policies of government and conduct."[34]

In the context of international politics, democracy meant for Du Bois the abolition of European colonialism and American corporate domination of nonwhite nations and full self-determination for oppressed peoples. Americans must "stop making income by unholy methods," Du Bois declared in a commencement address at Talledega College in June 1944. "The great majority of men, the poverty-stricken and diseased are the *real workers* of the world. . . . Their future path is clear. It is to accumulate such knowledge and balance of judgment that they can reform the world, so that the workers of the world, receive just share of the wealth which they make and that all human beings who are capable of work, shall work." Democracy in Asia meant political freedom for China, the end of British colonialism in India, and the destruction of the "imperialism of Japan." "The greatest color problem in the world is that of India," Du Bois wrote in February 1944. Du Bois demanded the release of Mohandas K. Gandhi and Jawaharlal Nehru, who had been imprisoned by British authorities during the war.[35] Nothing outraged Du Bois more than the Holocaust of European Jews under the Nazi regime. In 1942, Du Bois observed that the Jewish people were related to other oppressed groups "composed of Chinese, Japanese, East Indians, African Negroes, American Negroes, and American Indians" who had been deliberately "excluded from fellowship with the world aristocracy." In January 1944, Du Bois commented in the *Amsterdam News:* "Let Negroes remember one thing: the greatest evil of this evil war, is the attack on the Jewish people. It is the most unforgiveable and unwarranted result of this collapse of civilization. The man or race that condones it, is lost." The war reinforced Du Bois's conviction that the survival of the Jewish people depended upon the development of a Zionist state in Palestine. "What the wretched and scourged Jew would have done without Zion in this modern revival of race hatred is inconceivable," Du Bois noted.[36]

Even before the outbreak of war, Du Bois thought that the conflict could revive the basis for the Pan-African movement. Pan-Africanism is a "movement to begin a leadership of the exploited among the most exploited," Du Bois wrote in June 1937, "with the idea of its ultimate expansion to the colored laboring class of the world and to the laboring class of all colors throughout the world." In June 1940, Du Bois first proposed the scheduling of a fifth Pan-African Congress, to be held in Haiti tentatively in 1942. Historian Rayford Logan, a participant in the 1923 Pan-African Congress, endorsed Du Bois's proposal for a conference "as soon as it is practical after the close of the present war." In late 1942, Randolph also suggested independently the initiation of a black people's conference that would be held during the peace negotiations at the conclusion of the war. Du Bois contemplated Africa's postwar prospects and projected a political program of self-determination that was to the left of his earlier concepts. "Do we want to keep Africa in subjection just as long as it is physically possible?" he inquired in a lecture at Vassar College in April 1942. "If we do, are we not planting right here inevitable seeds of future hatred, struggle and war?" Africa's land, natural resources, and industries must be controlled by Africans themselves. In a July 1943 article for *Foreign Affairs,* Du Bois insisted that Africa's socioeconomic development in the postwar period must take precedence over "European profit." The principles of race and class emancipation that informed Du Bois's Pan-Africanism also applied to the situation of black Americans. In a 1944 lecture in Haiti, Du Bois suggested that American Negroes "do not form a separate nation" but nevertheless "resemble in their economic and political condition a distinctly colonial status." The future of blacks in the United States "depends to a degree on the development of the colonial status among other peoples of the world." These lectures and essays formed the basis of Du Bois's book *Color and Democracy: Colonies and Peace,* published in early 1945.[37]

But the central political insight advanced by Du Bois during the war was the direct connection between peace, national liberation, and democracy. "Without worldwide democracy applied to the majority of people, it is going to be impossible to establish universal peace," Du Bois stated in Haiti in 1944. "Democracy is tapping the great possibilities of mankind from unused and unsuspected reservoirs of human greatness." If oppressed people were "released from poverty, ignorance and disease," world peace would be possible. "There will be no need to fight for food, for healthy homes, for free speech," Du Bois reasoned, "for these will not depend on force, but increasingly on knowledge, reason and art." "Democracy" had to be redefined as the representative government of the vast majority of workers, nonwhites, and the poor. Any society "ruled for the benefit of the minority" would have no democracy, "and peace for any long time will be utterly impossible." The great danger in the postwar period was the possibility that the United States would retreat from the democratic reforms of the New Deal. Writing in the *American Journal of Sociology* in March 1944, Du Bois noted that growing political pressures to outlaw "'Communistic' propaganda" had nearly halted "efforts at clear thinking on economic reform." Peace and democracy were threatened by "a combination of Northern investors and Southern Bourbons desiring not simply to overthrow the New Deal but to plunge the United States into fatal reaction."[38] The "fatal reaction" of McCarthyism and the Cold War was only several years ahead.

Despite Du Bois's extensive academic and professional activities, administrators at Atlanta University were not pleased with his role in campus life. For nearly a decade, Du Bois had engaged in an open feud with Florence M. Read, president of Atlanta's Spelman College. Du Bois had even informed her in 1940 that she had sheltered Spelman students from his radical ideas and that her "determined opposition to any university periodical has cut five irreplaceable years from my creative life." Atlanta University president Clement increasingly viewed Du Bois as "uncooperative" and "antagonistic." He criticized Du Bois for not consulting with him directly about *Phylon.* In early 1941, New York University asked Du Bois to spend one semester as a visiting professor—an invitation that would have been a major victory in the desegregation of white higher education. But Clement refused to allow Du Bois to accept the offer. In the winter of 1943 rumors began to surface that Du Bois was about to leave Atlanta University. Du Bois wrote to one friend in March 1943: "If there is any rumor of my leaving Atlanta, I have not heard it. Of course there is always the possibility of being kicked out but I am not expecting it yet."[39]

In 1939 Du Bois had signed a five-year contract with the university that included the provision that "professors shall serve continuously until such time as they reach the age of retirement," which was sixty-five years. Since Du Bois had returned to Atlanta University at age sixty five, and before the school had adopted the provision on mandatory retirement, it seemed to Du Bois that the new contractual terms were merely a formality. They were not. At the board of trustees' meeting of Atlanta University on 16 November 1943, Read moved that Du Bois "be retired from the active faculty" effective 30 June 1944. Clement seconded the motion, and the trustees approved it without debate. "Without a word of warning I found myself at the age of 76 without employment and with less than $5,000 of savings," Du Bois commented in his *Autobiography*. "Not only was a great plan of scientific work [the Negro Land Grant college program] killed at birth, but my own life was thrown into confusion." Du Bois's situation was critical. Nina had lived primarily with their daughter in Baltimore since 1934 and was in poor health. Yolande's early marriage to Cullen had been dissolved years before, and her second marriage was quite unhappy. Although Yolande's modest income as a school teacher provided some support for her daughter and elderly mother, they still depended on Du Bois's steady income. Du Bois had lost about $15,000 in life insurance and real estate in the depression and owed $3,000 on the family's home in Baltimore. In great despair, he appealed to Atlanta University alumni and the black community generally for support. Within months, offers for employment came from Howard University, North Carolina College for Negroes, and Fisk University. After significant national protests, Atlanta University's board of trustees voted to grant Du Bois one year's salary, amounting to $4,500, for the academic year 1944–45 and approved a small stipend for the remainder of his life. However, he was not permitted to teach after June 1944.[40]

In the middle of this academic turmoil, Du Bois received an unexpected letter from Walter White. On 8 May 1944, the NAACP's board of directors voted to ask Du Bois to accept a "full or part time" position to prepare "material to be presented on behalf of the American Negro and the colored peoples of the world to the Peace Conference." Du Bois saw this as an opportunity to return permanently to the NAACP. After negotiations with White and NAACP board members Louis T. Wright and Arthur Spingarn, Du

Bois received a formal offer to become "Director of Special Research." The NAACP board granted Du Bois the freedom to collect data "concerning peoples of Africa and their descendants" and stipulated that he would "continue in this work as long as his health permits and his services are, in the judgement of the Directors, of value to the Association."[41]

During the preceding decade, Du Bois had not severed all ties with the NAACP. In 1942, White had suggested to the British ambassador to the United States, Lord Halifax, that Du Bois be sent to India with several other distinguished Americans to negotiate an independence settlement with Gandhi and Nehru. White had also defended Du Bois during his conflict with the Atlanta University board of trustees. But the bitterness from the early 1930s had not been forgotten. When White had been proposed in January 1939 as a possible Atlanta University trustee, Du Bois termed the move a potential "calamity." Writing to one trustee, Du Bois had described White as "utterly selfish," devoid of "principle and broad ideals," and "dangerous and difficult to deal with." Subsequently, White was not selected. The motivation behind the Association's reappointment of Du Bois can be understood retrospectively. Spingarn, Wright, and other board members assumed "my life work was done," Du Bois later observed. They believed that "what I wanted was leisure and comfort and for that I would willingly act as window dressing, say a proper word now and then and give the Association and its secretary moral support." White simply wanted Du Bois to write formal documents, to draft speeches, and to appear "for him on such public occasions as he wished." It seems that all parties seriously misjudged the situation. Nevertheless, Du Bois returned to work for the NAACP in September 1944.[42]

Du Bois's principal activities for the NAACP in late 1944 and 1945 revolved primarily around the development of the United Nations. In October 1944 he attended a meeting chaired by Undersecretary of State Edward R. Stettinius in Washington, D.C. that reviewed postwar international policies. Du Bois became worried when he learned that the Roosevelt administration had no progressive position concerning colonialism. Du Bois's fears increased in San Francisco, where he served as a consultant with White and black educator Mary McLeod Bethune to the U.S. delegation at the 1945 founding of the United Nations. Du Bois wrote several dozen newspaper articles and lobbied aggressively with U.S. officials to support anticolonialist positions. Although unsuccessful in efforts to influence representatives of the new president Harry S. Truman, Du Bois sensed that the United Nations would eventually become a force for national independence in Asia, Africa, and the Caribbean. But he also perceived the potential for the United States and other capitalist states to align themselves against the Soviet Union. "I seem to see outlined a third World War based on the suppression of Asia and the strangling of Russia," Du Bois wrote in June 1945. "Perhaps I am wrong. God knows I hope I am."[43]

More fruitful was the mobilization to revive the Pan-African Congress movement. Du Bois later described the fifth Pan-African Congress, which was held in Manchester, England, in October 1945, as the result of a "spontaneous call" at the meeting of black labor leaders attending the International Trades Union convention in Paris one month before. More accurately, the congress was the direct result of the intense organizing of George Padmore. For over a decade, Padmore and his associates in England had cultivated firm political relationships with black trade unionists and nationalist leaders throughout the Caribbean and Africa, particularly in the British colonies. Padmore discussed the concept of a Pan-African Congress with black labor union leaders at the February 1945 conference of the World Federation of Trade Unions in London. In early March a steering committee was established, with Padmore and a young Gold Coast nationalist, Kwame Nkrumah, serving as "joint political secretaries," and Jomo Kenyatta acting as "assistant secretary." Du Bois did not learn about Padmore's plans until mid-March 1945, when the *Chicago Defender* published an announcement of the pending Congress. One could speculate why Padmore had not directly contacted Du Bois. Padmore was now strongly anti-Communist, and Du Bois had become quite close politically to the party. Perhaps the bitter polemics Padmore had engaged in fifteen years earlier against Du Bois and the NAACP were another factor. Du Bois's initial letter to Padmore on 22 March 1945 reflected slight irritation. Du Bois asked Padmore to postpone the congress until six months after the war and suggested that it "be held in Africa." Within several weeks, however, Du Bois wrote to Padmore that he was "in complete sympathy" with his proposal, and he had also changed his mind about the timing of the congress. During the next six months, both men worked closely in coordinating the event.[44]

The Manchester congress was a pivotal event in black political history. A broad selection of leading trade unionists, politicians, and radical intellectuals from the African diaspora came together to chart the agenda for their postwar nationalist movements. Key individuals attended the sessions: from Jamaica, Amy Jacques-Garvey and barrister Norman Manley, who was elected the island's first premier in 1957; Jomo Kenyatta, who later became Kenya's first president; Wallace Johnson, secretary of the Sierra Leone Youth League; Mangus Williams of the National Council of Nigeria and the Cameroons. The most charismatic African spokesman was Nkrumah, but Padmore and Peter Milliard, president of the Negro Association of Manchester, were the essential coordinators of the congress. The guiding spirit of the sessions, however, was Du Bois. As Padmore later wrote: "Even among the older delegates there were many who were meeting the 'Father' of Pan-Africanism in the flesh for the first time. . . . He entered into all the discussions and brought to the deliberations a freshness of outlook that greatly influenced the final decisions; the implementations of which are already shaping the future of the African continent." The two hundred delegates had little difficulty drafting resolutions for political action. They demanded the right to organize free labor unions, denounced the poverty, illiteracy, and starvation of African people as endemic to colonialism, and called for the granting of home rule. Du Bois best articulated the political challenge to Western colonialism: "it is perfectly clear . . . what the African peoples want. They want the right to govern themselves. . . . We must impress upon the world that it must be Self Government."[45]

8

THE
POLITICS
OF PEACE

The iron curtain was not invented by Russia; it hung between Europe and Africa half a thousand years. . . . If a world of ultimate democracy, reaching across the color line and abolishing race discrimination, can only be accomplished by the method laid down by Karl Marx, then that method deserves to be triumphant.

W. E. B. Du Bois,
The World and Africa, 1947

The intent of science is to ease human existence. If you give way to coercion, science can be crippled. . . . I have betrayed my profession. Any man who does what I have done must not be tolerated in the ranks of science.

Bertolt Brecht,
"Galileo," 1938

Those who do not believe in the ideology of the United States, shall not be allowed to stay in the United States.

Attorney General Tom Clark,
1948

World War II left an indelible impact upon black American political life and thought. The mobilization and war against fascism, combined with the domestic struggles for racial equality, tended to increase popular involvement in democratic movements of all kinds. The most prominent Afro-American leaders—noted artist and progressive activist Paul Robeson, A. Philip Randolph, Walter White, and Du Bois—seemed to advance a common policy of social justice. Randolph's initiation of the 1941 Negro March on Washington movement, for example, had forced the Roosevelt administration to sign Executive Order No. 8802, outlawing racial discrimination by defense industry contractors. Through the militant labor organizing activities of Communists and other progressives, the number of Afro-Americans in unions soared from barely 150,000 in 1935 to 1.25 million a decade later. The Association directly benefited from this mass activism. From a national membership of 50,556 and 355 branches in 1940, the NAACP had nearly 450,000 members and 1,073 branches in 1946. Even White, certainly one of the most conservative of all major black leaders, took public positions favorable to domestic social reform and anticolonialist movements. Padmore was invited to write a series of *Crisis* articles between 1942 and 1947 that criticized the Anglo-American posture on Africa and praised the Soviet Union's policies "in the sphere of inter-racial relations." Throughout 1944 and 1945, White aggressively attacked imperialism and favored the continuation of the Soviet-United States détente into the postwar period. When Du Bois's *Color and Democracy* was published, the NAACP distributed copies to members of the U.S. delegation at the United Nations founding conference in San Francisco.[1]

For these reasons, Du Bois attempted at first to overlook certain tensions that marked his relationship with White. Initially, the problems seemed relatively minor. Although promised adequate office space, Du Bois found to his consternation that the Association had made no provisions for him. After many months, Du Bois was forced to spend nearly five hundred dollars of his own money to rent office space. Subsequently, White refused to pay for Du Bois's office furniture and bookshelves, which he judged "too expensive." In January 1945, Du Bois noticed that mail and telegrams addressed to him personally had been opened by NAACP staff members, and he promptly complained to Roy Wilkins, White's assistant. More troubling to Du Bois was the nearly complete absence of any "vestige of democratic method and control" within the organization. During his years in Atlanta, the NAACP "had become a big business, smoothly run and extraordinarily influential." White dominated the Association's board and largely dictated major policies. With White's consent, even Villard was dropped as an Association vice-president in early 1946. Du Bois was "ashamed" of this decision and personally apologized to Villard for the NAACP action.[2]

These disagreements soon escalated to matters of policy. In August 1945, a group of citizens from Dayton, Ohio, contacted Du Bois concerning his position on segregated schools. He replied that such schools were "undemocratic and discriminatory," but that where they did exist, Negroes had the obligation to "make the best of a bad situation." White later learned of Du Bois's correspondence and charged him with "seriously interfer[ing] with the smooth operation of the NAACP as a whole." On 30 August 1946, Robeson asked Du Bois to participate on a national antilynching committee, and Du Bois quickly accepted the invitation. Three weeks later, White informed Du Bois that the NAACP had already initiated its own antilynching organization in early August and that Du Bois had created "headaches" for the Association by endorsing a "competing group." Du Bois replied briefly that no one in the NAACP had bothered to inform him previously about their "new Anti-Lynching movement," and had he been asked, "I would gladly have cooperated. . . . The fight against mob law is the monopoly of no one person—no one organization." White thought otherwise. Without responding to Du Bois's major point, the lack of political courtesy exhibited toward him by the Association's leaders, White noted critically "that the tone of your memorandum was distinctly surprising in its tartness." Additionally, Du Bois was dismayed by the distinct absence of enthusiasm of the NAACP board and White for Pan-Africanism. Only after "great difficulty and delay," Du Bois informed Padmore in July 1946, was he "finally able to take the trip to England." At the end of 1946, Du Bois wrote Padmore: "Any effort now to get Mr. White to recommend an appropriation of money for printing the report of its Fifth Pan African Congress would, I am sure, be quite in vain."[3]

By mid-1946, relations between Du Bois and White had become nearly as strained as they had been in 1934. White suspected that Du Bois was leaking internal memos to George Streator, then a writer for the *New York Times,* and to journalist George S. Schuyler. Du Bois complained that he had written many memoranda at the secretary's request but seldom received any subsequent information on their status or disposition. Du Bois comprehended that his differences with White were, at root, conflicts over the future political orientation of the NAACP. In a lengthy memorandum on 10 October 1946, Du Bois outlined his ideas for White and other Association staff members. The NAACP had to transcend White's "negative program of resistance to discrimination, and unite with the best elements of the nation in a position constructive program for rebuilding civilization," Du Bois began. The NAACP had an obligation to fight for a progressive economic agenda, to eliminate poverty, to "curb monopoly and the rule of wealth, spread education and practice democracy." Du Bois argued that the NAACP should not be "diverted by witch-hunting for Communists, or by fear of the wealthy" in advocating its revised program. Most important, the Association could not lead democratic causes if it was not truly democratic in its structure. "Power and authority" were too highly concentrated among "a small tight group which issues directives to the mass of members." The NAACP had to "hand down and distribute authority to regions and branches." As in the early 1930s, nothing came of Du Bois's call to democratize the Association. "I saw the handwriting on the wall," Du Bois later observed in his *Autobiography*. Nevertheless, he was certain that his "two sponsoring friends," Arthur Spingarn and Louis Wright, the board chairman, "would see the attack being made on me and stand by me."[4]

Publicly, Du Bois tried to work harmoniously with White on United Nations activities. In August 1946, Du Bois secured White's approval to draft a petition "touching the situation of American Negroes" for consideration by the United Nations. Within three months, Du Bois had coordinated the writing of much of the petition with contributions from Rayford W. Logan, Chicago attorney Earl B. Dickerson, and others. After many delays, the NAACP finally printed *An Appeal to the World* in 1947; perhaps only Du Bois knew that the title of the petition had also been used in his historic statement at the London Pan-African conference of 1900. In the autumn of 1947, Du Bois obtained the support of Madame Vijaya Lakshmi Pandit, the head of India's UN delegation and sister of Jawaharlal Nehru, for the NAACP's petition. Du Bois and White presented the petition to the assistant of UN Secretary General Trygve Lie in October 1947. The petition received wide international coverage, much to the chagrin of the Truman administration. Consequently, when Soviet delegates proposed that the petition be received by a UN subcommission on human rights in December 1947, it was summarily rejected by the Americans and their allies. Unfortunately, Eleanor Roosevelt was the U.S. delegate on the human rights commission—and also a member of the NAACP's national board. Du Bois discussed this issue personally with Roosevelt and appealed to her basic commitment to civil rights. But she replied that the petition on American racism "would be embarrassing; that it would be seized upon by the Soviet Government." Geopolitics took precedence over racial justice, and the U.S. government had decided to bury the NAACP petition.[5]

In the late forties, Du Bois aggressively toured the nation, advancing his ideas on foreign and domestic affairs. Between 1944 and 1948, he gave at least 150 public lectures or speeches. In one 1946 speaking tour, which included stops in Montgomery, Knoxville, Philadelphia, and Springfield, he lectured on the necessity of cooperation between the American and Soviet governments. Many of the speeches focused directly on the relationship between democracy and racism. Before a New York audience in February 1946, Du Bois insisted that "no attack upon social problems by free democratic methods" could occur in the United States, so long as the Negro people were bound "by the color line." America's democratic ideals were compromised by the government's "alliance with colonial imperialism and class dictatorship in order to enforce the denial of freedom to the colored peoples of the world." Using a more academic style, Du Bois again criticized the structural limitations of Western democracy before a convention of the American Education Fellowship in 1947. But two of Du Bois's most important speeches of the period occurred in Columbia, South Carolina, in October 1946, and at the June 1947 NAACP convention in Washington, D.C. The former was a conference of nearly nine hundred black and white activists, sponsored by the Southern Negro Youth Congress, a progressive formation led by Louis E. Burnham and James E. Jackson. Given the location of this address, the event was truly remarkable. With characteristic presence, Du Bois argued, "The future of American Negroes is in the South." The region would become "the battleground of a great crusade" for democracy in the near future. But to "rescue this land," institutional racism, lynching, poverty, and the "monopoly of wealth in the whole South" would have to be challenged. Before the NAACP convention, Du Bois sought to persuade leaders to support the struggle against colonialism and world poverty. "Socialism is an attack on poverty. We can by our knowledge, by the use of our democratic power, prevent the concentration of political and economic power in the hands of the monopolists who rule colonies," Du Bois declared. "Every leading land on earth is moving toward some form of socialism, so as to restrict the power of wealth, introduce democratic methods in industry, and stop the persistence of poverty and its children, ignorance, disease and crime." Not surprisingly, this was Du Bois's last major address before an NAACP convention.[6]

A steady torrent of newspaper and magazine articles also came from Du Bois. In January 1945 the *Chicago Defender* began running his "Winds of Time" column, and by mid-1948 Du Bois had contributed about 170 popular essays to the publication. Many of these articles focused on the necessity for world peace and presented a sympathetic view of progressive movements and of the Soviet Union. The "Colored and Colonial World" had to develop its own policy toward atomic technology, Du Bois noted in 1946. Peaceful and constructive uses of atomic energy were possible, but the bomb's destructive power should be permanently prohibited.[7] In several columns, Du Bois reiterated his support for the creation of economic cooperatives. But he also looked abroad for models of socialism that might spark effective domestic reforms. The postwar parliamentary victory of the British Labour party over the Conservatives indicated the potential for left political movements in the United States. "We have got to work hard for a new organization of industry and a new distribution of wealth," Du Bois wrote in August 1945. "In no other way can real freedom come to the American people."[8]

Any transitional strategy toward an American socialism required cordial relations with the Soviet people. The Soviet Union, not the United States, had become the greatest proponent for colonial independence, and it offered a model for the elimination of poverty and unemployment. The country was certainly not perfect or "without mistakes," Du Bois observed, but it still represented "the most hopeful state in the world today." Writing for the *Christian Register* in August 1946, Du Bois condemned American politicians who favored conflict with the Soviets.[9] Although Du Bois's foreign policy positions later appeared "radical" by Cold War standards, it must be emphasized that his views and similar statements by Paul Robeson expressed the dominant opinion of black Americans, certainly until 1948. Most Afro-Americans were less enthusiastic about the Truman administration's Marshall Plan to Western Europe than many whites and were less critical about communism in general. Many black workers deeply respected the Communist party's contributions to their labor union and civil rights organizing efforts. One indication of this was the election of black Communist Benjamin J. Davis, Jr., in 1943 and 1945, to the New York City Council. Another was the testimony of Harlem congressman Adam Clayton Powell, Jr., in 1945: "There is no group in America, including the Christian church, that practices racial brotherhood one-tenth as much as the Communist Party."[10]

Peace and socialism were directly linked to Pan-Africanism. "The emancipation of the black masses of the world," Du Bois declared in January 1947, "is one guarantee of a firm foundation for world peace." With Padmore's support, Du Bois drafted a petition "supporting the rights of African Negroes and descendants of Africans" for the United Nations. This petition was endorsed by major figures throughout the African diaspora: Padmore and Milliard in England; Jomo Kenyatta of Kenya; Nnamdi Azikiwe of Nigeria; Wallace Johnson of Sierra Leone; and Richard Hart, Secretary of the Caribbean Labor Congress. From the United States, endorsement came from Mary McLeod Bethune; Earl Dickerson, president of the National Bar Association; Congressman Adam Clayton Powell, Jr.; and D. W. Jemison, president of the National Baptist Convention. Regrettably, White refused to sign the petition, and the statement had little success in gaining broad support at the United Nations. Attempts by Du Bois to coordinate his activities with the Council on African Affairs, led by Robeson and Max Yergan, were also frustrated by the Association. As Du Bois explained to Padmore, "I wanted their cooperation but was not able to ask them." Although the council "has a constituency and is doing good work," the NAACP was fearful that it was "financed by the Communists."[11]

Despite the NAACP's hostility, Du Bois was determined to generate broad support for Pan-Africanism inside the United States. From March 1947 until March 1948, Du Bois authored a series of fifty-one popular essays on African politics for the *People's Voice* newspaper, published in New York. More influential was his 1947 book *The World and Africa*. Building upon his previous research but including new information from Padmore, Leo Hansberry, Rayford Logan, and others, Du Bois attempted to interpret the dynamics of colonialism and imperialism in the continent. The text is an historical, political—and ethical—condemnation of the "democracy" and rule over nonwhite people of the capitalist West. "If this nation could not exist half slave and half free," Du Bois observed, "then the world in which this nation plays a larger and larger part also cannot be half slave and half free, but must recognize world democracy. . . . The iron curtain was not invented by Russia; it hung between Europe and Africa half a thousand years." Robeson and other American supporters of African self-determination found *The World and Africa* an invaluable source. As Robeson later explained, "*The World and Africa* was one of the first important books on modern postwar Africa and helped to point out and focus attention on the continuing exploitation of Africa by the 'free world.'"[12]

As international tensions between the American and Soviet governments increased in 1947 and early 1948, Du Bois spoke out frequently against "red-baiting" and the danger of a domestic purge of real or imaginary leftists from public life. Anti-Soviet and anti-Communist propaganda, he observed in the *Chicago Defender* in February 1947, was designed "to distract the thought of the people of the United States" from the basic contradictions that faced the nation—"poverty, ignorance and private monopoly." Du Bois joined the "Committee of One Thousand," whose members included playwright Lillian Hellman and physicist Albert Einstein, which lobbied for the abolition of the House Un-American Activities Committee. He also became a member-at-large of the progressive National Council of Arts, Sciences and Professions.[13] Both major political parties seemed to Du Bois hopelessly committed to sterile anti-Communism, colonial rule, and the preservation of Jim Crow. In April 1947, he characterized President Truman's support for the suppression of Greek leftists as "the most stupid and dangerous proposal ever made by the leader of a great modern nation." Truman's Marshall Plan was criticized as an attempt to establish American corporate hegemony over European markets. What did the development of a "Cold War" mean for black America? Writing in the *Negro Digest* in April 1947, Du Bois suggested that Negroes had to reconsider their strategic priorities. Even with the removal of racial segregation in most of the United States over the next two decades, blacks would have to confront even more fundamental tasks. "Are we going to try to increase the wealth of the richest by climbing on the faces of the poorest among us?" Du Bois wondered. "With the right to vote, what are we going to vote for?" Black Americans had the latent capacity to ignite a social transformation, but would their leaders commit themselves to the next stages of radical democracy? Speaking before the Sigma Pi Phi fraternity, to which he belonged, Du Bois fundamentally revised his Talented Tenth thesis. The new "passport to leadership," Du Bois suggested, would include "willingness to sacrifice and plan for such economic revolution in industry and just distribution of wealth, as would make the rise of our group possible."[14]

From White's point of view, Du Bois's advocacy of socialism, Pan-Africanism, and peace made the Association vulnerable to charges that it was a "Communist organization." Marxists had joined the NAACP during the depression, in order to help build the black freedom movement—but in virtually no branch were leftists predominant. Southern segregationists needed no evidence, however, to smear all Association leaders as "reds." Unfortunately, these undocumented charges were repeated by many intellectuals and "Cold War liberals." Historian Arthur Schlesinger, Jr., warned in *Life* magazine that the Communists were "sinking tentacles" into the NAACP; in early 1947, Michigan governor Kim Sigler declared that the organization was nothing but a "communist front." To his credit, White's initial response was to condemn these red-baiting tactics. "If we go around denying that we are Communists," White explained to Wilkins in April 1947, "there will be suspicious people who will say where there is smoke there must be fire." But the political pressure from the right escalated. In 1947 and early 1948, some NAACP members were fired from their jobs or denied federal government posts because of their "pinkist tendencies." In mid-1947 an NAACP southern regional conference consisting of over two hundred delegates approved a resolution voicing their opposition to "communism or communist tactics." In late 1947, White joined the Citizens Committee for the Support of the Marshall Plan. Within months, the pages of the *Crisis* assumed an anti-Communist tone.[15]

The ideological crisis inside the Association was part of a broader rupture within American liberalism in general over the Cold War. A number of New Deal liberals created the Progressive Citizens of America (PCA) as a force to the left of the Truman administration. Ultimately, this movement germinated into the Progressive party, which was led by former vice-president Henry Wallace. Du Bois became an early supporter of Wallace as a potential third-party presidential candidate and viewed the campaign as a means to stem the tide of anti-Communist reaction. In his *Chicago Defender* columns, Du Bois admitted that Wallace probably could not be elected. Both major parties seemed virtually identical on most issues, however, and a new political movement that favored social reforms and opposed racial discrimination might ultimately succeed. Du Bois had correctly gauged the political sentiments of many black Americans. Thousands of black artists, civil rights leaders, and trade unionists rallied behind the Wallace movement. Paul Robeson, actress/singer Lena Horne, Shirley Graham, and newspaper publisher George Murphy served on the PCA national board. Former UNIA activist Charlotta Bass, then publisher of the *California Eagle*, mobilized blacks in Los Angeles for the new party. Heavyweight boxing champion Joe Louis gave money to the campaign. Because Wallace refused to speak before segregated audiences and advocated major civil rights reforms, a number of young blacks in the Progressive party were encouraged to seek public office. Margaret Bush Wilson, who became the NAACP national president in the 1970s, first ran for a congressional seat in Missouri on the Progressive party ticket in 1948. The young black director of the Progressive party in Michigan sought election to the state senate that same year. Although defeated this first time, a quarter century later Coleman Young would be elected mayor of Detroit as a liberal Democrat.[16]

White learned to his discomfort that "70 percent of the staff" in the Association's national office "favored Wallace." In late February 1948, he reminded the national staff by memo that Association officers were "prohibited from any partisan activity" and that "they may not speak at meetings called by partisan political groups." The board had adopted this rigid restriction in 1944, and White soon demanded to know why Du Bois's name had appeared on Wallace's campaign literature. Du Bois was "bewildered" by White's latest inquisition and promptly complained to Arthur Spingarn. When he was invited to return to the Association, "there was no warning that my usual freedom of expression was to be curtailed, except of course general conformity with the NAACP program." He had endorsed Wallace as an individual, but never in the name of the Association. Du Bois viewed the board's policy as a violation of simple democratic rights. If the order was "narrowly applied," it "practically closes my mouth and stops my pen, with about the sharpest threat a man can face at the end of his life." The Wallace campaign peaked in the late summer of 1948, but Truman was successful in defeating his opponents in the general election in November. Two tactics were decisive. Wallace and the Progressives were repeatedly condemned for permitting Communists to participate inside their campaign, and these red-baiting efforts had the effect of driving several million liberals back into the Democratic party. Second, Truman realized that he would need a substantial majority of the black vote to be reelected, and the Democratic National Convention that year adopted a civil rights plank in its platform, the first in its history. Under White's supervision, the 1948 NAACP national convention was turned largely into a Truman campaign rally. Pressured by Randolph, Truman also signed an executive order desegregating the armed forces. These concessions to civil rights, created in part by Wallace's appeals to blacks, produced victory for the incumbent. About two-thirds of the black electorate voted for Truman.[17]

But before the November election, the final confrontation between White and Du Bois exploded. White asked Du Bois to draft a memorandum that would be used in his discussions at a UN meeting in Paris. On 7 September 1948, Du Bois refused to "comply with his request" and wrote a lengthy memorandum to White and Association board members. Most of his previous memos, he complained, had been ignored or unanswered. More important, the NAACP had never taken a policy toward the "reactionary, warmongering colonial imperialism of the present administration." If the Association was "to be loaded on the Truman bandwagon, with no chance for opinion or consultation, we are headed for a tragic mistake." Du Bois insisted upon copies of Association board meetings in the future and requested that the organization clarify its muddled foreign policy objectives. The Du Bois memorandum was sent to all national board members and office staff. One of these individuals—not Du Bois—leaked the information to the *New York Times,* which published most of Du Bois's criticisms on 9 September. Four days later, the board voted to terminate Du Bois's employment as of 31 December 1948. The grounds for his removal were technical, as in 1934. Du Bois had refused "to cooperate" with White's request for a memorandum, and he had "made public" the memo prior to the board's consideration.[18] In reality, Du Bois had become a casualty of the Cold War.

Many black editors, labor leaders, educators, and old friends of the Association publicly and privately deplored the removal of Du Bois. The main figure in this dissident movement was Shirley Graham. Organizing the Emergency Committee for Dr. Du Bois and the NAACP, she obtained endorsements from Alain Locke, E. Franklin Frazier, educator Horace Mann Bond, and other leaders. Many friends urged Du Bois to lead a national campaign to reorganize the Association. He could not bear to do this. "White was not wholly responsible for what had happened," Du Bois reflected later. Spingarn, Wright, and other board members had probably made an agreement with White in 1944 that Du Bois would be dismissed if he created any difficulties for the secretary. Again, Du Bois foundered in difficult financial straits. The NAACP had promised to pay him $2,400 as a pension in 1949. His annual retirement funds from Atlanta University amounted to $1,200. Du Bois's book royalties yielded under $150 annually. And his debts seemed nearly overwhelming. Nina experienced a paralytic stroke in 1946, and nursing care for his wife amounted to $2,600 a year. His own modest apartment cost another thousand dollars annually. Du Bois had virtually no funds for his own food, clothing, travel, and research. Through Henry Wallace and Robeson, he obtained a gift of $5,000 from a liberal philanthropist, Anita McCormick Blaine, in May 1949. But this sorely needed donation did little to redress his feelings of deep outrage and sadness about the NAACP.[19]

Robeson invited Du Bois to serve as honorary vice-chairman of the Council of African Affairs, and he readily accepted the position. Robeson had been Du Bois's friend for nearly three decades, and the council's secretary, Alphaeus Hunton, was as dedicated as Du Bois to the study of African culture and history. The council had experienced its own turmoil in 1948, with the removal of its anti-Communist cofounder Max Yergan. The council could not afford to pay Du Bois's salary but granted him secretarial assistance and free office space. With this new measure of security and fraternal support, the eighty-year-old man felt quite energetic. Between 1948 and 1950 he contributed ten articles for the council's *New Africa* publication, thirty-one political columns under his old title "As the Crow Flies" to the *Chicago Globe* newspaper, and about one dozen essays to the independent left newsweekly, the *National Guardian*. In 1949–50, he completed a book-length manuscript tentatively entitled "America and Russia" that documented his travels in the Soviet Union and appealed for American cooperation with the Marxist government.

The one positive side of Du Bois's dismissal from the NAACP was that he was now completely free to participate in national and international peace movements against the Cold War. In early February 1949, Du Bois was asked to participate in the Cultural and Scientific Conference for World Peace by Oetje John Rogge, a liberal lawyer and former assistant attorney general in the Roosevelt administration. The conference was held at the Waldorf-Astoria Hotel in New York on 25–27 March 1949 and was sponsored by 550 influential scholars and artists. Du Bois's paper "The Nature of Intellectual Freedom" was presented on a panel whose members included Harvard University professor F. O. Matthiessen, Shirley Graham, and novelists Howard Fast and Norman Mailer. Du Bois briefly commented that humanity stood "this instant tiptoe on the threshold of infinite freedoms, freedoms which outstretch this day of slavery as the universe of suns outmeasures our little earthly system. . . . Even the chained and barred fields of work and food and disease today will yield to vaster freedoms when men are let to think and talk and explore more widely in regions already really free." Du Bois's appeal here was not for socialism but against intellectual "barbarism." Such barbarism was openly displayed outside the "Waldorf Conference." Right-wing fanatics picketed the hotel, and the *New York Times* described the sessions as "the most controversial meetings in recent New York history." Pablo Picasso, as well as other international artists, were denied visas by the U.S. government to attend the conference.[20]

In April 1949, Du Bois, Graham, Rogge, and approximately sixty other Americans attended the Paris World Congress for Peace. The sessions attracted two thousand delegates, and to Du Bois, the conference was more impressive than the founding of the United Nations. Much of the American press coverage focused on Robeson's controversial speech at the congress: he had declared that "the black folk of America will never fight against the Soviet Union." Du Bois's plenary address, which was similar to Robeson's appeal for peace, was also well received. But what truly surprised Du Bois was the massive applause and cheering he heard at his introduction to the assembly. He informed Graham later that "as he stood waiting for the waves of acclamation to subside he was overwhelmed with amazement that these peoples from the far corners of the earth 'seemed to know me.'" Graham understood completely: "these people did know that the slight, dignified gentleman that they were seeing for the first time had been their champion" for decades. Upon their return to the United States, Robeson and to a lesser extent Du Bois had become political pariahs in the national press. Robeson's concert appearances and public lectures were cancelled. Walter White denounced Robeson's speech in the *Negro Digest,* and Du Bois penned a counterargument in his defense. In March 1949, Martin D. Jenkins, president of Morgan State College in Baltimore, had invited Du Bois to be the school's commencement speaker that spring, for an honorarium of one hundred dollars plus expenses. After the Paris congress, Jenkins hastily cancelled the engagement: "Your appearance with Mr. Paul Robeson . . . and, particularly, your failure to condemn his treasonable statement made at that meeting have linked you in the public mind with the Communist movement in this country."[21]

Du Bois appeared before the House Committee on Foreign Affairs on 8 August 1949 to testify against the Truman administration's request for $1.5 billion to finance the North Atlantic Treaty Organization and to suppress leftist movements in Greece and Turkey. Before a hostile audience, Du Bois warned Congressmen: "if you vote this blank check, gentlemen, do not assume that you will decide when and where to fight." More receptive was Du Bois's audience in Moscow, where one thousand delegates from 14 countries participated in the 25–27 August 1949 Peace Congress. Du Bois surveyed the gathering: "They were artisans, miners, peasants, workers, intellectuals and professional men. . . . This was no crowd of cringing slaves nor fearful followers of command." All the speakers emphasized the need to maintain peace. Du Bois was particularly moved by a "Polish woman of amazonian proportions" who spoke from the "rostrum with tears in her eyes, 'Every drop of blood in my heart shouts, "Never again War."'" Du Bois's speech in Moscow was significant in that he was the only American present. "I represent millions of citizens of the United States who are just as opposed to war as you are," Du Bois declared. He briefly analyzed the historical evolution of America's political economy and suggested that the domestic peace movement's prospects were directly related to the redefinition of democracy. "No great American industry admits that it could or should be controlled by those who do its work. But unless democratic methods enter industry, democracy fails in other paths of life." The only way to achieve peace and social reform for Negroes, Du Bois stated, "is for the

American people to take control of the nation in industry as well as government."[22]

Years before the rise of "McCarthyism," Federal and state governments had adopted anti-Communist statutes. In 1939–41, the Alien Registration Act, widely called the Smith Act, was used to imprison Communists and Trotskyists. But the serious offensive against the left in the postwar years was initiated largely by Garvey's old nemesis, FBI director J. Edgar Hoover. On 5 February 1948, Hoover submitted a massive document to U.S. Attorney General Tom Clark, entitled "Brief to Establish the Illegal Status of the Communist Party of the United States of America." Although the FBI could not "cite a single case of the advocacy or use of violence" by Communists against the American government, the administration had decided to destroy the Marxist movement. On 20 July 1948, twelve key leaders of the Communist party were indicted by a federal grand jury for violating the Smith Act. Eleven of them were convicted on 14 October 1949 and received the maximum sentence of five years in prison and a ten-thousand-dollar fine each. Within several years, 146 Communists were indicted, and thousands lost their jobs or were forced underground. This was just the beginning of the reaction against the American left. At the CIO's 1949 convention, the fifty-thousand-member United Electrical, Radio, and Machine Workers of America was expelled on the grounds that the union had endorsed Henry Wallace in 1948 and that it opposed the Truman administration's foreign policies. Ten other progressive unions, with a combined membership of nearly one million workers, were soon expelled from the CIO. In the motion picture industry, major producers voted to ban any employment of "Communists"—a term that increasingly meant liberal New Dealers as well as Marxists. The most dramatic manifestation of Cold War terror in 1949 occurred at Peekskill, New York. Vigilantes attacked the audience at a Robeson outdoor concert on 27 August. One week later a second Robeson performance was held, despite fierce physical intimidation and mob violence.[23]

Du Bois was appalled by the upsurgence of political intolerance. "This is a time when any man who sincerely questions the efficiency of industrial organization of the United States is liable to be called a revolutionist, a traitor, and a liar," Du Bois noted in a 1949 essay published in the *Midwest Journal*. "If he attempts to defend his position he may lose his friends, his influence, and what is more important, he may lose his chance to earn a decent living. Such a situation is one of the greatest dangers, not only to the person himself but even more to his family, his nation, and the civilization in which he lives." Americans were being taught to regard Marxism as "not only dangerous but malevolent," yet no free and open study of its "accomplishments" were tolerated. Blinders were being placed before the "pursuit of knowledge," and the cause of civil rights and all political liberties would soon be curtailed. Du Bois publicly protested the persecution of the "Hollywood Ten," progressive writers and directors who had been cited for contempt of Congress by the House Un-American Activities Committee. In the fall of 1949 he campaigned for the unsuccessful reelection of Benjamin Davis, Jr., to the New York City Council. "This country has gone stark crazy," Du Bois lamented to Padmore in March 1950. "Our Civil Rights are only glimmering."[24]

Du Bois's principal involvement in the peace movement during 1950 was his work as chairman of the Peace Information Center. Initiated by O. John Rogge on 3 April, the small center printed and circulated the "Stockholm Appeal," an international statement adopted by the World Partisans of Peace in Stockholm in March 1950. The appeal simply called for the "absolute banning" of atomic weapons. Nearly one-half billion people throughout the world signed this peace statement in 1950–52. The Peace Information Center was a small operation. Members of its advisory board, which included Rogge, Robeson, Graham, and John T. McManus, were extensively involved in other progressive activities. From April through mid-October 1950, the center received a total of only $23,000, mostly from small donations and the sale of literature. Although the center maintained no structural connections with foreign peace organizations or domestic formations, it was able to secure the signatures of 2.5 million Americans on the Stockholm appeal.

The initial attack against the Peace Information Center was launched by Secretary of State Dean Acheson on 12 July 1950. Acheson termed the Stockholm pledge "a propaganda trick in the spurious 'peace offensive' of the Soviet Union." In a press statement, Du Bois replied to Acheson: "Must any proposals for averting atomic catastrophe be sanctified by Soviet opposition? . . . Today in this country it is becoming standard reaction to call anything 'communist' and therefore subversive and unpatriotic, which anybody for any reason dislikes. We feel strongly that this tactic has already gone too far; that it is not sufficient today to trace a proposal to a communist source in order to dismiss it with contempt." With the remarkable success of the center in securing endorsements for the Stockholm appeal, the federal government decided to act. FBI agent John J. Kearney was assigned to attend a Peace Information Center public meeting to collect evidence. A young medical student, William B. Reed, was hired by the FBI to visit the center's offices. During four occasions at the center he procured materials and listened at least once to a private telephone conversation. Reed gave the evidence to J. B. Matthews, formerly the chief investigator for the House Un-American Activities Committee. When Du Bois attempted to obtain a visa to attend a meeting of the Bureau of World Partisans of Peace, held in Prague in August 1950, he was harrassed and nearly denied his passport.[25]

During this latest political turmoil, Nina Du Bois died on 1 July 1950, after almost five years as an invalid. Du Bois buried his beloved wife next to the grave of their son, Burghardt, in Great Barrington. He also wrote an eloquent tribute to Nina in the *Chicago Globe*. Padmore learned of Du Bois's latest sorrow and extended a thoughtful letter of condolence: "Please accept my heartfelt sympathy in the loss you have sustained. . . . [we] rejoice in the knowledge that, in spite of advancing age, you are still with us to inspire and lead the struggle for African liberation." Perhaps for the first time, Du Bois keenly felt his age and limitations. "I was lonesome because so many boyhood friends had died, and because a certain illogical reticence on my part had never brought me many intimate friends," Du Bois observed. Shirley Graham, now his closest friend and coworker, provided much valuable support. By the end of the year, she "finally persuaded herself" that Du Bois "needed her help and companionship" permanently. Overcoming his reluctance, Du Bois agreed that they should be married. A wedding date was planned for late February 1951.[26]

In August 1950, the American Labor Party (ALP) of New York, a progressive organization, asked Du Bois to run as its candidate for the U.S. Senate. He laughed when he first heard the proposal. But Du Bois recognized that his candidacy might help to reelect Congressman Vito Marcantonio of New York, an ALP member who had led the fight against the Cold War in the House of Representatives. In his 1952 book *In Battle For Peace,* Du Bois commented: "I found myself increasingly proscribed in pulpit, school and platform. My opportunity to write for publication was becoming narrower and narrower, even in the Negro press. I wondered if a series of plain talks in a political campaign would not be my last and only chance to tell the truth as I saw it." Du Bois agreed to run for the Senate, "knowing well from the first" that he had no chance to win and that the campaign "would bring me ridicule at best and jail at worst." In the fall of 1950 Du Bois canvassed the state, giving ten major addresses and seven radio broadcasts. Robeson was proud of his friend but a little worried about the "grueling pace of the campaign." "In the usual free-for-all scramble which American political campaigns involve, Dr. Du Bois always remained calm and dignified," Robeson wrote later. "He never descended to shrill attack or name-calling, but discussed the real issues with brilliant speeches in which he combined his keen intelligence and trenchant humor." With almost no advertising budget and a virtual press boycott of the campaign, Du Bois plugged away. Mass meetings were held in Harlem, the Bronx, Brooklyn, and Queens. A Madison Square Garden rally on 24 October attracted seventeen thousand people. Du Bois's basic theme was an appeal for peace and civil rights: "The most sinister evil of this day is the widespread conviction that war is inevitable and that there is no time left for discussion. . . . In modern world war all contestants lose and not only lose the immediate causes of strife, but cripple the fundamental bases of human culture."[27]

Both Du Bois and Marcantonio were defeated in the November 1950 elections. There have been several attempts to minimize Du Bois's accomplishments during this campaign.[28] Du Bois had hoped to obtain at least 10,000 votes and was pleasantly surprised to receive almost 210,000, 4 percent of the electorate. In black communities, Du Bois did best—receiving about 12.6 percent of all votes cast in Harlem. The campaign illustrated that thousands of Americans could withstand Cold War propaganda and support a peace candidate who had absolutely no chance of being elected. In January 1951, Du Bois evaluated his recent experiences in the democratic process before a Yale University Law School audience. Both South Carolina and Connecticut, he observed, had the same number of Congressmen. "But South Carolina needed but 100,000 votes, to elect hers, while it took 800,000 to elect yours. Thus in the leading democracy in the world members of the Congress are not elected by majority vote." Du Bois's electoral total from his senate campaign was far greater than many southern "Dixiecrats" who sat on powerful congressional committees. The racial "caste system, still strong, far-reaching, and cruel," undermined democratic government and fed the movement toward economic and political reaction. Part of the problem resided with the failure of educators and intellectuals to adhere to their democratic convictions. "Today our rightful intelligentsia is curiously dumb and our political leadership, sunken to a low level. We seem unable to think, reason clearly or act with decision." Du Bois had become convinced that the United States, despite its rhetoric, "never has been a democracy. . . . Our industrial enterprise is dominated by vast monopolies and our freedom of thought increasingly chained by law, police spies and refusal to let anybody earn a decent living who does not think as he is told to think."[29]

Du Bois's continued agitation against Cold War repression placed government authorities in a difficult position. Despite his removal from the NAACP, Du Bois was still the most prominent black intellectual in the country. Even in 1948, John Gunther's *Inside U.S.A.* noted that Du Bois "has a position almost like that of Shaw or Einstein, being the most venerable and distinguished of leaders in his field." But Du Bois's circulation of the Stockholm appeal and his senatorial race pushed the government to take punitive measures. On 11 August 1950, the Department of Justice demanded the Peace Information Center to register "as an agent of a foreign principal." The center's attorney, Gloria Agrin, replied that the group "was conceived and formed" by Americans and had no external ties to foreign agencies or governments. On 19 September the Justice Department again ordered the center to register "without further delay." The center was dissolved on 12 October 1950, during the middle of Du Bois's senatorial campaign. But this failed to satisfy the government. A federal grand jury was formed in Washington, D.C., to investigate possible indictments against the center's principal officers. On 9 February 1951, the Peace Information Center was indicted for "failure to register as agent of a foreign principal." Five defendants were named: Elizabeth Moos, a teacher; Sylvia Soloff, the center's secretary; Abbott Simon, an attorney; Kyrle Elkin, a Harvard University graduate and small businessman; and Du Bois. All five faced a possible fine of ten thousand dollars each and five years in federal prison.[30]

Shirley Graham first learned about the indictments from Du Bois on the evening of February ninth. In her own words, she insisted that their marriage occur immediately: "This, I knew was no time for maiden coyness. . . . With him in jail, only a wife could carry the case to the people. *I must be in a position to stand at his side*—this I felt was essential." Shirley Graham and Du Bois were married on the night of February fourteenth. Two days later, in the Federal District Court in Washington, the indicted peace activists were arraigned. Du Bois did not know precisely what to expect: his only previous court appearance had been in 1918, when he was fined twenty-five dollars for speeding. The experience was an unnecessary humiliation. Du Bois and the others were fingerprinted; their clothing was searched for concealed weapons. Then the eighty-two-year-old man was manacled for ten minutes. After vigorous protests from Du Bois's attorneys, the marshal reluctantly removed the handcuffs and bail was set at one thousand dollars each. At his arraignment, Du Bois calmly read a statement: "It is a sad commentary that we must enter a courtroom today to plead Not Guilty to something that cannot be a crime—advocating peace and friendship between the American people and the peoples of the world. . . . In a world which has barely emerged from the horrors of the Second World War and which trembles on the brink of an atomic catastrophe, can it be criminal to hope and work for peace?"[31]

Months before Du Bois's indictment, friends at the Council on African Affairs had planned to celebrate his eighty-third birthday at a public gathering. Donations would be used to print some of Du Bois's unpublished manuscripts, to reprint older works, and to subsidize his research at the council. The Essex House in New York City was reserved, and E. Franklin Frazier volunteered as chairman of the sponsoring committee. Honorary chairs for the occasion included Mary Church Terrell; Alain Locke; Mary White Ovington; Mordecai Johnson, the president of Howard University; and Rabbi Abba Hillel Silver, formerly president of the Zionist Organization of America. By early February 1951, about three hundred people had reserved seats and had paid over two thousand dollars. When the Peace Information Center's officers were indicted, the press quickly convicted them without waiting for the trial. Typical was one *New York Herald Tribune* editorial, published on 11 February: "The Du Bois outfit was set up to promote a tricky appeal of Soviet origin, poisonous in its surface innocence, which made it appear that a signature against the use of atomic weapons would forthwith insure world peace. It was, in short, an attempt to disarm America and yet ignore every form of Communist aggression." The banquet's major speakers—Rabbi Silver, Mordecai Johnson, and President Charlotte Hawkins Brown of the Palmer Memorial Institute in North Carolina—immediately withdrew. Brown apologized by telegram, explaining that her most influential trustee would resign "if I appear on [the] Du Bois program." There was simply "great fear of Communist influence." Ralph Bunche, the Nobel Peace Prize recipient in 1950, had also declined the invitation, as did Arthur Spingarn and many original sponsors. The Essex House cancelled the contract and returned the deposit for the dinner. "I can stand a good deal," Du Bois confessed later, "but this experience was rather more than I felt like bearing, especially as the blows continued to fall. . . . I was more than ready to drop all thought of the birthday dinner."[32]

But Shirley Graham, Robeson, Frazier, and other friends refused to buckle beneath this repression. No white hotel in Manhattan would accommodate the testimonial banquet. But a modest restaurant in Harlem was secured and new speakers were scheduled—Robeson and Bedford Lawson, head of Du Bois's graduate fraternity Alpha Phi Alpha. In a room filled to capacity, seven hundred people, who contributed over $6,500 in fees and donations, were in attendance. The mood was festive and defiant, and Robeson spoke "courageously and feelingly." Dozens of birthday cakes had been baked. Letters and cablegrams were read from well-wishers. From the United States, messages were received from President Benjamin E. Mays of Morehouse College, Catholic Archbishop William H. Francis, Langston Hughes, Judge Hubert T. Delany, Mary McLeod Bethune, and many more. From abroad, birthday greetings were forwarded by the Reverend Hewlett Johnson, dean of Canterbury Cathedral; Soviet composer Dmitri Shostakovitch; Frederic Joliot-Curie, president of the World Peace Council and former French high commissioner for atomic energy; Marxist philosopher Georg Lukács of Hungary; Vice-Premier Kuo Mo Jo of the People's Republic of China, and others. In honoring Du Bois, these women and men were affirming their commitment to world peace and social justice. Du

Bois later thanked Frazier for his "courageous stand" and added: "We are still in of course for the rather nasty fight in the matter of this indictment, but we are going to fight to the end. It's a big opportunity and I am willing to go to jail in order to make the courts face the issue and make the United States and especially Negro Americans know what they are up against."[33]

The trial was postponed several times and did not begin until 8 November 1951. This gave Du Bois and the other defendants sufficient time to prepare their defense and to mobilize popular support. They were fortunate to obtain the counsel of several excellent attorneys, including Gloria Agrin and the black law firm of Cobb, Howard and Hayes in Washington, D.C. As chief counsel, Marcantonio volunteered his services without a fee. Technically, the government's case was at best extremely weak, even spurious. Had the prosecution ever admitted that the Peace Information Center had been formally dissolved before the indictment was rendered, no case would exist. Du Bois and his associates were not being tried as Communists—although the press and much of the general public drew this conclusion. The entire case rested on the government's claim that the center had "acted as an agent or in a capacity similar to that for a foreign organization or foreign political power." This would be literally impossible to prove, because there was no formal or financial connection between the center and any other body, beyond its circulation of peace literature.[34]

When Du Bois, Graham, and other supporters explained the specific details of the case, most observers were shocked that the government had been able to secure indictments. But few were willing to jeopardize their careers to defend Du Bois. Arthur Garfield Hays, national director of the American Civil Liberties Union, attempted to persuade his organization's board to assist Du Bois. In April, Hays forwarded Du Bois a letter of apology: "The general opinion seemed to be that we should take no position in connection with the indictment. . . . Since we did not oppose the indictment where unpopular Nazi groups were involved we should not oppose it now merely because friends of ours are involved." A petition was prepared that defended Du Bois's "integrity and absolute sincerity" and described his indictment as government "intimidation." Du Bois was "deeply disappointed" when his supporters were unable to obtain enough "signatures to this statement to warrant its circulation." One black leader refused to sign the petition in order to protect his son's government job. Others gave no excuses or were simply silent. The black press was generally supportive, but a *Chicago Defender* editorial deplored that Du Bois "should have become embroiled in activities that have been exposed as subversive." Du Bois's Sigma Pi Phi fraternity refused to extend greetings at the birthday celebration, and only one chapter of the fraternity defended his integrity in a public statement before the trial. The National Baptist Convention did nothing; among the black college presidents, only Charles S. Johnson of Fisk—whose selection in 1946 Du Bois had opposed—publicly expressed support for him.[35]

The behavior of the NAACP's leaders was malignant. When Shirley Graham appealed directly to Arthur Spingarn for support, he stated that "of course the Soviet Union was furnishing funds for the Peace Information Center, although . . . 'possibly' [Du Bois] might not be aware of it." Branches of the Association demanded that the organization extend "active, tangible aid" to Du Bois. At the NAACP board meeting of 12 March 1951, White claimed to have consulted the attorney general's office and had been assured that "definite evidence of guilt" existed. The board finally issued a bland statement of token support that included a disclaimer on "the merits of the recent indictment." The national office ordered locals "not to touch" the case or to extend any moral or material support to Du Bois. Complaints continued to surface from Association branches. In July 1951, sixty-five branches came to the national convention with resolutions on Du Bois's behalf, and a strong statement of solidarity was ratified. But White did not leave matters alone. Even the day before Du Bois's acquittal, White claimed in Milwaukee that "irrefutable proof" existed that funds for the Center "came from Moscow."[36]

One major difficulty for Du Bois and his colleagues was financial: the trial cost the defendants thirty-five thousand dollars. A defense committee was established, headed by Robeson and former Minnesota governor Elmer Bensen. Doxey Wilkerson carried out many of the committee's tasks. In June and September Du Bois toured the country. Crowds became larger and more receptive during the second tour, although in Detroit Du Bois was placed under a "continuous body-guard" by his hosts, and the local NAACP refused to cosponsor his speech. In Chicago, local Negro leaders pledged $1,100 toward Du Bois's defense—but after he left town, only $445 was finally contributed, "despite many reminders from the committee." In Denver, however, two thousand people attended a church rally in Du Bois's behalf, and the NAACP branch voted unanimously to oppose their leader's "persecution by the government." Local "Defense Committees for Dr. Du Bois" were initiated at Fisk, Wilberforce, the University of Texas, the University of Chicago, and other colleges. Hundreds of letters and telegrams were forwarded both to President Truman and the Justice Department denouncing the trial. Although it is difficult to assess who were the various constituencies supporting Du Bois, it is clear that the vast majority of black workers—and significant numbers of white trade unionists—comprised the core of his defense movement. Thirteen national and international unions led by Ben Gold of the Fur and Leather Workers Union, for example, held a banquet that raised twenty-three hundred dollars for Du Bois's defense. The Talented Tenth was divided, and a majority of black leaders in education, politics, and business were either silent or critical of Du Bois. Gordon B. Hancock, a conservative black sociologist and journalist, best described the situation in late 1951: "The important Negroes of this country, the head-liners, the highly positioned, the degreed Negroes stayed off the petition by droves. Negroes who claim to be race champions . . . actually deserted Dr. Du Bois in the hour of his greatest trial."[37]

More impressive was Du Bois's international support. The International Committee in Defense of Dr. W. E. B. Du Bois and his Colleagues was initiated; it quickly grew to include two hundred prominent members. Lead-ers of the world peace movement issued letters of solidarity; Pablo Neruda and Jorge Amado circulated a protest statement throughout Latin America; student associations in China and Vietnam forwarded protests to the United States; even Bulgarian Orthodox priests drafted a protest letter, "since our Lord Jesus Christ himself preached world peace for all men of good will." The Soviets responded to Du Bois's indictment "with a sense of profound indignation," according to one reporter. The trial was widely viewed as "an act of inhumanity." The International Union of Students, with five million members in seventy-two nations, wrote the Justice Department: "Prose-cution is an attack upon peace supporters, upon Negro people and upon [the] right of professors and students to act for peace." Padmore used his invaluable connections with black workers' movements to assist Du Bois. "We consider this attempt to blackmail you into silence an outrage against the fundamental principles of democracy and an insult to Africans and peo-ples of African descent throughout the world," Padmore wrote Du Bois in March 1951. "For in you, sir, we see the finest representative of our peo-ple's hopes, dream and ambition." In several months, protests and appeals came from the black Caribbean; letters of solidarity arrived from the Pro-gressive Syndicalists of Djibouti and French Somaliland; rallies of support were held by workers in the General Federation of Trade Unions of Marti-nique and by trade unionists in Madagascar. What had started as a simple court case was rapidly becoming an international incident.[38]

One simple measure of Du Bois's importance as a democratic leader was the "generous offer" of Albert Einstein to do "anything" he could to defend Du Bois.[39] After the arraignment, the Justice Department tried to persuade Marcantonio to allow Du Bois to plead "nolo contendere" and receive a sus-pended sentence. Convinced of his innocence, Du Bois refused to compro-mise. When the trial began, the prosecution called only seven of its twenty-seven witnesses. The major prosecution witness was O. John Rogge, who had broken with the peace movement in the previous year. Rogge testified that the center he had helped to initiate was definitely connected with in-ternational groups that promoted "the foreign policy of the Soviet Union."

But Rogge was fatal for the prosecution's case: he was admittedly a "paid agent" for the Yugoslavian government; he had visited and spoken in the Soviet Union; and he presented no evidence proving any concrete link between the center and other peace organizations. Desperately, the government's lawyers tried to establish their case on circumstantial evidence, by comparing the center's literature with the "propaganda" of foreign peace advocates. Judge James McGuire, a political conservative, failed to accept the government's arguments. Marcantonio's motion for a directed acquittal was granted on 20 November, before the defense had called its witnesses. [40]

Why was the Justice Department "so arrogant, determined, and certain?" Du Bois asked in *In Battle For Peace.* "Why did it so impudently brush off my offer to explain our whole work?" Marcantonio had raised the same questions with the federal prosecutors in Judge McGuire's chambers. "You have no case and why don't you admit it?" Marcantonio exploded with anger. Apologizing for his remarks, he still insisted that the "prosecution wants to convict these defendants on their political views."[41] In retrospect, it seems probable that the Justice Department sought primarily to discredit and silence Du Bois, rather than place an eighty-three-year-old man in a federal prison. Most prominent black leaders, with the "notorious" exception of Robeson, had already fallen into line behind the anticommunist campaign. Charles S. Johnson, for example, had fired Giovanni Rossi Lomanitz from Fisk's faculty in 1949, when the professor refused to testify against himself before the House Un-American Activities Committee. Johnson later dismissed Fisk mathematics professor Lee Lorch, a civil rights activist, on similar grounds.[42] Randolph had become, second only to White, a leader of black anticommunisim. In 1952, he toured Asia under the auspices of the Congress of Cultural Freedom, denouncing the Soviet Union's "slavery" and stressing the racial progress achieved in the United States. Only in 1967 was it revealed that Randolph's speeches had been subsidized indirectly by the Central Intelligence Agency. The Congress of Racial Equality (CORE), founded in 1941 by black social democrats Bayard Rustin and James Farmer, initiated its own "purge" of suspected Marxists in 1948, and openly denounced any association with "Communist-controlled" groups.[43] The Department of Justice may have expected Du Bois to accept the "nolo contendere" plea and to acquiesce to the politics of Cold War conformity.

But Du Bois could never do this. The trial was a symbolic test of his personal integrity and morality, as well as his politics. The key to Du Bois's behavior during the Cold War is revealed in his 1908 lecture "Galileo Galilei" at the Fisk University commencement. Like Du Bois, Galileo had been viewed as "a dangerous soul." As a scientist, he had "started to know, to observe, to prove, to dream. In doing so he met the Opposition—the obstacles that ever block the way of the man who proposes in thought or deed, something New." The Catholic Church considered Galileo's studies heretical and threatened him with torture. Finally, at the age of seventy, Galileo renounced his life's work. Du Bois asked: "Did it pay? Was the truth worth a lie?. . . . The verdict of civilization must be that not even the splendor of the service of Truth done by Galileo Galilei can wipe away the blot of his cowardly lie. By that lie, civilization was halted, science was checked, and bigotry was more strongly enthroned on its crimson glory." The meaning of Galileo's tragedy for black America was obvious. "A stubborn determination at this time on the part of the Negro race, to uphold its ideals . . . means victory," Du Bois declared. "But a course of self-abasement and surrender . . . means indefinite postponement of the true emancipation of the Negro race."[44] Du Bois would accept imprisonment, and possibly death, for the sake of his ideals. This was the message of John Brown and Nat Turner; this was the ultimate meaning of the lives of Douglass and Crummell. As Du Bois stated in 1946, happy is the man "who fights in despair and in defeat still fights."[45]

But the persecution was not finished. Du Bois was acquitted, but his punishment had barely begun. In 1951, the NAACP reduced his annual pension without notice from $2400 to $1200. In February 1952, Du Bois and Graham applied for visas to attend a peace conference in Brazil. The State Department denied permission, claiming that "your proposed travel would be contrary to the best interests of the United States." Graham's passport was also "retained" by the department. Several months later, Du Bois was invited to address the national conference of the Canadian Peace Congress, held in Toronto. Arriving at the Toronto airport, Graham and Du Bois were prohibited from entering Canada. They were forcibly placed on the next airplane back to the United States.[46]

Prestigious periodicals such as *Foreign Affairs,* the *American Journal of Sociology, New Republic,* and the *Journal of Negro Education* no longer solicited Du Bois's essays. Harcourt, Brace and Company, the publishers of *Darkwater, Dark Princess, Black Reconstruction, Dusk of Dawn,* and *Color and Democracy,* rejected Du Bois's manuscript "America and Russia." The volume was circulated to several publishing houses, and all eventually turned it down. It was never published. Du Bois was trapped in a Kafkaesque situation: he had committed no crime; he had achieved great national recognition as a writer, researcher, and civil rights leader; and he was not yet a member of the Communist party. Nevertheless, he was "rejected of men, refused the right to travel abroad and classed as 'controversial figure' even after being acquitted of guilt by a Federal court of law." Du Bois's mail was "tampered with or withheld"; police interrogated his neighbors "asking about my visitors"; universities and churches no longer requested his lectures; black newspapers generally refused to publish his essays. The leaders of the civil rights group he had founded were among the first to condemn him even before his trial. It was like being buried alive. "It was a bitter experience and I bowed before the storm," Du Bois confessed later. "But I did not break."[47]

9

STERN PROPHET, FLAMING ANGEL

The last two decades of Dr. Du Bois's life cannot be ignored or written off. They contain, both in his actions and in writings, the most valuable lessons of his long life, the peaks of his wisdom and understanding. . . . The enemies of Dr. Du Bois and Black freedom understand this.

David Graham Du Bois,
1982

I hope you will not either over-stress that earlier part of my career or forget that latter part. There seem to be a considerable number of persons who think that I died when [Booker T.] Washington did, which is an exaggeration.

W. E. B. Du Bois to Arna Bontemps,
3 November 1952

"Blessed are the Peacemakers for they shall be called Communists," observed Du Bois in 1952. "Is this shame for the Peacemakers or praise for the Communists?"[1] Du Bois and the members of the Peace Information Center had challenged the government in court and had won. But other progressives, Marxists and liberals alike, were usually less fortunate. Many of Du Bois's friends paid a heavy penalty for their ideals. Robeson's passport was seized in August 1950, and like Du Bois, he was even refused permission to enter Canada. The secretary of the Council on African Affairs, Alphaeus Hunton, served five months in jail for "refusing to act as an informer" for the government. The national executive secretary of the progressive

Civil Rights Congress, William L. Patterson, was jailed in April 1954; Claude Lightfoot, a black Communist leader in Illinois, was arrested in June 1954 and later received a five-year prison sentence and a five-thousand-dollar fine. Black Marxist organizer Claudia Jones, whose political commitment and activities Du Bois particularly admired, was imprisoned and later deported to England. Black Communist leader Henry Winston was sentenced to eight years in prison; gross neglect by prison authorities led to his loss of sight during his incarceration. Despite these hardships, these women and men showed remarkable courage. Benjamin Davis, Jr., for example, persistently challenged prison officials. At the federal penitentiary in Terre Haute, Davis initiated a court case against racial segregation inside the facility.[2]

The national hysteria of the Red Scare, promulgated by both the Truman and Eisenhower administrations and by the extreme right, led to an unprecedented series of laws that fundamentally compromised American democracy. The number of congressional investigations into communism reached twenty four in 1949–50 and peaked at fifty one during the Eighty-third Congress of 1953–54. By late 1950, the Communist party was specifically outlawed from electoral participation in seventeen states. Michigan sanctioned life imprisonment "for writing or speaking subversive words"; Massachusetts approved a penalty of three years' imprisonment for any individual permitting Marxists to meet in their homes or on their property. Convicted Communists in Georgia were subject to twenty years' imprisonment; and in 1954, Texas governor Allan Shivers asked his state legislature to make membership in the Communist party a capital offense, punishable by execution. Local police departments initiated "red squads" that investigated "subversives" among municipal employees and school teachers. Controversial groups such as the Progressive party were denied the right to use public auditoriums and even parks for open meetings. Most colleges quickly accommodated themselves to McCarthyism. In 1948–49, the presidents of Harvard and Yale Universities informed their alumni and legislators that no Communists would ever be appointed to their respective faculties. In 1950, the University of California demanded that all faculty sign an oath stating that "Communists should not be allowed to teach." Many refused to sign, and within less than one year the university lost 110 professors.[3]

Political intolerance is often contagious. Many Negro middle-class leaders did their best to cooperate with reaction. The NAACP endorsed the deployment of U.S. troops in Korea "to halt Communist aggression." But the suppression of the left did not end with the Communist party or its friends. Robeson was banned, but he was not alone. Lena Horne was also briefly "blacklisted" as a "subversive." Black actors William Marshall and Canada Lee were virtually destroyed professionally. At least fifteen hundred artists were "blacklisted" from television and radio by 1954. Du Bois was a pariah within the academy, but others soon experienced the weight of the great fear. Professor Forest O. Wiggins, a black philosophy professor at the University of Minnesota, was constantly harassed by the FBI for his socialist views and membership in the Progressive party. Some students who openly defended Wiggins were later denied employment. In December 1952, Ira De A. Reid was accused of being a Communist party member by one paid informant at a congressional hearing. Reid was forced to deny his membership under oath. One former Communist swore before a loyalty board that Ralph Bunche, then a member of the United Nations Secretariat, was a member of the Communist party. After some difficulty, Bunche was finally cleared of the charges. Some black intellectuals, fearful that their careers might be ruined, made compromises in their academic and professional work. Even Langston Hughes—an artist who had once written a poem praising Stalin during the Depression—was not immune from this pressure. In 1955, Hughes prepared a text, *Famous Negro Music Makers,* that inexplicably deleted Robeson's contributions to black music. Du Bois had received an advance copy of Hughes's book and promptly contacted the publisher about the omission of Robeson. Du Bois learned sadly that Hughes had "decided that it would be unwise" to include Robeson, because it would mean that the book would be eliminated from "a good many school libraries, state adoption lists, etc."[4]

Du Bois refused to be intimidated by the moral obscenity of the Red Scare. He was seen by many as "a tower of strength," Shirley Graham later related. "He was constantly being called upon: to speak to some embattled harassed group, to appear as a witness before some committee or even in court, to sign a petition, to visit a family bowed in grief because one of its members had been 'taken away.'" Du Bois demanded amnesty for all Smith Act political prisoners. He campaigned for the release of Benjamin Davis, Jr., and actively challenged all repressive legislation. Before Charles S. Johnson dismissed Lee Lorch from the Fisk University faculty, Du Bois drafted a strong letter in the professor's defense. Lorch's removal, Du Bois argued, would be "an unwarranted attack upon a man of high character and of learning, and a denial of freedom of thought and expression in a nation founded to protect liberty."[5] Du Bois was prominent in the political defense of Ethel and Julius Rosenberg, who were charged by the government for allegedly conspiring to conduct espionage for the Soviets. After their execution, Du Bois gave a moving eulogy at their funeral services. His open defiance led to increased surveillance and political harassment. Du Bois's books were seized by postal authorities without explanation. Invitations to appear on academic programs were rudely withdrawn. When Du Bois was scheduled to speak at Levittown Hall on Long Island, local authorities banned the meeting on the grounds of Du Bois's "Communist-front affiliations." Shirley Graham's novel on Aaron Burr, the product of six years' research, was rejected by seventeen publishers before she received a contract. And within several months, this publishing house refused to print the book, although she had received an advance on royalties. The fear of any connection with radicalism was simply too great.[6]

Politically, Du Bois viewed McCarthyism as a repudiation of America's democratic heritage. "I believe in Socialism as well as Democracy," Du Bois wrote in *In Battle For Peace*. "I have obeyed my country's laws even when I thought some of these laws barbarous." The political reaction, however, against all liberal and progressive thought threatened civil liberties and the very existence of democracy. The jailing of Americans because of their political opinions was ultimately dangerous to all citizens: "Such reasoning in the past would have hanged Washington and Jefferson; sent Garrison, Douglass and Phillips to jail for life, and imprisoned Eugene O'Neill and Harry Hopkins."[7] Tactically, the task of progressives was to radically reform the American two-party system; in the long term, this also meant a structural change within the apparatus of government.

Americans are "ruled by one party under two names," Du Bois observed. In a series of public lectures and articles, Du Bois outlined the necessity to "restore democracy to America." At an American Labor party rally of seventeen thousand people held in New York City on 13 May 1952, Du Bois delivered a stirring address on this topic. The country was confronted with tremendous problems, yet Americans "are allowed no free discussion on platform or over the radio; in newspapers or periodicals." All the major party candidates were controlled by the corporations. "All of them listen to their master's voice. . . . They are united in that supercongress of which the National Association of Manufacturers in the upper house and the United States Chamber of Commerce is the lower, which are preparing world war to rule mankind and reduce again the worker not simply to slavery but to idiocy." The Progressive party nominated attorney Vincent Hallinan and black newspaper publisher Charlotta Bass as their national candidates in 1952, and Du Bois actively supported their campaign. His partisan speech at Madison Square Garden in New York City on 27 October 1952 drew parallels between the South's struggle to maintain slavery and the national suppression of the left in the Cold War. "If you want to throw away your vote," Du Bois noted, "give it to [Dwight] Eisenhower or [Adlai] Stevenson." Both major party candidates could only "kowtow to the new slavery and kiss its blood-stained feet. . . . If you want to win, vote right, vote right and still vote right, if it takes a hundred years." Du Bois concluded by quoting (somewhat incorrectly) a stanza from a poem by Frederick William Faber, "On the Field," which linked the fight for democracy with moral

193

reformation: "For right is right, if God is God / And right the day shall win / To doubt it would be blasphemy / To falter would be sin."[8]

The majority of Du Bois's journalistic and political essays in the 1950s focused on three topics: the necessity to build the "third party" movement; the struggle for world peace and constructive relations with the Soviet Union; and assessments of the various African liberation movements. Repeatedly, he emphasized that democratic debate was hindered by the absence of a strong socialist or "Commonsense Party." Without effective alternatives, American voters had become "prisoners of propaganda." The 1956 presidential election was at best "a farce. We had no chance to vote for the questions in which we were really interested," Du Bois observed. The major parties' nominees "shadowboxed with the false fanfare and advertisement for the same policies, with infinitesimal shades of difference and with spurious earnestness."[9] Du Bois continued to support the international efforts for peace, despite his travel ban by the U.S. State Department. He contributed essays on the necessity for peaceful coexistence between the United States and the Soviet Union to the *New World Review,* the *National Guardian,* and *Jewish Life.* In January 1953, the World Peace Council awarded its annual peace prize to Du Bois, for his sacrifices and contributions to the cause of peace. In his letter of acceptance, Du Bois mentioned his embarrassment in receiving the award, given his "few and ineffective efforts for Peace. . . . Before this brutal Juggernaut of Wealth and Force my words have been fruitless and futile; but at least they have been spoken." Of course, the State Department prohibited Du Bois from traveling to Europe to accept this honor.[10]

The topic of Africa continued to dominate much of Du Bois's work. At the Jefferson School of Social Science in New York City, Du Bois gave a weekly seminar on comparative African politics and history in 1953. He donated much time to the Council on African Affairs and defended the organization against government repression. Both the Jefferson school and the council were finally forced to close in the mid-1950s because of federal harassment. However, Du Bois continued to write on African politics for Robeson's *Freedom* newspaper and in the *National Guardian.* Two of Du Bois's more important essays were "American Negroes and Africa," which appeared in the *National Guardian* in February 1955, and "Africa and the American Negro Intelligentsia," published later that same year in *Présence Africaine.* The termination of the council, Du Bois explained in the *National Guardian,* was a product of the federal government's hostility toward any progressive efforts by Afro-Americans on behalf of African independence and a result, as well, of the impact of antileft repression. Du Bois also suggested that many Afro-American middle-class leaders and the Negro press tacitly accepted the procolonialist policies of the U.S. government regarding Africa.

This argument was expanded more fully in the *Présence Africaine* article. "Leading American Negroes are today widely ignorant of the history and present situation in Africa and indifferent to the fate of African Negroes," Du Bois observed critically. "This represents a great change from the past." Reviewing the rich history of black America's cultural and political identity with the continent of Africa, Du Bois argued that the Negro intelligentsia had begun to repudiate this legacy. Black Americans after enfranchisement "turned entirely toward achieving citizenship and equality in the United States. . . . They were taught that Africa had no history and no culture and they became ashamed of any connection with it." Despite the rise of a Pan-African movement in the early twentieth century, the "black bourgeoisie" had lost all interest in Africa. "Today the American interest in Africa is almost confined to whites." Du Bois suggested that these "fatal trends" among black Americans would be reversed by the political emancipation of Africa and the impact of world socialism. "American Negroes, freed of their baseless fear of Communism, will again begin to turn their attention and aim their activity toward Africa." They would soon recognize the role of American capitalism in the exploitation of African people. "When once the blacks of the United States, the West Indies, and Africa work and think together," Du Bois concluded hopefully, "the future of the black man in the modern world is safe."[11]

As indicated by his essays on Africa, Du Bois continued to reevaluate some of his basic assumptions during the Cold War. The clearest indications of this were his critical reflections on the social class composition and political character of black America, and especially his view of the Talented Tenth. In a January 1953 speech, Du Bois explicitly denied that the "American Negro group" was a "nation" and added that blacks "do not even form a complete cultural unit." With increased racial integration, "it is difficult to say how far there is today a distinct American Negro culture and in what direction it will probably grow." Du Bois not only repudiated his own "nation in a nation" analogy of the 1930s but also the position taken as late as 1947 in his *Appeal to the World* document for the United Nations. Du Bois anticipated the acceleration of a national movement by blacks to abolish Jim Crow laws and looked forward to "increasing cooperation between white and colored union labor, especially in the South, until complete integration is reached." But Du Bois also worried that an "exploiting class is beginning to appear among Negroes. Its extreme development must be opposed."[12] The concern about class stratification within the Afro-American community was expressed several times by Du Bois. In *In Battle For Peace,* he admitted being "astonished to find well-to-do and educated American Negroes cow-ardly and dishonest." His Talented Tenth thesis had "naively" assumed that "trained members of the learned professions would supply leadership for the working classes." Although some black intellectuals had lived up to his expectations, most had not. Real leadership for black laborers came "mainly from intelligent and better paid workers." In the *National Guardian,* Du Bois remarked that a "choice" confronted black America—it could unite with other oppressed peoples to attack "poverty, ignorance and disease," or it could acquiesce to capitalism. Class divisions within the black population were a potential threat to political and social cohesion. [13]

What sustained Du Bois during these difficult years of government har-assment and political isolation? The supportive presence of Shirley Graham was of course most important. She shared her husband's ordeals and with grace and vigor gave unselfishly toward his ideals. The friendship of Marxist historian Herbert Aptheker was also of particular importance to Du Bois. After World War II Aptheker had begun to organize Du Bois's massive cor-respondence for publication, and the project drew them together. Du Bois valued Aptheker's scholarly writings, and the young historian's political views closely paralleled his own. [14] And as in previous decades, a generation of talented, young black intellectuals constantly sought Du Bois's advice and wisdom. In June 1954, a twenty-four-year-old writer, Lorraine Hansberry, asked Du Bois to speak at an Independence Day picnic. Du Bois had a delightful time, as did those in attendance. Elliott Skinner—later chair of the Columbia University anthropology department—first contacted Du Bois in May 1957. The young college instructor nervously explained: "I want to see and speak to the person who started to fight for me before I was even born. You can even say that I want to make a pilgrimage to see . . . one of the most important men in the world today." Du Bois graciously admitted Skin-ner into his home and engaged him "at length" about his research on Africa. Several months later, a young black historian, Sterling Stuckey, was warmly entertained in the Du Bois home. In his letter of gratitude, Stuckey noted: "You remain now as always my greatest single inspiration, for you represent . . . the New Negro in his finest form." [15]

The most important new element in constant contact with Du Bois, how-ever, was hundreds of white and black activists involved in the Progressive party, the peace movement, and the Communist party. David Graham Du Bois, Shirley Graham's son by a previous marriage, explains: "my mother gradually drew Dr. Du Bois into contact with leading figures of this new progressive movement. . . . In his presence, they behaved like disciples at the feet of the prophet. Slowly Dr. Du Bois found these white Americans to be of a different breed from those who early in his career had discouraged him from seeking out or desiring white company." [16] He praised their political courage, and he acquired a better understanding of the Communist party's theoretical and programmatic positions. In 1953, Du Bois publicly protested the imprisonment of Communist writer V. J. Jerome as "obscene" and "sacrilegious." He soon began to study Lenin's *Imperialism*, although admitting to Aptheker that the book left him "a little at sea in my own thinking." Du Bois became increasingly critical of black intellectuals who expressed anti-Marxist positions. In early 1955 Du Bois read Richard Wright's *Black Power*, and he complained to Padmore: "I don't like Wright . . . to write a book to attack Communism in Africa when there has been no Communism in Africa, and when the degradation of Africa is due to that Capitalism which Wright is defending—this is sheer contradiction." Nevertheless, Du Bois had certain intellectual and political reservations about identifying himself as a Marxist-Leninist. There were still occasions where he parted political company with the Communists. For example, in early 1958 he joined a number of independent leftists, ex-Communists, and Trotskyists to propose a "united Independent-Socialist" slate for the New York state elections. Benjamin Davis soon denounced the group, specifically objecting to the participation of "viciously anti-Soviet Trotskyists." But Du Bois refused to break from the left-wing electoral coalition. More fundamental, however, was Du Bois's belief that he was simply "too old" to claim any identity as a Marxist. "Most of my books were written before I read deeply of Marxism," Du Bois informed black Communist leader James E. Jackson. "I would have to rework, or append afterthoughts to each of them. I couldn't possibly live so long. No. They will have to judge me with the contemporaries of my generation against the then dominant philosophy—bourgeois democracy."[17]

Du Bois's general opinion of the Soviet Union continued to be positive—which was another important factor in his evolution as a Marxist. In 1953, he noted that the Soviets and other socialist states voted consistently for "non-white" interests at the United Nations. The Communists were the strongest defenders of national independence and antiracist movements throughout the world.[18] Even the events of 1956—the Khrushchev denunciation of Stalin, the major internal debates over policy inside the American Communist party, and political turmoil in Eastern Europe—did not shatter Du Bois's respect for the Communist movement. Du Bois had never idolized Stalin, and he tried to place the former leader's crimes into a broader political context of social achievement. Stalin was "not perfect" and "probably too cruel," Du Bois observed in July 1956. "If in his last years he became an irresponsible tyrant, that was very bad. . . . But he was not the first tyrant in the world and will not be the last." Stalin did, however, achieve "three things: he established the first socialist state; he broke the power of the kulaks; and he conquered Hitler." Du Bois defended the accomplishments of the "Stalin era" in several political journals in early 1957, and contributed a note of congratulations to the *Literary Gazette* in Moscow on the fortieth anniversary of the Bolshevik Revolution. "I am quite prepared to believe that Stalin was at times a cruel taskmaster; I do not doubt that suspicion and unjust punishment have been rife in the Soviet Union when tolerance and justice would have served better," Du Bois wrote. "On occasion, human nature is horrible and human beings beastly, but the world progresses; men reel and stagger forward; and never before in the history of man, have they made so gallant and successful a struggle as in the Soviet Union."[19]

The most significant literary works of Du Bois during the Cold War were his revision of *The Souls of Black Folk* and the completion of his *Black Flame* trilogy. In 1953, the Blue Heron Press of New York City prepared to print a fiftieth anniversary edition of *The Souls of Black Folk,* and Du Bois reviewed his old classic "for the first time in years." He was disturbed to find several incidental references to Jews that might be interpreted by some as anti-Semitic. "As I re-read these words today, I see that harm might come if they were allowed to stand as they are," Du Bois wrote Aptheker in February 1953. "By stressing the name of the group instead of what some members of [it] may have done, I was unjustly maligning a people in exactly the same way my folk were then and are now falsely accused." Du Bois had long despised anti-Semitism; in 1952 he had contributed a powerful attack on Jewish oppression to the journal *Jewish Life.* During the summer of 1953 Du Bois deleted any negative or questionable references to Jews in his book. In the new edition, which was limited to one thousand copies, these revisions were not explicitly discussed. But Du Bois did comment on two other theoretical shortcomings of *The Souls of Black Folk* in his introduction. "As a student of James, Santayana and Royce, I was not unprepared for the revolution in psychology," Du Bois noted. Nevertheless, *Souls* did not "adequately allow for unconscious thought and the growth and influence of race prejudice." More serious was his failure to include the thought of Marx in his interpretation of the black experience. The "color line" still remained "a great problem of this century," Du Bois observed. But behind the dilemma of racism "lies a greater problem which both obscures and implements it: and that is the fact that so many civilized persons are willing to live in comfort even if the price of this is poverty, ignorance and disease of the majority of their fellowmen." In short, the struggle against racism was an aspect of the larger effort to transform the capitalist political economy.[20]

Du Bois had begun to write the initial volume of the *Black Flame* trilogy, *The Ordeal of Mansart,* in the 1940s. By the time he was fired from the NAACP in 1948, about 150 rough manuscript pages had been completed. Published between 1957 and 1961, the three volumes—which also included

Mansart Builds a School (1959) and *Worlds of Color* (1961)—comprised over one thousand pages. The trilogy documents the fictional life of Manuel Mansart, a black intellectual who becomes the president of a small black college in Georgia, and the lives of his four children. Through these central characters, Du Bois presents his own changing perceptions over eight decades of black history. In vivid detail, Du Bois's characters are constantly confronted with racist violence: Mansart's father is lynched; Mansart's youngest son Bruce is forced to commit suicide after confessing to a murder; Douglas, Mansart's oldest child, kills white American officers at the battlefront during World War I. Most critics have found *The Black Flame* series the least successful of all of Du Bois's major works. Arnold Rampersad describes the trilogy as occasionally "sluggish" and as presenting a view of history "seen from the dark underside of America." Less charitably, Jack B. Moore wrote that *The Black Flame* was "by any conventional measure an artistic flop" and that its characters "are too often ridiculous, one-dimensional, inconsistent, and erratic." When contrasted with *The Quest of the Silver Fleece,* the later novels seem more pessimistic and are often harsh in their interpretations of black middle-class leaders and organizations. Booker T. Washington's demise as a leader is interpreted rather unfairly as the outcome of his New York City assault. In *Worlds of Color,* Du Bois criticizes the Negro press for ignoring "the mass of workers while glorifying the pushers and social climbers." The NAACP is blamed for failing to initiate a program for "economic justice"; and black politicians are characterized as "nonentities" who have "almost no weight politically." Nevertheless, the ordeal of the Mansart family leads to an optimistic conclusion. At Mansart's death, Africa had begun its emergence as a world power, marking "the end of white supremacy." Perhaps the most valuable feature of the novels was Du Bois's meticulous characterization of real figures, from Franklin D. Roosevelt to Kwame Nkrumah, which lends a striking sense of authenticity to the works. *The Black Flame* merits analysis as one of the most candid perspectives left by Du Bois about his own life and his views of other leaders.[21]

In the mid-1950s, the repressive political environment inside the United States gradually began to subside. Senator Joseph McCarthy was censured by the Senate in late 1954, and some politicians who had advanced their careers solely by anti-Communist rhetoric became less influential. Political suppression of the left still continued: in 1956 the progressive National Negro Labor Council, founded five years before by black labor leaders William R. Hood and Coleman Young, was destroyed as a "Communist-front organization." But on 17 May 1954, the Supreme Court ruled that any racial segregation in public schools was unconstitutional in the *Brown v. Board of Education* decision, which explicitly outlawed the "separate-but-equal" thesis of Jim Crow. In December 1955, blacks in Montgomery, Alabama, led by a young minister, Martin Luther King, Jr., initiated a mass, nonviolent boycott of the city's segregated buses. Du Bois quickly sensed that a new phase of black resistance was beginning and that the older generation of leaders from the pre–World War II period was rapidly being replaced. This feeling of transition was reinforced by the deaths of many of Du Bois's former associates during these years. Among the NAACP leaders, Ovington died in 1951, followed by Louis Wright in 1952 and Walter White in 1955. Four of Du Bois's major critics during the 1930s also expired—Charles S. Johnson (1956), George Streator (1955), Carter G. Woodson (1950), and Alain Locke (1954). Most grievous to Du Bois was the sudden death of Marcantonio in August 1954. Du Bois had outlived his adversaries and many of his comrades; but with fresh vigor he attempted to provide some direction to the new democratic movements and young leaders that had emerged in the post-McCarthy era.[22]

The *Brown* decision represented a major step forward toward the "complete freedom and equality between black and white Americans," Du Bois wrote in May 1954. But blacks had to "go further" to achieve full justice. In a February 1955 essay in *Jewish Life,* Du Bois reviewed the history of racial segregation in American schools. He congratulated the NAACP for leading the fight to challenge the legality of Jim Crow education. But he predicted several problems that the Afro-American community had not fully anticipated. With "successfully mixed schools," black children would be forced to "suffer for years from southern white teachers, from white hoodlums who sit beside them and under school authorities . . . who hate and despise them." Du Bois feared that many excellent Negro teachers would be fired "because they will not and cannot teach what many white folks will long want taught. Much teaching of Negro history will leave the school and with it that brave story of Negro resistance." Du Bois insisted that full desegregation had to be supported despite these difficulties, as part of "the price of liberty." But implicit in his observations was a lingering concern that Negro Americans might achieve integration while sacrificing their unique history of social protest and cultural gifts. Du Bois's assessment of King's nonviolent, direct-action campaigns was similarly subtle and complex. He praised King as an American "Gandhi," a moral crusader who led a political movement for justice. But there were potential limitations to the method of *satyagraha,* Du Bois noted in the *National Guardian* in February 1957. White racists in the South could not be convinced to change solely by moral suasion or by logical arguments. Du Bois reflected that "it is possible any day" that a nonviolent leader like King could be murdered.[23]

As the political struggles for democracy increased across the South, Du Bois's old prestige among many Afro-Americans was restored. Local Association chapters and black universities began to request speaking engagements from the black scholar. In 1958, Fisk University gave Du Bois an honorary degree, and named a new campus dormitory in his honor. Two years later, Morgan State College president Martin D. Jenkins awarded an honorary degree to Du Bois and invited him to present a commencement address. When a group of prominent black artists and entertainers, led by Sidney Poitier and Harry Belafonte, collected funds to send Kenyan students to American colleges, they solicited Du Bois's opinions and assistance. The continued veneration of Du Bois by black Americans proved vexing to the NAACP leaders. The *Crisis* failed to request a contribution from Du Bois for its special issue on the Gold Coast in 1957. When challenged by an irate member, Roy Wilkins explained: "there is no policy to exclude Dr. Du Bois . . . however I would be less than frank if I did not say that the present views of Dr. Du Bois are not deemed fitting" for the *Crisis*. The Association also refused to invite him to participate in its fiftieth anniversary celebration in 1959. Nevertheless, even the NAACP was forced on rare occasions to acknowledge Du Bois's restored popularity. In early 1956, the Association requested Du Bois's presence at a program held at the University of California-Los Angeles. In 1956 and 1959, Du Bois was invited to take part in the Spingarn Medal presentations. The Association's national leadership was still too anticommunist and antileft to embrace their founder and intellectual mentor. Yet they were ashamed to deny his singular contributions to the growing national movement for civil rights and desegregation.[24]

Events in the Gold Coast and throughout Africa presented different opportunities and questions for Du Bois. Nkrumah's Convention People's party (CPP) had won an overwhelming victory in the February 1951 elections, obtaining thirty four out of a possible thirty eight legislative seats. Nkrumah was led directly from a British prison to form the new parliamentary government. Du Bois was overjoyed at his success. At the 1945 Manchester Congress, Du Bois later observed, "I did not then dream that Nkrumah had the stamina and patience for this task. . . . Nkrumah was shabby, kindly, but earnest, and he and others called for justice . . . and freedom for the Gold Coast." But from the beginning, Du Bois detected certain problems with the young Pan-Africanist leader. Writing Padmore in October 1951, Du Bois politely complained that many of Nkrumah's "friends could not get in touch with him" during his recent visit to the United States. More disturbing was a report Du Bois received from a Gold Coast colleague that claimed Nkrumah's government "is no longer a resistance movement nor a revolutionary people's movement since its leaders have been captured thru luxury and flattery." Du Bois urged Padmore to initiate plans for a sixth Pan-African Congress under Nkrumah's direction as quickly as possible. Padmore later informed Du Bois that Nkrumah could not press ahead with his Pan-Africanist agenda "as we don't want to create undue alarm before we have full power in our hands." Nkrumah and Padmore were plotting "a skillful game of manoeuvering and we cannot afford at this stage of the struggle to give the imperialists any excuse to intervene as in British Guiana." Du Bois expressed strong reservations about Padmore's strategy in December 1954: "The power of British and especially American capital when it once gets a foothold is tremendous. . . . Once political power is in your hands you can curb capital, providing your own bourgeoisie permits it." Du Bois kept many of his doubts to himself. Like Padmore, Du Bois attributed most of Nkrumah's domestic opposition in 1951–57 to Ashanti "tribalism and provincialism," as well as to the intrigues of the British colonial office. Following the July 1956 Gold Coast elections, Du Bois congratulated Nkrumah for having "increased his majority."[25]

Du Bois's analysis of Gold Coast politics was seriously flawed. At the Manchester Pan-African Congress, Du Bois had also met two future CPP leaders who were sympathetic to Marxism: historian J. C. De Graft Johnson and attorney Kurankyi Taylor. By 1952, Johnson, Taylor, and many trade union militants in the CPP's left wing began to criticize Nkrumah's procapitalist economic policies and the government's cordial relations with the British. At Padmore's urging, Nkrumah expelled these leftists from the CPP in late 1953. Padmore observed that "disciplinary action" was essential to protect Nkrumah's government from "Communist infiltration. . . . The oppressed Negro workers and peasants are regarded by Communists as 'revolutionary expendables' in the global struggle of Communism against Western capitalism." Nkrumah's popular support had actually declined sharply in the mid-1950s, and in the 1956 elections over forty three percent of all voters opposed the CPP—a high figure by African electoral standards.[26] Du Bois accepted Nkrumah's socialist rhetoric at face value, without undertaking a detailed critique of the economic policies of the society. Even after Ghana's (Gold Coast) formal independence was declared in March 1957, Nkrumah's chief economic architects had little sympathy with socialism, and looked to the West for capital investments in the tradition of British colonial development. Du Bois's only criticisms of Padmore's anti-Communist policies, implemented by Nkrumah, appeared in his October 1956 review of Padmore's *Pan-Africanism or Communism?* Du Bois deplored Padmore's call for an "American Marshall Plan" in Africa and also suggested that his friend had failed to address the possible dangers of "a rising black bourgeoisie" in postcolonial states.[27] It seems unlikely that Du Bois ever recognized Padmore's rigid correlation between black anti-Communism and contemporary Pan-Africanism. As late as 1961, in a critique of an essay by Immanuel Wallerstein on Pan-Africanism, Du Bois defended his late associate: "The Communists did not oppose Pan-Africanism. They did not, for some time, realize its existence and did not pay proper attention to advice of men like Padmore. . . . I am convinced that had [Padmore] lived, he and the Soviet Union would have come to closer understanding."[28]

Du Bois was anxious to acquire firsthand information on various socialist states and revolutionary movements throughout the world—but he could not do so while confined to the United States. In 1953, the State Department demanded that Du Bois and Shirley Graham submit sworn statements "as to whether you are now or ever have been communists." Both indignantly refused. My political beliefs, Du Bois replied in the press, "are none of your business." In 1958 the Supreme Court ruled that the State Department had no legal right to require anticommunist affidavits "as prerequisite to issuing a passport." Robeson finally obtained his passport after an eight-year battle and promptly left for Europe. Du Bois and Shirley Graham made plans to depart on 8 August 1958. Although this was his fifteenth trip abroad, Du Bois noted in his *Autobiography,* "I felt like a released prisoner." Their extensive world journey, which finally ended 1 July 1959, was to Du Bois "one of the most important trips that I have ever taken, and had wide influence on my thought."[29]

Western Europe was a major disappointment for Du Bois. "I came to Europe to learn if now European imperialism was about to disappear, and what hope we had of a future. Was a world of peace and racial equality about to emerge?" Du Bois asked. American capital and political influence was omnipresent, and Western Europeans seemed indifferent to international trends of democracy and peace. The British "were determined to maintain their comforts and civilization by using cheap labor and raw materials, seized without rightful compensation." In Sweden, Du Bois attended a World Peace Council meeting and was surprised to find that "her press and pulpit ignored it." Europe's social democratic parties were not sympathetic to "the workers of Asia and Africa. On the contrary," Du Bois observed, "all are willing to take higher wages based on colonial profits; and to fight wars waged to defend those profits." But France provided the greatest disheartenment. For four years, France had been waging war against the Algerian National Liberation Front. Thousands of Arabs had been tortured, killed, or herded into Algerian detention centers. The impact of France's colonial war upon its domestic life was unmistakable. "The gates of my most loved of public parks, the Luxembourg Gardens, were guarded by police armed with machine guns," Du Bois noted. "I saw Algerian boys searched on the public streets. Fear, hate and despair rode the streets of Paris."[30]

Radically different was Du Bois's reception in Eastern Europe. During his travels in Czechoslovakia, the rectors of the Charles University in Prague awarded Du Bois an honorary doctorate of historical science. Genuinely surprised, Du Bois later noted: "No American university (except Negro institutions in understandable self-defense) had ever recognized that I had any claim to scholarship. I had no reason to think that Charles University even knew my name." On 23 October 1958, Du Bois accepted his degree and delivered an address on "The American Negro and Communism." Summarizing his views over the previous two decades, Du Bois declared that "the salvation of American Negroes lies in socialism." It was possible that the socialist "methods which were right and clear in Russia and China" might not "fit our circumstances," Du Bois noted. However, he expected that growing numbers of blacks would support measures to expand "the welfare state" and to "favor strict regulation of corporations or their public ownership."[31] On 3 November, Du Bois "fulfilled one of the highest ambitions" of his youth when he was awarded an honorary doctorate from Humboldt University of East Berlin, formerly Friedrich Wilhelm University. His brief stay in the city revived half-forgotten memories of his student days and on at least one occasion provided a sad reminder of his current political status in the United States. Traveling by foot through East Berlin, Du Bois decided to visit his old student lodgings. But he suddenly stopped. The old house was in West Berlin, "and if I had entered, American soldiers might arrest me on any pretext they invented. I turned back."[32]

Du Bois spent five months in the Soviet Union. As in his previous trips, he "marveled" at the advances of the country in education, science, and industrial development. Du Bois was awarded an honorary doctorate from Moscow University and received the Lenin Peace Prize. In January 1959, he held discussions with Soviet leader Nikita Khrushchev. During their two-hour talk, Du Bois suggested the development of an institute of African studies that would "aim at the promotion of scientific research" on the "cultural, political, and economic organizations" of African people. Khrushchev was impressed with the concept and appointed a group of scholars to investigate the possible development of the institute. Before the end of the year, the Soviets had established an "Institute on Africa'" as a component of their national Academy of Sciences.[33]

Du Bois had an opportunity to examine Soviet society in some detail. At Leningrad University, Du Bois discussed his plans for an African institute with professors; four thousand miles away in Tashkent, Uzbekistan, he attended an international writers' conference; he talked with hundreds of teachers, working people, and political leaders. Still the sociologist, Du Bois observed with approval that dogmatic religion had been "dethroned" in the nation's schools. The social role of women had vastly improved, as more females were employed at all levels of the labor force. Equally impressive was the Soviet attitude toward people of color. "The Soviet Union seems to me the only European country where people are not taught and encouraged to despise and look down on some class, group or race," Du Bois noted. "I know countries where race and color prejudice show only slight manifestations, but no white country where race and color prejudice seems so absolutely absent." Du Bois had never viewed the Soviet political system as being "qualitatively" different from other states: all governments were one form of "dictatorship" or another. What the Soviet Union was attempting to achieve differed "only in quantity, not in quality, from every other modern country," in terms of state intervention and control of economic and social forces. Du Bois tried not to minimize the problem areas within the society: "There is power rivalry and personal jealousy; all things in the Soviet Union are not perfect." Overall, however, his confidence in the Leninist state and its socioeconomic structure had increased. "The Soviet Union is great and growing greater, and, as it seems to believe, it belongs to this two hundred million folk about me," Du Bois concluded. "I am strongly inclined to agree with them."[34]

Although Du Bois was a veteran traveler, little had prepared him for his "amazing" journey into the People's Republic of China. Du Bois and Shirley Graham spent two months touring the nation, traveling five thousand miles and visiting all major cities. Du Bois spent four hours in discussions with Mao Tse-tung, and scheduled two dinners with Prime Minister Chou En-lai. Long the outcasts of American foreign policy, the Chinese appreciated Du Bois's sense of political defiance. Upon Du Bois's arrival, the Chinese inquired whether any publicity concerning his trip should be released. Du Bois's response was characteristic: "So far as we are concerned you can tell the whole world." Here was "a land of colored people" that had survived feudalism, European colonialism, Japanese occupation, and civil war—yet seemed to be building a remarkable socialist state. Du Bois was less reserved, and clearly less accurate, in his appraisal of Chinese communism compared to other socialist societies. "Their officials are incorruptible, their merchants are honest, their artisans are reliable," Du Bois remarked. "China has no rank or classes; her universities grant no degrees. . . . But she has leaders of learning and genius." One high point of the tour occurred at Peking University, where Du Bois gave a lecture on his ninety-first birthday. Graham recalled: "We expected an assembly of faculty and university students, but when we turned onto the campus grounds we saw multitudes of students in every direction. . . . They hailed him by name and applauded until we were swallowed up inside the building." Du Bois's speech, broadcast over national radio, contained elements of bitterness created by Cold War suppression and expressions of hope for the socialist future of all humanity: "I speak with no authority; no assumption of age or rank; I hold no position, I have no wealth. One thing alone I own and that is my own soul. . . . In my own country for near a century I have been nothing but a 'nigger.'" Du Bois's perceptions of China were blurred by the fact that the Chinese were "people of color," part of those oppressed nations behind the "veil." Mao, among others, shrewdly sensed this. Upon meeting Du Bois, the party chairman declared, "You are no darker than I am. Who could tell which one of us is darker?" Mao announced to the Chinese nation: "Du Bois [is] a great man of our time. His deeds of heroic struggle for the liberation of the Negroes and the whole of mankind, his outstanding achievements in academic fields and his sincere friendship toward the Chinese people will forever remain in the memory of the Chinese people." Du Bois scholar Gerald Horne accurately suggested that Du Bois was "seduced by certain precursors of the disastrous cultural revolution."[35] In his fervent desire to perceive another non-European people transcending the barriers between colonialism and socialism, Du Bois ignored the contradictory signals that were already evident within Chinese communism. Three months after returning from "Red China," Du Bois's and Graham's passports were seized by the State Department and held until mid-1960.

Du Bois continued to write the draft manuscript of his *Autobiography.* In several public lectures, however, he also attempted to explain how this last trip "completely transformed my thinking." Speaking before an audience at the University of Wisconsin in May 1960, Du Bois stated that before his 1958–59 travels he had believed that both capitalism and socialism were "successful" forms of government. Although capitalism "might degenerate into fascism," the experience of Roosevelt's New Deal had illustrated the "progressive" potential of the existing system. "I returned with completely changed ideas," Du Bois commented. Socialism was certainly "the most successful form of government today possible," while capitalism had become "a force so destructive, that it cannot be endured." The majority of the world's people "live under socialism. . . . In my mind," Du Bois declared, "there is no doubt that the world of the 21st century, will be overwhelmingly communistic." Du Bois had identified his lifelong commitment to radical democracy with the new socialist societies he had seen. To embrace communism, for Du Bois, was to stand with the worldwide social movements for national liberation, peace, and socialist development. In his *Autobiography,* Du Bois acknowledged that "the triumph of communism will be a slow and difficult task, involving mistakes of every sort." His advocacy of communism was also conditional; he would support the movement "in every honest way . . . without deceit or hurt and in any way possible, without war." He had not yet become a member of the Communist party, but he now "frankly and clearly" supported its goals: "I believe in communism."[36]

Du Bois's criticisms of Afro-American society and politics had become sharper. In early 1960, Du Bois argued that "class divisions" within Negro communities had so divided blacks "that they are no longer [one] single body. They are different sets of people with different sets of interests." At the University of Wisconsin, Du Bois indicated that the civil rights movement's strategy of nonviolent demonstrations and sit-ins "does not reach the center of the problem" confronting blacks. Nearly alone among major civil rights leaders, Du Bois urged the proponents of desegregation to chart "the next step" of their collective struggle. The abolition of Jim Crow meant little if Negroes were unemployed. Blacks must "insist upon the legal rights which are already theirs, and add to that, increasingly a socialistic form of government, an insistence upon the welfare state." The demand for civil rights must ultimately check the power "of those corporations which monopolize wealth." Du Bois now recognized that full equality for Negroes was not possible beneath the capitalist system.[37] Du Bois also cautioned black Americans not to surrender their unique heritage of cultural and political resistance as society became more desegregated. Speaking at Johnson C. Smith College in North Carolina in April 1960, Du Bois made a critical distinction between cultural pluralism and complete racial assimilation:

> I am not fighting to settle the question in America by the process of getting rid of the Negro race; getting rid of black folk; not producing black children, forgetting the slave trade and slavery, and the struggle for emancipation. . . . No! What I have been fighting for and am still fighting for is the possibility of black folk and their cultural patterns existing in America without discrimination; and on terms of equality. . . . We must accept equality or die. What we must do is to lay down a line of thought and action which will accomplish two things: The utter disappearance of color discrimination in American life and the preservation of African history and culture as a valuable contribution to modern civilization.

Du Bois again urged black Americans to recognize that "democracy has almost disappeared" inside the United States. Negroes had to help "lead" the fight for socialism, and in doing so, "restore the democracy of which we have boasted so long and done so little."[38]

During Ghana's first two years of formal independence, it took few steps toward a socialist and Pan-Africanist foreign policy. Until his death in September 1959, Padmore largely dominated Ghana's external affairs, and he was determined to cement fraternal ties with the West. No agreement for a Soviet ambassador to Ghana was even signed until April 1959. Ghana defended South Africa's membership in the British Commonwealth; it provided political and financial support to pro-Western African nationalists, such as Joseph Kasavubu of the Congo and Holden Roberto of Angola. During Nkrumah's tour of the United States in the summer of 1958, he declared that Communism would not be permitted "any fruitful set-up in our country." Amazingly, Nkrumah also stated that "the racial question in the United States" had been "exaggerated deliberately."[39] His statement reflected a policy of appeasement to the West that brought few tangible results. It is doubtful that Du Bois was fully aware of Nkrumah's early moderate policies. While visiting Tashkent, Du Bois received a cable inviting him to participate in an "All-African Peoples Conference," to be held in Accra in December 1958. The conference "call" was curiously worded: "this conference will formulate and proclaim the philosophy of Pan-Africanism as the ideology of the African Non-Violent Revolution." No personal notes from Padmore or Nkrumah were initially forwarded, and there was no mention about Du Bois's expenses. "I sensed immediately that opposition had arisen in Africa over American Negro leadership of the African peoples," Du Bois observed. Actually, it was over Padmore's objections that the term "Pan-Africanism" was deleted from the conference title; Nkrumah wanted to establish a "new tradition." Fatigued from his travels, Du Bois was represented at the Accra conference by Shirley Graham. Du Bois continued to advise Nkrumah to avoid "borrowing capital from the West. . . . Buy of the Soviet Union and China as they grow able to sell at low prices. Save thus your own capital and drive the imperialists into bankruptcy or into Socialism."[40]

By 1960, the politics of Ghana had changed dramatically. The CPP's strongest advocate of Western investment, K. A. Gbedemah, had lost considerable influence and would go into exile in late 1961. The selection of Tawia Adamafio as the CPP's general-secretary and Ako Adjei, a veteran of the Manchester Congress, as Ghana's foreign minister in 1959, pushed domestic and external policies to the left. These and other events—the death of Padmore, and the political crisis in the Congo—led Nkrumah to adopt a more nonaligned, socialist agenda. Through a national plebiscite, Ghana became a republic, and Nkrumah's inauguration as president was held in July 1960. Nkrumah invited Du Bois and Graham to be his "personal private guests" at the ceremonies. Through their lawyer, they obtained new passports and spent six weeks in Ghana in July and August 1960. Nkrumah then made a surprising offer to Du Bois: that he consider directing a major scholarly project, an *Encyclopedia Africana,* with its headquarters in Ghana. Du Bois declined, observing that he was ninety-two years old. But Nkrumah was insistent; only Du Bois's leadership would be sufficient. Several considerations prompted Nkrumah's offer. The invitation to Du Bois was an "overture" to the left, in the broadest political sense. After all, Du Bois was widely viewed as the "Father of Pan-Africanism" and the leading advocate of socialism in the black world. The venerable scholar would add immense prestige to the project. In the end, Du Bois could not refuse the proposal. He saw in Nkrumah the next generation's leadership for Pan-Africanism. He had contemplated the encyclopedia for over half a century. Du Bois was prepared to give his remaining years to the project.[41]

In September 1960, Du Bois began to work nearly full-time on the *Encyclopedia Africana*. He hired secretarial assistance, and in four months spent over $1,300 of his limited funds on supplies, postage, and wages. With great enthusiasm, Du Bois contacted dozens of scholars with expertise in Afro-American, African, and Caribbean Studies—including Melville Herskovits, Basil Davidson, Eric Williams, Arthur Lewis, and Louis S. Leakey. By April 1961, Du Bois had outlined a tentative schedule for the project. Within several years, he hoped, members of an editorial board should be selected, under the direction of the Ghana Academy of Learning. The first volume of the *Encyclopedia* should be available "not later than 1970." As in the 1930s, several scholars voiced reservations about the project. Frazier again raised objections with Du Bois, complaining that it was "premature" to publish such a volume. In May 1961, Charles H. Wesley, then president of Central State University in Ohio and leader of the Association for the Study of Negro Life and History, proposed a "co-editorship in Africa and the United States so that our two groups would be equally represented" on the projected board of the *Encyclopedia*. Sensitive to the claims of African intellectuals and Nkrumah's sponsorship, Du Bois had to decline Wesley's offer. "This work must be done in Africa and mainly by African scholars," Du Bois informed Wesley. "There can be no question of division of control or authority." Following Woodson's tradition, the Association's executive council voted to launch its own *Encyclopedia*. Unfortunately, neither project was ever completed.[42]

As Du Bois's work on the *Encyclopedia* progressed, his contacts with representatives of the new generation of African leaders and intellectuals were expanded. He was constantly surprised and pleased to learn how many of these new heads of state, trade unionists, and officials had studied his writings for decades, and sought his advice. From Kenya, Jomo Kenyatta corresponded to Du Bois from prison; his lieutenants Oginga Odinga and labor leader Tom Mboya consulted with the American Negro scholar in 1960 and 1961. W. O. Goodluck, the leader of the Nigerian Trade Union Congress, and nationalist leader Nnamdi Azikiwe invited Du Bois to Nigeria in late 1960 during independence ceremonies. Goodluck informed Du Bois: "You can be assured that there awaits you a tremendous welcome from the Nigerian workers, the progressives, intellectuals and a large section of the

Nigerian community." During his brief stay in Nigeria, Azikiwe asked Du Bois to draft a booklet, later entitled "A Path for Nigeria," that would develop a political strategy "from the Socialist point of view of the steps which Nigeria ought to take." For other African comrades, Du Bois wrote "Africa and the French Revolution," which was also printed in Nigeria. To Tanganyika's new president Julius Nyerere, Du Bois cautioned against reliance on U.S. investments and the presence of the Peace Corps in that country: "I hope you watch these persons carefully. Most of them will be . . . filled with ideas of white superiority." And from South Africans engaged in mass campaigns against the apartheid regime, Du Bois received word in 1961 that he was "greatly admired and inspire those who carry on in Capetown and Johannesburg."[43]

In the summer of 1961 Du Bois was able to travel to Rumania for two months to obtain medical treatment. His tentative plans were to continue working on the *Encyclopedia* in Brooklyn and to move to Accra sometime in 1962. This timetable was upset by a federal court decision that required the Communist party to register under the Subversive Control Act. The provisions of this law made it likely that Du Bois's and Graham's passports would be seized again. In late August 1961, they both urgently contacted Nkrumah, requesting permission to arrive in Ghana "about the middle of October." This correspondence arrived at a difficult moment for the Nkrumah government. The president and his chief advisers were touring the Soviet Union. That September, thousands of railroad and dock workers initiated a seventeen-day strike against the government; and the following month, in concession to the Ghanaian working class, Nkrumah finally confronted and eliminated the corrupt, conservative wing of the CPP inside his administration. In these later events, according to St. Clair Drake and L. C. Lacy, "the Government saw its very existence implicitly challenged." Striking workers had made Nkrumah understand that "if Parliament did not give way to the demands of the people, they would disband that body by force." For several weeks, the state was nearly paralyzed. E. E. Boateng, acting secretary of the Ghana Academy of Learning, informed Du Bois on 16 September that his arrival would have to be "delayed for a few weeks." Du Bois promptly explained that he had no other alternative: "there is grave possibility that if we wait until a later date, we would not be allowed to leave at all." After Nkrumah's return to Ghana on 18 September, he resolved the matter personally. Alex Quaison-Sackey, Ghana's representative at the United Nations, soon contacted Du Bois with a message from the president: "Much regret impression created by Boateng for which he had no authority whatever. Please come as soon as ever you are ready. Let nothing stop you."[44]

Du Bois was not absolutely certain that his departure from the United

States would be permanent. But with Yolande's death in late 1960, there were fewer reasons to remain. His Brooklyn house was sold; most of his private papers and unpublished manuscripts were entrusted to Herbert Aptheker. Yet one important political act had to be completed. As Aptheker relates, "Du Bois had come to the decision that the program and ideas of the Communist Party of the United States were nearest to his own ideas. With the warlike policy of Washington and its policy of persecuting radicals and Communists, Du Bois decided that it might be some contribution to peace and sanity if he were not only to join the Party but to do with a public announcement of the fact."[45]

Perhaps another factor influencing Du Bois's decision was the continued anti-Communist stance of the NAACP, and its growing alienation from many domestic progressive currents that were taking the lead in combating segregation. In 1959, for example, twenty thousand college student activists took part in a national mobilization for school desegregation. The Association not only opposed the march, which included some independent socialists and Communists, but pressured its youth members not to participate. In February 1961, Afro-American activists demonstrated before the United Nations to condemn the murder of leftist Congolese prime minister Patrice Lumumba. Roy Wilkins criticized the protest and warned that "Belgium colonizers should not be replaced with Soviet colonizers." Three months later, the *Crisis* published a harsh attack on the new Cuban government that described Fidel Castro as a "master of deceit" and a "dictator." The controversial essay appeared only weeks after the unsuccessful "Bay of Pigs" invasion of Cuba. Du Bois's attitude toward the Cuban revolution was, of course, extremely positive. He criticized the U.S.-backed invasion of Cuba as a "crazy, ill-judged scheme. The work that Castro is doing in Cuba is marvelous and inspiring and the mass of people utterly support it." Du Bois was fully convinced that the Association's capitulation to anti-Communist rhetoric and Cold War liberalism limited its ability to pursue its domestic reform agenda. By openly joining the Communist party, he might move the ideological boundaries of black American politics further left.[46]

There were other elements that logically led Du Bois to his conclusion. For nearly two decades the Communists had gained his admiration for defending their political beliefs and in suffering extreme repression. On 7 September 1961, Du Bois spoke at a Harlem banquet in celebration of black Communist leader Henry Winston's release from a federal prison. Blinded during his ordeal but still defiant, Winston symbolized the moral courage that Du Bois had seen in Douglass, Crummell, and other Afro-American leaders. "More than most men, Henry Winston had suffered for his determination to think and act in accord with what he believed was right," Du Bois stated. "It is a great honor to stand in the presence of this man, and beholding his wounded body and undaunted soul." There was also the matter of Du Bois's scholarship, which few white American universities viewed with credibility. Harvard University had never asked him to lecture on its campus; indeed, as a Negro, he was not even permitted to belong to the Harvard Club in New York. The contrast with socialist countries was striking. A Czech translation of *In Battle For Peace* had been published in Prague in December 1954. In 1959, a Chinese language edition of *The Souls of Black Folk* was printed in Peking, and Du Bois contributed seven short articles to Soviet publications during the year, including an essay on "Lenin and Africa." Du Bois's *Black Flame* trilogy was translated and published in Hungarian and Russian; a Soviet edition of *John Brown* appeared in 1960; and his final *Autobiography* would later be translated into German, Russian, and Rumanian. At a period when many American libraries refused to circulate his works, millions of people across the socialist world were being introduced to his ideas. Du Bois's last collection of essays, *An ABC of Color,* was initially released by Seven Seas Publishers in Berlin in 1963.[47]

But these personal considerations were at best secondary. Du Bois was now convinced that the path of radical democracy led to socialism, and by joining the Communist party he would confirm the central ideals he had cherished throughout most of his adult life. On 1 October 1961, Du Bois applied for membership to the Communist party general secretary Gus Hall. "I have been long and slow in coming to this conclusion," Du Bois noted, "but at last my mind is settled." Du Bois briefly reviewed his long affinity for socialism, tracing his involvement with the left. After decades of research and political engagement, he had come to "a firm conclusion":

> Capitalism cannot reform itself; it is doomed to self-destruction. No universal selfishness can bring social good to all. Communism—the effort to give all men what they need and to ask of each the best they can contribute—this is the only way of human life. It is a difficult and hard end to reach, it has and will make mistakes, but today it marches triumphantly on in education and science, in home and food, with increased freedom of thought and deliverance from dogma. In the end communism will triumph. I want to help bring that day. The path of the American Communist Party is clear: It will provide the United States with a real Third party and thus restore democracy to this land.[48]

Four days later, Aptheker drove Du Bois and Graham to the airport. One reporter waiting at the terminal asked Du Bois how many volumes his encyclopedia would contain. When Du Bois responded that about "ten stout volumes would be sufficient," the reporter inquired how long it would take to complete each volume. Du Bois smiled slightly: "I should think it will take me about ten years per volume."[49]

Du Bois and Graham arrived in Accra, after a short stop in London, on 7 October 1961. Nkrumah was a thoughtful host and had begun to prepare a quaint cottage outside of Accra for the couple. Without hesitation, Du Bois proceeded to work on the *Encyclopedia Africana* project. As his chief assistant, Du Bois selected the son of Alphaeus Hunton, who was then teaching in Guinea. Alphaeus Hunton, Jr., had established his academic credentials with an excellent survey on African politics; the young scholar performed his new responsibilities with the same dedication as his father. In May 1962, Du Bois was formally named director of the project's secretariat, and a preliminary report of the *Encyclopedia Africana* was prepared for the president. Nkrumah became particularly attached to Du Bois during this time; he later described the elder man as "a real friend and father to me." Du Bois and Graham occasionally entertained guests from the small but lively Afro-American expatriate community living in Accra. As much as his physical condition permitted, Du Bois endeavored to establish close contacts with Ghanaian intellectuals. On 18 December 1962, Du Bois presented a lecture at the University of Ghana. As if answering Frazier, Du Bois urged his colleagues not to view the encyclopedia as "premature" or "too ambitious." The project "is long overdue," Du Bois remarked. But it was only "logical that such a work had to wait for independent Africans to carry it out."[50]

Despite all his preparations for the project and a carefully controlled way of life, Du Bois could not transcend the limitations of his failing health. In July 1962, Du Bois was forced to request a leave of absence from the secretariat. Following a painful prostate gland operation in London, Du Bois recuperated in Switzerland and China for several months. His recovery was "slow and tedious," he wrote Hunton in September 1962, "and it has taken me a long time to be myself again." By late 1962, Du Bois had resumed work. But any plans to return to the United States were dashed when the American consulate in Accra refused to renew Du Bois's passport. As a member of the Communist party, it was illegal to possess a passport, and Du Bois was now subject to ten years' imprisonment for his "crime." He had no choice except to renounce his American citizenship. On 17 February 1963, Du Bois became a citizen of Ghana. As Hunton observed, Du Bois had "simply formalized the fact that he was also a son of Africa."[51]

In March 1963, Du Bois had become physically incapable of performing his duties at the secretariat, and with reluctance he retired. On 27 August 1963, at the age of ninety-five, Du Bois died. Nkrumah authorized a state funeral in Du Bois's honor and delivered his eulogy in a national broadcast: "We mourn the death of Dr. William Edward Burghardt Du Bois, a great son of Africa. . . . He was an undaunted fighter for the emancipation of colonial and oppressed people, and pursued this objective throughout his life. . . . It was the late George Padmore who described Dr. Du Bois as the greatest scholar the Negro race has produced, and one who always upheld

213

the right of Africans to govern themselves." For the African diaspora and the entire socialist world, the loss of Du Bois was monumental. "It was this great leader who predicted that the 'Problem of the twentieth century is the problem of the color line,'" wrote Nnamdi Azikiwe, president of Nigeria. Du Bois's Pan-African Congresses "led ultimately to the political emancipation of this continent." Nearly every embassy and consulate in Accra sent representatives to pay their respects to the "Father of Pan-Africanism." There was only one exception—the consulate of the United States of America.[52]

The news of Du Bois's death reached the United States on the morning of 28 August 1963. Over one quarter of a million people had come that day to the historic March on Washington to demonstrate for civil rights and jobs. NAACP leader Roy Wilkins informed the gathering: "Remember that this has been a long fight. We were reminded of it by the news of the death yesterday in Africa of Dr. W. E. B. Du Bois. Now, regardless of the fact that in his later years Dr. Du Bois chose another path, it is incontrovertible that at the dawn of the twentieth century his was the voice that was calling to you to gather here today in this cause." On 9 September the NAACP board adopted a resolution mourning Du Bois's death, calling their former leader "the prime inspirer, philosopher and father of the Negro protest movement." The NAACP resolution was curiously selective in listing Du Bois's achievements. It praised *The Philadelphia Negro* and *The Souls of Black Folk,* but failed to mention *The World and Africa* or his greatest work, *Black Reconstruction.* It briefly mentioned Du Bois's role as "a fierce and uncompromising foe of colonialism, and promoter of the Pan-African Congresses," but was silent on Du Bois's Pan-Africanist and antiimperialist activities after 1940. Du Bois's endeavors in the peace movement, his membership in the Communist party, and the circumstances relating to his untimely exits from the Association in 1934 and 1948 were not discussed.[53] The central issue was eschewed by Wilkins and the Association. Did Du Bois choose "another path," as Wilkins asserted? Or did the quest for radical democracy lead Du Bois further down the path than his former associates were willing to tread?

There is no need for an apologia of Du Bois's career. He was a writer of rare grace and power. As Eugene O'Neill once observed: "Ranking as [Du Bois] does among the foremost writers of true importance in the country, one sometimes wishes . . . that he would devote all of his time to the accomplishment of that fine and moving prose which distinguishes his books."[54] He was the major human rights leader in the United States for half a century; a cultural pluralist who helped spark the movement for African liberation. But Du Bois never held himself above criticism. Like any leader, he committed serious errors in judgment. Du Bois was sometimes plagued by moments of theoretical uncertainty. Individuals of lesser ability often defeated him. Washington was superior as a political tactician; White excelled in bureaucratic maneuvers. Du Bois's legacy to black scholarship was fundamental but certainly not exclusive. E. Franklin Frazier and Charles S. Johnson were more influential than Du Bois in the field of black sociology after the 1920s. Woodson played a greater role in shaping the profession of Afro-American historiography; Locke was a more highly respected literary critic. Similar judgements must be made concerning Du Bois's political work. His grand theoretical formulations were sometimes ahead of their time, or were unsuitable to the immediate circumstances facing Negroes. His decision to "close ranks" during World War I was a disaster; his segregated cooperatives plan was unworkable; his assessments of Japanese imperialism in the 1920s–30s were faulty; and his understanding of Ghanaian society under Nkrumah during the 1950s was too uncritical. Du Bois remained essentially a man of letters, a scholar who fought in the arena out of a firm moral and political dedication to human equality. As Aptheker has observed, in 1907 Du Bois actually wrote two letters of resignation from the Niagara Movement—but never sent them.[55]

Among Du Bois's chief shortcomings as a socialist theorist were his tendency to equate any type of state-dominated economies with the process of socialist construction, and his uncertainty concerning the relationship between nationalism and socialism. Societies in which the government controls the major means of production are not necessarily socialist—if "socialism" is also assumed to mean the fullest expansion of democracy in the workplace and the creation of egalitarian social and political institutions. Du Bois's general definition of socialism—"the idea that the government should direct the production of goods and control the wage contract and the distribution of consumers' goods"—underestimated the decisive issue of state power and class relations within the state. In other words, the fundamental variable within any society, whether it claims to be capitalist or socialist, is the question of state authority: which social classes dominate the state apparatus, and what specific class interests are hegemonic over others. Consequently, Du Bois's critiques of various social formations often appear contradictory or at best naive. One glaring example was his curious analysis of Nazi Germany. In July 1950, Du Bois defined "fascism" in his correspondence as the "leadership of a small group with total power supported by the capitalists and run for their benefit, but allaying the complaints of the workers by full employment, better wages and many social gifts like housing and social medicine." This sketchy outline failed to comprehend the central features of the German fascist state: the destruction of trade unions and all opposition parties, the systematic suppression of civil liberties, and the direct relationship between German capital, the Nazi party, and the state. Even worse was Du Bois's glowing assessment of Ethiopia's feudal regime. Writing in 1955, Du Bois praised Haile Selassie as a "conscientious" ruler. "Ethiopia is a state socialism under an Emperor with almost absolute power." The evidence for the authoritarian state's "socialism" was nonexistent, nor was there any justification for Du Bois's belief that "there is no race or color prejudice" in Ethiopia's multiethnic society.[56] Du Bois did not anticipate the Sino-Soviet split that divided Communist parties across the world in the early 1960s, and it is not clear whether he fully appreciated the role of nationalism in directing Chinese international policies. In October 1962, after the Soviets broke relations with the Chinese, Du Bois visited the People's Republic to participate in the thirteenth anniversary of the founding of the regime. Immediately following Du Bois's second journey to China, the government initiated a major polemical attack against American racism. Du Bois was deeply disturbed by the worsening relations between the two major Communist states, and in 1963 he wrote a letter to the leaders of both nations urging reconciliation: "The joy of the imperialist is great as they see differences arising among Communist leadership." But Du Bois never drafted an extensive criticism of "Maoism" or attended to the limitations and contradictions of other socialist states, such as Ghana after 1960.[57]

Nevertheless, many interpretations of Du Bois's social thought and role in Afro-American history remain distorted, primarily because of one central conceptual flaw—the refusal to draw any correlation between Marxism and democracy. C. L. R. James has observed that Du Bois can only be understood as "a true son of the intellectuals who founded the United States in 1776. Devoted as he was to righting the injustices of coloured people, he came in time to see his famous aphorism, that the problem of the twentieth century was the problem of the colour line, in a wider context."[58] The political trajectory of liberation movements predicted by Du Bois—embodied by leaders such as Maurice Bishop, Amilcar Cabral, Agostinho Neto, and Nelson Mandela—project new types of democratic social systems. The social movements for women's equality, peace, civil rights, and a more equitable restructuring of economic and political power within the United States, to which Du Bois devoted his life, have accelerated since his death. In these contexts, the living symbol of Du Bois as a black radical democrat will continue to flourish. As Lorraine Hansberry stated in 1964, Du Bois is "an institution in our lives, a bulwark of our culture. . . . And, without a doubt, his ideas have influenced a multitude who do not even know his name."[59]

Perhaps the best interpretation of the historical significance of Du Bois was presented by Martin Luther King, Jr., at a Carnegie Hall tribute to Du

216

Bois held on 23 February 1968. King suggested that Du Bois's "singular greatness lay in his quest for truth about his own people." But Du Bois was more than a gifted social scientist of the black experience. "He was proud of his people, not because their color endowed them with some vague greatness but because their concrete achievements in struggle had advanced humanity and he saw and loved progressive humanity in all its hues, black, white, yellow, red, and brown." King also emphasized that Du Bois's democratic vision embraced Marxism: "Some people would like to ignore the fact that he was a communist in his later years. . . . It is time to cease muting the fact that Dr. Du Bois was a genius and chose to be a communist. Our irrational obsessive anticommunism had led us into too many quagmires to be retained as if it were a mode of scientific thinking." King concluded that Du Bois's image would continue to inspire movements for social justice and peace: "Dr. Du Bois has left us, but he has not died. The spirit of freedom is not buried in the grave of the valiant. . . . Dr. Du Bois's greatest virtue was his committed empathy with all the oppressed and his divine dissatisfaction with all forms of injustice."[60]

CHRONOLOGY

1868	Born in Great Barrington, Massachusetts, 23 February.
1883–1885	Correspondent for T. Thomas Fortune's *New York Age* and other newspapers.
1884	June, graduation from Great Barrington High School.
1885–1888	Attends Fisk University, Nashville; receives B.A.; teaches in rural Tennessee.
1888–1890	Attends Harvard University; receives B.A., cum laude.
1891	Receives M.A. in history, Harvard University.
1892–1894	Study at University of Berlin; travels extensively in Europe.
1894–1896	Professor of classics, Wilberforce University, Ohio.
1895	Receives Ph.D. in history, Harvard University.
1896	*The Suppression of the African Slave-Trade to the United States of America, 1638–1870.*

1896–1897	Assistant instructor of sociology, University of Pennsylvania.
1897–1903	Extensive involvement in the American Negro Academy, founded in Washington, D.C.
1897	Summer research in Farmville, Virginia.
1897–1910	Professor of economics and history, Atlanta University; co-ordinates annual Atlanta University Studies conferences and edits annual publications.
1899	*The Philadelphia Negro.*
1900	Pan-African Conference held in London.
1903	*The Souls of Black Folk.*
1905–1910	Edits the *Moon* (1905–1906) and the *Horizon* (1907–1910).
1905–1910	Cofounder and general secretary of the Niagara Movement.
1909	*John Brown.*
1910–1934	Member of Board of Directors of the National Association for the Advancement of Colored People (NAACP); serves as director of publicity and research; edits the *Crisis*.
1911–1912	Member of the Socialist party.
1911	*The Quest of the Silver Fleece.*
1915	*The Negro.*
1917–1918	Supports American entry into World War I; lobbies for black officers and better treatment for black soldiers.
1919	First Pan-African Congress, Paris.
1920	*Darkwater: Voices from within the Veil;* awarded Spingarn Medal from NAACP.
1921	Second Pan-African Congress, London, Brussels, Paris.
1923	Third Pan-African Congress, London, Paris, Lisbon.
1924–1925	Forces resignation of Fayette McKenzie, president of Fisk University.
1924	*The Gift of Black Folk.*
1924–1928	Patron and critic of the Harlem Renaissance literary movement.
1926	First extensive travel in the Soviet Union (six weeks).
1927	Fourth Pan-African Congress, New York City.

1928	*Dark Princess.*
1930–1934	Attempt to democratize NAACP; proposes the development of black economic cooperatives; resigns from *Crisis* and NAACP (1934).
1934–1944	Professor and chairman of sociology department, Atlanta University.
1935	*Black Reconstruction: An Essay toward a History of the Part Which Black Folk Played in the Attempt to Reconstruct Democracy in America, 1860–1880.*
1936	Extensive world tour, including Nazi Germany, Soviet Union, China and Japan.
1939	*Black Folk Then and Now.*
1940	*Dusk of Dawn: An Essay toward an Autobiography of a Race Concept.*
1940–1944	Founder and editor of *Phylon,* a quarterly journal published at Atlanta University.
1944	Return to NAACP as director of special research.
1945	Consultant to U.S. delegation at founding of the United Nations.
1945	*Color and Democracy: Colonies and Peace.*
1945	Fifth Pan-African Congress, Manchester.
1947	*The World and Africa: An Inquiry into the Part Which Africa Has Played in World History.*
1947	Edits and presents an NAACP appeal against racism to the United Nations.
1948–1949	Dismissed from NAACP; joins the Council on African Affairs as vice-chairman.
1950	Chairs Peace Information Center; candidate for U.S. senator in New York on American Labor party ticket.
1951	Indicted by federal grand jury as "unregistered foreign agent"; arrested, tried, and acquitted.
1952	*In Battle for Peace: The Story of My 83rd Birthday.*
1952–1958	Denied U.S. passport; unable to travel abroad.
1957–1961	*Black Flame* trilogy: *The Ordeal of Mansart* (1957); *Mansart Builds a School* (1959); and *Worlds of Color* (1961).

221

1958–1959   World tour, including USSR, England, France, Sweden and China; receives Lenin Peace Prize.

1961   At invitation of President Kwame Nkrumah, travels to Ghana to direct work on *Encyclopedia Africana;* joins U.S. Communist party.

1963   Becomes citizen of Ghana, dies in Ghana on 27 August at age ninety-five.

NOTES AND REFERENCES

1. A GREAT AMBITION

1. The quotation is a description of Blessed Alwyn's cultural identity, which also accurately characterizes Du Bois's own self-consciousness. See W. E. B. Du Bois, *The Quest of the Silver Fleece* (Chicago: A. C. McClurg, 1911), 265.

2. W. E. B. Du Bois, *Darkwater: Voices from within the Veil* (New York: Schocken, 1969), 5.

3. W. E. B. Du Bois, *The Autobiography of W. E. B. Du Bois: A Soliloquy on Viewing My Life from the Late Decade of Its First Century* (New York: International Publishers, 1968), 61–65.

4. Ibid., 72–73.

5. Ibid., 84–87, 94, 279.

6. Ibid., 92–93.

7. Ibid., 75, 78, 80, 91.

8. Ibid., 83, 95, 96.

9. W. E. B. Du Bois, "Something About Me," (3 October 1890), in *Against Racism: Unpublished Essays, Papers, Addresses, 1887–1961*, ed.

Herbert Aptheker (Amherst: University of Massachusetts Press, 1985), 16–17.

10. W. E. B. Du Bois, "The Lash," *Horizon* 1 (May 1907):6.

11. W. E. B. Du Bois, "Great Barrington Notes," *New York Globe,* 14 April 1883.

12. W. E. B. Du Bois, "Great Barrington Notes," *New York Globe,* 29 September 1883.

13. Du Bois, *The Autobiography of W. E. B. Du Bois,* 71.

14. W. E. B. Du Bois to Mary Burghardt Du Bois, 21 July 1883, in *The Correspondence of W. E. B. Du Bois,* 3 vols., ed. Herbert Aptheker, vol. 1, *Selections, 1877–1934* (Amherst: University of Massachusetts Press, 1973), 3–4.

15. Du Bois, *Autobiography,* 99.

16. Du Bois, "Great Barrington Notes," *New York Globe,* 8 September 1883.

17. Du Bois, *Autobiography,* 107.

18. Ibid., 108–9, 280.

19. W. E. B. Du Bois to the Reverend Evarts Scudder, 3 February 1886; Du Bois to Edward Van Lennep, 29 September 1892, in *Correspondence,* 1:5, 18–19.

20. Du Bois, *Autobiography,* 110–11, 127.

21. Ibid., 109.

22. Ibid., 108, 112, 123.

23. Ibid., 114.

24. Ibid., 115–16.

25. W. E. B. Du Bois, *The Souls of Black Folk: Essays and Sketches* (Chicago: A. C. McClurg, 1903), 60–74.

26. Du Bois, *Autobiography,* 118–20, 280.

27. Ibid., 114, 119–20; and Du Bois, *Souls of Black Folk,* 189–91, 250–64.

28. Du Bois, *Autobiography,* 124, 127.

29. Jack B. Moore, *W. E. B. Du Bois* (Boston: Twayne Publishers, 1981), 22; and W. E. B. Du Bois, "An Open Letter to the Southern People" (1887), in *Against Racism,* 4.

30. Francis L. Broderick, *W. E. B. Du Bois: Negro Leader in a Time of Crisis* (Stanford: Stanford University Press, 1959), 8.

31. Erastus M. Cravath to "the Faculty of Harvard University," 10 April 1888; and Frederick A. Chase to secretary of Harvard College, no date, in *Against Racism,* 5.

32. Du Bois, *Autobiography,* 126.

33. W. E. B. Du Bois, Editorial, *Fisk Herald,* December 1887, 8–9.

34. W. E. B. Du Bois, Editorial, *Fisk Herald,* February 1888, 8–9.

35. Du Bois, *Darkwater,* 111–13; and Du Bois, *Autobiography,* 128–29.

36. Du Bois, *Autobiography,* 132.

37. Arnold Rampersad, *The Art and Imagination of W. E. B. Du Bois* (Cambridge: Harvard University Press, 1976), 29, 33, 36–38.

38. Du Bois, *Autobiography,* 138–39.

39. Broderick, *W. E. B. Du Bois,* 20.

40. W. E. B. Du Bois, "Jefferson Davis as a Representative of Civilization" 25 June 1890 in *Against Racism,* 12–16; and *Nation,* 3 July 1890, 14–15.

41. W. E. B. Du Bois, "The American Girl" (10 April 1891) in *Against Racism,* 19–20.

42. W. E. B. Du Bois to Rutherford B. Hayes, 4 November 1890; Du Bois to Hayes, 19 April 1891; Du Bois to Hayes, 6 May 1891; Du Bois to Hayes, 25 May 1891, in *Correspondence,* 1:10–14.

43. Du Bois, *Autobiography,* 153.

44. Ibid., 160–62; and W. E. B. Du Bois to D. C. Gilman, 28 October 1892, in *Correspondence,* 1:20–21.

45. Broderick, *W. E. B. Du Bois,* 26.

46. Peter Gay, *The Dilemma of Democratic Socialism* (New York: Collier Books, 1962), 62, 117.

47. Du Bois, *Autobiography,* 172–75.

48. W. E. B. Du Bois, *Fisk Herald,* September 1893, 5–7.

49. Broderick, *W. E. B. Du Bois,* 21.

50. Du Bois, *Autobiography,* 177, 277, 280, and W. E. B. Du Bois, "The Art and Art Galleries of Modern Europe" (1896?) in *Against Racism,* 33–43.

51. Du Bois, "Celebrating His Twenty-fifth Birthday" (23 February 1893) in *Against Racism,* 27–29.

52. W. E. B. Du Bois to the trustees of the John F. Slater Fund, 10 March 1893, in *Correspondence,* 1:23–25.

53. D. C. Gilman to W. E. B. Du Bois, 13 April 1894, in *Against Racism,* 29.

54. Du Bois, *Autobiography,* 181.

55. Du Bois, *Darkwater,* 16.

56. Broderick, *W. E. B. Du Bois,* 31.

2. THE IVORY TOWER OF RACE

1. W. E. B. Du Bois to Booker T. Washington,, 27 July 1894, in *Correspondence,* 1:37.

2. Booker T. Washington to W. E. B. Du Bois, 25 August 1894, in *Correspondence,* 1:38.

3. Du Bois, *Autobiography,* 186.

4. Broderick, *W. E. B. Du Bois,* 33.

5. Du Bois, *Autobiography,* 187.

6. W. E. B. Du Bois, *The Suppression of the African Slave-Trade to the United States of America, 1638–1870, Harvard Historical Studies no. 1* (New York: Longmans, Green, 1896; reprint ed., Williamstown, Mass.: Corner House Publishers, 1970), 6.

7. Ibid., 56, 61, 62, 70, 198.

8. Quoted in *The Unfolding Drama: Studies in U.S. History by Herbert Aptheker,* ed. Bettina Aptheker (New York: International Publishers, 1978), 147.

9. Du Bois, *Suppression of the African Slave-Trade,* 153–154, 194, 199.

10. Jessie P. Guzman, "W. E. B. Du Bois—The Historian," *Journal of Negro Education,* 30 (Fall 1961):379.

11. Du Bois, *Autobiography,* 187–88, 280–81.

12. Ibid., 190, 192.

13. C. C. Harrison to W. E. B. Du Bois, 15 August 1896, in *Correspondence,* 1:40.

14. Du Bois, *Autobiography,* 197.

15. Ibid., 198.

16. Gunnar Myrdal, *An American Dilemma: The Negro Problem and Modern Democracy* (New York: Harper & Brothers, 1944), 1132.

17. W. E. B. Du Bois, "The Study of the Negro Problems," *Annals of the American Academy of Political and Social Science,* 11 (January 1898):12.

18. See W. E. B. Du Bois, *The Philadelphia Negro* (New York: Schocken, 1967), 127–136, 212, 215.

19. Du Bois, *Autobiography,* 198–99.

20. Ibid., 208, 210, 213, 285.

21. W. E. B. Du Bois, "The Negroes of Farmville, Virginia: A Social Study," *Bulletin of the Department of Labor* 3 (January 1898):1–38.

22. See W. E. B. Du Bois, "The Negro in the Black Belt: Some Social Sketches," *Bulletin of the Department of Labor* 4 (May 1899):401–17.

23. See W. E. B. Du Bois, "The Negro Landholder of Georgia," *Bulletin of the Department of Labor* 6 (July 1901):647–777.

24. Du Bois, *Dusk of Dawn,* 61–62.

25. See W. E. B. Du Bois, ed., *Some Efforts of American Negroes for Their Own Social Betterment* (Atlanta: Atlanta University Press, 1898).

26. See W. E. B. Du Bois, ed., *The Negro in Business* (Atlanta: Atlanta University Press, 1899).

27. See W. E. B. Du Bois, ed., *The College-Bred Negro* (Atlanta: Atlanta University Press, 1900).

28. W. E. B. Du Bois, ed., *The Negro Artisan* (Atlanta: Atlanta University Press, 1902), 5–7.

29. C. Vann Woodward, *The Strange Career of Jim Crow* (New York: Oxford University Press, 1974), 94, 103.

30. Du Bois, *Autobiography,* 218–19.

31. Du Bois, "The Study of the Negro Problems," 20–23.

32. See "General and Industrial Education" hearings, *Immigration and Education,* vol. 15 (Washington, D.C.: Government Printing Office, 1901), 159–175.

33. W. E. B. Du Bois, "Memorial to the Legislature of Georgia," in *A Documentary History of the Negro People in the United States,* 2 vols., ed Herbert Aptheker. (Secaucus, N.J.: The Citadel Press, 1951), 1:784–86.

34. C. Vann Woodward, *Origins of the New South, 1877–1913* (Baton Rouge: Louisiana State University Press, 1951), 351–55.

35. Woodward, *Strange Career of Jim Crow,* 99.

36. Du Bois, *Souls of Black Folk,* 207–14.

37. Du Bois, *Autobiography,* 281.

38. W. E. B. Du Bois, "The Religion of the American Negro,"*New World* 9 (December 1900):614–25.

39. Cornel West, *Prophesy Deliverance! An Afro-American Revolutionary Christianity* (Philadelphia: Westminster Press, 1982), 72–73.

40. Alexander Crummell, *The Greatness of Christ and other Sermons* (New York: Thomas Whittaker, 1882), 294–311.

41. Du Bois, *Souls of Black Folk,* 215–27.

42. Alfred A. Moss, Jr., *The American Negro Academy: Voice of the Talented Tenth* (Baton Rouge: Louisiana State University Press, 1981), 19–34.

43. Ibid., 44.

44. Alexander Crummell, "Civilization, the Primal Need of the Race," Occasional Paper no. 3 (Washington, D.C.: American Negro Academy, 1898), 3–7.

45. W. E. B. Du Bois, "The Conservation of Races," Occasional Paper no. 2 (Washington, D.C.: American Negro Academy, 1897), 7–10, 12–14.

46. See Rampersad, *The Art and Imagination of W. E. B. Du Bois,* 61; and Joseph P. De Marco, *The Social Thought of W. E. B. Du Bois* (Lanham, Md.: University Press of America, 1983), 31, 36–37.

47. Du Bois, "The Conservation of Races," 12–15.

48. Moss, *The American Negro Academy,* 50, 52, 54–57.

49. W. E. B. Du Bois, "Striving of the Negro People," *Atlantic Monthly* 80 (August 1897):194–98.

50. August Meier, *Negro Thought in America, 1880–1915* (Ann Arbor: University of Michigan Press, 1963), 30, 66–67.

51. W. E. B. Du Bois, Memorandum to Paul Hagemans (1897), in *Against Racism,* 44–49.

52. P. Olisanwuche Esedebe, *Pan-Africanism: The Idea and Movement, 1776–1963* (Washington, D.C.: Howard University Press, 1982), 49–54.

53. W. E. B. Du Bois, "To the Nations of the World," in *Report of the Pan-African Conference* (London: 1900), 10–12.

54. George V. Plekhanov, *Fundamental Problems of Marxism* (New York: International Publishers, 1975), 176.

55. Louis R. Harlan, *Booker T. Washington: The Making of a Black Leader, 1856–1901* (New York: Oxford University Press, 1972), viii.

56. Booker T. Washington, *Up From Slavery* (1901), in *Three Negro Classics* (New York: Avon, 1965), 146–150.

57. Harlan, *Booker T. Washington,* 222–27.

58. Meier, *Negro Thought in America,* 111.

59. Moss, *The American Negro Academy,* 61.

60. W. E. B. Du Bois to Booker T. Washington, 24 September 1895, in *Correspondence,* 1:39.

61. Du Bois, *Dusk of Dawn,* 55.

62. Harlan, *Booker T. Washington,* 265, 360.

63. Ibid., 266–67.

64. Booker T. Washington to W. E. B. Du Bois, 11 March 1900, in *Correspondence,* 1:44.

65. Rudwick, *W. E. B. Du Bois,* 59.

66. Booker T. Washington to W. E. B. Du Bois, 15 July 1902, in *Correspondence,* 1:46.

67. W. E. B. Du Bois, "Careers Open to College-Bred Negroes," *Two Addresses Delivered by Alumni of Fisk University, in Connection with the Anniversary Exercises of Their Alma Mater, June, 1898* (Nashville: Fisk University, 1898), 1–14.

68. Meier, *Negro Thought in America,* 214.

69. Manning Marable, "Booker T. Washington and African Nationalism," *Phylon* 35 (December 1974):398.

70. Esedebe, *Pan-Africanism,* 48.

71. Louis R. Harlan, *Booker T. Washington: The Wizard of Tuskegee, 1901–1915* (New York: Oxford University Press, 1983), 267–69, 273, and Manning Marable, "A Black School in South Africa," *Negro History Bulletin,* 37 (June/July 1974):258–61.

72. Harlan, *Booker T. Washington: 1856–1901,* 227.

73. Joel Williamson, *The Crucible of Race: Black-White Relations in*

the American South since Emancipation (New York: Oxford University Press, 1984), 75.

74. Du Bois, *Autobiography*, 239.

75. Meier, *Negro Thought in America*, 174—212.

76. Harlan, *Booker T. Washington: 1901–1915*, 36–38.

77. Harlan, *Booker T. Washington: 1856–1901*, 267.

78. Harlan, *Booker T. Washington: 1901–1915*, 40.

79. Du Bois, *Autobiography*, 242.

80. W. E. B. Du Bois, "The Evolution of Negro Leadership," *Dial* 31 (1 July 1901):53–55.

81. W. E. B. Du Bois, "Hopeful Signs for the Negro," *Advance* 44 (2 October 1902):327–28.

82. W. E. B. Du Bois, "First Meeting of Persons Interested in the Welfare of the Negroes in New York City" (1903), in *Against Racism*, 72–74.

83. Du Bois, *Autobiography*, 243.

84. Booker T. Washington to W. E. B. Du Bois, 8 November 1903, in *Correspondence*, 1:53, 54.

85. Ida B. Wells-Barnett to W. E. B. Du Bois, 30 May 1903, in *Correspondence*, 1:55–56.

86. Casely Hayford to W. E. B. Du Bois, 8 June 1904, in *Correspondence*, 1:76.

87. Rampersad, *The Art and Imagination of W. E. B. Du Bois*, 74–76.

88. Du Bois, *Souls of Black Folk*, 78–84.

89. Ibid., 1–12, 68.

90. See Eugene D. Genovese, *In Red and Black: Marxian Explorations in Southern and Afro-American History* (New York: Vintage, 1971), 154.

91. Du Bois, *Souls of Black Folk*, 41–59.

92. James Weldon Johnson, *Along This Way* (New York: Viking, 1935), 203.

93. Rudwick, *W. E. B. Du Bois*, 69-70.

94. Du Bois, *Autobiography*, 247.

95. Harlan, *Booker T. Washington: 1901–1915*, 50–51.

96. W. E. B. Du Bois to George Foster Peabody, 28 December 1903, in *Correspondence*, 1:67–69.

97. W. E. B. Du Bois, "The Talented Tenth," in Booker T. Washington et al., *The Negro Problem* (New York: Arno, 1969), 31–75.

98. Harlan, *Booker T. Washington: 1901–1915*, 134.

99. W. E. B. Du Bois, "Lecture in Baltimore" (December 1903), in *Against Racism*, 75–77.

3. TUSKEGEE AND THE NIAGARA MOVEMENT

1. Booker T. Washington to W. E. B. Du Bois, 8 November 1903, in *Correspondence*, 1:54.

2. Harlan, *Booker T. Washington: 1901–1915*, 70.

3. Herbert Aptheker, "The Washington-Du Bois Conference of 1904," *Science and Society* 13 (Fall 1949):349.

4. Du Bois, *Autobiography*, 246–47.

5. Harlan, *Booker T. Washington: 1901–1915*, 79.

6. W. E. B. Du Bois, "The Parting of the Ways," *World Today* 6 (April 1904):521–23.

7. W. E. B. Du Bois, "To Solve the Negro Problem," *Collier's*, 18 June 1904, 14.

8. W. E. B. Du Bois, "Debit and Credit. The American Negro the Year of Grace Nineteen Hundred and Four," *Voice of the Negro* 2 (January 1905):677.

9. Rudwick, *W. E. B. Du Bois*, 88, 90.

10. Oswald Garrison Villard to W. E. B. Du Bois, 7 February 1905; Du Bois to Villard, 9 March 1905; Villard to Du Bois, 13 March 1905; Du Bois to William Monroe Trotter, 15 March 1905; Trotter to Du Bois, 18 March 1905; Du Bois to Villard, 24 March 1905; Villard to Du Bois, 18 April 1905; and Du Bois to Villard, 20 April 1905, in *Correspondence*, 1:97–105.

11. Harlan, *Booker T. Washington: 1901–1915*, 90–91.

12. Du Bois, *Autobiography*, 248–49.

13. Elliott M. Rudwick, "The Niagara Movement," *Journal of Negro History* 42 (July 1957):181.

14. Harlan, *Booker T. Washington: 1901–1915*, 88.

15. W. E. B. Du Bois to Isaac Max Rubinow, 17 November 1904, in *Correspondence*, 1:82.

16. W. E. B. Du Bois, "The Georgia Equal Rights Convention, 1906," in *The Selected Writings of W. E. B. Du Bois*, ed. Walter Wilson (New York: New American Library, 1970), 311–12.

17. W. E. B. Du Bois, "Niagara Address of 1906," in *Documentary History of the Negro People*, 1:907–10.

18. James Weldon Johnson to W. E. B. Du Bois, 16 December 1905, in *Correspondence*, 1:115–16.

19. Meier, *Negro Thought in America*, 255.

20. Louis R. Harlan, "The Secret Life of Booker T. Washington," *Journal of Southern History* 37 (August 1971):409.

21. Du Bois, *Autobiography*, 252–53.

22. Harlan, *Booker T. Washington: 1901–1915*, 153–55.

23. Meier, *Negro Thought in America*, 240.

24. Harlan, *Booker T. Washington: 1901–1915*, 57, 94.

25. Ibid., 89. See also Allison Blakely, "Richard T. Greener and the 'Talented Tenth's' Dilemma," *Journal of Negro History* 59 (October 1974):305–21.

26. Oliver C. Cox, "The Leadership of Booker T. Washington," *Social Forces* 30 (1951):91–97.

27. Ray Stannard Baker, *Following the Color Line: An Account of Negro Citizenship in the American Democracy* (1908; reprint ed., Williamstown, Mass.: Corner House Publishers, 1973), 13.

28. Harlan, *Booker T. Washington: 1901–1915,* 300–1.

29. Du Bois, *Darkwater,* 27.

30. Du Bois, *Autobiography,* 286.

31. W. E. B. Du Bois, "The Tragedy of Atlanta. From the Point of View of the Negroes," *World Today* 11 (November 1906):1173–75.

32. Du Bois, *Dusk of Dawn,* 94.

33. See W. E. B. Du Bois, ed., *A Select Bibliography of the Negro American* (Atlanta: Atlanta University Press, 1905).

34. See W. E. B. Du Bois, ed., *The Health and Physique of the Negro-American* (Atlanta: Atlanta University Press, 1906).

35. See W. E. B. Du Bois, ed., *Economic Co-Operation among Negro Americans* (Atlanta: Atlanta University Press, 1907).

36. W. E. B. Du Bois, "The Laboratory in Sociology at Atlanta University," *Annals of the American Academy of Political and Social Science* 21 (May 1903):160–63.

37. W. E. B. Du Bois, "The Atlanta University Conferences," *Charities* 10 (2 May 1903):435–39.

38. W. E. B. Du Bois, "Atlanta University" (1905), in *Writings by W. E. B. Du Bois in Non-Periodical Literature Edited by Others,* ed. Herbert Aptheker (Millwood, N.Y.: Kraus-Thomson, 1982), 44–59.

39. Richard Lloyd Jones to W. E. B. Du Bois, 7 January 1904, in *Correspondence,* 1:72–73.

40. Harlan, *Booker T. Washington: 1901–1915,* 51.

41. W. E. B. Du Bois, "The Atlanta Conferences," *Voice of the Negro* 1 (March 1904):85–90.

42. Du Bois, *Dusk of Dawn,* 94.

43. Max Weber to W. E. B. Du Bois, 30 March 1905, in *Correspondence,* 1:106–7.

44. W. E. B. Du Bois, "The Economics of Negro Emancipation in the United States," *Sociological Review* 4 (October 1911):303–13.

45. W. E. B. Du Bois, "Diminishing Negro Illiteracy," *Nation* 78 (25 February 1904):147–48.

46. W. E. B. Du Bois, "The Color Line Belts the World," *Collier's,* 20 October 1906, 20.

47. W. E. B. Du Bois, "Race Friction Between Black and White," *American Journal of Sociology* 13 (May 1908):834–38.

48. W. E. B. Du Bois, "The Souls of White Folk," *Independent* 69 (18 August 1910):339–42.

49. W. E. B. Du Bois, "The Beginning of Slavery," *Voice of the Negro* 2 (February 1905):104–6; Du Bois, "Slavery in Greece and Rome, *Voice of the Negro* 2 (May 1905):320–23; Du Bois, "The Beginning of Emancipation," *Voice of the Negro* 2 (June 1905):397–400; and Du Bois, "Serfdom," *Voice of the Negro* 2 (July 1905):479–81.

50. W. E. B. Du Bois, "Slavery and Its Aftermath," *Dial* 40 (1 May 1906):294–95.

51. W. E. B. Du Bois, "Garrison and the Negro," *Independent* 59 (7 December 1905):1316–17.

52. J. R. L. Diggs to W. E. B. Du Bois, 12 July 1909, in *Correspondence,* 1:150–51.

53. W. E. B. Du Bois, "Reconstruction and Its Benefits," *American Historical Review* 15 (July 1910):781–99.

54. W. E. B. Du Bois to J. Franklin Jameson, 2 June 1910; Jameson to Du Bois, 10 June 1910; Du Bois to Jameson, 13 June 1910; and Du Bois to Jameson, 5 July 1910, in *Correspondence,* 1:171–72.

55. Ellis Paxson Oberholtzer to W. E. B. Du Bois, 11 November 1903; Du Bois to Oberholtzer, 18 November 1903; Oberholtzer to Du Bois, 21 November 1903; Oberholtzer to Du Bois, 25 January 1904; and Du Bois to Oberholtzer, 30 January 1904, in *Correspondence,* 1:61–64.

56. W. E. B. Du Bois, *John Brown* (New York: International Publishers, 1962), 18, 25, 61, 96, 356, 375, 383, 395.

57. Oswald Garrison Villard to W. E. B. Du Bois, 26 November 1909, in *Correspondence,* 1:158–59.

58. W. E. B. Du Bois, "The Negro in Literature and Art," *Annals of the American Academy of Political and Social Science* 49 (September 1913):233–37.

59. W. E. B. Du Bois, *A Bibliography of Negro Folk Songs* (Atlanta: Atlanta University Press, 1903).

60. See W. E. B. Du Bois, *The Quest of the Silver Fleece: A Novel* (Chicago: A.C. McClurg, 1911): Du Bois, *Dusk of Dawn,* 269; and Arlene A. Elder, "Swamp Versus Plantation: Symbolic Structure in W. E. B. Du Bois' *The Quest of the Silver Fleece,*" *Phylon* 34 (December 1973):358–67.

61. W. E. B. Du Bois, "Credo," *Independent* 57 (6 October 1904):787.

62. W. E. B. Du Bois, "The Song of the Smoke," *Horizon* 1 (February 1907):4–6.

63. W. E. B. Du Bois, "The Horizon," *Horizon* 4 (July 1908):1–4.

64. Charles W. Puttkammer and Ruth Worthy, "William Monroe Trotter, 1872–1934," *Journal of Negro History* 43 (October 1958):304.

65. Du Bois, *Dusk of Dawn,* 94.

66. William H. Ferris, *The African Abroad,* (New Haven: Tuttle, Morehouse & Taylor, 1913),1:273–77.

67. Hallie E. Queen to W. E. B. Du Bois, 11 February 1907, in *Correspondence,* 1:125–26.

68. W. E. B. Du Bois, "Bryan," *Horizon* 3 (March 1908):7.

69. August Meier, "Booker T. Washington and the Rise of the NAACP," *Crisis* 60 (February 1954):74–75.

70. Rudwick, *W. E. B. Du Bois,* 105–6.

71. W. E. B. Du Bois, "Union," *Horizon* 3 (June 1908):506.

72. Rudwick, *W. E. B. Du Bois,* 104, 110, 116.

73. Technically Washington did not veto Du Bois's job offer. He informed Howard University president W. P. Thirkield that he opposed the appointment and hinted: "in the last analysis," the president "bears the burden and should have the credit or censure for success or failure." Poor Thirkield understood completely. Howard University made no offer to Du Bois. See Harlan, *Booker T. Washington: 1901–1915,* 178–79.

74. Ibid., 100–1, 105–6.

75. David R. Wallace to W. E. B. Du Bois, 16 October 1908, in *Correspondence,* 1:142.

76. John Hope to W. E. B. Du Bois, 17 January 1910; and Du Bois to Hope, 22 January 1910, in *Correspondence,* 1:165–67.

77. Mary White Ovington, "The National Association for the Advancement of Colored People," *Journal of Negro History* 9 (April 1924):107–11.

78. Rudwick, *W. E. B. Du Bois,* 121–22.

79. Ibid., 124–25.

80. W. E. B. Du Bois, "National Committee on the Negro," *Survey* 22 (12 June 1909):407–9.

81. Harlan, *Booker T. Washington: 1901–1915,* 361–62.

82. Du Bois, "The National Committee on the Negro," 409.

83. Rudwick, *W. E. B. Du Bois,* 131.

84. Harland, *Booker T. Washington: 1901-1915,* 364, 372, 373, 393.

85. Du Bois, *Darkwater,* 21.

86. W. E. B. Du Bois, *Prayers for Dark People,* ed. Herbert Aptheker (Amherst: University of Massachusetts, 1980), 15, 21.

4. THE *CRISIS* AND THE NAACP

1. Du Bois, *Dusk of Dawn,* 225–26.

2. W. E. B. Du Bois, "The Second Birthday," *Crisis* 5 (November 1912):27–28.

3. W. E. B. Du Bois, "The Crisis," *Crisis* 1 (November 1910):10.

4. W. E. B. Du Bois, "Except Servants," *Crisis* 1 (January 1911):21.

5. W. E. B. Du Bois, "Social Equality," *Crisis* 2 (September 1911):197; Du Bois, "Social Equality," *Crisis* 3 (November 1911):25; and Du Bois, "Forward Backward," *Crisis* 2 (October 1911):243–44.

6. W. E. B. Du Bois, "Lies," *Crisis* 6 (September 1913):236.

7. W. E. B. Du Bois, "Southerners," *Crisis* 7 (November 1913):337.

8. W. E. B. Du Bois, "Civilization in the South," *Crisis* 13 (March 1917):215–16.

9. See Benjamin R. Tillman to W. E. B. Du Bois, 23 July 1914, in *Correspondence,* 1:197–98, and "Radical Agitation Aimed at Negro Labor," Memorandum of the Office of Naval Inspector of Ordnance, 14 June 1919, in *The Marcus Garvey and Universal Negro Improvement Association Papers,* 4 vols., ed. Robert A. Hill (Berkeley: University of California Press, 1983), 1:433–34.

10. W. E. B. Du Bois, "Civil Service," *Crisis* 2 (May 1911):21; Du Bois, "Allies," *Crisis* 2 (July 1911):112–13; Du Bois, "Ross," *Crisis* 9 (January 1915):134; and Du Bois, "Organization," *Crisis* 9 (March 1915):235.

11. W. E. B. Du Bois, "Triumph," *Crisis* 2 (September 1911):195.

12. W. E. B. Du Bois, "Separation," *Crisis* 1 (February 1911):20–21; Du Bois, "The Strength of Segregation," *Crisis* 7 (December 1913):84.

13. Irene Diggs, "Du Bois—Revolutionary Journalist Then and Now: Part I," *A Current Bibliography on African Affairs,* 4 (March 1971):95–117.

14. Moss, *The American Negro Academy,* 168–69. The academy had a "change of heart" in March 1911 and for a very brief period advertised in the *Crisis.* After 1911, however, the academy placed no advertisements in the *Crisis* for its occasional papers series.

15. Harlan, *Booker T. Washington: 1901–1915,* 365, 367, 375–78.

16. Ibid., 427.

17. Benjamin Quarles, *Frederick Douglass,* (New York: Atheneum, 1969), 78.

18. W. E. B. Du Bois to Oswald Garrison Villard, 18 March 1913, in *Correspondence,* 1:181.

19. Paul U. Kellogg to W. E. B. Du Bois, 17 December 1913, in *Correspondence,* 1:186–87.

20. W. E. B. Du Bois, "Work for Black Folk in 1914," *Crisis* 7 (February 1914):186–87.

21. W. E. B. Du Bois to Joel Spingarn, 28 October 1914, in *Correspondence,* 1:203–7.

22. W. E. B. Du Bois to Mary White Ovington, 9 April 1914, in *Correspondence,* 1:188–91.

23. Joel E. Spingarn to W. E. B. Du Bois, 24 October 1914, in *Correspondence,* 1:200–2.

24. Broderick, *W. E. B. Du Bois,* 100–1.

25. Du Bois to Spingarn, 28 October 1914, in *Correspondence,* 1:206.

26. W. E. B. Du Bois to James Weldon Johnson, 1 November 1916, in *Correspondence,* 1:219–20.

27. Rudwick, *W. E. B. Du Bois,* 176–77.

28. Du Bois, *Autobiography,* 261.

29. Harlan, *Booker T. Washington: 1901–1915,* 379–404, 430–31, 451–55.

30. W. E. B. Du Bois, "Booker T. Washington," *Crisis* 11 (December 1915):82.

31. W. E. B. Du Bois, "An Open Letter to Robert Russa Moton," *Crisis* 12 (July 1916):136–37.

32. Rudwick, *W. E. B. Du Bois,* 192–93.

33. W. E. B. Du Bois, "The Amenia Conference: An Historic Negro Gathering," in *W. E. B. Du Bois Speaks: Speeches and Addresses, 1920–1963,* ed. Philip S. Foner (New York: Pathfinder Press, 1970), 21–31.

34. W. E. B. Du Bois to Walter F. White, 12 June 1923, in *Correspondence,* 1:265–67.

35. Lois Palken Rudnick, *Mabel Dodge Luhan: New Woman, New Worlds* (Albuquerque: University of New Mexico Press, 1984), 90.

36. Robert Rives La Monte, "The New Intellectuals," *New Review,* 2 (January 1914), 35–53.

37. Walter Lippmann to W. E. B. Du Bois, 17 January 1916, and Lippmann to Du Bois, 20 February 1919, in *Correspondence,* 1:214, 233.

38. Edwin Seaver to W. E. B. Du Bois, 13 February 1925, and Du Bois to Seaver, 19 February 1925, in *Correspondence,* 1:302–3.

39. Margaret Sanger to W. E. B. Du Bois, 7 February 1925, and Du Bois to Sanger, 14 February 1925, in *Correspondence,* 1:301–2; "As the Crow Flies," *Crisis* 36 (August 1929):257; and W. E. B. Du Bois, "Black Folk and Birth Control," *Birth Control Review,* 16 (June 1932):166–67.

40. W. E. B. Du Bois, "Abraham Lincoln," *Voice of the Negro* 4 (June 1907):242–47.

41. W. E. B. Du Bois, "Votes for Women" *Crisis* 4 (September 1912):234.

42. W. E. B. Du Bois, "Hail Columbia!" *Crisis* 5 (April 1913):289–90.

43. W. E. B. Du Bois, "Woman Suffrage," *Crisis* 9 (April 1915):284–85.

44. W. E. B. Du Bois, "Woman Suffrage," and Kelly Miller, "The Risk of Woman Suffrage," *Crisis* 11 (November 1915):29–30, 37–38.

45. Angela Y. Davis, *Women, Race and Class,* (New York: Random House, 1981), 122–25; and Belle Kearney, "The South and Woman Suffrage," in *Up From the Pedestal: Selected Writings in the History of American Feminism,* ed. Aileen S. Kraditor (Chicago: Quadrangle Books, 1968), 262–65.

46. W. E. B. Du Bois, "Forward Backward," *Crisis* 2 (October 1911):243–44.

47. W. E. B. Du Bois, "Votes for Women," *Crisis* 15 (November 1917):8.

48. W. E. B. Du Bois, "The Woman," *Crisis* 2 (May 1911):19, and Du Bois, "The Black Mother," *Crisis* 5 (December 1912):78.

49. W. E. B. Du Bois, "The Burden of Black Women," *Crisis* 9 (November 1914):31.

50. W. E. B. Du Bois, "Men of the Month," *Crisis* 3 (March 1912):190; 4 (June 1912):67; 5 (November 1912):16; 5 (December 1912):67; 5 (March 1913):225; 7 (January 1914):121; 8 (July 1914):117; and 8 (August 1914):169.

51. Du Bois, *Darkwater,* 172.

52. Philip S. Foner, *Organized Labor and the Black Worker, 1619–1981* (New York: International Publishers, 1981), 64, 75, 100–7.

53. Ibid., 80–81.

54. W. E. B. Du Bois, "Organized Labor," *Crisis* 4 (July 1912):131.

55. W. E. B. Du Bois, "The Pullman Porter," *New York Times,* 16 March 1914, 5; and A. Philip Randolph to W. E. B. Du Bois, 28 December 1927, in *Correspondence,* 1:371.

56. W. E. B. Du Bois, "I.W.W.," *Crisis* 18 (June 1919):60.

57. De Leon campaigned for Henry George in New York City's mayoral race of 1886, while still a member of the Columbia university faculty. By 1890 he had broken with George's theories, left the academy, and joined the small Socialist Labor party as a newspaper editor. Du Bois first mentions George's work in the June 1907 issue of the *Horizon.* As late as 1944, Du Bois continued to quote George as an authority on the structural inequalities of the capitalist system. See David Herreshoff, *The Origins of American Marxism: From the Transcendentalists to De Leon* (New York: Monad Press, 1973), 108–114; W. E. B. Du Bois, "Books," *Horizon* 1 (June 1907):9–10; Du Bois, "The Single Tax," *Crisis* 22 (October 1921):248; Du Bois, "Colored Editors on Communism," *Crisis* 39 (June 1932):190–91; Du Bois, "Kelly Miller—Who Owns the Earth," New York *Amsterdam News,* 20 January 1940, 1, 14; and Du Bois, "Jacob and Esau," *Talladegan* 62 (November 1944):1–6.

58. John P. Diggins, *The American Left in the Twentieth Century* (New York: Harcourt, Brace, Jovanovich, 1973), 66.

59. Herreshoff, *Origins of American Marxism,* 168.

60. James Theodore Holly, "Socialism from the Biblical Point of View," *AME Church Review* 9 (1892–93):244–58.

61. Reverdy C. Ransom, "The Negro and Socialism," AME *Church Review* 13 (1896–97):192–200.

62. Philip S. Foner, ed., *Black Socialist Preacher* (San Francisco: Synthesis Publications, 1983), 8.

63. Ray Ginger, *Eugene V. Debs: A Biography* (New York: Collier, 1962), 275.

64. Du Bois, *Autobiography,* 133, 142.

65. W. E. B. Du Bois, "The Magazines," *Horizons* 2 (August 1907):3.

66. W. E. B. Du Bois, "Socialist of the Path" and "Negro and Socialism," *Horizon* 1 (February 1907):7–8.

67. W. E. B. Du Bois, "To Black Voters," *Horizon* 3 (February 1908):17–18.

68. W. E. B. Du Bois, "Opinion," *Crisis* 1 (March 1911):11–14; and Ginger, *Eugene V. Debs,* 352.

69. W. E. B. Du Bois, "Christmas Gift," *Crisis* 3 (December 1911):68.

70. Du Bois, *Darkwater,* 138.

71. W. E. B. Du Bois, "Politics," *Crisis* 4 (August 1912):180–81.

72. W. E. B. Du Bois to Carolina M. Dexter, 6 November 1912, in *Correspondence,* 1:180.

73. W. E. B. Du Bois, "The President," *Crisis* 9 (February 1915):181.

74. W. E. B. Du Bois, "A Field for Socialists," *New Review* 1 (11 January 1913):54–57; Du Bois, "Socialism and the Negro Problem," *New Review* 1 (1 February 1913):138–41; and Du Bois, "The Problem of Problems," *Intercollegiate Socialist* 6 (December 1917–January 1918):5–9.

75. W. E. B. Du Bois to J. Ramsay MacDonald, 10 January 1914, and MacDonald to Du Bois, 6 February 1914, in *Correspondence,* 1:187–88.

76. Upton Sinclair to W. E. B. Du Bois, 8 September 1914; Sinclair to Du Bois, 2 October 1914; and Du Bois to Sinclair, 19 October 1914, in *Correspondence,* 1:198–200.

77. Rudnick, *Mabel Dodge Luhan,* 86–87.

78. W. E. B. Du Bois, "The Star of Ethiopia," *Crisis* 11 (December 1915):91–93, and Du Bois, "A Negro Art Renaissance," *Los Angeles Times,* 14 June 1925, 26–27.

79. Du Bois, *Darkwater,* 103.

80. Herbert Aptheker, "W. E. B. Du Bois and the Struggle Against Racism" (pamphlet) (New York: United Nations Centre Against Apartheid, 1983), 4.

81. W. E. B. Du Bois, "Africa", *Horizon* 1 (June 1907):5–7; Du Bois,

"The Magazines for November", *Horizon* 2 (November 1907):1; and Du Bois, "An African on His Race", *Horizon* 4 (July 1908):7–8.

82. W. E. B. Du Bois, "Edward Wilmot Blyden", *Crisis* 3 (January 1912):103; Du Bois, "The Military Attaches to Liberia", *Crisis* 4 (May 1912):16; Du Bois, "The Minister to Liberia", *Crisis* 7 (November 1913):326–27; and Du Bois, "Menelik", *Crisis* 7 (February 1914):185.

83. W. E. B. Du Bois, "The Story of Africa", *Crisis* 8 (September 1911):234–35.

84. Du Bois, *Darkwater,* 166.

85. W. E. B. Du Bois to Edward Wilmot Blyden, 5 April 1909, in *Correspondence,* 1:146.

86. W. E. B. Du Bois, "The Races Congress", *Crisis* 2 (September 1911):200–9.

87. W. E. B. Du Bois, *The Negro* (New York: Oxford University Press, 1970), 80, 113–14.

88. Ibid., xxi, 145–46.

89. W. E. B. Du Bois, "Of the Children of Peace," *Crisis* 8 (October 1914):289–90.

90. W. E. B. Du Bois, "World War and the Color Line," *Crisis* 9 (November 1914):28–30.

91. W. E. B. Du Bois, "The African Roots of the War," *Atlantic Monthly* 115 (May 1915):707-14.

92. Robert C. Tucker, ed., *The Lenin Anthology* (New York: W. W. Norton, 1975), 261.

93. W. E. B. Du Bois, "Ireland," *Crisis* 12 (August 1916):166–77; and Du Bois, "'Refinement and Love,'" *Crisis* 13 (December 1916):63.

94. W. E. B. Du Bois, "The World Last Month," *Crisis* 13 (January 1917):111.

95. W. E. B. Du Bois, "The Negro's Fatherland," *Survey* 39 (10 November 1917):141; Du Bois, "The Future of Africa," *Crisis* 15 (January 1918):114; and Du Bois, "The Black Soldier," *Crisis* 16 (June 1918):60.

96. Albert Fried, ed., *Socialism in America: From the Shakers to the Third International,* (Garden City, N.Y.: Anchor Books, 1970), 506–9, and Diggins, *American Left in the Twentieth Century,* 82–86.

97. W. E. B. Du Bois to Newton D. Baker, 6 December 1917, and Baker to Du Bois, 13 December 1917, in *Correspondence,* 1:224–25.

98. Du Bois, *Dusk of Dawn,* 247–57.

99. W. E. B. Du Bois, "Close Ranks," *Crisis* 16 (July 1918):111.

100. Byron Gunner to W. E. B. Du Bois, 25 July 1918; and Du Bois to Gunner, 10 August 1918, in *Correspondence,* 1:228.

101. W. E. B. Du Bois, "A Philosophy in Time of War," *Crisis* 16 (August 1918):164–65.

102. Garrett Distributing Company to W. E. B. Du Bois, 20 August 1917, and Du Bois to Garrett Distributing Company, 29 August 1917, in *Correspondence*, 1:223.

103. Rudwick, *W. E. B. Du Bois*, 191.

104. Broderick, *W. E. B. Du Bois*, 120.

105. Du Bois, *Autobiography*, 269.

106. Ibid., 283.

107. Johnson, *Along This Way*, 203.

5. PAN-AFRICANISM, SOCIALISM, AND GARVEYISM

1. Esedebe, *Pan-Africanism*, 61.

2. W. E. B. Du Bois, "The Peace Conference," *Crisis* 17 (January 1919):111–12.

3. J. P. Tumulty to W. E. B. Du Bois, 29 November 1918, in *Correspondence*, 1:232.

4. Du Bois, *Dusk of Dawn*, 260.

5. W. E. B. Du Bois, "The Future of Africa," *Advocate of Peace* 81 (January 1919):12–13; and "Letters From Dr. Du Bois," "Africa," "Reconstruction and Africa," and "Not 'Separatism,'" *Crisis* 17 (February 1919):163–66.

6. F. B. Schoonmaker to Intelligence Officers, Secret Memo, 1 January 1919, in *Correspondence*, 1:232. Du Bois soon acquired a copy of this secret order, which was stamped by division headquarters.

7. W. E. B. Du Bois, "The Pan-African Movement," in *W. E. B. Du Bois Speaks*, 163.

8. Du Bois, *Dusk of Dawn*, 261.

9. George Padmore, *Pan-Africanism or Communism* (Garden City, N.Y.: Anchor Books, 1972), 98.

10. C. L. R. James, *The Future in the Present: Selected Writings* (Westport, Conn.: Lawrence Hill, 1980), 207.

11. Of the heroic conduct of French West African troops during the war, Du Bois wrote: "Against the banked artillery of the magnificent German Army were sent untrained and poorly armed Senegalese. They marched at command in unwavering ranks, raising the war cry in a dozen different Sudanese tongues. When the artillery belched they shivered, but never faltered. They marched straight into death; the war cries became fainter and fainter and dropped into silence as not a single black man was left living on that field." W. E. B. Du Bois, *The World and Africa: An Inquiry into the Part Which Africa Has Played in World History* (New York: International Publishers, 1965), 7.

12. Padmore, *Pan-Africanism or Communism*, 98–99.

13. Du Bois, *The World and Africa,* 10.

14. Du Bois, *Dusk of Dawn,* 262.

15. Du Bois, *The World and Africa,* 10. Padmore noted that "the American officials in President Wilson's entourage were afraid that the Congress might discuss, among other things, the lynching of Negroes in the United States and the treatment of Afro-American troops in France. The American statesmen had good reason to be alarmed, for apart from maintaining racial segregation between black and white troops serving under the Stars and Stripes, the U.S. Army authorities in France tried to impose their racial prejudices on the French people." Padmore, *Pan-Africanism or Communism,* 99–100. Also see "The Denial of Passports," *Crisis* 17 (March 1919):237–38.

16. Ibid., 10.

17. Esedebe, *Pan-Africanism,* 82.

18. Du Bois, *The World and Africa,* 11–12; and W. E. B. Du Bois, "The Pan-African Congress," *Crisis* 17 (April 1919):271–74.

19. Kwame Nkrumah, *Africa Must Unite* (New York: International Publishers, 1970), 103.

20. W. E. B. Du Bois, "An Essay toward a History of the Black Man in the Great War," *Crisis* 18 (June 1919):63–87.

21. W. E. B. Du Bois, "Returning Soldiers," *Crisis* 18 (May 1919):13–14.

22. W. E. B. Du Bois, "Let Us Reason Together," *Crisis* 18 (September 1919):231.

23. James F. Byrnes, Statement of August 1919, in *W. E. B. Du Bois,* ed. William M. Tuttle, Jr. (Englewood Cliffs, N.J.: Prentice-Hall, 1973), 124–25.

24. W. E. B. Du Bois, "The Black Majority," *Crisis* 18 (September 1919):232–33; and Du Bois, "Byrnes," *Crisis* 18 (October 1919):284–85.

25. W. E. B. Du Bois, "Forward," *Crisis* 18 (September 1919):234–35.

26. W. E. B. Du Bois to Charles Evans Hughes, 23 June 1921, in *Correspondence,* 1:250–51.

27. W. E. B. Du Bois, "To the World," *Crisis* 23 (November 1921):5–10, and Esedebe, *Pan-Africanism,* 83–89.

28. Du Bois, "The Pan-African Movement," 169–70.

29. Du Bois, *The World and Africa,* 240–241, and Padmore, *Pan-Africanism or Communism,* 112.

30. Du Bois, *The World and Africa,* 240.

31. Padmore, *Pan-Africanism or Communism,* 110–11.

32. Esedebe, *Pan-Africanism,* 90–91.

33. Du Bois, "To the World," 5–10, and Du Bois, "A Second Journey to Pan-Africa," *New Republic,* 7 December 1921, 39–41.

34. Du Bois, *The World and Africa,* 241.

35. J. Ramsay MacDonald to W. E. B. Du Bois, 6 November 1923, in *Correspondence,* 1:276–77.

36. Esedebe, *Pan-Africanism,* 95.

37. Du Bois, *The World and Africa,* 242; Padmore, *Pan-Africanism or Communism,* 117–120; and W. E. B. Du Bois, "Pan-Africa in Portugal," *Crisis,* 27 (February 1924):170.

38. Nkrumah, *Africa Must Unite,* 133.

39. W. E. B. Du Bois, "Pan-Africa," *Crisis* 27 (December 1923):57–58.

40. William H. Lewis to W. E. B. Du Bois, 4 October 1923, in *Correspondence,* 1:277–78.

41. W. E. B. Du Bois, "The Negro Mind Reaches Out," in *The New Negro,* ed. Alain Locke (New York: Atheneum, 1977), 385–414.

42. W. E. B. Du Bois to C. D. B. King, 21 January 1924; King to Du Bois, 30 June 1924; and Du Bois to King, 29 July 1924, in *Correspondence,* 1:279–83; W. E. B. Du Bois, "The Primitive Black Man," *Nation,* 17 December 1924, 675–76; and W. E. B. Du Bois, "Liberia and Rubber," *New Republic,* 18 November 1925, 326–29.

43. Du Bois, "The Negro Mind Reaches Out," 406–7.

44. W. E. B. Du Bois, "Kenya," *Crisis* 27 (February 1924):151–52.

45. W. E. B. Du Bois, "The World and Us," *Crisis* 24 (May 1922):7, and Du Bois, "The Prayer-Book," *Crisis* 35 (February 1928):61.

46. W. E. B. Du Bois, "Italy and Abyssinia," *Crisis* 32 (June 1926):62–63.

47. Du Bois, *Dusk of Dawn,* 275.

48. W. E. B. Du Bois, "The Answer of Africa" (1926), in *Writings by W. E. B. Du Bois in Non-Periodical Literature,* 150–55.

49. W. E. B. Du Bois, "Dying," *Horizon* 1 (May 1907):8–9.

50. In *Prayers for Dark People,* 22.

52. W. E. B. Du Bois, "Migration," *Crisis* 12 (October 1916):270.

52. Du Bois, "World War and the Color Line," 28–30.

53. W. E. B. Du Bois, "The World Last Month," *Crisis* 13 (March 1917):215.

54. Du Bois, *Darkwater,* 159.

55. W. E. B. Du Bois, "After the War," *Crisis* 17 (January 1919):114; and "Political Straws," *Crisis* 26 (July 1923):124–26.

56. W. E. B. Du Bois, "Egypt and India," *Crisis* 18 (June 1919):62.

57. W. E. B. Du Bois, "Socialism and the Negro," *Crisis* 22 (October 1921):245–47.

58. W. E. B. Du Bois, "The Unreal Campaign," *Crisis* 21 (December 1920):54–56.

59. See W. E. B. Du Bois, "Co-operation," *Crisis* 16 (October

1918):268; Du Bois, "Co-operation" *Crisis* 17 (November 1918):9–10; Du Bois, "Consumers' Co-operation," *Crisis* 17 (January 1919):114–15; Du Bois, "Cooperation," *Crisis* 19 (February 1920):171–72; and Du Bois, "Cooperation," *Crisis* 23 (January 1922):107.

60. A. Philip Randolph and Chandler Owen, "A Thanksgiving Homily to Revolution" (December 1919), and Chandler Owen, "The Failure of the Negro Leaders" (January 1918), in *Voices of a Black Nation: Political Journalism in the Harlem Renaissance,* ed. Theodore G. Vincent (San Francisco: Ramparts Press, 1973), 46–47, 48–50; and "Du Bois as Reactionary," in *W. E. B. Du Bois,* ed. Tuttle, 125–30.

61. Manning Marable, *From the Grassroots: Social and Political Essays towards Afro-American Liberation* (Boston: South End Press, 1980), 68–69.

62. W. E. B. Du Bois, "Radicals," *Crisis* 19 (December 1919):46.

63. W. E. B. Du Bois, "The Class Struggle," *Crisis* 22 (August 1921):151–52.

64. W. E. B. Du Bois, "Socialism and the Negro," *Crisis* 22 (October 1921):245–47.

65. Chandler Owen, "Du Bois on Revolution: A Reply" (1921), in *Voices of a Black Nation,* 88–92.

66. William H. Harris, *The Harder We Run: Black Workers since the Civil War* (New York: Oxford University Press, 1982), 81–82.

67. W. E. B. Du Bois, "The Black Man and Labor," *Crisis* 31 (December 1925):60; Du Bois, "Pullman Porters," *Crisis* 31 (January 1926):113; Du Bois, "Again, Pullman Porters," *Crisis* 31 (April 1926):271; and Du Bois, "Unions," *Crisis* 33 (January 1927):131.

68. Du Bois, *Autobiography,* 284.

69. Wilfred D. Samuels, "Hubert H. Harrison and 'The New Negro Manhood Movement,'" *Afro-Americans in New York Life and History* 5 (January 1982):29–41.

70. Theodore G. Vincent, *Black Power and the Garvey Movement* (San Francisco: Ramparts Press, 1972), 72–87, and Robert A. Hill, ed., *Marcus Garvey Papers,* 1:521–27.

71. W. E. B. Du Bois, "The Negro and Radical Thought," *Crisis* 22 (July 1921):102–4.

72. W. E. B. Du Bois, "Communists Boring Into Negro Labor," *New York Times,* (17 January 1926).

73. W. E. B. Du Bois, "Communists and the Color Line," *Crisis* 38 (September 1931):315.

74. George Padmore, "The Bankruptcy of Negro Leadership" (1931), in *Voices of a Black Nation,* 184–89.

75. W. E. B. Du Bois, "A Labor Program," *Crisis* 25 (April

1923):249–50; Du Bois, "As the Crow Flies," *Crisis* 36 (July 1929):223; and Du Bois, "Socialism in England," *Crisis* 39 (April 1932):132.

76. W. E. B. Du Bois, "The World and Us," *Crisis* 24 (June 1922):55–56.

77. James C. Jackson to W. E. B. Du Bois, 15 July 1924, in *Correspondence,* 1:289–90.

78. Du Bois, "The Negro Mind Reaches Out," 408.

79. Du Bois, "The Black Man and Labor," 60.

80. Theodore G. Vincent, introduction to *Voices of a Black Nation,* 93.

81. See E. U. Essien Udom, Introduction to *Philosophy and Opinions of Marcus Garvey,* ed. Amy Jacques-Garvey (London: Frank Cass, 1967), xxvi; Hollis R. Lynch, Introduction to *Philosophy and Opinions of Marcus Garvey* (reprint ed., New York: Atheneum, 1977), 11–12; and Rudwick, *W. E. B. Du Bois,* 216.

82. Robert A. Hill, ed. *Marcus Garvey Papers,* 1:529; Harold Cruse, *Crisis of the Negro Intellectual,* 120–21; E. Franklin Frazier, "Garvey: A Mass Leader" (1926), and Kelly Miller, "After Marcus Garvey—What of the Negro?", in *Marcus Garvey and the Vision of Africa,* ed. John Henrik Clarke (New York: Vintage Books, 1974), 236–41, 242–46.

83. Hill, *Marcus Garvey Papers,* 1:1xxviii.

84. Marcus Garvey, "UNIA Memorial Meeting for Booker T. Washington", 24 November 1915, in *Marcus Garvey Papers,* 1:166, and Garvey to R. R. Moton, 29 February 1916, in *Marcus Garvey Papers,* 1:166, 177–83.

85. Frazier, "Garvey: A Mass Leader," 236–41.

86. Richard B. Moore, "The Critics and Opponents of Marcus Garvey," in *Marcus Garvey and the Vision of Africa,* 210–35.

87. Quoted in *Marcus Garvey Papers,* 1:lxxxiii.

88. Garvey speech, 18 December 1918, in *Marcus Garvey Papers,* 1:332.

89. Cadet's initial charges against Du Bois had been sent on either 22 or 23 March 1919, but Du Bois left France on 22 March. Cadet quickly tired of pursuing the UNIA agenda at the peace conference, and for most of the remainder of the year worked in Paris as an auto mechanic. He returned to Haiti in late 1919, and eventually "became a vodun high priest of the cult of Damballah (the serpent god)." Hill, *Marcus Garvey Papers,* 1:308, 392–400.

90. Hill, *Marcus Garvey Papers,* 1:200–11; Moss, *The American Negro Academy,* 239, 276; and Vincent, *Black Power and the Garvey Movement,* 40, 74.

91. Garvey speech, 3 August 1920, and Marcus Garvey interview

with Charles Mowbray White, 18 August 1920, in Robert A. Hill, ed., *Marcus Garvey Papers*, 2:525–26, 602–3.

92. Truman K. Gibson to W. E. B. Du Bois, 24 July 1920, and W. E. B. Du Bois to H. L. Stone, 24 July 1920, in *Marcus Garvey Papers*, 2:434–35.

93. Hill, *Marcus Garvey Papers*, 1:cxv–cxvii. In the United States, Garvey was under the active surveillance of J. Edgar Hoover, then special assistant to the attorney general and of the General Intelligence Division of the federal government. Hill, *Marcus Garvey Papers*, 1:406.

94. W. E. B. Du Bois interview with Charles Mowbray White, 22 August 1920, in *Marcus Garvey Papers*, 2:620–21.

95. Du Bois, "Radicals," 46, and W. E. B. Du Bois, "The Rise of the West Indian," *Crisis* 20 (September 1920):214–15.

96. W. E. B. Du Bois, "Marcus Garvey," *Crisis* 21 (December 1920):58, 60, and Du Bois, "Marcus Garvey," *Crisis* 21 (January 1921):112–15.

97. Marcus Garvey, "What Garvey Thinks of Du Bois" (1 January 1921), in *Voices of a Black Nation*, 97–99.

98. Du Bois to Hughes, 23 June 1921, in *Correspondence*, 1:250–51.

99. Du Bois, *Dusk of Dawn*, 277–78.

100. Hill, General Introduction, *Marcus Garvey Papers*, 1:lxxviii–lxxxi; Frank Burke to George F. Lamb, Bureau of Investigation, 15 September 1919; and Garvey to White, 18 August 1920, in *Marcus Garvey Papers*, 2:19, 603.

101. A. Philip Randolph, "Garveyism" (September 1921), in *Voices of a Black Nation*, 114–17.

102. Cyril Briggs, "The Decline of the Garvey Movement," in *Marcus Garvey and the Vision of Africa*, 174–79.

103. See Kenneth T. Jackson, *The Ku Klux Klan in the City, 1915–1930* (New York: Oxford University Press, 1967).

104. Marcus Garvey, "The Negro, Communism, Trade Unionism," in *Philosophy and Opinions of Marcus Garvey*, 71.

105. W. E. B. Du Bois, "Ku Klux Klan," *Crisis* 23 (November 1921):10–11; Du Bois, "The Ku Klux Klan," *Crisis* 24 (August 1922):155; Du Bois, "Travel," *Crisis* 28 (September 1924):202–03; Du Bois, "The Election," *Crisis* 29 (December 1924):55; and Du Bois, "The Shape of Fear," *North American Review* 223 (June 1926):291–304.

106. W. E. B. Du Bois, "Back to Africa," *Century Magazine* 105 (February 1923):539–48.

107. Marcus Garvey, "W. E. B. Du Bois as a Hater of Dark People" (13 February 1923), in *Voices of a Black Nation*, 99–105.

108. W. E. B. Du Bois, "A Lunatic or a Traitor," *Crisis* 28 (May 1924):8–9.

109. A. Philip Randolph, "Battling Du Bois Vs. Kid Garvey" (June 1924), in *Voices of a Black Nation,* 122.

110. Du Bois, "A Lunatic or a Traitor," 8–9.

111. W. E. B. Du Bois, "Pan-Africa," *Crisis* 36 (December 1929):423–24.

112. W. E. B. Du Bois, "Pan-Africa," *Crisis* 32 (October 1926):284, and "The Pan-African Congresses," *Crisis* 34 (October 1927):263–64.

113. Du Bois, "Pan-Africa" (1929), 423–24.

114. W. E. B. Du Bois, "Marcus Garvey," *Crisis* 35 (February 1928):51.

115. W. E. B. Du Bois to Amy Jacques-Garvey, 9 February 1944; Jacques-Garvey to Du Bois, 4 April 1944; Du Bois to Jacques-Garvey, 8 April 1944; and Jacques-Garvey to Du Bois, 24 April 1944, in *The Correspondence of W. E. B. Du Bois,* 3 vols., ed. Herbert Aptheker, vol. 2, *Selections, 1934–1944* (Amherst: University of Massachusetts Press, 1976), 375–83.

116. Vincent, *Black Power and the Garvey Movement,* 58.

117. Padmore, *Pan-Africanism or Communism,* 106.

6. THE NEW NEGRO

1. Rudwick, *W. E. B. Du Bois,* 240–41.

2. W. E. B. Du Bois, "Correspondence," *Crisis* 25 (March 1923):201–2.

3. Charles Mowbray White, Interview with Chandler Owen and A. Philip Randolph, 20 August 1920, and White, Interview with Frederick Moore, 23 August 1920, in *Marcus Garvey Papers,* 2:611, 623.

4. W. E. B. Du Bois to M. V. Boutté, 27 December 1927, in *Correspondence,* 1:369–70.

5. Vincent, *Voices of a Black Nation,* 30–31, 37.

6. Du Bois, *Dusk of Dawn,* 281.

7. W. E. B. Du Bois to James Weldon Johnson, 15 April 1924; Johnson to Du Bois, 17 April 1924; and Du Bois to Joel Spingarn, 16 July 1924, in *Correspondence,* 1:286–89, 291–92.

8. Du Bois, *Autobiography,* 295.

9. W. E. B. Du Bois, "Woman Suffrage," *Crisis* 19 (March 1920):234; Du Bois, "Triumph," *Crisis* 20 (October 1920):261; Du Bois, "A Question of Facts," *Crisis* 21 (February 1921):150–52; and Du Bois, "As the Crow Flies," *Crisis* 41 (January 1934):5.

10. W. E. B. Du Bois, "The American Jew," *Crisis* 24 (August 1922):152; Du Bois, "The Wide Wide World," *Crisis* 34 (April 1927):39; Du

Bois, "As the Crow Flies," *Crisis* 34 (September 1927):219; Du Bois, "Exclusion," *Crisis* 35 (January 1928):23; and Du Bois, "The Jews," *Crisis* 40 (May 1933):117.

11. W. E. B. Du Bois to the Reverend Samuel H. Bishop, 1 May 1907, in *Correspondence*, 1:131.

12. W. E. B. Du Bois, "The Methodists," *Crisis* 12 (July 1916):137; Du Bois, "Bishops," *Crisis* 20 (August 1920):166; and Du Bois "Methodists", *Crisis* 29 (November 1924):7.

13. Joseph B. Glenn to W. E. B. Du Bois, 18 February 1925; Du Bois to Glenn, 18 March 1925; Glenn to Du Bois, 20 March 1925; and Du Bois to Glenn, 24 March 1925; in *Correspondence*, 1:308–11; and Du Bois, "The Church," *Crisis* 11 (June 1916):302.

14. W. E. B. Du Bois, "The Episcopal Church," *Crisis* 7 (December 1913):83–84; and Du Bois, "The Sermon on the Tower," *Crisis* 31 (December 1925):59.

15. Du Bois, *Darkwater,* 123–33.

16. W. E. B. Du Bois, "Darrow," *Crisis* 35 (June 1928):203; Du Bois, "The Aax-Wealth-Dewey and Taft," New York *Amsterdam News,* 30 December 1939, 1, 6; and Du Bois, "A 'Missionary' From S. Africa," New York *People's Voice,* 7 February 1948, 14.

17. W. E. B. Du Bois, "Dives, Mob and Scab, Limited," *Crisis* 19 (March 1920):235–36; Du Bois, "The American Scene," *Crisis* 28 (May 1924):7–8; and Du Bois, "As The Crow Flies," *Crisis* 36 (August 1929):257.

18. W. E. B. Du Bois, "The Black Man and the Unions," *Crisis* 15 (March 1918):216–17.

19. Edward P. Clarke to W. E. B. Du Bois, 8 February 1930, and Du Bois to Clarke, 18 February 1930, in *Correspondence*, 1:418; and Du Bois, "The A.F. of L" *Crisis* 40 (December 1933):292.

20. W. E. B. Du Bois, "An Open Letter to Warren Gamaliel Harding," *Crisis* 21 (March 1921):197–98; Du Bois, "Kicking Us Out," *Crisis* 24 (May 1922):11; "How Shall We Vote? A Symposium," *Crisis* 29 (November 1924):13; Du Bois, "A New Party," *Crisis* 37 (August 1930):282; and Du Bois to Devere Allen, 24 June 1929, in *Correspondence*, 1:405–6.

21. W. E. B. Du Bois, "How Shall We Vote?" *Crisis* 35 (October 1928):346; Du Bois, "As the Crow Flies," *Crisis* 35 (August 1928):257; Du Bois, "De Priest," *Crisis* 36 (February 1929):57; and Du Bois to Margaret Deland, 12 December 1928, in *Correspondence*, 1:383–84.

22. W. E. B. Du Bois, "Ferdinand Q. Morton," *Crisis* 30 (July 1925):115–16, and W. E. B. Du Bois to Ferdinand Q. Morton, 18 February 1930, in *Correspondence*, 1:416–17.

23. Rudwick, *W. E. B. Du Bois,* 264.

24. Richard E. Enright to W. E. B. Du Bois, 2 June 1922, and Du Bois to Enright, 3 April 1923, in *Correspondence*, 1:257–58, 264.

25. Du Bois, *Autobiography*, 280–82; and Du Bois, "So the Girl Marries," *Crisis* 35 (June 1928):192–93, 207–9.

26. Du Bois, *Dusk of Dawn*, 315.

27. W. E. B. Du Bois, "William Monroe Trotter," *Crisis* 41 (May 1934):134.

28. W. E. B. Du Bois, "Paul LeRoy Robeson," *Crisis* 15 (March 1918):229–31.

29. James W. Ford to W. E. B. Du Bois, 20 February 1925; Abram L. Harris to Du Bois, 21 November 1925; Ralph J. Bunche to Du Bois, 11 May 1927; Richard Barthé to Du Bois, 5 August 1928; St. Clair Drake to Du Bois, 10 August 1930; Robert C. Weaver to Du Bois, 29 January 1931; and William Leo Hansberry to Du Bois, 13 July 1933, in *Correspondence*, 1:306–7, 327–28, 353–54, 376–77, 428–29, 434–35, 466–67.

30. William H. Ferris, "Review of *Darkwater*" (June 1920), in *Voices of a Black Nation*, 342–48.

31. W. E. B. Du Bois, "History," *Crisis* 18 (May 1919):11; Du Bois to John Hope, 25 March 1925, and Du Bois to Raymond B. Fosdick, 18 November 1927, in *Correspondence*, 1:312, 365–67.

32. W. E. B. Du Bois, "The Negro Church," *The Freeman* 6 (4 October 1922):92–93; and Carter G. Woodson, *The Mis-education of the Negro* (Washington, D.C.: Associated Publishers, 1969), 186–87.

33. Du Bois, "A Portrait of Carter G. Woodson," *Masses and Mainstream*, 3 (June 1950):19–25; Du Bois to Rayford Logan, 26 April 1950, in *The Correspondence of W. E. B. Du Bois*, 3 vols., ed. Herbert Aptheker, vol. 3, *Selections 1944–1963* (Amherst: University of Massachusetts Press, 1978), 282–93; and Herbert Aptheker, ed., "Douglass as a Statesman," *Journal of Negro History*, 49 (October 1964):264–68.

34. Alain Locke and W. E. B. Du Bois, "The Younger Literary Movement," *Crisis* 27 (February 1924):161–63; Du Bois to Jesse E. Moorland, 5 May 1927, in *Correspondence*, 1:352; Du Bois, "Our Book Shelf," *Crisis* 31 (January 1926):140–41; and Du Bois, "The Passing of Alain Locke," *Phylon* 15, no. 3 (1954):251–52.

35. W. E. B. Du Bois, "The Browsing Reader," *Crisis* 35 (May 1928):165; Alain Locke, "The New Negro," and Charles S. Johnson, "The New Frontage on American Life," in *The New Negro*, 3–16, 278–98.

36. W. E. B. Du Bois, "Negro Art," *Crisis* 22 (June 1921):55–56; and Du Bois, "Truth and Beauty," *Crisis* 25 (November 1922):7–8.

37. W. E. B. Du Bois, "A Composer," *Crisis* 3 (March 1912):190; Du Bois, "Can the Negro Serve the Drama?", *Theatre Magazine* 38 (July 1923):12, 68; Du Bois, "Krigwa," *Crisis* 30 (June 1925):59; "John Work:

Martyr and Singer," *Crisis* 32 (May 1926):32–34; Du Bois, "Krigwa," *Crisis* 32 (June 1926):59; Du Bois, "Musicians," *Crisis* 34 (July 1927):168; and Du Bois, "The Black Man Brings His Gifts," *Survey Graphic* 53 (1 March 1925):655–57.

38. W. E. B. Du Bois, "The Social Origins of American Negro Art," *Modern Quarterly* 3 (October-December 1925):53–56; and Du Bois, "Criteria of Negro Art," *Crisis* 32 (October 1926):290, 292, 296–97.

39. W. E. B. Du Bois, "The Browsing Reader," *Crisis* 34 (June 1927):129; Du Bois, "Mencken," *Crisis* 34 (October 1927):276; Du Bois, "The Browsing Reader," *Crisis* 35 (June 1928):202, 211; and Claude McKay to Du Bois, 18 June 1928, in *Correspondence,* 1:374–75.

40. Alain Locke, "A Retrospective Review" (January 1929), and Marcus Garvey, "'Home to Harlem': An Insult to the Race" (29 September 1928), in *Voices of a Black Nation,* 353–56, 357–59.

41. W. E. B. Du Bois, "The Field and Function of the Negro College," in *The Education of Black People: Ten Critiques by W. E. B. Du Bois,* ed. Herbert Aptheker (New York: Monthly Review Press, 1973), 95–96.

42. W. E. B. Du Bois, *Dark Princess: A Romance* (New York: Harcourt, Brace, 1928); and George S. Schuyler to W. E. B. Du Bois, 11 October 1928, in *Correspondence,* 1:382.

43. W. E. B. Du Bois, "Mixed Schools," *Crisis* 22 (August 1921):150–51; and Du Bois to Frank J. Goodnow, 21 November 1925, in *Correspondence,* 1:326–27.

44. W. E. B. Du Bois, "The Negro and the Northern Public Schools," *Crisis* 35 (March 1923):205–8, and *Crisis* 35 (April 1923):262–65; Du Bois, "The Segregated Negro World," *World Tomorrow* 6 (May 1923):136–38; Du Bois, *Dusk of Dawn,* 307; J. A. Walden to W. E. B. Du Bois, 18 July 1923, and Du Bois to Walden, 25 July 1923, in *Correspondence,* 1:272–73; and Du Bois, "Does the Negro Need Separate Schools?" *Journal of Negro Education* 4 (July 1935):328–35.

45. W. E. B. Du Bois, "Galileo Galilei," in *The Education of Black People,* 18, 30; Du Bois to Paul H. Hanus, 19 June 1916, in *Correspondence,* 1:126; Du Bois, "The Hampton Strike," *Nation,* 2 November 1927, 471–72; and Du Bois, "The Hampton Strike," *Crisis* 34 (December 1927):347–48.

46. W. E. B. Du Bois, "Diuturni Silenti," in *The Education of Black People,* 41–60.

47. Ibid., 59–60; Du Bois, "Fisk," *Crisis* 29 (April 1925):247–51.

48. W. E. B. Du Bois, *The Gift of Black Folk: Negroes in the Making of America* (Boston: Stratford, 1924); Du Bois, *Africa, its Geography, People and Products,* and Du Bois, *Africa—Its Place in Modern History* (Girard,

Kans.: Haldeman-Julius, 1930): and Du Bois, "The Field and Function of the Negro College," in *The Education of Black People,* 83–102.

49. Du Bois, *Autobiography,* 29; Du Bois, "Judging Russia," *Crisis* 33 (February 1927):189–90; Du Bois, "As The Crow Flies," *Crisis* 35 (January 1928):3; Du Bois, "As The Crow Flies," *Crisis* 35 (May 1928):149; Du Bois, "As The Crow Flies," *Crisis* 36 (February 1929):41; Du Bois, "As The Crow Flies," *Crisis* 36 (August 1929):257; and Du Bois, "As The Crow Flies," *Crisis* 37 (June 1930):185.

50. W. E. B. Du Bois, "Prejudice," *Crisis* 34 (November 1927):311; Du Bois, "Marxism and the Negro Problem," *Crisis* 40 (May 1933):103–4, 118.

51. Charles Edward Russell, *Unchained Russia* (New York: D. Appleton, 1918); Diggins, *American Left,* 90; W. E. B. Du Bois, "The American Federation of Labor and the Negro," *Crisis* 36 (July 1929):241; Foner, *Organized Labor and the Black Worker,* 175; Du Bois, "The Denial of Economic Justice to Negroes," in *W. E. B. Du Bois Speaks,* 43–46; and Du Bois, "As The Crow Flies," *Crisis* 40 (February 1933):29.

52. Langston Hughes, *The Big Sea* (New York: Hill & Wang, 1967), 247.

53. Mary White Ovington to W. E. B. Du Bois, 20 December 1930; and Du Bois to Ovington, 24 December 1930, in *Correspondence,* 1:430–31.

54. See Edward E. Waldron, *Walter White and the Harlem Renaissance* (Port Washington, N.Y.: Kennikat Press, 1978); Walter White, *Rope and Faggot* (New York: Arno Press, 1969); and Walter White, *A Man Called White* (New York: Viking Press, 1948).

55. Du Bois, *Autobiography,* 293.

56. W. E. B. Du Bois, "Our Program," *Crisis* 37 (May 1930):174; Du Bois to John W. Davis, 21 September 1931, in *Correspondence,* 1:441–42; and Remarks (from speech by Du Bois, 18 May 1932), *Crisis* 39 (July 1932):218.

57. Du Bois, *Dusk of Dawn,* 291, 312; and Abram L. Harris to W. E. B. Du Bois, 6 January 1934, in *Correspondence,* 1:471–73.

58. W. E. B. Du Bois, "Segregation," *Crisis* 41 (January 1934):20; Walter White, "Segregation—A Symposium," *Crisis* 41 (March 1934):80–81; Du Bois, "Separation and Self-Respect" and "History of Segregation Philosophy," *Crisis* 41 (March 1934):85–86; and Du Bois, "Segregation in the North," "'No Segregation,'" and "Objects of Segregation," *Crisis* 41 (April 1934):115–16.

59. Rudwick, *W. E. B. Du Bois,* 279–80; W. E. B. Du Bois, "Ethics in Education" and "The Board of Directors on Segregation," *Crisis* 41 (May

1934):148–49; Du Bois to the Board of Directors of the NAACP, 21 May 1934, in *Correspondence,* 1:478–79.

60. W. E. B. Du Bois to the Board of Directors of the NAACP, 26 June 1934, in *Correspondence,* 1:479–81, Du Bois, "'Don't You Remember Me?'," *Crisis* 36 (March 1929):94; Dorothy Cowser Yancy, "William Edward Burghardt Du Bois' Atlanta Years: The Human Side—A Study Based upon Oral Sources," *Journal of Negro History* 63 (January 1978):62; Harrison S. Jackson to Du Bois, 18 August 1934, and Du Bois to Jackson, 22 August 1934, in *Correspondence,* 2:5–6; and Foner, *Organized Labor and the Black Worker,* 213–14.

61. W. E. B. Du Bois, "Communist Strategy," *Crisis* 38 (September 1931):313–14; Du Bois, "Praise—Negro Lodges," Pittsburgh *Courier,* 20 June 1936, 1–2; Du Bois, "Cooperation and Communism—The Education of the Proletariat—Cooperatives in Various Lands," Pittsburgh *Courier,* 14 August 1937, 11; Du Bois, *Dusk of Dawn,* 205, 301; and Du Bois, "The Negro Bourgeoisie,"*Crisis* 38 (September 1931):314.

62. Du Bois, *Dusk of Dawn,* 311–12, 314–15.

7. THE GREAT DEPRESSION AND WORLD WAR

1. George W. Crawford to W. E. B. Du Bois, 1 October 1934; and Du Bois to Trevor Arnett, 13 June 1944, in *Correspondence,* 2:11, 405–7.

2. Yancy, "Du Bois' Atlanta Years," 60–63.

3. As early as 1935, Du Bois began to plan a "three-volume novel," which became his *Black Flame* trilogy in 1957–61. He continued to revise his massive manuscript on the "history of the Negro in the World War" but was unable to obtain funding for its completion and publication. In 1937, he proposed to write a two-hundred-page volume, "A Search for Democracy," that would have contrasted and compared "Democracy, Fascism, and Communism." In 1939–40 Du Bois wrote a collection of short stories, "The Sorcery of Color," which was described by William Sloane of Henry Holt and Company as representing work "as fine as anything you have ever done." Du Bois also proposed editing a collection of essays similar to Locke's *New Negro* that was to have included contributions by Abram Harris, Ira Reid, E. Franklin Frazier, Countee Cullen, Langston Hughes, and Sterling Brown. See W. E. B. Du Bois to John Farrar, 9 February 1935; Du Bois to Edwin R. Embree, 8 November 1935; Du Bois to James T. Shotwell, 16 January 1935; Du Bois to Alfred Harcourt, 11 February 1937; and Du Bois to William Sloane, 9 December 1940, in *Correspondence,* 2:50–51, 73–76, 126–28, 137–38, 259–60.

4. Alfred Harcourt to W. E. B. Du Bois, 8 November 1934; Du Bois to Harcourt, 12 November 1934; Du Bois to Harcourt, 17 November 1934;

and Du Bois to Jackson Davis, 7 December 1939, in *Correspondence,* 2:16–18, 201–2.

5. Sterling A. Brown to W. E. B. Du Bois, 29 January 1935, in *Correspondence,* 2:22–23.

6. W. E. B. Du Bois, *Black Reconstruction in America: An Essay toward a History of the Part Which Black Folk Played in the Attempt to Reconstruct Democracy in America, 1860–1880* (New York: Atheneum, 1971), 13, 281–83, 605, 612, 694–95, 702, 706; and Herbert Aptheker, "Du Bois as Historian," *Negro History Bulletin* 32 (April 1969):6–16.

7. Emmett J. Scott to W. E. B. Du Bois, 27 June 1935; and Walter White to Du Bois, 13 September 1935, in *Correspondence,* 2:24–25; Guzman, "W. E. B. Du Bois—The Historian," 381–82; and Aptheker, "Du Bois as Historian," 6–16.

8. W. E. B. Du Bois, "A Negro Nation within the Nation," *Current History* 42 (June 1935):265–70; and Du Bois, "The Present Economic Problem of the American Negro" (1935), in *A W. E. B. Du Bois Reader,* ed. Andrew G. Paschal (New York: Macmillan, 1971), 163–79.

9. W. E. B. Du Bois, "The Siege—The Foundations—The First Assault—The Second Assault—The Third Assault," *Pittsburgh Courier,* 17 April 1937, 11, 15; Du Bois, "Who Are Our Allies?—The Day of Consultation—Earning a Living—The Minority Group—Mistakes," *Pittsburgh Courier,* 24 April 1937, 11; Du Bois, "The Talented Tenth—Segregation—Paradox—Self-Grouping—The Philosophy of Segregation," *Pittsburgh Courier,* 1 May 1937, 11; and Du Bois, "Cooperation Without—Cooperation Within—Economic Cooperation," *Pittsburgh Courier,* 12 June 1937, 11.

10. George Streator to W. E. B. Du Bois, 9 April 1935; Du Bois to Streator, 24 April 1935; and Streator to Du Bois, 29 April 1935, in *Correspondence,* 2:86–87, 90–96.

11. W. E. B. Du Bois, "The Negro and Social Reconstruction" (1936), in *Against Racism,* 103–58.

12. Alain Locke to W. E. B. Du Bois, 4 June 1935; Du Bois to Locke, 27 February 1936; Locke to Du Bois, 6 March 1936; Du Bois to Locke, 22 May 1936; Locke to Du Bois, 30 May 1936; and Locke to Du Bois, 30 November 1936, in *Correspondence,* 2:81–85.

13. W. E. B. Du Bois to Edwin R. Embree, 24 April 1935; Embree to Du Bois, 30 April 1935; Du Bois to George Foster Peabody, 4 October 1935; Roscoe Pound to Du Bois, 16 October 1935; Ira De A. Reid to Du Bois, 12 September 1935; and Du Bois to Anson Phelps-Stokes, 19 May 1937, in *Correspondence,* 2:64–67, 69, 109–10, 145–46.

14. W. E. B. Du Bois, "On the Scientific Objectivity of the Proposed *Encyclopedia of the Negro* and on Safeguards against the Intrusion of Prop-

aganda" (1939?), in *Against Racism,* 164–68; Du Bois to Carter G. Woodson, 29 January 1932; and Woodson to Du Bois, 11 February 1932, in *Correspondence,* 1:448–49; E. Franklin Frazier to Du Bois, 7 November 1936; Du Bois to Robert E. Park, 3 March 1937; and Du Bois to Anson Phelps-Stokes, 17 December 1942, in *Correspondence,* 2:71–72, 141, 340; Charles H. Wesley to Du Bois, 17 October 1956; and Du Bois to Wesley, 22 October 1956, in *Correspondence,* 3:403–5.

15. W. E. B. Du Bois to Edwin R. Embree, 10 April 1936; Jackson Davis to Du Bois, 2 December 1939; Du Bois to Davis, 7 December 1939; Du Bois to Rufus E. Clement, 1 March 1940; and F. P. Keppel to Du Bois, 17 April 1940, in *Correspondence,* 2:133, 200–1, 224–26, 232; Du Bois, "Apology," *Phylon* 1 (1940):3–5; and "On the Roots of *Phylon*" (1937) in *Against Racism,* 168–73.

16. J. McFarline Ervin to W. E. B. Du Bois, 18 January 1935; Du Bois to Ervin, 31 January 1935; Madeline Morgan to Du Bois, 10 September 1941; and Du Bois to Morgan, 23 September 1941, in *Correspondence,* 2:47–48, 298; and *Committee on Education, House of Representatives, 75th Congress, Hearings on Federal Aid for the Support of Public Schools* (Washington, D.C.: Government Printing Office, 1937), 284–95.

17. W. E. B. Du Bois, "A Negro Book-of-the-Year Club—Our Political History—The Depression," *Pittsburgh Courier,* 15 August 1936, 1–2; John W. Studebaker to Du Bois, 1 November 1938; Du Bois to Studebaker, 4 November 1938; Studebaker to Du Bois, 7 November 1938; and Du Bois to Cromwell, 6 May 1941, in *Correspondence,* 2:174–76, 280–81.

18. W. E. B. Du Bois, "The Revelation of Saint Orgne the Damned," in *The Education of Black People,* 103–26.

19. W. E. B. Du Bois, "The Position of the Negro in the American Social Order: Where Do We Go From Here?" *Journal of Negro Education* 8 (July 1939):551–57; Du Bois, "The Future of the Negro State University," in *The Education of Black People,* 129–38; Du Bois to Charles Dollard, 14 January 1942, in *Correspondence,* 2:349–52.

20. W. E. B. Du Bois, *Black Folk Then and Now: An Essay in the History and Sociology of the Negro Race* (New York: Henry Holt, 1939); Du Bois to Charles Edward Russell, 25 November 1938, in *Correspondence,* 2:173; and Du Bois, *Dusk of Dawn,* 192, 198, 217, 305.

21. Shirley Graham to W. E. B. Du Bois, 7 November 1934; Du Bois to Graham, 17 November 1934; A. Philip Randolph to Du Bois, 24 May 1935; Gunnar Myrdal to Du Bois, 26 November 1938; E. Franklin Frazier to Du Bois, 2 August 1939; John Hope Franklin to Du Bois, 26 March 1940; and Cy Wilson Record to Du Bois, 31 December 1942, in *Correspondence,* 2:33–35, 99–100, 177, 193–94, 229–30, 352–53.

22. W. E. B. Du Bois, "Haiti," *Crisis* 20 (October 1920):251–62; Du

Bois, "As The Crow Flies," *Crisis* 38 (September 1931):296; Du Bois, "As The Crow Flies," *Crisis* 39 (February 1932):44; and "As The Crow Flies," *Crisis* 39 (August 1932):246.

23. W. E. B. Du Bois, "Prolegomena—The Search For Employment—Inside Industry in the South—The Way Out—The Obstacles," *Pittsburgh Courier*, 21 March 1936, sec. 2, 2; Du Bois, "Income," *Pittsburgh Courier* (19 September 1936), sec. 2, 1; Du Bois, "The Campaign," New York *Amsterdam News*, 10 August 1940, 8; Du Bois, "Social Security," *Amsterdam News*, 24 August 1940, 1; Du Bois, "The Democrats," *Amsterdam News*, 23 November 1940 1; 8; Du Bois to Jesse H. Sterling, 10 March 1937, in *Correspondence*, 2:142; and "For the Reelection of Franklin Delano Roosevelt" (14 October 1944), in *Against Racism*, 253–54.

24. W. E. B. Du Bois to Wilber K. Thomas, 3 May 1935; Thomas to Du Bois, 9 May 1935; Thomas to Du Bois, 12 June 1935; and Du Bois to Robert L. Vann, 4 January 1936, in *Correspondence*, 2:57–59, 121–22; Du Bois, *Dusk of Dawn*, 169–70; Du Bois, "Germany—Germany and Hitler—The Background—Depression and Revolution," *Pittsburgh Courier*, 5 December 1936, sec. 2, 1–2; Du Bois, "The Hitler State—National Socialism" *Pittsburgh Courier*, 12 December 1936, sec. 2, 1, 3; Du Bois, "Race Prejudice in Germany—Anti-Semitism—The Present Plights of the German Jew," *Pittsburgh Courier*, 19 December 1936, sec. 2, 1, 3; Du Bois, "How Long Will Hitler Last?—Hitler's Danger—Profit," *Pittsburgh Courier*, 26 December 1936, sec. 2, 1, 3; and Du Bois, "Neuropa. Hitler's New World Order," *Journal of Negro Education* 10 (July 1941): 380–86.

25. Du Bois, *Autobiography*, 31–32; Du Bois, "Moscow—Comfort—Present Methods," *Pittsburgh Courier*, 16 January 1937, sec. 2, 1, 3; Du Bois, "Capital—Economic Planning—Results," *Pittsburgh Courier*, 30 January 1937, sec. 2, 1, 3.

26. Warren Lerner, *Karl Radek: The Last Internationalist* (Stanford: Stanford University Press, 1970), 134, 166–171; W. E. B. Du Bois, "As The Crow Flies," *Crisis* 36 (March 1929):77; and Du Bois, "Russia," New York *Amsterdam News*, 24 February 1940, 1.

27. Du Bois, *Autobiography*, 44–45; Du Bois, "As The Crow Flies," *Crisis* 25 (February 1928):39; Du Bois, "As The Crow Flies," *Crisis* 36 (July 1929):223; Du Bois, "China and Japan—The Failure of China—China and Russia—The World Attack on Japan," *Pittsburgh Courier*, 25 September 1937, 11.

28. W. E. B. Du Bois, "The World and Us," *Crisis* 23 (April 1922):247; Du Bois, "As The Crow Flies," *Crisis* 34 (June 1927):111; Du Bois, "As The Crow Flies," *Crisis* 39 (April 1932):116; Du Bois, "Japan," *Pittsburgh Courier*, 22 February 1936, sec. 2, 2; Du Bois, "Yosuke Mat-

suoka—Japanese Colonialism—Conference," *Pittsburgh Courier*, 13 February 1937, 1, 18; Du Bois, "Shrines of Japan—Shinto—Hospitality—Two Weeks—Nara and Kyoto—Tokyo," *Pittsburgh Courier*, 13 March 1937, 11–15; Du Bois, "What Japan Has Done—Japan's Present Position—Japan's Danger," *Pittsburgh Courier*, 27 March 1937, 10; Yusaku Ozawa, *Theory of Education of the Nations* (Tokyo: Meiji-Tosho, 1967); and Masako Sasamoto Nakamura, "Educational Thought of W. E. B. Du Bois: Power and Self-Realization in the Liberation of Black People," *Historical Research of Education in Japan* 24 (1980):80–97.

29. W. E. B. Du Bois to Harry F. Ward, 7 October 1937; Waldo McNutt to Du Bois, 13 February 1939; Du Bois to McNutt, 25 February 1939; Du Bois to Andrew J. Allison, 3 February 1941, in *Correspondence*, 2:147, 184–85, 272–73; Du Bois, "India," New York *Amsterdam News*, 2 December 1939, 1; Du Bois, "Negro Youth," *Amsterdam News*, 31 May 1941, 1; and Foner, *Organized Labor and the Black Worker*, 278.

30. W. E. B. Du Bois to George Streator, 24 April 1935; Du Bois to George W. Cook, 7 November 1938, in *Correspondence*, 2:90–93, 170; Du Bois, "In Darkest Mississippi," New York *Amsterdam News*, 2 March 1940, 1; Du Bois, "As The Crow Flies," *Amsterdam News*, 23 March 1940, 1, 14; and Du Bois, "Freedom of Speech," *Amsterdam News*, 9 November 1940, 1.

31. Nell Irvin Painter, *The Narrative of Hosea Hudson: His Life as a Negro Communist in the South* (Cambridge: Harvard University Press, 1979), 271.

32. Cyril V. Briggs and Harry Haywood, *Is Japan the Champion of the Colored Races?* (New York: Workers' Library Publishers, 1938); Esedebe, *Pan-Africanism*, 123–24; "Cyril V. Briggs," in *Marcus Garvey Papers*, 1:526.

33. W. E. B. Du Bois, "European Alliances," *Amsterdam News*, 18 November 1939, 1; Du Bois, "As The Crow Flies," *Amsterdam News*, 12 April 1941, 1, 16; Du Bois, "Russia and German," *Amsterdam News*, 26 July 1941, 14; Du Bois, "The Negro and the War," *Amsterdam News*, 9 May 1942, 6; Du Bois, "Riots," *Amsterdam News*, 3 July 1943, 10; Du Bois, "My Evolving Program for Negro Freedom," in *What the Negro Wants*, ed. Rayford W. Logan (Chapel Hill: University of North Carolina Press, 1944), 31–70; James W. Ford to Du Bois, 8 January 1945, in *Correspondence*, 3:28.

34. Du Bois, *Dusk of Dawn*, 169; Du Bois, "Fight Against Poverty—Unequal Wealth," New York *Amsterdam News*, 19 September 1942, 6; Du Bois, "Washington Not Democracy," *Amsterdam News*, 3 October 1942, 6; Du Bois, "Voting—What About Education," *Amsterdam News*, 8 May 1943, 6; Du Bois, "Coming Events—Sterile Results—Emancipation in Sight,"

Amsterdam News, 11 September 1943, 10–A; and Du Bois, "The Release of Earl Browder," in *Against Racism,* 198—202.

35. Du Bois, "Jacob and Esau," 1–6; Du Bois, "Should Settle Differences—Who Will Pay Cost?" New York *Amsterdam News,* 20 February 1943, 6; Du Bois, "As The Crow Flies," *Amsterdam News,* 1 July 1944, 1, 5.

36. W. E. B. Du Bois, Book Review, *Annals of the American Academy of Political and Social Science,* 223 (September 1942):199–200; Du Bois, "As The Crow Flies," New York *Amsterdam News,* 8 January 1944, 1–2; and Du Bois, "Zionism," *Amsterdam News,* 11 May 1940, 1, 16.

37. W. E. B. Du Bois, "Race as Class—Pan-Africa—Dictatorship of the Proletariat," *Pittsburgh Courier,* 5 June 1937, 23; Du Bois, "Again Pan-Africa," New York *Amsterdam News,* 22 June 1940, 1, 10; Du Bois, "Recalls Former Experience," *Amsterdam News,* 26 December 1942, 8; Du Bois, "The Future of Europe in Africa," and "The Colonial Groups in the Postwar World," in *Against Racism,* 184–98, 229–36; Du Bois, "The Realities in Africa: European Profit or Negro Development?" *Foreign Affairs,* 21 (July 1943):721–32; and Du Bois, *Color and Democracy: Colonies and Peace* (New York: Harcourt, Brace, 1945).

38. W. E. B. Du Bois, "Democracy and Peace," in *Against Racism,* 236–44; and Du Bois, "Prospect of a World Without Race Conflict," *American Journal of Sociology,* 49 (March 1944):450–56.

39. W. E. B. Du Bois to Florence M. Reed, 6 May 1940; Du Bois to W. R. Banks, 18 April 1941; Ruth Anna Fisher to Du Bois, 17 March 1943; Du Bois to Fisher, 29 March 1943; and B. M. Phillips to Du Bois, 16 May 1944, in *Correspondence,* 2:234–36, 282–83, 358–60, 402–3.

40. Du Bois, *Autobiography,* 323; and Rufus E. Clement to W. E. B. Du Bois, 23 November 1943; Du Bois to W. R. Banks, 11 January 1944; and Du Bois to Louis T. Wright, 6 June 1944, in *Correspondence,* 2:390–91, 393–94, 396, 404–5.

41. Walter White to W. E. B. Du Bois, 17 May 1944; Arthur B. Spingarn to Du Bois,, 23 May 1944; Du Bois to Louis T. Wright and Spingarn, 1 June 1944; Du Bois to White, 23 June 1944; Du Bois to White, 5 July 1944; and White to Du Bois, 21 July 1944, in *Correspondence,* 2:409–15.

42. W. E. B. Du Bois to W. R. Banks, 11 January 1939; Walter White to Du Bois, 28 April 1942; White to Atlanta University Board of Trustees, 28 April 1944; White to Du Bois, 22 September 1944, in *Correspondence,* 2:181–82, 320–21, 395, 418; and Du Bois, *Autobiography,* 327.

43. W. E. B. Du Bois, "Colonial Question Ignored at Dumbarton Oaks Peace Session," *Pittsburgh Courier,* 28 October 1944, 4; Du Bois, "Recognition at Frisco—Colonies Seen Key to Parley—Economic Background,"

Chicago Defender, 28 April 1945, 13; Du Bois, "The Future of Colonies—What's the Lineup—Anti-Colonial Forces Grow," *Chicago Defender,* 19 May 1945, 13; and Du Bois, "UNCIO Dodges Colonial Issue—U.S. Becomes Colonial Power—World War III?" *Chicago Defender,* 23 June 1945, 13.

44. W. E. B. Du Bois, "The Pan-African Movement" (1945), in *Writings by W. E. B. Du Bois in Non-Periodical Literature,* 242–52; Padmore, *Pan-Africanism or Communism,* 132–33; Du Bois to Padmore, 22 March 1945; Du Bois to Padmore, 11 April 1945; and Padmore to Du Bois, 12 April 1945, in *Correspondence,* 3:56–57, 60–61, 62–65.

45. Du Bois, "The Pan-African Movement," 252; and Padmore, *Pan-Africanism or Communism,* 139–148.

8. THE POLITICS OF PEACE

1. See George Padmore, "Race Relations: Soviet and British," *Crisis* 50 (November 1943):345–48; Padmore, "Anglo-American Plan for Control of Colonies," *Crisis* 51 (November 1944):355–57; Padmore, "Review of the Paris Peace Conference," *Crisis* 53 (November 1946):331–33, 347–48; Richard Dalfiume, "The 'Forgotten Years' of the Negro Revolution," in *The Negro in Depression and War: Prelude to Revolution,* ed. Bernard Sternsher (Chicago: Quadrangle Books, 1969), 298–316; and Manning Marable, *Race, Reform and Rebellion: The Second Reconstruction in Black America, 1945–1982* (Jackson: University Press of Mississippi, 1984), 12–17.

2. W. E. B. Du Bois to Roy Wilkins, 31 January 1945; Du Bois to Walter White, 10 April 1945; Du Bois to NAACP Board of Directors, 5 July 1945; White to Du Bois, 26 December 1945; and Du Bois to Villard, 13 February 1946, *Correspondence,* 3:95, 97–98, 100–1, 106; and Du Bois, *Autobiography,* 328.

3. Marian S. Williams to W. E. B. Du Bois, 6 August 1945; Du Bois to Williams, 31 August 1945; Walter White to Du Bois, 21 December 1945; Paul Robeson to Du Bois, 30 August 1946; Walter White to Du Bois, 19 September 1946; Du Bois to White, 23 September 1946; White to Du Bois, 2 October 1946; Du Bois to Padmore, 12 July 1946; and Du Bois to Padmore, 30 December 1946, in *Correspondence,* 3:48–50, 99–100, 112–15, 141–44, 159.

4. Walter White to W. E. B. Du Bois, 23 October 1946; White to Du Bois, 25 October 1946; Du Bois to White, 10 October 1946, in *Correspondence,* 3:105–6, 120–24; and Du Bois, *Autobiography,* 331–32.

5. W. E. B. Du Bois to Walter White, 1 August 1946; White to Du Bois, 1 August 1946; Du Bois to White, 21 November 1946; Du Bois to Vijaya Lakshmi Pandit, 18 September 1947; Pandit to Du Bois, 25 Septem-

ber 1947; Du Bois to White, 1 July 1948, in *Correspondence*, 3:163–66, 180, 188–89; and Du Bois, ed., *An Appeal to the World: A Statement on the Denial of Human Rights to Minorities in the Case of Citizens of Negro Descent in the United States of America and an Appeal to the United Nations for Redress* (New York: NAACP, 1947).

6. Du Bois, *Autobiography*, 330; Du Bois, "Bound by the Color Line," *New Masses* 58 (12 February 1946):8; Du Bois, "No Second Class Citizenship," *Progressive Education* 25 (January 1948):10–14, 21; Du Bois, "Behold the Land," in *W. E. B. Du Bois Speaks*, 195–201; Du Bois, "In 1909—The Firing Line," *Chicago Defender*, 16 November 1946, 15; Du Bois, "Enormous Opportunities—Consumer Co-ops—Belong to Worker," *Chicago Defender*, 23 November 1946, 15; Du Bois, "At San Francisco—A Statement on Race and Colonies—The NAACP," *Chicago Defender*, 19 July 1947, 15; and Du Bois, "We Must Know The Truth," in *W. E. B. Du Bois Speaks*, 222–27.

7. W. E. B. Du Bois, "Atom Bomb and the Colored World," *Chicago Defender*, 12 January 1946, 13; Du Bois, "Reasoning Deficiency—Soviet Proposal Realistic," *Chicago Defender*, 6 July 1946, 15; Du Bois, "The Atom Bomb–Atomic Energy," *Chicago Defender*, 5 July 1947, 15.

8. W. E. B. Du Bois, "Growth of Cooperatives—Opposed to Private Enterprise," *Chicago Defender*, 31 March 1945, 13; Du Bois, "Labor Victory Democracy's Gain—England Joins Russia—Turned Toward Socialism," *Chicago Defender*, 18 August 1945, 13; and Du Bois, "Duty to Buy?—Begins With Consumer," *Chicago Defender*, 10 August 1946.

9. W. E. B. Du Bois, "Common Objectives," *Soviet Russia Today* 15 (August 1946):13, 32–33; Du Bois, "Democracy's Opportunity," *Christian Register* 125 (August 1946):350–51; and Du Bois, "The Most Hopeful State in the World Today," *Soviet Russia Today* 16 (November 1947):24.

10. Alfred O. Hero, "American Negroes and U. S. Foreign Policy: 1937–1967," *Journal of Conflict Resolution* 8 (June 1969):220–51; Foner, *Organized Labor and the Black Worker*, 280.

11. W. E. B. Du Bois, "Nobel Committee Banquet," *Chicago Defender*, 4 January 1947, 15; Du Bois to Trygve Lie, 4 September 1946; Du Bois to George Padmore, 12 July 1946; and Du Bois to Padmore, 30 December 1946, in *Correspondence*, 3:141–44, 153–56, 159.

12. W. E. B. Du Bois, *The World and Africa: An Inquiry into the Part Which Africa Has Played in World History*, enl. ed. (New York: International Publishers, 1965), 256–57; Paul Robeson, "Tribute," in *Black Titan: W. E. B. Du Bois*, ed. John Henrik Clarke, Esther Jackson, Ernest Kaiser, and J. H. O'Dell (Boston: Beacon Press, 1970), 34–38.

13. W. E. B. Du Bois, "Witch Hunting and Red-Baiting," *Chicago De-*

fender, 8 February 1947, 15; Harlow Shapley to Du Bois, 17 February 1948; Van Wyck Brooks to Du Bois, 15 February 1948, in *Correspondence*, 3:195–97.

14. W. E. B. Du Bois, "A Technique of Duplicity," *Chicago Defender*, 5 October 1946, 15; Du Bois, "'Stupid and Dangerous,'" *Chicago Defender*, 19 April 1947, 15; Du Bois, "Marshall Plan," *Chicago Defender*, 9 August 1947, 15; Du Bois, "Can the Negro Expect Freedom by 1965?," *Negro Digest* 5 (April 1947):4–9; and Du Bois, "The Talented Tenth Memorial Address," *Boulé Journal* 15 (October 1948):3–13.

15. See Gerald Horne, *Black and Red: W. E. B. Du Bois and the Afro-American Response to the Cold War, 1944–1963* (Albany: State University of New York Press, 1986), 57–82.

16. W. E. B. Du Bois, "Write to Wallace," *Chicago Defender*, 3 January 1948, 14; Du Bois, "Truman on Discrimination," *Chicago Defender*, 7 February 1948), 15; Du Bois, "Negroes Should Vote for Wallace," *Chicago Defender*, 21 February 1948, 15; Du Bois, "Wallace," *Chicago Defender*, 20 March 1948, 15; and Horne, *Black and Red*, 97–111.

17. Du Bois, *Autobiography*, 334; Walter White to the staff, 25 February 1948; White to Du Bois, 29 March 1948; Du Bois to Arthur Spingarn, 2 April 1948, in *Correspondence*, 3:238–41; and Marable, *Race, Reform and Rebellion*, 24–25.

18. W. E. B. Du Bois to the Secretary and Board of Directors of the NAACP, 7 September 1948; Motion Passed by NAACP Board of Directors, 13 September 1948, in *Correspondence*, 3:243–46.

19. Shirley Graham, "Why Was Du Bois Fired?" *Masses and Mainstream*, 8 (November 1948):15–26; Du Bois, *Autobiography*, 335; Du Bois to Anita McCormick Blaine, December 1948; Du Bois to Blaine, 15 December 1948; Du Bois to Blaine, 7 January 1949; Du Bois to Henry Wallace, 18 January 1949; and Blaine to Du Bois, 18 May 1949, in *Correspondence*, 3:230–36.

20. Du Bois, *Autobiography*, 344–45; W. E. B. Du Bois, *In Battle For Peace: The Story of My 83rd Birthday (With Comment by Shirley Graham)* (New York: Masses & Mainstream, 1952), 26–28, and Du Bois, "The Nature of Intellectual Freedom," in *Writings by W. E. B. Du Bois In Non-Periodical Literature*, 267–68.

21. W. E. B. Du Bois, "None Who Saw Paris Will Ever Forget," *National Guardian* 1 (16 May 1949):12; Du Bois, "Paul Robeson. Right or Wrong?—Right, says W. E. B. Du Bois," *Negro Digest* 7 (March 1950):8, 10–14; Du Bois, *In Battle For Peace*, 30–31; Martin D. Jenkins to Du Bois, 23 March 1949, in *Correspondence*, 3:257, 259.

22. *Committee on Foreign Affairs,, House of Representatives*, Hearings on Mutual Defense Assistance Act of 1949, 81st Congress, 1st session

(Washington, D.C.: Government Printing Office, 1949), 261–70; W. E. B. Du Bois, "An Appreciation," in *Writings by W. E. B. Du Bois in Non-Periodical Literature,* 275–79; Du Bois, *In Battle For Peace,* 182–86.

23. David Caute, *The Great Fear: The Anti-Communist Purge under Truman and Eisenhower* (New York: Simon & Schuster, 1978), 25; Gil Green, *Cold War Fugitive: A Personal Story of the McCarthy Years* (New York: International Publishers, 1984), 24–29, 53; and Foner, *Organized Labor and the Black Worker,* 283.

24. W. E. B. Du Bois, "The Freedom to Learn," *Midwest Journal* 2 (Winter 1949):9–11; Herbert Biberman to Du Bois, 29 December 1947; Du Bois to Biberman, 12 January 1948; Open Letter by Du Bois for the Reelection of Benjamin J. Davis, 7 October 1949; Du Bois to Davis, 14 November 1949; Davis to Du Bois, 22 November 1949; and Du Bois to Padmore, 17 March 1950, in *Correspondence,* 3:175, 270–71, 280.

25. Du Bois, *In Battle For Peace,* 37–42, 134–35.

26. W. E. B. Du Bois, "As The Crow Flies," *Chicago Globe,* 15 July 1950, and George Padmore to Du Bois, 21 August 1950, in *Correspondence,* 3:289–90, and Du Bois, *In Battle For Peace,* 62.

27. Du Bois, *In Battle For Peace,* 43–44, 46–49; Robeson, "Tribute," 36–37; "There Can Be No Progress Without Peace," *National Guardian* 2 (4 October 1950):8; and "U.S. Needs No More Cowards," *National Guardian* 3 (25 October 1950):1.

28. The latest attempt to diminish Du Bois's 1950 campaign was in Hanes Walton, Jr., *Invisible Politics: Black Political Behavior* (Albany: State University of New York Press, 1985), 148–50. Walton argues, "Du Bois ran on the American Labor Party ticket, seeking to capture black support. He polled fewer black votes in every district than a white Progressive two years earlier. In all, Du Bois, who placed third in the race, received 11,522 fewer votes than Wallace had in 1948." Walton also attributed Du Bois's defeat to the black community's "limited access to the American Labor Party's organizational structure." This analysis fails to note: (1) the domestic political climate had become far more repressive against the left by 1950, and that even Wallace had repudiated the Progressive party; (2) the media gave Du Bois's campaign little objective coverage; and (3) that Du Bois ran *ahead* of the ALP's gubernatorial candidate, John T. McManus, by nearly two thousand votes in Harlem. See Arthur Schutzer to W. E. B. Du Bois, 28 January 1952, in *Correspondence,* 3:331–32.

29. W. E. B. Du Bois, "The Social Significance of These Three Cases," in *Against Racism,* 276, 279, 283.

30. Du Bois, *In Battle For Peace,* 11, 51–56; William E. Foley to the Peace Information Center, 11 August 1950; Du Bois to Foley, undated; and Foley to Du Bois, 2 February 1951, in *Correspondence,* 3:306–9.

31. Du Bois, *In Battle For Peace*, 58–59, 70–71, and Du Bois, Statement, 16 February 1951, in *Correspondence*, 3:310–11.

32. Du Bois, *In Battle For Peace*, 18–19, 62–64, 73; Charlotte Hawkins Brown to Alice Crawford, 21 February 1951; and Abba Hillel Silver to E. Franklin Frazier, 15 February 1951, in *Correspondence*, 3:325.

33. Du Bois, *In Battle For Peace*, 64–65, 186–91; Du Bois to E. Franklin Frazier, 11 April 1951, in *Correspondence*, 3:327.

34. Du Bois, *In Battle For Peace*, 92–93, 122–23.

35. Arthur Garfield Hays to W. E. B. Du Bois, 26 April 1951; Du Bois to Arthur Elmes, 27 November 1951; and John S. Brown to Du Bois, 29 December 1951, in *Correspondence*, 3:314–15, 321–22; and Du Bois, *In Battle For Peace*, 72–74, 153.

36. W. E. B. Du Bois to Hubert T. Delaney, 21 December 1951, in *Correspondence*, 3:322–23, and Du Bois, *In Battle For Peace*, 90–91.

37. Du Bois, *In Battle For Peace*, 87–108, 191.

38. Ibid., 78–83, 107; and George Padmore to W. E. B. Du Bois, 21 March 1951, in *Correspondence*, 3:311–12.

39. W. E. B. Du Bois to Albert Einstein, 29 November 1951, in *Correspondence*, 3:321, and Du Bois, *In Battle For Peace*, 125.

40. Du Bois, *In Battle For Peace*, 116, 122, 136, 140–47.

41. Ibid., 133, 148.

42. Marable, *Race, Reform and Rebellion*, 30. Du Bois appreciated Johnson's statement of support during his ordeal but was under no illusions about Johnson's conservative orientation. As Du Bois informed Padmore: "(Johnson) is, if not reactionary, certainly very cautious." See W. E. B. Du Bois to George Padmore, 17 March 1950, in *Correspondence*, 3:280–81.

43. Marable, *Race, Reform and Rebellion*, 27–28, 33.

44. W. E. B. Du Bois, "Galileo Galilei" (1908), in *The Education of Black People*, 17–30.

45. Du Bois, "Behold the Land," 201.

46. R. B. Shipley to W. E. B. Du Bois, 12 February 1952; Du Bois to Mary Jennison, 30 April 1952; Ivy Stoetzer to Du Bois, 12 May 1952, in *Correspondence*, 3:332, 334–35.

47. W. E. B. Du Bois to George Padmore, 18 September 1950, in *Correspondence*, 3:290; Du Bois, *Autobiography*, 394–95.

9. STERN PROPHET, FLAMING ANGEL

1. Du Bois, *In Battle For Peace*, 160.

2. Du Bois, Appeal Letter for the Council on African Affairs, 18 June

1953, in *Correspondence,* 3:348–49; Caute, *The Great Fear,* 179, 180, 207, 209, 247; and Davis, *Women, Race and Class,* 167–71.

3. Caute, *The Great Fear,* 71–72, 85, 122, 161–62, 413, 423–24.

4. Ibid., 129, 421, 522, 530–31; W. E. B. Du Bois to Edward H. Dodd, Jr., 27 September 1955; and Dodd to Du Bois, 4 October 1955, in *Correspondence,* 3:387–88.

5. Shirley Graham Du Bois, *His Day Is Marching On: A Memoir of W. E. B. Du Bois* (Philadelphia: J. B. Lippincott, 1971), 210; W. E. B. Du Bois, "This Man I Know," *Masses and Mainstream* 7 (February 1954):43; Lee Lorch to Du Bois, 20 September 1954; Du Bois to Lorch, 24 September 1954, in *Correspondence,* 3:363–65.

6. Du Bois, "A Negro Leader's Plea to Save the Rosenbergs," *Worker,* 16 November 1952, 3, 6; W. E. B. Du Bois, "The Rosenbergs," *Masses and Mainstream* 6 (July 1953), 10–12; Caute, *The Great Fear,* 162; Du Bois to Yolande Du Bois Williams, 15 November 1954; Vojtech Strnad to Du Bois, 21 October 1955; Du Bois to Arthur E. Summerfield, 4 November 1955, in *Correspondence,* 3:372–73, 388–89.

7. Du Bois, *In Battle For Peace,* 162, 164, 174–75.

8. Ibid., 161; W. E. B. Du Bois, "Let's Restore Democracy to America," *National Guardian* 8 (2 January 1956):1, 3; Du Bois, *An ABC of Color: Selections Chosen by the Author from over a Half Century of His Writings* (New York: International Publishers, 1971), 202–5; and "Address at American Labor Party Election Rally" (27 October 1952), in *Against Racism,* 283–88.

9. W. E. B. Du Bois, "The Commonsense Party," *National Guardian* 5 (6 April 1953):8; Du Bois, "A Third Party—or Even a Second," *National Guardian* 6 (17 May 1954):1; Du Bois, "The Theory of a Third Party," *National Guardian* 8 (26 March 1956);4; and Du Bois, "The Negro and Socialism" (1958), in *Writings by W. E. B. Du Bois in Non-Periodical Literature,* 289, 292.

10. W. E. B. Du Bois, "America and World Peace," *New World Review* 20 (November 1952):49–52; Du Bois, "Formosa and Peace," *Jewish Life* 9 (March 1955):20; Du Bois, "The World Peace Movement," *New World Review* 23 (May 1955):9–14; Du Bois, "Cannot This Paralyzed Nation Awake?" *National Guardian* 6 (12 April 1954):1; Du Bois to Ruth B. Shipley, 28 March 1953; Shipley to Du Bois, 6 April 1953; and Du Bois, Statement to World Peace Council, 14 October 1953, in *Correspondence,* 3:345–46, 352.

11. W. E. B. Du Bois, "American Negroes and Africa," *National Guardian* 7 (14 February 1955):5; and Du Bois, "Africa and the American Negro Intelligentsia," *Présence Africaine* (December 1955–January 1956), 34–51.

12. W. E. B. Du Bois, "One Hundred Years in the Struggle for Negro Freedom," *Freedom* 3 (January 1953):6–7.

13. Du Bois, *In Battle For Peace,* 173, 178; Du Bois, "The Choice That Confronts America's Negroes," *National Guardian* 4 (13 February 1952), 7.

14. See W. E. B. Du Bois to Herbert Aptheker, 12 August 1947; Du Bois to Aptheker, 18 December 1947; Aptheker to Du Bois, 5 January 1948; and Du Bois to Aptheker, 8 January 1948, in *Correspondence,* 3:175–77; Du Bois, Review of Herbert Aptheker, *To Be Free: Studies in Negro History, Masses and Mainstream* 1 (June 1948):76–79; and Du Bois, "The Rise of American Negroes, *National Guardian* 4 (2 January 1952):8.

15. Lorraine Hansberry to W. E. B. Du Bois, 15 June 1954; Du Bois to Hansberry, 22 June 1954; Hansberry to Du Bois, 25 June 1954; Du Bois to Hansberry, 7 July 1954; Elliott P. Skinner to Du Bois, 1 May 1957; and Sterling Stuckey to Du Bois, 6 August 1957, in *Correspondence,* 3:361–62, 407, 410.

16. David G. Du Bois, "W. E. B. Du Bois: The Last Years," *Race and Class* 24 (Autumn 1982):178–183.

17. W. E. B. Du Bois, Statement in Defense of V. J. Jerome, 9 March 1953; Du Bois to Herbert Aptheker, 21 December 1954; Aptheker to Du Bois, 24 December 1954; Du Bois to George Padmore, 27 January 1955, in *Correspondence,* 3:344–45, 375, 378; James E. Jackson, "Tribute," in *Black Titan,* 18–21; and Horne, *Black and Red,* 297.

18. W. E. B. Du Bois, "Color Lines," *National Guardian* 5 (12 February 1953):7; and Du Bois, "Colonialism and the Russian Revolution," *New World Review* 24 (November 1956):18–22.

19. W. E. B. Du Bois to Anna Melissa Graves, 8 July 1956; and Du Bois to the Foreign Editor of the *Literary Gazette,* 26 September 1957, in *Correspondence,* 3:402–3, 412–15; Du Bois, "The Stalin Era," *Masses and Mainstream* 10 (January 1957):1–5; and Du Bois, "Socialism and Democracy," *American Socialist* 4 (January 1957):6–9.

20. W. E. B. Du Bois to Herbert Aptheker, 27 February 1953, in *Correspondence,* 3:343; Du Bois, "The Negro and the Warsaw Ghetto," *Jewish Life* 6 (May 1952):14–15; and Aptheker, "The Souls of Black Folk: A Comparison of the 1903 and 1952 editions," *Negro History Bulletin* 34 (January 1971):15–17. Aptheker has observed that "at the time the original edition of *Souls* appeared, blatant anti-Semitism in the United States in conduct and language was intense, especially in the South. In this connection it is noteworthy that so far as the present writer knows, no reviewer of the book alluded to this feature of it. Of course, in his own conduct, the Doctor was quite incapable of anything so gross as anti-Semitic

behavior; on the contrary, he often denounced it." (16).

21. Rampersad, *The Art and Imagination of W. E. B. Du Bois,* 270, 275; Moore, *W. E. B. Du Bois,* 148, 151; and W. E. B. Du Bois, *The Black Flame: A Trilogy* (New York: Mainstream Publishers): *The Ordeal of Mansart* (1957): *Mansart Builds a School* (1959); *World of Color* (1961).

22. See W. E. B. Du Bois, "A Portrait of Carter G. Woodson," *Masses and Mainstream* 3 (June 1950):19–25; Du Bois, "The Passing of Alain Locke," *Phylon* 15, no. 3 (1954):251–52; and Du Bois, "Politician in the Finest Sense," *Freedom* 4 (August 1954):3.

23. W. E. B. Du Bois, "We Rejoice and Tell the World . . .," *National Guardian* 6 (31 May 1954):5; Du Bois, "200 Years of Segregated Schools," *Jewish Life* 9 (February 1955):7–9; and Du Bois, "Will the Great Gandhi Live Again?" *National Guardian* 9 (11 February 1957):6–7.

24. Horne, *Black and Red,* 241–48.

25. W. E. B. Du Bois, "The Saga of Nkrumah," *National Guardian* 8 (30 July 1956):8; Du Bois to George Padmore, 27 October 1951; Padmore to Du Bois, 3 December 1954; Du Bois to Padmore, 10 December 1954, in *Correspondence,* 3:329–30, 373–75.

26. Esedebe, *Pan-Africanism,* 163; Padmore, *Pan-Africanism or Communism,* 319; and Dennis Austin, *Politics in Ghana, 1946–1960* (London: Oxford University Press, 1964), 168. In the 1951 general elections, the CPP received ninety five percent of the urban vote and about eighty percent of all rural votes cast in the Gold Coast. By 1956, the CPP's popular vote had declined to fifty seven percent. If the Colony region of the Gold Coast (which includes Accra) is excluded, the anti-Nkrumah opposition won a clear victory in the rest of the country, both in legislative seats and total votes. See Austin, *Politics in Ghana,* 320–23, 351.

27. W. E. B. Du Bois, "Africa's Choice," *National Guardian* 9 (29 October 1956):10. Perhaps the best evidence of Nkrumah's economic conservatism during the period 1951–59 is provided by Ras Makonnen, an organizer of the 1945 Pan-African Congress and an associate of Nkrumah's until the 1966 coup. At independence, Makonnen observes, none of the CPP "elite" knew the "difference between a plantation and a collective farm. . . . [The leaders] had a simple conviction, that if there were going to be any capitalist millionaires around, then they might as well be Ghanaian ones." See Kenneth J. King, ed., *Ras Makonnen: Pan-Africanism From Within* (London: Oxford University Press, 1973), 22.

28. Horne, *Black and Red,* 335–36.

29. Ruth B. Shipley to Du Bois, 6 April 1953, in *Correspondence,* 3:346; Du Bois, "My Beliefs Are None of Your Business," *National Guardian* 7 (10 October 1955):10; and Du Bois, *Autobiography,* 12.

30. Du Bois, *Autobiography,* 14–21.

31. Ibid., 24–25; W. E. B. Du Bois, "The American Negro and Communism," (23 October 1958), in *Against Racism*, 294–98.

32. Du Bois, *Autobiography*, 23, and Du Bois, "Humboldt University at Berlin" (3 November 1958), in *Against Racism*, 299.

33. W. E. B. Du Bois, "Moscow University" (22 January 1959), and Du Bois, "A Scientific Study of Africa" (December 1960), in *Against Racism*, 299–300, 316–17.

34. Du Bois, *Autobiography*, 35, 38–39, 42–43.

35. Ibid., 47, 51, 405; Graham, *His Day Is Marching On*, 277–80; W. E. B. Du Bois, "The Vast Miracle of China Today," *National Guardian* 11 (8 June 1959):6; and Horne, *Black and Red*, 324–25.

36. W. E. B. Du Bois, "Socialism and the American Negro" (May 1960), in *Against Racism*, 303–7, 312–15; Du Bois, *Autobiography*, 57–58; and Du Bois, "Race Pride: Comments" (27 February 1960), in *A W. E. B. Du Bois Reader*, 135–36.

37. Du Bois, "Socialism and the American Negro," 312.

38. W. E. B. Du Bois, "Whither Now and Why" (2 April 1960), in *The Education of Black People*, 149–58.

39. W. Scott Thompson, *Ghana's Foreign Policy, 1957–1966* (Princeton: Princeton University Press, 1969), 28, 42–43, 100, 120, 223.

40. Ibid., 58–60; and Du Bois, *Autobiography*, 401–2.

41. Kwame Nkrumah to W. E. B. Du Bois, 18 June 1960; and Du Bois to Nkrumah, 10 October 1960, in *Correspondence*, 3:443–44.

42. E. Franklin Frazier to W. E. B. Du Bois, 5 December 1960; Du Bois to Kwame Nkrumah, 4 January 1961; Nkrumah to Du Bois, 23 January 1961; Du Bois to A. A. Kwapong, 7 April 1961; Charles H. Wesley to Du Bois, 24 May 1961; Du Bois to Wesley, 13 June 1961; and Wesley to Du Bois, 20 September 1961; in *Correspondence*, 3:446–47, 449–50, 452–53.

43. Horne, *Black and Red*, 336–38.

44. W. E. B. Du Bois to Ghana Academy of Science and Learning, 23 May 1961; Du Bois to Kwame Nkrumah, 28 August 1961; E. A. Boateng to Du Bois, 21 September 1961; Alex Quaison-Sackey to Du Bois, September 1961, in *Correspondence*, 3:451, 453–56; Thompson, *Ghana's Foreign Policy*, 181–85; St. Clair Drake and L. C. Lacy, "Government Versus the Unions: The Sekondi-Takoradi Strike, 1961," in *Politics in Africa*, ed. G. Carter (New York: Harcourt, Brace, 1966), 68, 99.

45. Herbert Aptheker, "W. E. B. Du Bois and Africa," *Political Affairs* 60 (March 1981):29.

46. Horne, *Black and Red*, 237, 327, 335.

47. W. E. B. Du Bois, "Henry Winston" (7 September 1961), in *Against Racism*, 320; Paul G. Partington, *W. E. B. Du Bois: A Bibliography*

of His Published Writings (Whittier, Calif.: Penn Lithographics, 1979), 165–69; W. E. B. Du Bois to Gertrude Gelbin, 10 July 1963, in *Correspondence,* 3:463–64.

48. W. E. B. Du Bois to Gus Hall, 1 October 1961, in *Correspondence,* 3:439–40.

49. Aptheker, "W. E. B. Du Bois and Africa," 29.

50. W. E. B. Du Bois to Sekou Touré, 16 January 1962; and Kwame Nkrumah to Du Bois, 9 June 1962, in *Correspondence,* 3:457–59; Du Bois, "Conference of Encyclopedia Africana," *Freedomways* 3 (Winter 1963):28–30; and Kwame Nkrumah, "Tribute to W. E. B. Du Bois" (29 August 1963), in *W. E. B. Du Bois Speaks,* 327–28.

51. W. E. B. Du Bois to W. Alphaeus Hunton, Jr. 14 September 1962, in *Correspondence,* 3:459; David Graham Du Bois, "W. E. B. Du Bois," 183; Aptheker, "W. E. B. Du Bois and Africa," 29; and W. Alphaeus Hunton, "W. E. B. Du Bois: the Meaning of his Life," in *Black Titan,* 131–37.

52. Aptheker, "W. E. B. Du Bois and Africa," 29; Nkrumah, "Tribute to W. E. B. Du Bois," 327–28; and Nnamdi Azikiwe, "Tribute," in *Black Titan,* 4.

53. Daniel Walden, ed., *W. E. B. Du Bois: The Crisis Writings* (Greenwich, Conn.: Fawcett, 1972), 13–14; and "NAACP Mourns Passing of Dr. Du Bois, A Founder," *Crisis* 70 (October 1963):472–73.

54. Tuttle, ed., *W. E. B. Du Bois,* 52.

55. Herbert Aptheker, *Afro-American History: The Modern Era* (Secaucus, N.J.: Citadel Press, 1973), 156.

56. Du Bois to Du Bois Williams, 17 July 1950; and W. E. B. Du Bois, "Ethiopia: State Socialism Under an Emperor," *National Guardian* 7 (21 February 1955), 4.

57. The cordial relationship between Shirley Graham and the Communist Chinese also merits additional study. Unlike her husband, Graham seems to have taken the People's Republic's position in its conflict with the Soviets. "Inside China," she observed critically, "the straight line towards the ultimate goal is clearer and simpler than inside the U.S.S.R." As late as 1975 she was favorably quoting the sayings of Chairman Mao. See Kenneth Ray Young and Dan S. Green, "Harbinger to Nixon: W. E. B. Du Bois in China," *Negro History Bulletin* 35 (October 1972):125–28; Shirley Graham, "Hail the People's Republic of China," *Political Affairs* 38 (October 1959):25–34; Shirley Graham Du Bois, "Together We Struggle; Together We Win," *Black Scholar* 6 (April 1975):36–40; and Horne, *Black and Red,* 328–29.

58. C. L. R. James, *The Future in the Present* (Westport, Conn.: Lawrence Hill, 1980), 212.

59. Lorraine Hansberry, "Tribute," in *Black Titan*, 17.

60. Martin Luther King, Jr., "Honoring Dr. Du Bois," in *Black Titan*, 176–83; David L. Lewis, *King: A Critical Biography* (Baltimore: Penguin, 1970), 376; and William Robert Miller, *Martin Luther King, Jr.* (New York: Avon, 1969), 277–78.

BIBLIOGRAPHIC ESSAY

Few American scholars have been as prolific as W. E. B. Du Bois. The sheer magnitude of his oeuvre and the complexity of his thought complicates matters for any researcher. Generally, the bulk of Du Bois's writings may be divided into several categories. One major field consists of political journalism and contemporary social criticism. Prominently, the essays in the *Crisis* would be located here. But this area also includes Du Bois's voluminous essays in newspapers and popular magazines: the *Moon, Voice of the Negro, Horizon, Pittsburgh Courier, Chicago Defender, Amsterdam News, National Guardian, Atlantic Monthly, New Republic, Negro Digest,* and the *Nation.* The second major field consists of Du Bois's scholarly and academic writings. Subdivided into four broad disciplinary groups, they include sociology, social and political history, education, and literary and cultural studies. The major sociological studies by Du Bois are *The Philadelphia Negro* (1899) and the *Atlanta University Publications on the Study of Negro Problems* (1898–1913). Additional sociological studies appeared in the *Southern Workman,* the *American Journal of Sociology, Phylon,* and other periodicals. Du Bois's major historical works are *The Suppression of the African Slave-Trade* (1896), *John Brown* (1909), *The Negro* (1915), *Black Reconstruction* (1935), and *The World and Africa* (1947). Du Bois's writings in the field of education were also quite extensive. He contributed articles to the *Journal of Negro Education* and the *Quarterly Review of Education among Negroes,* and for a half century was the nation's leading proponent for black higher education. The best single source of Du Bois's ideas on education was edited by Herbert Aptheker: W. E. B. Du Bois, *The Education of Black Peo-*

ple, Ten Critiques, 1906–1960 (1973). Du Bois's most important literary works were his novels *The Quest of the Silver Fleece* (1911), *Dark Princess* (1928), and the *Black Flame* trilogy, *The Ordeal of Mansart* (1957), *Mansart Builds a School* (1961), and *Worlds of Color* (1961). The three books of Du Bois that are absolutely essential to understanding his evolving social thought are the seminal collection of essays, *The Souls of Black Folk* (1903), *Black Reconstruction* (1935), and *The Autobiography of W. E. B. Du Bois* (1968).

Interpretations of Du Bois have varied tremendously. Some have erred by focusing almost exclusively on one phase of his career at the expense of other periods or have placed greater emphasis on certain texts, especially *The Souls of Black Folk,* while nearly ignoring his books published after 1940. Most studies on Du Bois written during the Cold War of the 1950s and early 1960s minimized the black scholar's intellectual achievements and focused primarily on his career in the Niagara Movement and as leader of the NAACP. The best work of this period, with the exception of Herbert Aptheker, was that of historian August Meier. While working first as an assistant to Charles S. Johnson at Fisk University, and later as a professor at Morgan State College, Meier completed a number of important studies on both Washington and Du Bois. In "From 'Conservative' to Radical: The Ideological Development of W. E. B. Du Bois, 1885–1905" (1959), Meier advanced the thesis that "it was only beginning about 1901 that Du Bois gradually moved from a conciliatory to a protest ideology." For Meier, Du Bois's ideas represented a "paradox" between racial separatism and a desire for full democratic rights. In *Negro Thought in America* (1963), Meier termed Du Bois "a mystic and materialist . . . and equalitarian who apparently believed in innate racial differences, a Marxist who was fundamentally a middle-class intellectual . . . the epitome of the paradoxes in American Negro thought." Meier corrected the popular misconception that Du Bois's and Washington's educational and political ideologies were diametrically opposite each other. But Meier did overstate the "radical" shift in Du Bois's thought between the 1897 "Conservation of Races" address and the publication of *The Souls of Black Folk,* and by using the "paradox" theme he underestimated the theoretical coherence of Du Bois's general outlook. Meier also failed to give adequate or comprehensive emphasis to the role of socialism and the advocacy of women's rights in Du Bois's politics before 1915.

Elliott Rudwick's *W. E. B. Du Bois* (1960) generally shared Meier's basic interpretation of Du Bois. The biography detailed the major issues and controversies surrounding Du Bois during his debates with Washington. Its chief limitations were its treatment of Du Bois's Pan-Africanism, its review of the Garvey-Du Bois debate, and its failure to discuss adequately or accurately Du Bois's post-1934 career. Despite its conceptual flaws, Rudwick's study was superior to the writings of Harold Isaacs and Francis L. Broderick. A former Trotskyist, Isaacs retained a deep hostility towards communism, and his Cold War biases distorted his treatment of Du Bois in his book *The New World of Negro Americans* (1963). Du Bois was described sarcastically as a "breakfast-table autocrat," whose "half-digested Marxism" and elitism had culminated "in a close embrace-indeed, a marriage-with totalitarian Communist world power," Isaacs declared. Du Bois had the potential for greatness but fell short of the mark, because he was unable "to set himself resolutely all his life against *all* forms of tyranny over the minds of men." As Isaacs reviewed Du Bois's earlier career, he found other shortcomings. His Pan-African Congresses were "unsuccessful" and manifested his "romantic racism." Du Bois's segregated cooperative economics concepts of the 1930s were "a confused interval" that "took him all the way back into the shadow of Booker T. Washington." Isaacs was also dissatisfied with Du Bois's literary writings. *Dark Princess,* for instance, was "one of the most forgotten of his many books, and as a work of literature deserves no other fate." In summary, "Du Bois is hardly to be classed as a world shaker or world changer," Isaacs insisted. "Other Negroes have been far greater as leaders and played much larger historic roles."

More acrid was Broderick, author of *W. E. B. Du Bois: Negro Leader in a Time of Crisis* (1959). Although Du Bois permitted him to examine his personal papers for a time, Broderick's study is one of the best examples of a denunciatory biography in American historiography. Nearly every facet of Du Bois's life was subjected to polemical attack. Broderick described Du Bois's personality as being "handicapped . . . by righteous, tempestuous arrogance." Du Bois was driven by "racist tendencies," and during his 1892–94 studies in Germany he appeared "to have absorbed some anti-Semitism." Broderick wrote that Du Bois's Pan-Africanism was a type of "racial nationalism" that "led nowhere." Reviewing Du Bois's novels and poetry, Broderick suggested that his "style fell between sociological prose and vague grandiloquence." *Dark Princess* contained "exalted nonsense" and "labored, obtuse metaphors . . . his plots went beyond even the limits of fantasy." Du Bois's famous "Litany at Atlanta" was dismissed as "a frenzied clamor." Critiquing Du Bois's sociological and historical studies, Broderick noted: "no single work, except *The Philadelphia Negro,* is first-class. . . . *Black Reconstruction* will be remembered, but more because of its eccentric racist-Marxist interpretations than because of its assemblage of new material." Broderick's book is still cited as a definitive source on Du Bois. Jack B. Moore's *W. E. B. Du Bois* (1981) refers to Broderick as "perhaps [Du Bois's] most perceptive, thorough and objective critic."

The Broderick-Isaacs thesis was not effectively challenged by many of

Du Bois's former colleagues. A few were also eager to bury the Du Bois legacy. At Atlanta University, several professors claimed that Du Bois's conversion to Leninism was due to "senility." Two black authors who had known Du Bois for forty years, historian Rayford W. Logan and journalist Henry Lee Moon, lamented their mentor's turn to the left. According to Logan's introduction in his edited collection, *W. E. B. Du Bois: A Profile* (1971), by the 1950s Du Bois "had abandoned hope" that he could achieve "equal rights" in America. He had retreated to Africa as a "disillusioned expatriate." Moon presented Du Bois as a fallen titan, a leader who had betrayed his own ideals, in his edited volume, *The Emerging Thought of W. E. B. Du Bois* (1972). Du Bois was "a Renaissance man . . . seer and poet, teacher and historian, man of letters," Moon related. At his pinnacle of power, he had "soundly" condemned "the antics of the American Communists." But in his "declining years he was a foremost American advocate of peace on Soviet terms." As Du Bois became entrapped "in Marxism-Leninism, his vision inevitably narrowed," Moon commented. Du Bois had come to believe that racial equality was "unobtainable within the framework of the American constitutional system." Moon believed that Du Bois's advocacy of socialism would not lead to "the abolition of racial and color distinctions." In Moon's description of Du Bois's termination from the NAACP in 1948, he clearly sided with the Association: "By the time that he and the NAACP finally parted company in 1948, it was abundantly evident that he was basically in accord with the Communist Party line."

Historian Herbert Aptheker was the focal point of much of the anti-Du Bois hostility during these years. As a leading communist intellectual, editor of Du Bois's final *Autobiography,* and the executor of Du Bois's papers, he was widely attacked. Although Aptheker's academic publications were extensive, he was unable to obtain a permanent position in an American university for over three decades. In numerous instances, he was not permitted to lecture on college campuses—even on Du Bois. Some even dared to question his integrity. Jay Saunders Redding has written that some black intellectuals "objected" to Aptheker's work on Du Bois on racial and anti-Communist grounds: "Herbert Aptheker was white, and editing the [Du Bois] correspondence . . . was a job for a Negro American, they said." Others argued that Aptheker was "an avowed Marxist" and that Du Bois "did not know what he was doing" by selecting him. Logan insisted that "Aptheker's discussion of Du Bois as an historian" was an "example of casting Du Bois in the writer's own image." He also raised several questions about "the reasons for the change in the language" of material printed in an earlier work which appeared in the *Autobiography*. "What is even more necessary," Logan added, "is an explanation why Du Bois, 'a radical democrat' all his life, became a Communist." Jack B. Moore has termed the *Autobiog-*

raphy a "highly uneven text, which sometimes does not seem to be a finished book at all, but rather some passages from various sources that might be assembled into a book with rigorous reworking." Moore was also troubled that Du Bois "never submitted the book for publication nor revised it as he always did, usually extensively, in proof." Moore was displeased, in short, with "the murkiness surrounding some elements of the *Autobiography*."

With the eruption of the modern civil rights movement, Du Bois's treatment by some historians and sociologists became more objective. But the generally negative consensus on his post-1945 career continued. Literary critic and social democrat Irving Howe, for example, applauded Du Bois as a "remarkable" leader in a 1968 essay in *Harper's* magazine. But Du Bois was also severely censured for succumbing to Marxist totalitarianism. Howe declared that the elder Du Bois's remarks on politics looked "as if they came from the very heart of a mimeograph machine." S. P. Fullinwider's *The Mind and Mood of Black America* (1969) relied upon Broderick's earlier interpretation. "It does not seem likely that Du Bois believed in God," Fullinwider cautiously observed. Du Bois was always "the humanist and the racist—these were his two selves, forever in conflict." Fullinwider explained Du Bois's detour to Marxism as an act of "bitterness. . . . He turned his back on the civil rights movement."

As Black Power and the renaissance of black nationalism supplanted integrationism, the image of Du Bois was again transformed. Scores of black social scientists turned to Du Bois's works and echoed many of his ideas. In his 1969 essay, "W. E. B. Du Bois and the Black Messanic Vision," Vincent Harding argued that Du Bois "was likely the most significant voice to prepare the way for this current, newest stage of blackness. He is the proper context for an adequate understanding of Malcolm, of Fanon, of Stokely Carmichael and Martin Luther King." Lerone Bennett's *Black Power U.S.A.* (1967) affirmed that Du Bois had charted the "fundamental principles" of the contemporary liberation struggle—"Economic Security, Political Liberty, and Light for all bondsmen of America, black and white." Black political scientist Chuck Stone observed in his 1970 text *Black Political Power in America* that Du Bois was "one of the intellectual forerunners of the Black Power movement . . . [a] brilliant writer and scholar." With the institutionalization of Black Studies in the early and mid-1970s, a revisionist and highly favorable criticism of Du Bois's works became dominant. Clarence Contee's "Emergence of Du Bois as an African Nationalist" (1969) presented a sympathetic view of the black intellectual's part within Pan-Africanism; Stanley Brodwin's "The Veil Transcended: Form and Meaning in W. E. B. Du Bois's *The Souls of Black Folk*" (1972) examined the literary style and philosophical orientation of Du Bois's most popular work; Arlene

Elder's "Swamp Versus Plantation: Symbolic Structure in W. E. B. Du Bois's *The Quest of the Silver Fleece*" (1973) drew critical attention to and praise of Du Bois's first novel; Jean Yellin's "Du Bois's *Crisis* and Woman's Suffrage" (1973) noted correctly that Du Bois "used the pages of the N.A.A.C.P. magazine to champion woman's rights" and that he also consistently exposed "white racism within the woman's movement"; and Wilson J. Moses's "Poetics of Ethiopianism: W. E. B. Du Bois and Literary Black Nationalism" (1975) presented the literary connections between Du Bois and the black nationalist cultural tradition.

The political environment of the Black Power period also had a negative consequence: some scholars and writers frequently placed excessive emphasis on the "black nationalist dimensions" of Du Bois's work, while diminishing his support for desegregation and Marxism. Black political scientist Charles V. Hamilton, for instance, used Du Bois's 1934 polemics against Walter White to argue against what he termed "structural integration," in a 1970 essay. At no time during Du Bois's political career did he embrace an unqualified position in behalf of black nationalism or complete racial separatism. Yet Hamilton insisted, without evidence, that Du Bois endorsed black nationalism "when he was advocating the building of strong black political and economic institutions." Another "nationalist-oriented" treatment of Du Bois appeared in Andrew G. Paschal's *W. E. B. Du Bois Reader* (1971). The majority of the volume's selections focus on the themes "African Culture," "Black Power," and "Race Solidarity and Economic Cooperation," while nearly excluding materials on Marxism, women's rights, peace, and the need for desegregation. Moreover, Paschal accepts the Broderick-Isaacs thesis on the detrimental role of the Communists. "Were [Du Bois] alive today, Soviet Socialism would not be too venerable for deserved criticism," Paschal observed. The Party continued "to endeavor to present him as a showpiece of the Soviet Union." To Paschal, Du Bois had retained "his deep black culture," but all other black Marxists had "disposed of it for the sake of ideology. They seem to have thought and think that a visit to the Kremlin held the salvation of mankind, including black people."

In recent years, conservatives and "Cold War liberals" alike have been forced to accept Du Bois as a major intellectual figure. But they have continued to attempt to reinterpret his ideas and programs to fit their own ends. In 1975, black conservative Thomas Sowell published *Race and Economics,* a text that was critical of liberal policies, such as affirmative action, and the use of federal government programs to promote full equality. Yet here we find the black Marxist Du Bois respectfully cited on the black family and on American Negro slavery. Sowell also added carefully that Du Bois and Washington "were not nearly as far apart in substance as popular stereotypes sometimes suggest." The NAACP *Crisis* has generally interpreted Du

Bois in a manner similar to that of Sowell. In 1974, an article by Wesley C. Pugh declared that the Du Bois-Washington conflict was an "inflated controversy. . . . Their ideas were not basically contradictory." Pugh claimed that Washington's Atlanta Compromise simply attempted "to make the most" of the "employer-employee relationship" between most Southern whites and blacks. He also insisted that Du Bois's economic commonwealth program of the 1930s was "similar to Washington's ideas on black economics." William D. Wright's 1978 essay in the *Crisis* suggested that "the 1920s and early 1930s marked the height of [Du Bois'] leadership . . . and were the years of his most imaginative and productive social thinking." Wright explained that Du Bois's theory of "political democracy" was central to his entire work. Yet in a confused final paragraph, Wright asserted that Du Bois advocated "a social democratic society" at the end of his life. Understandably, the Association was still reluctant to address the root causes for Du Bois's expulsion in 1948 and the organization's near-capitulation to McCarthyism during the Cold War.

Gerald Horne's *Black and Red: W. E. B. Du Bois and the Afro-American Response to the Cold War, 1944–1963* (1986) marks a new phase of Du Bois historiography. Horne effectively refutes Rudwick's charge that Du Bois was a "prophet in limbo" during the postwar period and Broderick's assertion that Du Bois "abandoned the struggle for Negro rights." He illustrates convincingly that Du Bois's later years were a culmination of the theoretical and programmatic positions that he had maintained for nearly half a century, and that Du Bois was a primary target of domestic anticommunism. The accomplishments of Horne's thesis, however, only begin to provide the detailed analytical work that remains to be completed on Du Bois's life and social thought.

As theorist George Plekhanov once observed, "every man of talent who becomes a social force, is the product of social relations." The achievements and contradictions inherent in Du Bois's ideology were part of the broader fabric of Afro-American society at a particular moment in history. From a contemporary perspective, the theoretical work of Du Bois requires the same rigorous assessment that he clearly demanded of himself. Du Bois's theories of "double consciousness" and cultural pluralism, his efforts to achieve connections between peace, socialism, and African liberation, and his understanding of the relationship between racial equality and political democracy, merit extensive scrutiny and reappraisal, in the light of late twentieth-century social realities. Du Bois's finest legacy as an activist and scholar was his effort to comprehend the full possibilities of democracy, in the broadest social context. The future task is to build upon his monumental intellectual achievement without minimizing the problems inherent in this social project.

SELECTED BIBLIOGRAPHY

PRIMARY SOURCES

The Suppression of the African Slave-Trade to the United States of America, 1638–1870. New York: Longmans, Green, 1896.

Atlanta University Publications on the Study of Negro Problems. The initial publication of the Atlanta University conferences was *Mortality Among Negroes in Cities,* printed at Atlanta University in 1896. From 1898 until 1913, Du Bois edited the conference proceedings.

The Philadelphia Negro: A Social Study. Boston: Ginn and Company, 1899. Includes a report on domestic service by Isabel Eaton.

The Souls of Black Folk: Essays and Sketches. Chicago: A. C. McClurg, 1903.

John Brown. Philadelphia: George W. Jacobs, 1909.

The Quest of the Silver Fleece: A Novel. Chicago: A. C. McClurg, 1911.

The Negro. New York: Henry Holt, 1915.

Darkwater: Voices from within the Veil. New York: Harcourt, Brace & Howe, 1920.

The Gift of Black Folk: Negroes in the Making of America. Boston: Stratford, 1924.

Dark Princess: A Romance. New York: Harcourt, Brace, 1928.

Africa—Its Place in Modern History. Girard, Kans.: Haldeman-Julius, 1930.

Africa—Its Geography, People and Products. Girard, Kans.: Haldeman-Julius, 1930.

Black Reconstruction: An Essay toward a History of the Part Which Black

Folk Played in the Attempt to Reconstruct Democracy in America, 1860–1880. New York: Harcourt, Brace, 1935.

Black Folk Then and Now: An Essay in the History and Sociology of the Negro Race. New York: Henry Holt, 1939.

Dusk of Dawn: An Essay toward an Autobiography of a Race Concept. New York: Harcourt, Brace, 1940.

Color and Democracy: Colonies and Peace. New York: Harcourt, Brace, 1945.

The World and Africa: An Inquiry into the Part Which Africa Has Played in World History. New York: Viking, 1947.

In Battle For Peace: The Story of My 83rd Birthday, With Comment by Shirley Graham. New York: Masses & Mainstream, 1952.

The Ordeal of Mansart. New York: Mainstream, 1957.

Mansart Builds a School. New York: Mainstream, 1959.

Worlds of Color. New York: Mainstream, 1959.

An ABC of Color: Selections from over a Half Century of the Writings of W. E. B. Du Bois. Berlin: Seven Seas, 1963.

The Autobiography of W. E. B. Du Bois: A Soliloquy on Viewing My Life from the Last Decade of Its First Century. Edited by Herbert Aptheker. New York: International Publishers, 1968.

Most of Du Bois's works have been reprinted by a number of publishers. There are at least seven reprints of *The Suppression of the African Slave-Trade,* and seven "versions" of *The Souls of Black Folk.* Most reprints, notably those done by Kraus-Thomson, are excellent. But some reprints, especially those of *The Souls of Black Folk,* have numerous errors.

SECONDARY SOURCES

BIBLIOGRAPHIES

Comprehensive selected bibliographies of Du Bois's writings include: Ernest Kaiser, "A Selected Bibliography of the Published Writings of W. E. B. Du Bois," in *Black Titan,* ed. Clarke et al., 309–30; Daniel Walden, "A Selected Bibliography," in *W. E. B. Du Bois,* ed. Walden, 431–47; and Meyer Weinberg, "A Selected Bibliography of W. E. B. Du Bois," in *W. E. B. Du Bois,* ed. Weinberg, 445–59. Rayford W. Logan, "Bibliographical Note" in *W. E. B. Du Bois,* ed. Logan, 294–318 is also helpful.

The two essential bibliographies of Du Bois's writings are: Herbert Aptheker, *Annotated Bibliography of the Published Writings of W. E. B. Du Bois* (Millwood, N.Y.: Kraus-Thomson, 1973); and Paul G. Partington,

W. E. B. Du Bois: A Bibliography of His Published Writings, rev. ed. (Whittier, Calif.: Printed by Penn Lithographics for Paul G. Partington, 1979). Of the two bibliographies, Aptheker's is superior. His thoughtful commentaries on the bulk of Du Bois's newspaper columns, magazine and journal articles, and books are extremely helpful. Aptheker also includes extremely rare materials—for example, Du Bois's 1950 articles in the *Chicago Globe*—that are virtually unavailable.

BOOKS AND EDITED VOLUMES

Aptheker, Herbert, ed. *The Correspondence of W. E. B. Du Bois.* 3 vols. Amherst: University of Massachusetts Press, 1973–78.

———, ed. *Writings by W. E. B. Du Bois in Non-Periodical Literature Edited by Others.* Millwood, N.Y.: Kraus-Thomson, 1982.

———, ed. *Writings by W. E. B. Du Bois in Periodicals Edited by Others.* 4 vols. Millwood, N.Y.: Kraus-Thomson, 1982.

———, ed. *Writings in Periodicals Edited by W. E. B. Du Bois: Selections from the "Crisis."* 2 vols. Millwood, N.Y.: Kraus-Thomson, 1983.

———, ed. *Writings in Periodicals Edited by W. E. B. Du Bois: Selections from the "Horizon."* Millwood, N.Y.: Kraus-Thomson, 1985.

Broderick, Francis, L. *W. E. B. Du Bois: Negro Leader in a Time of Crisis.* Stanford: Stanford University Press, 1959.

Clarke, John Henrick; Jackson, Esther; Kaiser, Ernest; and O'Dell, J. H., eds. *Black Titan: W. E. B. Du Bois.* Boston: Beacon Press, 1970.

De Marco, Joseph P. *The Social Thought of W. E. B. Du Bois.* Lanham, Md.: University Press of America, 1983.

Du Bois, Shirley Graham. *His Day is Marching On: A Memoir of W. E. B. Du Bois.* Philadelphia: J. B. Lippincott, 1971.

Foner, Philip S., ed. *W. E. B. Du Bois Speaks: Speeches and Addresses.* 2 vols. New York: Pathfinder Press, 1970.

Fullinwider, S. P. *The Mind and Mood of Black America: Twentieth Century Thought.* Homewood, Ill.: Dorsey Press, 1969.

Green, Dan S., and Driver, Edwin D., eds. *W. E. B. Du Bois on Sociology and the Black Community.* Chicago: University of Chicago Press, 1978.

Horne, Gerald. *Black and Red: W. E. B. Du Bois and the Afro-American Response to the Cold War, 1944–1963.* Albany: State University of New York Press, 1986.

Isaacs, Harold R. *The New World of Negro Americans.* New York: John Day Co., 1963.

Lacy, Leslie Alexander. *Cheer the Lonesome Traveler: The Life of W. E. B. Du Bois.* New York: Dell Publishing, 1972.

Lester, Julius, ed. *The Seventh Son: The Thought and Writings of W. E. B. Du Bois.* 2 vols. New York: Random House, 1971.

Logan, Rayford, W., ed. *W. E. B. Du Bois: A Profile.* New York: Hill & Wang,, 1971.

Moon, Henry Lee, ed. *The Emerging Thought of W. E. B. Du Bois.* New York: Simon & Schuster, 1972.

Moore, Jack B. *W. E. B. Du Bois.* Boston: Twayne Publishers, 1981.

Paschal, Andrew G., ed. *A W. E. B. Du Bois Reader.* New York: Macmillan Co., 1971.

Rampersad, Arnold. *The Art and Imagination of W. E. B. Du Bois.* Cambridge: Harvard University Press, 1976.

Rudwick, Elliott M. *W. E. B. Du Bois, A Study in Minority Group Leadership.* Philadelphia: University of Pennsylvania Press, 1960.

Stone, Chuck. *Black Political Power in America.* New York: Delta, 1970.

Tuttle, William M., ed. *W. E. B. Du Bois.* Englewood Cliffs, N.J.: Prentice-Hall, 1973.

Walden, Daniel, ed. *W. E. B. Du Bois: The Crisis Writings.* Greenwich, Conn.: Fawcett Publications, 1972.

Weinberg, Meyer, ed. *W. E. B. Du Bois: A Reader.* New York: Harper & Row, 1970.

Wilson, Walter, ed. *The Selected Writings of W. E. B. Du Bois.* New York: New American Library, 1970.

ARTICLES

Note: Articles cited in the notes are not listed below.

Aptheker, Herbert. "Dr. Du Bois and Communism." *Political Affairs* 40 (December 1961):13–20.

———. "Du Bois: The Final Years." *Journal of Human Relations* 14 (1966):149–55.

———. "To Dr. Du Bois—With Love." *Political Affairs* 42 (February 1963):35–42.

———. "W. E. B. Du Bois and Religion: A Brief Reassessment." *Journal of Religious Thought* 59 (Spring-Summer 1982):5–11.

Bontemps, Arna. "Tribute to Du Bois." *Negro Digest* 13 (July 1964):42–44.

Breathett, George. "William Edward Burghardt Du Bois: An Address to the Black Academic Community." *Journal of Negro History* 60 (January 1975):45–52.

Brewer, William M. "Some Memories of Dr. W. E. B. Du Bois." *Journal of Negro History* 53 (October 1968):345–48.

Broderick, Francis L. "The Tragedy of W. E. B. Du Bois." *Progressive* 22 (February 1958):29–32.

————. "W. E. B. Du Bois: History of an Intellectual." In *Black Sociologists: Historical and Contemporary Perspectives,* edited by James E. Blackwell and Morris Janowitz, 3–24. Chicago: University of Chicago Press, 1974.

Brodwin, Stanley. "The Veil Transcended: Form and Meaning in W. E. B. Du Bois' *The Souls of Black Folk." Journal of Black Studies* 2 (March 1972):303–21.

Butler, B. N. "Booker T. Washington, W. E. B. Du Bois, Black Americans and the NAACP." *Crisis* 85 (August 1978):222–30.

Contee, Clarence G. "A Crucial Friendship Begins: Du Bois and Nkrumah, 1935–1945." *Crisis* 78 (August 1971):181–85.

————. "Du Bois, the NAACP, and the Pan-African Congress of 1919." *Journal of Negro History* 57 (January 1972):13–28.

————. "The Emergence of Du Bois as an African Nationalist." *Journal of Negro History* 54 (January 1969):48–63.

————. "W. E. B. Du Bois and *Encyclopedia Africana." Crisis* 77 (November 1970):375–79.

De Marco, Joseph P. "The Rationale and Foundation of Du Bois's Theory of Economic Cooperation." *Phylon* 35 (March 1974):5–15.

Dennis, Rutledge M. "Du Bois and the Role of the Educated Elite." *Journal of Negro Education* 46 (Fall 1977):388–402.

Diggs, Irene. "Du Bois and Children." *Phylon* 37 (December 1976):370–99.

————. "Du Bois and Women: A Short Story of Black Women, 1910–1934." *Current Bibliography on African Affairs* 7 (Summer 1974):260–307.

Duberman, Martin. "Du Bois as Prophet." *New Republic,* 23 March 1968, 36–39.

Du Bois, David Graham. "The Du Bois Legacy under Attack." *Black Scholar* 9 (January-February 1978):2–12.

Fletcher, Diorita C. "W. E. B. Du Bois' Arraignment and Indictment of White Civilization." *Black World* 22 (May 1973):16–22.

Gorman, William. "W. E. B. Du Bois and His Work." *Fourth International* 2 (May-June 1950):80–85.

Green, Dan S. "Bibliography of Writings About W. E. B. Du Bois." *College Language Association Journal* 20 (March 1977):410–21.

————. "W. E. B. Du Bois' Talented Tenth: A Strategy for Racial Advancement." *Journal of Negro Education* 46 (Summer 1977):358–66.

Green, Dan S., and Driver, Edwin D. "W. E. B. Du Bois: A Case in the Sociology of Sociological Negation," *Phylon* 37 (December 1976):308–33.

Green, Dan S., and Smith, Earl. "W. E. B. Du Bois and the Concepts of Race and Class." *Phylon* 44 (December 1983):262–72.

Hamilton, Charles V. "Black Americans and the Modern Political Struggle." *Black World* 19 (May 1970):5–9, 77–79.

Harding, Vincent. "W. E. B. Du Bois and the Black Messianic Vision." *Freedomways* 9 (1969):44–58.

Henderson, Lennfals. "W. E. B. Du Bois, Black Scholar and Prophet." *Black Scholar* 1 (January-February 1970):48-57.

Henderson, Vivian W. "Race, Economics, and Public Policy with Reflections on W. E. B. Du Bois." *Phylon* 37 (March 1976):1–11.

Howe, Irving. "Remarkable Man, Ambiguous Legacy." *Harper's,* March 1968, 143–49.

Hunton, W. Alphaeus. "Concerning the *Encyclopedia Africana.*" *Freedomways* 7 (Spring 1967):139–149.

———. "The Meaning of His Life." *Freedomways* 3 (Fall 1963):490–95.

Ijere, Martin O. "W. E. B. Du Bois and Marcus Garvey as Pan-Africanists: A Study in Contrast." *Présence Africaine* 79 (1974):188–206.

Larue, H. C. "W. E. B. Du Bois and the Pragmatic Method of Truth." *Journal of Human Relations* 19 (1971):76–83.

McGill, Ralph. "W. E. B. Du Bois." *Atlantic Monthly,* November 1965, 78–81.

Marable, Manning. "Peace and Black Liberation: The Contributions of W. E. B. Du Bois." *Science and Society* 47 (Winter 1983–84):385–405.

———. "The Black Faith of W. E. B. Du Bois: Sociocultural and Political Dimensions of Black Religion." *Southern Quarterly* 23 (Spring 1985):15–33.

———. "W. E. B. Du Bois and the Struggle Against Racism." *Black Scholar* 16 (May-June 1985):43–44, 46–47.

Martin, Michael, and Yeakey, Lamont. "PanAfrican-Asian Solidarity: A Central Theme in Du Bois' Conception of Racial Stratification and Struggle on a World Scale." *Phylon* 43 (September 1982):202–17.

Meier, August. "From 'Conservative' to 'Radical'; The Ideological Development of W. E. B. Du Bois, 1885–1905." *Crisis* 66 (November 1959):527–36.

Moon, Henry L. "Leadership of W. E. B. Du Bois." *Crisis* 75 (February 1968):51–57.

Moses, Wilson J. "The Poetics of Ethiopianism: W. E. B. Du Bois and Literary Black Nationalism." *American Literature* 47 (November 1975):411–27.

Nelson, Truman. "A Life Style of Conscience." *Nation,* 29 April 1968, 574–75.

———. "W. E. B. Du Bois: Prophet in Limbo." *Nation,* 25 January 1958, 76–79.

Ofari, Earl. "W. E. B. Du Bois and Black Power." *Black World* 19 (August 1970):26–28.

Osofsky, Gilbert. "Master of the Grand Vision." *Saturday Review of Literature,* 24 February 1968, 42.

Paschal, Andrew G. "The Spirit of W. E. B. Du Bois." *Black Scholar* 2 (February 1971):38–50.

Pugh, Wesley C. "The Inflated Controversy: Du Bois vs. Washington." *Crisis* 81 (April 1974):132–33.

Redding, J. Saunders. "Portrait of W. E. Burghardt Du Bois." *American Scholar* 18 (Winter 1948–49):93–96.

————. "The Correspondence of W. E. B. Du Bois: A Review Article." *Phylon* 40 (June 1979):119–22.

Rogers, Ben F. "William E. B. Du Bois, Marcus Garvey, and Pan-Africa." *Journal of Negro History* 40 (April 1955):154–65.

Romero, Patricia W. "W. E. B. Du Bois, Pan-Africanists and Africa, 1963–1973." *Journal of Black Studies* 6 (June 1976):321–36.

Shipley, W. Maurice. "Reaching Back to Glory: Comparative Sketches in the Dreams of W. B. Yeats and W. E. B. Du Bois." *Crisis* 83 (June-July 1976):195–98.

Stewart, James B. "The Legacy of W. E. B. Du Bois for Contemporary Black Studies." *Journal of Negro Education* 53 (Summer 1984):296–311.

Taylor, Carol M. "W. E. B. Du Bois's Challenge to Scientific Racism." *Journal of Black Studies* 11 (June 1981):449–60.

Tuttle, William M. "W. E. B. Du Bois' Confrontation with White Liberalism during the Progressive Era." *Phylon* 35 (September 1974):241–58.

Walden, Daniel. "W. E. B. Du Bois: Pioneer Reconstruction Historian." *Negro History Bulletin* 26 (February 1963):159–60, 164.

Walker, S. Jay. "Du Bois' Uses of History: On Nat Turner and John Brown." *Black World* 24 (February 1975):4–11.

Wesley, Charles H. "W. E. B. Du Bois, Historian." *Freedomways* 5 (Winter 1965):59–72.

Wright, William. "Du Bois' Theory of Political Democracy." *Crisis* 85 (March 1978):85–89.

INDEX

ABOUT THE AUTHOR

Manning Marable was born in Dayton, Ohio, in 1950. He received the A.B. from Earlham College in 1971, the M.A. from the University of Wisconsin–Madison in 1972, and the Ph.D. in American history from the University of Maryland–College Park in 1976. He is currently professor of political science and sociology at Purdue University, West Lafayette, Indiana. His political column "Along the Color Line" regularly appears in 150 newspapers internationally. In the past decade Manning Marable has written more than one hundred articles for such periodicals as the *Black Scholar*, the *Nation*, the *New Statesman*, *Southern Quarterly*, *Phylon*, and *Temps Modernes*. He has written six books, including *How Capitalism Underdeveloped Black America* (1983), *Race, Reform and Rebellion: The Second Reconstruction in Black America, 1945–1982* (1984), and *Black American Politics: From the Washington Marches to Jesse Jackson* (1985). He is married to Hazel Ann Marable, and they have three children, Malaika, Sojourner, and Joshua.